Media Trust in a Digital World

Thomas Osburg · Stephanie Heinecke
Editors

Media Trust in a Digital World

Communication at Crossroads

Springer

Editors
Thomas Osburg
Faculty of Economy & Media
Fresenius University
of Applied Sciences
Munich, Germany

Stephanie Heinecke
Faculty of Economy & Media
Fresenius University
of Applied Sciences
Munich, Germany

ISBN 978-3-030-30773-8 ISBN 978-3-030-30774-5 (eBook)
https://doi.org/10.1007/978-3-030-30774-5

This Springer imprint is published by the registered company Springer Nature Switzerland AG
The registered company address is: Gewerbestrasse 11, 6330 Cham, Switzerland

Foreword

The last few years have changed the media industry in every aspect, more than the decades before. Traditional business models have been turned upside down, and the media industry has been oscillating between the demonization of online formats and free content. Everyone is suddenly able to publish and disseminate information that seemed important to him or her, making it difficult for readers to verify the facts as there was hardly any editing authority.

The German Chancellor Angela Merkel recently replied to a speaker in the "Bundestag," ironically pointing out the low level of quality that she saw in this speech, with the words: "The nice thing about liberal democracies is that everyone talks about what they consider important for the country." But while the Members of Parliament understood the irony of the statement, significant parts of citizens are often misled by (and thus trust) weird and false information.

In the discussion about trust in the media, however, we have to go much deeper than the verification of sources. The question arises as to how far changes in society influence the media and vice versa. Can television and newspapers still be considered leading media and what role do social media play for the political participation of citizens and the necessary trust in institutions? Is participation in the mediatized space a fundamental civil right that can be promoted and possibly also controlled by democracy-promoting structures?

Media change and media crisis can lead to scandalization and moralization in reporting. Media usage can contribute to everyone being more informed but also lead to the better educated benefitting even more. Eli Pariser ("Filter Bubble") describes in a TED Talk very vividly how the Internet first became a blessing—the dominance of publishers was broken, information was free for all, and constantly accessible. In recent years, however, more and more algorithms have taken control of what we read and see. The logic behind the news selection, however, is incomprehensible to many, stirs up fear, and thus also disintegrates part of the trust in the media.

We all have to ask the question of how the "old" and "new" media are used and what effects they have on trust in communication in general. Already now, the term "lying press" found its way into general German language and at the same time pushed a rejection of hierarchical communication (the powers that are) by the population. Some media houses were so focused on business models and payment models for content that they lost sight of a potentially much bigger storm brewing up on the horizon—the loss of trust in an entire industry.

This book could not come at a better time. It takes a deeper look at the role of trust in the media and in communication in general, and outlines approaches to how organizations should respond to the threat of loss of trust in communication and media.

May 2019

Prof. Dr. Tobias Engelsleben
President, Hochschule Fresenius
Cologne, Germany

Preface

In today's world, trust becomes a phenomenon, a new paradigm, and maybe a buzzword. A lot of people talk about it, in business, NGO's media, and government. Trust, as often said, is the new glue, holding together societies and the way we live and work. Especially in times when technology and digitalization become more and more important, a closer look is needed on what role trust will play. Digitalization and technologies can offer tremendous help and new opportunities for societies and people and solve problems in areas like health, education, inclusion, and environment—but also lead to new challenges like job security or responsibility of robots.

This book was a major undertaking at international levels, looking at concepts and question of trust in communication beyond traditional thinking. It is about Digital Worlds and New Technologies, but actually goes deeper. We have a lot of contributions highlighting challenges with trust in Digital Worlds that are often overlooked and ignored. We look at linguistic analysis and communication changes in general. We look at industries like the financial industry, or sectors like social entrepreneurship. And we look at concepts like branding, where brand trust is a common phenomenon to be successful.

We know that in today's world, trust is partially declining and that it plays a different role than what it used to. Artificial intelligence and computer algorithms will add to a level of complexity that often goes beyond the understanding by most people. Trust, as we know from the sociologist perspective, often is a mechanism to reduce that complexity. If we do not understand anymore what computers and machines decide, how can we build trust in so-called Smart Societies? We need to look at trust in urban living and future mobility spaces, as this impacts how we live and work together in the future. And we need to look at new competencies that are needed and how to build up that level of trusted competencies.

The opening chapter "The Game of Trust" from Stephanie Heinecke gives an overview of current challenges in the media system. Three key developments will be reflected: First, the topic of mediatization and how the media logic has gained influence on all areas of life; second, the question of truth and trust in journalism, and finally, the need for sustainable strategies and business models in our times of shifting power between traditional market participants and new competitors. All three developments are interconnected and will shape the trust in our future media system to a huge extend.

In his contribution about "Building Trust in Digital Worlds," Thomas Osburg focuses on the critical role; trust will play in new Digital Worlds. Current discussions are centered around possibilities and threats of technologies, with little focus on how the digital solutions are ultimately accepted by the users and citizens. And in order to be accepted, a new level of trust needs to be there. Trusting the unknown becomes a major challenge, especially in times of declining Institutional Trust. Companies remain, more than ever before, responsible for their impacts on society. And this responsibility goes far beyond concepts titled "Corporate Digital Responsibility (CDR)."

Jonas Bedford-Strohm analyzes the "Socio-Historical Contexts of Anti-Institutionalist Tendencies in Digital Media Transformation." Digital transformation is not only a matter of technology, but comes along with processes of social change and public debate. This chapter will identify and discuss five key factors for public trust: participation, information, consent, inclusion, and accountability.

"The Financial Value of Trust in the Media Business" is then examined by Harald Watzek. Trust is not a "nice-to-have" attribute for media companies, but is a strong driver of success with financial implications. Market players have to find the adequate strategy and ask themselves whether they better act as a price leader, a quality leader, or a speed leader.

Zhanna Belyaeva will focus on the responsibility of companies in her contribution about "Value CoCreation and CSR through Media Lenses." The purpose of her chapter is to examine the development of competences that force stronger trust and responsibility in Western (German) and Eastern (Russia) cultures. Trust, as a foundation for communication, embraces a variety of cross-functional and multidisciplinary concepts and goes beyond marketing theory aiming to advance both internal and external multistakeholder dialogue.

The contribution on "Communication and Trust: A Linguistic Analysis" by Anna-Maria Meck specifically looks at how exactly trust and communication are intertwined: Is it the voice or the content that are more trust building? And how does this change in times of Distributed Trust where Individual Trust is rising while Institutional Trust is declining?

"Shifts in Communication and Ego-Identity in Digital World" are then examined by Anke Werani. First, a brief overview of psycholinguistic aspects focusing on communication and the change of communication skills is given. Communication theories are presented, and the term *space of communication* is described. Finally, it is examined how communication is influenced by the use of social media and identity-constructing processes.

Following holistic and strategic concepts of trust, Part II of the book will then shift the focus to journalism and social media.

Influencer is an integral part of today's marketing strategies for young target groups. But to what end? "From Trusted Brand to Trusted Friend": Julia Kirn explains the specific relationship between influencers and their followers and shows some important factors in order to gain the most from this marketing approach: a transfer of credibility and trust.

Credibility is also a key topic for Thomas Mrazek, who points out the importance of “Truth and Trust in Journalism.” Which strategies can publishers and journalists use in times of discussions about fake news and distorted media coverage? Transparency is key in order to earn back the trust of recipients.

Jessica Kunert discusses a technological aspect of today’s journalism: “The Impact of Automation of Content Distribution and Content Creation in the Newsroom” challenges traditional newsrooms. This chapter gives insights on news personalization and automated journalism. Will machines take over? And how do the journalists and the recipients react?

Local journalism is a difficile area for trust: The audience knows best what is going on in their neighborhood. If local journalists do not keep in mind the special circumstances of news creation, credibility will be destroyed very quickly. Uwe Brueckner discusses the key aspects on how local TV can make the most of this situation and rise “Like the Phoenix from the Pixel.”

Usually, algorithms find recommendations by analyzing past behavior. However, this past-oriented approach has not been uncriticized as it leads to a so-called filter bubble. The contribution “The Filter Bubble in Social Media Communication” by Katharina Klug and Charlotte Strang sheds light to the filter bubble focusing on users’ perception and reaction. Communication has received much attention over the last two decades with the increasing use of social media. Taken together, the findings of the authors highlight the change in communication processes influenced by social media.

Online media has effects on our social behavior. Especially kids and teens often find themselves in communicative situations their parents have no access to—or just do not understand. Uwe Leest warns of the loss of control and explains how “Cyberbullying endangers our society.”

Part III of the book widens the focus from media to core competencies and whole market developments.

Artificial intelligence (AI) touches our lives every day. For most online actions, an AI algorithm has sorted out what it considers to be relevant for us. By the time you receive your search results in a Google, the advertising spaces on the results page have been auctioned by algorithms. This is based on your surfing habits stored in commercial databases, sociodemographic information collected from your social network profiles, and many other resources. Johannes Bruhn and Matthias Anderer look at the challenges of “Implementing Artificial Intelligence in Organizations and the special role of trust in this process.”

Natalie Buciek and Philipp Sandner focus on “The Blockchain Technology in the Media Sector.” What are smart contracts and how can a distributed ledger technology change the interdependencies in the media ecosystem? The authors give an overview on some key developments.

What competencies will we need in a Digital World? Stephanie Heinecke, Maria Berg, and Ludwig Hinkofer discuss the road we have come from conceptions of media competence to digital competence and give an outlook on the skills not only our children might need in the future. “Trust me if you can”: People will only feel confident with digital tools when they are equipped with corresponding knowledge.

A very special topic is introduced by Yuliya Aray and Anastasia A. Petrova-Savchenko. Their contribution about “Creating Societal Trust through Communication to Legitimize Social Entrepreneurship in Russia” is a role-model concept. Social entrepreneurs who set themselves both social and economic goals are the actors who may try to create and develop new business models in the areas of state and market failures. Trust plays a crucial role in this concept. People mostly judge social entrepreneurs by their intentions instead of judging by the social effects brought by their entrepreneurial activities. This is a very relevant challenge, as social entrepreneurs are usually characterized by a higher level of trust that comes from the different goals they have in finding solutions for society.

Concluding on the sector of social entrepreneurship and to understand how social enterprises use digital tools to market their offering to digitally connected stakeholders, Chinnoy Bandyopadhyay and Subhasis Ray interacted with four Indian social entrepreneurs described in their contribution “Digital Marketing and Communication for Social Enterprises.” Their study presented here reveals that social enterprises use innovative ways such as using an app to maintain transparency (and to create trust) about their offering and operations, showcasing their social impact, and offering through platforms like Facebook, Twitter, Instagram, and their own Web sites. WhatsApp videos featuring their innovative offering also go viral and let people know about these organizations. The results of the authors highlight that the digital marketing tools are more suitable for social enterprises to create trust in the face of challenges such as lack of resources, absence of well-established distribution or supply chain setup, and cumbersome to track and target customers in offline mode.

The editors sincerely hope that you enjoy this book as much as we did when bringing all these top-level authors together. We would like to thank them for their professional insight into very specific topics of Media and Communication Trust in Digital Worlds.

Munich, Germany
May 2019

Prof. Dr. Thomas Osburg
Prof. Dr. Stephanie Heinecke

Contents

Editors and Contributors

About the Editors

Thomas Osburg is an internationally experienced Professor, Entrepreneur, Advisor, and former Executive Director with over 25 years of experience in leadership positions working for global IT companies (i.e., Intel Corp. and Texas Instruments) in the USA, China, Germany, and France. During the last years, He has delivered more than 80 keynote speeches and written over 40 scientific publications, he is teaching bachelor, master, and MBA classes at leading European universities, and was elected on the Board of Directors at leading European associations. As an entrepreneur, he recently established a global Research Institute for Urban Live and Future Mobility and a Non-for-Profit NGO for Sustainable Development.

Stephanie Heinecke is a professor for communication studies and sports management at Hochschule Fresenius in Munich. Previously, she worked for 10 years as Head of Research and Knowledge Management at Solon Management Consulting, a strategy consultancy specialized in TIME markets. She studied communication science at Ludwig Maximilian University of Munich and did her Dr. Phil. in parallel to her work at Solon. Focus of her thesis were issues of mediatization in professional sports. In 2017, she joined Hochschule Fresenius. Her current work and research focus on media economy, development of digital strategy, and sports communication.

Contributors

Matthias Anderer Hochschule Fresenius, Munich, Germany

Yulia Aray Saint Petersburg State University, Saint Petersburg, Russian Federation

Chinmoy Bandyopadhyay Xavier Institute of Management, Xavier University, Bhubaneswar, Odisha, India

Jonas Bedford-Strohm Zentrum für Ethik der Medien und der digitalen Gesellschaft (zem::dg), Munich, Germany

Zhanna Belyaeva Graduate School of Economics and Management, Ural Federal University, GSEM-UrFU, Yekaterinburg, Russia

Maria Berg Hochschule Fresenius, Munich, Germany

Uwe Brückner muenchen.tv, Reichertshausen, Germany

Johannes Bruhn Hochschule Fresenius, Munich, Germany

Natalie Buciek Daimler AG, Stuttgart, Germany

Stephanie Heinecke Hochschule Fresenius, Munich, Germany

Ludwig Hinkofer Hochschule Fresenius, Munich, Germany

Katharina Klug Fresenius University of Applied Science, Munich, Germany

Jessica Kunert Universität Hamburg, Hamburg, Germany

Uwe Leest Bündnis gegen Cybermobbing e.V., Karlsruhe, Germany

Anna-Maria Meck VUI.agency, Munich, Germany

Julia Merz Hochschule Fresenius, Munich, Germany

Thomas Mrazek Bavarian Association of Journalists, Munich, Germany

Thomas Osburg Hochschule Fresenius, Munich, Germany

Anastasia Petrova-Savchenko Saint Petersburg State University, Saint Petersburg, Russian Federation

Subhasis Ray Xavier Institute of Management, Xavier University, Bhubaneswar, Odisha, India

Philipp Sandner Frankfurt School of Finance and Management gGmbH, Frankfurt am Main, Germany

Charlotte Strang University of Leipzig, Leipzig, Germany

Harald Watzek Hochschule Fresenius, Munich, Germany

Anke Werani LMU München, Munich, Germany

Part I
Trust and Communication

Chapter 1
The Game of Trust: Reflections on Truth and Trust in a Shifting Media Ecosystem

Stephanie Heinecke

1 Introduction

In many ways, trust has been a crucial component of the media industry for ages. History knows the full spectrum, from freedom of the press to the media serving as the fourth estate to suppression and misuse for propaganda. In today's modern society, trust in the media hasn't lost any relevance. On the contrary, in an ever more complex and digital world, trust is the crucial point not only for opinion making but also for business models. The term *media* covers much more than the traditional channels of mass media. Almost any kind of media content is only one click away, be it breaking news, marketing information from institutions and brands, or illegal activities. We can find anything online and make more or less deliberate decisions, believe the news or not, buy a product, or just forget about it. The competitive advantage is not necessarily with the journalists who produce objective and high-quality content but with those that have the best search engine marketing.

Traditionally, the media were agents that filter information. They were gatekeepers with an enormous impact on public opinion. As such, they had been subject to a lot of research in traditional communication science since the 1950s (overview in Pürer 2014). They may still be gatekeepers, but the rules and reach have changed significantly. Digitization has opened the door to alternative sources of information. How many people still appreciate journalistic standards and values? Why not just follow the politicians via Twitter, Facebook, and Instagram directly? Fulfilling increasingly divergent user expectations seems an impossible task for the media. The one-way flow of information is dead, the back channel is wide open, and user opinions stream in with all the consequences. If you are lucky, you go viral. Still, the next shitstorm is only one click away.

S. Heinecke (✉)
Hochschule Fresenius, Infanteriestr. 11a, 80797 Munich, Germany
e-mail: stephanie.heinecke@hs-fresenius.de

T. Osburg and S. Heinecke (eds.), *Media Trust in a Digital World*,
https://doi.org/10.1007/978-3-030-30774-5_1

Therefore, the old roles have eroded. Journalism faces existential problems on the content side, fighting against fake news and claiming its position against user-generated content. With digitization, traditional media companies ran into strategic difficulties. Tech companies from and outside of Silicon Valley disrupted key parts of their business and took away large parts of their advertising revenue. The old players' strong belief in their extensive industry experience, their quality content, and their traditional business models blinded them to new and innovative approaches to the customers. Even though they adopted digital technology, their mind-set was often limited. They underestimated the power of platforms, of communities, and of customer-centric approaches and lost large parts of their recipients.

As a consequence, shifts in the media system afflict not only journalism and media companies but also all parties along the value chain, starting from the people and institutions eager for media attention to do their job (politicians, stars, companies, etc.) and not ending with advertisers who use media as a platform to promote their products. The right message and the right channel are still crucial, but both aspects are no longer a privilege of traditional and professional media. User-generated content has moved from a niche for nerds to a broad audience. Professional social media influencers have made their way into the marketing mix, challenging traditional channels on both the content and the user sides and in terms of advertising revenues.

Let's get back to trust. All the aspects mentioned depend on credibility and reliability. Do we trust a source? Do we trust an institution? According to the 2018 edition of the Edelman Trust Barometer, the media have (for the first time) become the least trusted global institution (Edelman 2018). One has to check this carefully since there are differences by country, and *media*, in general, is defined as both platform and journalism. In the survey, journalism gains back trust as a source for news compared with the last years, probably not at least given the global worry about fake news. Still, the trust in platforms decreased in several countries. This introductory chapter will give an overview of the context *media–communication–trust* in a digital world.

2 Playgrounds and Battlefields

Several topics can be discussed in the context of this book's title as you will observe in the following chapters. If we look at the core of the media system, we will discover three key fields in the context of trust:

- Mediatization: how the media shape our society
- Journalism and social media: truth and trust
- Business models and strategy: money and/or trust?

The first aspect is based on a discourse in communication science and tries to explain the social implications of the increasing importance of media. The second point reflects an ongoing discussion both in research and in practice, pointing out the parallel existence of professional and user-generated media content and the users' expectations on credibility and trust. Economic aspects especially drive the third issue raised, which describes strategic shifts in the media system, both those we have already experienced and those likely to happen in the near future. All three aspects attempt to point out opportunities and conflicts shaping the media and communication landscape. This introductory chapter will raise some questions, to which the authors of this book have their own answers.

2.1 *Mediatization: How the Media Shape Our Society*

The concept of *mediatization* is a huge driver of today's media and information society. In communication science, it describes the increasing importance of media in all aspects of our lives (overview in Birkner 2017, Heinecke 2014, Meyen et al. 2014). The term includes different interpretations in terms of scope, theoretical background, and implications. Still, they all raise the question of how media of all kinds shape our society, our behavior, and our understanding of the world. Two major fields of research are to be distinguished mainly according to their different understanding of the term *medium*. In German literature, we find these differences even in the terminology: *Medialisierung* versus *Mediatisierung*. Even though the discussion has lost some of the initial sharpness, pointing out the key deliberations from both approaches is highly useful to show the relevance in the context of trust.

The first perspective is focused on mass communication, a traditional topic in communication science. In times of mediatization, all parts of society "become influenced by and dependent on the media" (Hjarvard 2012, 30). Media are the stage for everyone who wants to be heard: politicians, companies, stars, influencers, and activists. Public attention is the key for their business, no matter what the cost. To gain public attention, actors on all levels (individual, institutional, or system level) adapt their behavior to a specific media logic (which differs in each kind of medium). Mediatization, in this sense, can be understood as "second-order long-term mass media effects" (Meyen et al. 2014, 273). People believe in the power and importance of the media for their purpose and adapt their behavior. This is the huge difference compared with direct media effects often researched in an individual context (Kepplinger 2008).

Mediatization affects structures in our society and results in processes of social change. It has a long-term perspective; most authors focus on the last 30–40 years. Interactions are made with other social processes, such as economization, globalization, and digitization (Heinecke 2014). Several research results show the effects of mediatization in very different areas, such as politics or sports (e.g., Dohle and Vowe 2006, Kepplinger 2002, Heinecke 2014, Marcinkowski and Steiner 2010, Meyen 2014, Strömbäck and Van Aelst 2013, Vowe and Dohle 2008). Even though one must be careful not to interpret all changes as caused by mediatization, the research results clearly show that mediatization is happening, and adaptations to the logic of the media system become visible in several ways as listed below:

- *Individual level*: People present themselves according to the media logic and change their style, speech, and appearance. We see personalization strategies in communication, and people become human brands.
- *Institutional level*: Companies extend their PR, establish media strategies, and pay close attention to all aspects of corporate (media) communication.
- *System level*: Rules and circumstances (that usually define a system) change to create a media-friendly environment and make the system more attractive for media coverage (especially seen in sports when rules and places are adapted to the needs of the media: more action, strict timing, attractive event package, and perfect working conditions for journalists).

This list is far from complete but gives an idea of the effects of mediatization. In terms of trust, what does it mean to our understanding of the world when we are fully aware of the strategic part of communication in our society? Well, of course, most of us *are* aware somehow, but what consequences does this awareness have for our trust? What is actually *true* in a very basic sense?

These questions are closely connected to the concept of *media logic*, which, in general, describes the conditions for content creation. For Esser (2013), media logic comprises professional, commercial, and technological aspects. Neuberger (2013) differentiates a journalistic system logic from a media-related logic, while Landerer (2014) mentions normative and market considerations as key drivers of media logic. What they all try to capture is the controversial relationship between journalistic standards, values, and norms and the need to earn money and attract a broad audience. This discussion gains even more importance in times of social media, innumerable sources of information, and new market participants, all of which we will discuss in the next part of this text.

The second perspective of mediatization is focused not only on mass media but also on several media-related aspects of life. The representatives of this view define the terms *medium* and *communication* in a broader sense. Apart from mass communication, Krotz (2015) also mentions personal communication between people via a medium (such as a phone or chat) and interactive communication (such as human–computer/robot communication) as highly relevant parts of the mediatization discourse. Consequently, research approaches in this area are very broad and enclose very different topics. The effects permeate each area of our personal and social lives (Couldry and Hepp 2017), be it the mediatization of the home, private life, gaming, or religion. A broad selection of topics can be found in anthologies from the DFG project Mediatized Worlds (Krotz and Hepp 2012, Hepp and Krotz 2014, Krotz et al. 2014). Technological developments, especially the human–machine interaction, will become a key topic in the following years.

For our search for the role of trust, both approaches toward mediatization are highly relevant. The broader view is extremely valuable for our relationship to all aspects with increasing dependence on media of all kinds in a digital world. Human behavior and interaction with media, digital tools, and applications are key topics not only for communication science but also for education, the labor market, companies, and many other stakeholders. The mass media–centric perspective shows the importance of the media for many stakeholders and explains substantial changes in the public sphere and journalism. The mediatized world is the basis for the 24-7 multiple-source private and public flow of information that keeps us busy with all the advantages and challenges discussed below.

2.2 *Journalism and Social Media: Truth and Trust*

We see and reflect large parts of our world through media. Media knows the game, and the stakeholders do so as well. Journalistic coverage has always been a key path to public discourse. Even though the number of sources available has increased enormously, the media still filter how we see our world. We can't just easily look behind the scenes in politics or the economy. Global issues are too complex to learn about in detail without the help of well-informed explanations. Today, these explanations do not necessarily come from journalists. With the rise of digitization, blogs, and social media, everybody can speak directly to their audience, be it five followers or five million. The old gatekeeper function of traditional mass media has eroded.

In most cases, the debate focuses on the fight between journalism and social media. Neuberger (2014, 15) points out four key aspects regarding public communication in a digital environment:

- *Participation*: Everybody has access to public discourse via online channels—media users, PR departments, activists, minorities, or any other group of participants.
- *Interaction*: The roles of communicators and recipients are flexible. Many people with different backgrounds can take part in discussions.
- *Transparency*: Search functions and the user's usage selections enable them to compile their very own relevant set of media. By collecting usage data, information providers receive direct feedback on their reach and the behavior of their users.
- *Disintermediation*: both recipients and sources do not necessarily need journalists to get in touch. The traditional role of media companies as intermediary is eroding.

Today's digital communication platforms clearly have upsides (freedom of speech, diversity, communities) and downsides (fake news, manipulation, filter bubble). The relationship between journalism and social media can be a matter of competition, of complementariness, or of integration (Neuberger 2014). Media companies cannot do without social media channels if they want to be heard by relevant target groups. Still, there are differences in the users' perceptions and expectations.

Once again, trust is an important factor. Which sources and actors should we trust whether on traditional media channels or via social media? When it comes to credibility, surveys show that German media users rank public TV and radio the highest (WDR, infratest dimap 2018, a comprehensive overview of surveys in ARD 2018). Quality news outlets often form research collaborations, such as Süddeutsche Zeitung, NDR, and WDR or the initiative *European Investigative Collaborations* with several European magazines and newspapers. These efforts are a reaction to the increasingly diverse communication among all available media channels. Traditional editorial brands need to focus on their strength—objective and well-researched news and backgrounds—because alternative facts are only one click away. But do credible and quality news really have the highest market share when it comes to usage? Sometimes, the dark side just tells the better stories. Damage, conflict, and negativism have been key criteria for news selection since the very beginning of gatekeeper research (Lippmann 1922, Galtung and Ruge 1965, Schulz 1976). Even high-quality news outlets are not immune against journalistic fraud as the German magazine Der Spiegel had experienced in late 2018 with the case of the reporter Claas Relotius (Klusmann and Kurbjuweit 2018).

Another aspect of credibility is that marketing and branding have always been part of the game among rivaling professional players in the media sector. Still, social media has opened Pandora's box with millions of new competitors. Friends, PR departments, public persons, activists, and influencers compete for the users' attention. On social media platforms, all kinds of content stream into the users' news feeds. Cat content and family pictures follow political information. Influencers present brands and products. The logic of social media differs widely from journalistic standards. Objectivity? The separation of news from opinion? In particular, the separation of editorial content and advertising leads to absurdity when influencers try to follow obligations by labeling every post, even those without any advertising (just to be on the safe side). In most cases, the users don't care about it; it's part of the game. Regarding journalists, they have different expectations—journalists need to stick to their values while staying competitive in the battle for attention (which takes us back to the issue of journalistic norms and values versus the market logic). Is social media a friend or foe for trust?

2.3 *Business Models and Strategy: Money and/or Trust?*

We initially discussed the Edelman Trust Barometer and the shameful results for media in general. Still, while trust in platforms has decreased, journalism has gained back trust (Edelman 2018). In Germany, the research project Mainzer Langzeitstudie Medienvertrauen (Ziegele et al. 2018) shows that hysteria regarding fake news is slowing down. We already discussed that public broadcasting is especially recognized as a trustful source.

This could be the golden hour of these institutions. The question is, are people still listening? The request for information is still a key driver for media usage (Breunig and Engel 2015). User-centric news feeds and on-demand offerings from platforms such as Netflix have gained huge market shares and competed for our attention. Quality journalism requires attractive editorial formats and availability on demand and on mobile devices to attract recipients.

In 2017, ProSiebenSat.1 board member Conrad Albrecht openly asked for shares from the German broadcasting license fee for private TV stations to produce quality content. In his opinion, private TV accomplishes a huge part of the basic provision for all, especially young target groups that hardly use public broadcasting (Meier 2017). Even though Albrecht's approach was criticized heavily, he has a point. Quality content is expensive; the battle for user attention with players from Silicon Valley is on. But can an extended payment be the adequate solution? Public service and public value are hot topics in the political, legal, and regulatory environment of today's media systems. High-quality journalistic content may not disappear behind paywalls but should be accessible to everybody (low-income households are therefore excluded from public broadcasting license fees). But will we stick to our dual broadcasting system in the future, or will the system erode and content be exposed to the market logic only? In Switzerland's direct democracy, people voted to retain the current license fee system for public broadcasting in 2018, even though polls before the decision predicted the contrary (Agence France-Presse 2018). What results would such a popular vote produce in other countries?

As we already discussed, the ecosystem of media and communication has experienced massive shifts over the last few years. Companies from outside the media industry entered the stage, and they have come to stay. Today, FAANG (Facebook, Amazon, Apple, Netflix, and Google) controls large parts of our communication and media usage. Sure, we can always distinguish among journalistic content, clearly more entertaining editorial content, or user-generated content, but they all aim for the same recipients.

The new players follow a different logic than the old system (Klinger and Svensson 2015). The buzzword is *customer centricity*. The mind-set of these companies is based on customer satisfaction. Customers should get what they want anytime, anywhere, and if they don't know exactly what they want, the algorithm has some suggestions based on prior usage. The platforms already have detailed information on their customers. Artificial intelligence systems combine the data and make predictions on future buying decisions. The crucial point is that quality journalism seeking for the truth can only partly follow a customer-centric approach. Sure, one can edit the news in an appealing way, but hiding inconvenient news and challenging topics contradicts the journalistic claim in a democracy.

Since the 2000s, we have witnessed the rise of platforms at the expense of traditional media. Platforms took away both users and advertising customers. The consequences were financial difficulties and cost pressure in media companies, resulting in less money to invest in people and quality content and, at the same time, increasing the pressure to look for new revenue sources (for example, e-commerce activities and investments in start-ups).

The Edelman Trust Barometer talks about increasing trust in journalists but decreasing trust in platforms. Despite all user centricity, the platforms need trust for their data-driven business models of the future. In 2016 (before the public discussion of the Cambridge Analytica scandal), Facebook launched advertising campaigns to make the functionality more transparent, for example, with large explanatory advertisements on the usage of personal data or information on how to adapt the privacy settings (Brecht 2017). As a part of the fight against fake news, Facebook also introduced a nonpublic rating of the users' trustworthiness (Dwoskin 2018).

Another playground for trust in platforms might come from quality journalistic content itself. Instead of battling against traditional media, the platforms try to find synergies. Google set up the Digital News Initiative (Google 2018), while Facebook launched the Facebook Journalism Project (Facebook 2018). Both approaches are counterstrategies to fake news and promote quality journalism, starting on the educational level with training for journalists and not ending with efforts for traditional media and digital platforms to create products together.

The question is whether traditional media brands are ready for cooperation (Moses 2018, Dachwitz 2018). They might finally team up with their direct competitors to build a content alliance against the big players. We have seen similar approaches in the past, yet they either lacked the full support of all major players or failed because of legal and regulatory restrictions. Between 2010 and 2012, Germany's biggest private broadcasters, ProSiebenSat.1 and RTL, tried to create a joint OTT offering. Public broadcasters ARD and ZDF followed a similar approach. Still, the cartel office blocked both initiatives (Krieger 2018). Today, new collaboration initiatives in the German TV industry seem to find approval (for example Joyn, a joint-venture by ProSiebenSat.1 and Discovery). Alliances like these might be critical for the long-term survival of traditional media brands—maybe even cross-industry projects between broadcasters and publishing houses (Schade 2018).

3 Choices and Challenges

We just discussed three fields of trust in a shifting media ecosystem. First, the concept of mediatization describes processes of social change that come along with the enormously increased importance of media for all stakeholders. Second, in times of digital accessibility and social media, we are facing a diversity of content sources and interaction modes.

Journalists, users, brands, politicians, influencers, and many other voices try to get the users' attention. With open communication channels, misinformation and fake news have become serious problems with serious consequences on social coherence. In the battle for attention, competitors from the traditional media system start from very different positions, which brings us to the third aspect mentioned. Some of them are public funded, others private. They have different approaches and are still similarly affected by the rise of platforms, their different user logic, and their different business models. Still, when it comes to trust, traditional journalistic players are ahead (at a generally low level). This is, so far, the ecosystem. And what of the user?

Of course, we want to get whatever we ask from the media—information, entertainment, the full agenda. We still believe we have a choice, but we are trapped. If we want the best customer experience, some players leave us with no choice to agree to their terms and conditions. We always pay a price, be it money or data or both.

Having a choice might be an important factor of trust. In modern democracies, we never had that much choice before as we have today. At least, it seems like. Technological disruption is moving on; artificial intelligence plays a more and more important role in our lives and has come to stay. Will robots be the new journalists? Will algorithms decide on how we see the world—or do they already? Maybe it is even about time to trust data more than any human. But technology is not neutral; if the algorithms are trained on biased data, they will produce biased results.

Trust can only arise from something we understand. So we need to talk about skills. Which competences do we need to navigate through the digital media world? Having a choice is also about taking responsibility, not only for one's media usage but also for privacy protection, reasonable behavior in the online world, and security issues. Digital developments are challenging our trust. Do you accept the challenge?

References

Agence France-Presse (2018) Switzerland votes overwhelmingly to keep its public broadcaster. In: theguardian.com, 5 Mar 2018. https://www.theguardian.com/world/2018/mar/05/switzerland-votes-overwhelmingly-to-keep-its-public-broadcaster. Accessed 14 Dec 2018

ARD (2018) Studien zu Medienvertrauen und Glaubwürdigkeit der ARD. http://www.ard.de/home/die-ard/fakten/Studien_zu_Medienvertrauen_und_Glaubwuerdigkeit_der_ARD/4113572/index.html. Accessed 12 Dec 2018

Birkner T (2017) Medialisierung und Mediatisierung. Nomos, Baden-Baden

Brecht K (2017) “Mache Facebook zu deinem Facebook” geht in die zweite Runde. In: horizont.net, 17 Jul 2017. https://www.horizont.net/medien/nachrichten/Imagekampagne-Mache-Facebook-zu-deinem-Facebook-geht-in-die-zweite-Runde-159643. Accessed 14 Dec 2018

Breunig C, Engel B (2015) Massenkommunikation 2015: Funktionen und Images der Medien im Vergleich. Ergebnisse der ARD/ZDF-Langzeitstudien. In: Media Perspektiven 7-8/2015, pp 323–341. https://www.ard-werbung.de/fileadmin/user_upload/media-perspektiven/pdf/2015/07082015_Breunig_Engel.pdf. Accessed 14 Dec 2018

Couldry N, Hepp A (2017) The mediated construction of reality. Polity, Cambridge

Dachwitz, I (2018) News Initiative: Wohin Googles Millionen für die Medien in Deutschland fließen. In: netpolitik.org vom 26 Sep 2018. https://netzpolitik.org/2018/news-initiative-wohin-googles-millionen-fuer-die-medien-in-deutschland-fliessen/ Accessed 15 Dec 2018

Dohle M, Vowe G (2006) Der Sport auf der “Mediatisierungstreppe”? Ein Modell zur Analyse medienbedingter Veränderungen des Sports. In: Medien und Erziehung (merz), vol 50, pp 18–28

Dwoskin E (2018) Facebook is rating the trustworthiness of its users on a scale from zero to 1. In: washingtonpost.com, 21 Aug 2018. https://www.washingtonpost.com/technology/2018/08/21/facebook-is-rating-trustworthiness-its-users-scale-zero-one/?noredirect=on&utm_term=.42c1c3439a68. Accessed 15 Dec 2018

Edelman (2018) 2018 Edelman trust barometer. https://www.edelman.com/trust-barometer. Accessed 12 Dec 2018

Esser F (2013) Mediatization as a challenge. Media logic versus political logic. In: Kriesi H (ed) Democracy in the age of globalization and mediatization. Palmgrave Macmillan, Basingstoke, pp 177-201

Facebook (2018) Introducing: the Facebook journalism project. https://www.facebook.com/facebookmedia/blog/introducing-the-facebook-journalism-project. Accessed 14 Dec 2018

Galtung J, Ruge MH (1965) The structure of foreign news. J Peace Res 2(1):64–91

Google (2018) Google news initiative. https://newsinitiative.withgoogle.com/dnifund/. Accessed 14 Dec 2018

Heinecke S (2014) Fit fürs Fernsehen? Die Medialisierung des Spitzensports als Kampf um Gold und Sendezeit. Herbert von Halem, Köln

Hepp A, Krotz F (eds) (2014) Mediatized worlds: culture and society in a media age. Palgrave, London

Hjarvard S (2012) Doing the right thing. Media and communication studies in a mediatized world. Nordicom Rev 34(2):27–34

WDR, infratest dimap (2018) Glaubwürdigkeit der Medien. https://www1.wdr.de/unternehmen/der-wdr/unternehmen/glaubwuerdigkeitsstudie-2018-100.pdf. Accessed 12 Dec 2018

Kepplinger HM (2002) Mediatization of politics: theory and data. J Commun 52(4):972–986

Kepplinger HM (2008) Was unterscheidet die Mediatisierungsforschung von der Medienwirkungsforschung? Publizistik 53(3):326–338

Klinger U, Svensson J (2015) Network media logik: some conceptial considerations. In: Bruns A et al (eds) The Routledge companion to social media and politics. Routledge, New York, pp 23–38

Klusmann S, Kurbjuweit D (2018) Statement from DER SPIEGEL editors-in-chief. In: spiegel.de, 20 Dec 2018. https://www.spiegel.de/international/zeitgeist/der-spiegel-statement-on-relotius-fraud-case-a-1244896.html. Accessed 21 Dec 2018

Krieger J (2018) ZDF to approach cartel office on OTT platform prospects. In: broadbandtvnews.com, 30 June 2018. https://www.broadbandtvnews.com/2018/06/30/zdf-to-approach-cartel-office-on-ott-platform-prospects/. Accessed 15 Dec 2018

Krotz F (2015) Mediatisierung. In: Hepp A, Krotz F, Lingenberg S, Wimmer J (eds) Handbuch Cultural Studies und Medienanalyse. Springer VS, Wiesbaden, pp 439–451

Krotz F, Hepp A (eds) (2012) Mediatisierte Welten: Forschungsfelder und Beschreibungsansätze. VS Verlag für Sozialwissenschaften, Wiesbaden

Krotz F, Despotović C, Kruse M (eds) (2014) Die Mediatisierung sozialer Welten. Synergien empirischer Forschung. Springer VS, Wiesbaden

Landerer N (2014) Opposing the government but governing the audience? J Stud 15(3):304–320

Lippmann W (1922) Public Opinion. Harcourt, Brace and Company, New York

Marcinkowski F, Steiner A (2010) Was heißt "Medialisierung"? Autonomiebeschränkung oder Ermöglichung von Politik durch Massenmedien? In: Arnold K, Classen C, Kinnebrock S, Lersch E, Wagner HU (eds) Von der Politisierung der Medien zur Medialisierung des Politischen? Zum Verhältnis von Medien, Öffentlichkeiten und Politik im 20. Leipziger Universitätsverlag, Leipzig, Jahrhundert, pp 51–76

Meier C (2017) Eine Provokation. In: welt.de, 05.07.2017. https://www.welt.de/print/welt_kompakt/kultur/article166279076/Eine-Provokation.html. Accessed 14 Dec 2018

Meyen M (2014) Medialisierung des deutschen Spitzenfußballs. Eine Fallstudie zur Anpassung von sozialen Funktionssystemen an die Handlungslogik der Massenmedien. In: Medien & Kommunikationswisssenschaft, 62/3, pp 377-394

Meyen M, Thieroff M, Strenger S (2014) Mass media logic and the mediatization of politics. J Stud 15(3):271–288

Moses L (2018) One year in, Facebook journalism project gets mixed reviews from publishers. In: digiday.com, 06.01.2018. https://digiday.com/media/one-year-facebook-journalism-project-gets-mixed-reviews-publishers/ Accessed 15 Dec 2018

Neuberger C (2013) Journalismus und Medialisierung der Gesellschaft. In: Meier K, Neuberger C (eds) Journalismusforschung. Stand und Perspektiven. Nomos, Baden-Baden, pp 221–242

Neuberger C (2014) Social Media und Journalismus. In: Neuberger C, Langenohl S, Nuernbergk C (eds) Social Media und Journalismus. Landesanstalt für Medien Nordrhein-Westfalen (LfM), Düsseldorf, pp 15–33

Pürer H (2014) Publizistik und Kommunikationswissenschaft. UVK, Konstanz

Schade M (2018) Supermediathek: Wie realistisch ist eine gemeinsame Plattformlösung von Verlagen und TV? In: meedia.de, 9 Jul 2018. https://meedia.de/2018/07/09/supermediathek-wie-realistisch-ist-eine-gemeinsamen-plattformloesung-von-verlagen-und-tv/. Accessed 14 Dec 2018

Schulz W (1976) Die Konstruktion von Realität in den Nachrichtenmedien. Karl Alber, Freiburg/München

Strömbäck J, Van Aelst P (2013) Why political parties adapt to the media: Exploring the fourth dimension of mediatization. Int Commun Gaz 75:342–458

Vowe G, Dohle M (2008) Welche Macht wird den Medien zugeschrieben? Das Verhältnis von Medien und Politik im Spiegel der Mediatisierungsdebatte. In: Jäckel M, Mai M (eds) Medienmacht und Gesellschaft. Zum Wandel öffentlicher Kommunikation, Campus, Frankfurt, pp 11–36

Ziegele M, Schultz T, Jackob N et al (2018) Lügenpresse-Hysterie ebbt ab. Mainzer Langzeitstudie "Medienvertrauen". In: Media Perspektiven 4/2018, pp 150–162. https://www.ard-werbung.de/fileadmin/user_upload/media-perspektiven/pdf/2018/0418_Ziegele_Schultz_Jackob_Granow_Quiring_Schemer.pdf Accessed 14 Dec. 2018

Stephanie Heinecke is professor for communication studies at Hochschule Fresenius in Munich. Previously, she worked for 10 years as Head of Research and Knowledge Management at Solon Management Consulting, a strategy consultancy specialised in TIME markets. Stephanie studied communication science at Ludwig Maximilian University of Munich and did her Dr. phil. in parallel to her work at Solon. Focus of her thesis were issues of mediatization in professional sports. In 2017, she joined Hochschule Fresenius. Her current work and research includes both current issues of media economy and the impact of digital transformation on people, companies, and society.

Chapter 2
Changing Relevance of Trust in Digital Worlds

Thomas Osburg

1 Introduction

Some of us still recall the mid 1990s—a dial-up modem, a newsgroup reader and Netscape. It was the brave new world we adored, a magical universe of technology, transparency, freedom of expression and shared human experience.

For some time now, the utopian vision for the Internet has—among all the positive aspects—also partially given way to a frightening reality, with mass government surveillance, mass collection of personal data, constant data breaches, burgeoning fake messages and rampant commercialism. And instead of creating a trust structure, the economic incentives of today's Internet have created a system where privacy and profitability often contradict each other. We are no longer the users… we became the product!

Trust seems to decrease wherever you look. Several studies (Edelman 2019; GfK Verein 2017) have shown a continuing loss of trust between people and governments, NGOs, media and companies over the last few years. When consumers are asked about their expectations of the role of a CEO in any company, they often give top priority to 'securing trust' over all other factors, including the quality of products and services (Edelman 2019).

Trust is the foundation of trade and a critical factor in building strong brands and business models, but trust is at a historic low. The ongoing digitalization is to some extent complicit in this implosion of trust, but as so often, technology is both the problem and the solution.

This contribution will look at the complex concepts of trust, the current state of trust in general and what can be done to overcome this challenge in *Digital Times*.

T. Osburg (✉)
Hochschule Fresenius, Infanteriestr. 11a, D-80797 Munich, Germany
e-mail: thomas@thomasosburg.de

T. Osburg and S. Heinecke (eds.), *Media Trust in a Digital World*,
https://doi.org/10.1007/978-3-030-30774-5_2

2 The Need for Trust

For any kind of relationship to be successful, trust is a mandatory ingredient (Stelzig 2017). The exchange made between people and institutions must yield a comparable perceived value for all the parties involved (Covey 2009). Whether it is promises to clients, news on the media, good working environment for employees, or acceptable returns to investors, all relate on good communication and the trust placed on the exchange itself (Bruckner 2016).

We live in a highly interconnected world—connected to more things, ideas, news, organizations and humans, than we have been ever before. Technology bridges geographies and relationships and allows us to interact with more people every day. The act of trust involves a voluntary transfer of resources—emotional, physical, financial or material—with no visible, tangible or quantifiable commitment from the trustee. Trust only develops when the expected result of the interaction is perceived as 'beneficial' or 'useful' to the trustor. Leadership, law, economy, relationships, civilizations are all based on this bond of trust (Forcepoint 2019).

2.1 Different Perspectives of Trust

Trust can basically be understood from three different perspectives (Lewicki and Bunker 1995):

- The *sociological perspective* focuses on reduction of complexity and how to deal with the unknown (Luhmann 2014). This is a key approach to building trust in new environments, i.e. for unknown digital solutions.
- The *psychological perspective* builds on the sociological perspective and widens it by including previous experience and impacts on actions taken and results achieved. This perspective will ultimately become more relevant in Digital Worlds, as the usage and familiarity with new technologies increases.
- The *economic perspective*, among others, also deals with game theory, marketing and sales negotiations and puts the question of risk in the foreground (Lewicki and Bunker 1995).

This contribution will mainly look at trust from a sociological perspective. But despite the diverging perspectives, there are a few common elements among all trust perspectives (Bruckner 2016):

- Trust includes taking a *risk of possible disappointment*, increasing one's own vulnerability.
- Trust is built on a *positive future expectation* toward the trusted party that the trusted party will not exploit the respective situation to its advantage.
- Trust is usually built on the *interaction of at least two actors* (e.g. people or organizations) and, very important, the reciprocity of trust relationships.

- Trust usually always includes the notion of being a *reduction of complexity*—especially economic and technical complexity.

2.2 Levels of Trust

Depending on the duration and intensity of a relationship and on the basis of information, trust can further be distinguished into three different types, representing three different levels (Shapiro et al. 1992; Osterloh and Weibel 2006):

- *Calculation-based trust* is a rationalist-decision-oriented approach, i.e. when the value of a cooperation is greater than value of non-cooperation. This is usually considered to be the first or lowest level of trust given to individuals or institutions. The vendor of an immediately consumable product (i.e. ice-cream in a trailer on the street) needs trust regarding the immediate surrounding of the product—safe ingredients, hygiene standards, etc. There is no need to trust the sales person as a human being, nor the business model. Once consumed, trust is no longer needed.
- Going beyond the pure calculation-based approach, the *Knowledge-based trust* includes the expectation of competence, integrity and goodwill. It is usually very difficult to measure but more long-term oriented than a pure situation-based trust. This type of trust is also called the *Feature-based trust*, it is based on long-term experience with the vendor and can often be found in concepts of service-marketing. When you need a haircut, you need to have trust in the person performing it. The trust can come from previous experience, third-party-information, pictures in the store, etc. It goes beyond the pure transaction and often is the basis for successful Relationship Marketing.
- At the highest level, *Identification-based trust* (or Identity-based trust) deals with similar values, emotional attachment and the expectations of some kind of (sometimes virtual) community thinking. Only at the third level trust is built on similar values and beliefs. This could be the case when parents choose the right school for their child. Calculation-based trust (getting the child a good and solid education) and experience-based trust (school has a very good reputation for more than 100 years) are necessary, but not sufficient. Identity-based trust means that the values and goals of the trust-taker (parents) are identical to the ones of the trust-giver (school), the value system of the school has to match those of the parents.

2.3 From the 'What' to the 'How'

Adding to the intensity, negative trust incidents are becoming increasingly visible to the general public. The heightened transparency inherent in our digital world means trust is a highly flammable, ever-present concern. Managing trust cannot be relegated to simply addressing individual incidents with public relations as necessary. Instead, companies need to intentionally create a culture that builds, maintains and preserves trust. They must bake trust into their DNA, strategy, and day-to-day operations—'*Trusted by Design*' (Accenture 2016).

In this age of transparency, *how* a company does things has become as equally important as *what* it does. Trust must permeate relationships with all stakeholders—from employees, to customers, suppliers, investors, analysts and the media.

2.4 Personal and System Trust

A fundamental distinction in the tradition of research on trust refers to the separation of 'system trust' and 'personal trust' (Luhmann 2014). While (inter-)personal trust is aimed at the individual characteristics, conditions, influencing factors and effects of interpersonal trust in the most diverse life area-specific contexts, system trust refers to the phenomenon of an individual's trust in social systems or organizations and institutions (Cochrane 2018).

Luhmann (2014) diagnoses an increasing relevance of system trust in the context of social development towards modernity (Giddens 1991). This is characterized, for example, by spatial-temporal distance increases in our daily lives, the influence of complex systems, the disembodying and rearrangement of social relationships, and a steady increase in expertise (people trust purely the expertise of another person without knowing him or her), a change from personal to depersonalized, generalized relationships of trust can be observed in modern societies (Giddens 1991). Instead of personal trust relationships, trust in the functioning and reliability of a system and in the validity and reliability of structures and procedures takes the place of personal trust relationships (Vollmer et al. 2006).

Modern societies are becoming increasingly complex and confusing, interpersonal trust alone is no longer sufficient (Luhmann 2014). There are daily interactions with people and other actors such as companies or authorities, with whom there is no personal relationship and about whom the communicator can hardly know anything, but whom he must nevertheless place a certain amount of trust in, so that the interaction can be successful in the manner indicated (Zenger and Folkman 2019). Interpersonal trust must therefore be replaced or supplemented by so-called system trust. The expectations of the functioning of the system, of which the individual is a part, are stabilized by the fact that it can be trusted that the members of the system behave in accordance with the roles assigned to them (Lewicki and Bunker 1995).

If this system trust is given (Luhmann 2014), then trust can fulfil its central social function and serve as a decisive mechanism to reduce the complexity of our interactions with others within modern societies. In this way, trust makes it possible to cope with the uncertainties of future technologies. System trust makes this uncertainty tolerable and thus enables the individual, despite the opaque complexity that prevents certain predictions about the future from being made, to make decisions and thus to remain capable of action at all (Lahmann and Kreutzer 2017).

2.5 Importance of Identity-Based Trust

Trust comes at various levels and is highly dependent at the situational context and the personal involvement into the transaction (Lewicki and Bunker 1995).

While the bottom part of the pyramid (see Fig. 1) was often sufficient for defining B2C relationships, this is no longer the case. More and more people expect companies not only to deliver on products, service and all this based on previous experience, but institutions increasingly need to describe who they are, what their beliefs and value systems stand for and how they deliver value to the customer and society alike.

Hence, there are two levels of Identity-based trust we can observe today:

At the identity-based trust level, trust can first arise from trusting the company not to go against the individual's value system. (i.e. '*They might not really believe in things I do, but at least they don't go against my values*'). In a second step, common believe in similar goals (i.e. 'Saving the environment') can be a strong driver of identity-based trust and can even override temporary shortcomes of an institution's calculation-based trust (i.e. when issues arise but the consumer does not think this was on purpose to harm him).

The relevance of this concept in Digital Times is obvious. Smart Cities, Connected Homes, Autonomously Driven Cars and a lot of other solutions are partially able to promise and deliver on a calculation-based trust level, but yet still fail largely to deliver significantly on knowledge-based trust. Trust will be built in offering solutions and convenience with digital solutions, not contradicting the consumer's values and beliefs. Even better, if the same values of a person are reflected in a company's activities.

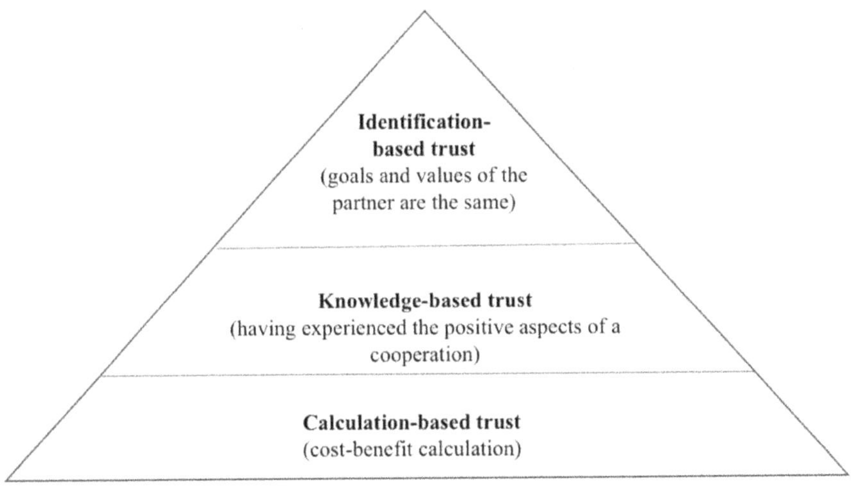

Fig. 1 Levels of trust. Own illustration, based on Osterloh and Weibel 2006

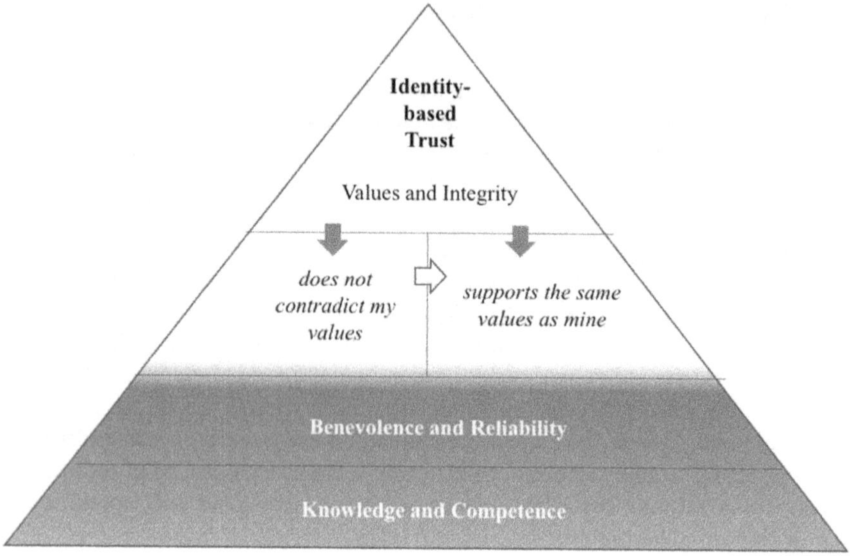

Fig. 2 Sub-levels to build Identity-based trust

Only time will help to build trust based on knowledge, experience or calculation—simply by the newness of the solutions offered and the levels of trust required to adopt them and integrate them in the people's lives (Fig. 2).

2.6 *Transparency*

The demand for transparency is very often cited as the basis for building trust, particularly as a result of the increasing economic scandals (Eccles and di Piazza 2003). Large companies like to use this paradigm to demand trust through communication (Zowislo and Schulz 2006). However, the question arises as to what role trust still plays in a completely transparent situation. When all information is available for customers, there is no room for mistrust. Complete transparency therefore does not require trust.

But where does the demand for confidence-building through transparency come from? Trust takes quite some time to be built up (Zowislo and Schulz 2006), and thus companies might be tempted to find faster ways to get a positive image again in the minds of the consumers. Genuine or fake transparency is faster and easier to create than the process of building consumer trust. Transparency can therefore only be a temporary tool for institutions to build trust (Fig. 3).

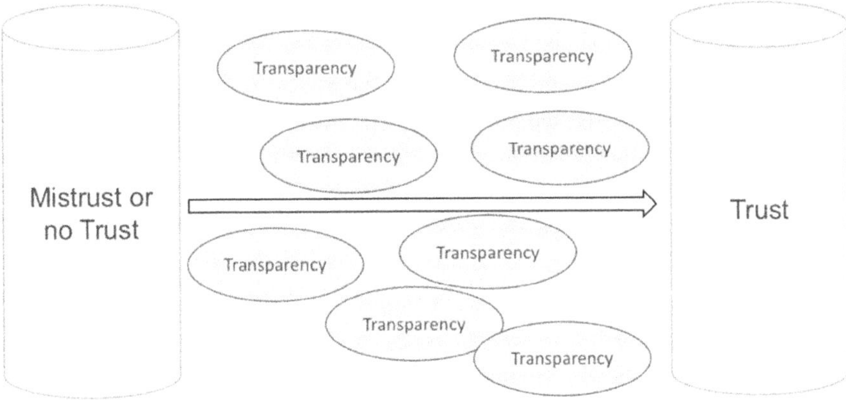

Fig. 3 Using transparency to create trust

3 The Current State of Trust

3.1 Shifting Trust to People and Employers

Over the last two decades, the Edelman Trust Barometer has researched and published significant opinion shifts in over 30 countries worldwide regarding trust of citizens towards Governments, Media, Business and NGO's (Edelman 2019). Recently, it was observing a continuous decline of trust in societal institutions, partially a result of the Financial Crisis, fears about increasing immigration not only in Europe, potential loss of jobs due to globalization and digitalization and many more. In 2018, more than 40% of the population distrusts Business and NGO's, more than half of the population distrusts Governments and Media (Fig. 4).

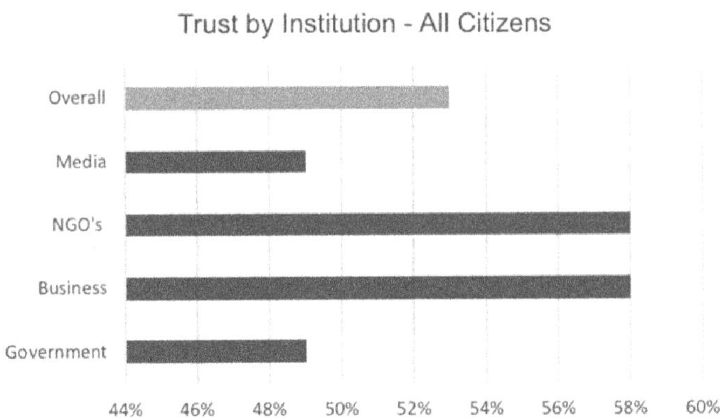

Fig. 4 Global trust in institutions (Edelman 2019)

3.2 Changes in Structure of Trust

At the same time, the growth of social media platforms combined with dialogue-oriented communication shifted people's general trust from a hierarchical top-down orientation to a more horizontal one, favoring friends and peers as more trustworthy. The shift towards moving trust to more local and personal sources still continues. The 2019 Edelman Trust Barometer also indicates that individual trust has shifted to the relationships within people's control—most importantly toward their employers.

Significant parts of the population have lost faith in brands, leaders and systems, but millions of people every day rent their homes to strangers, exchange cryptocurrency online, or get in the car of an unknown driver. Botsman (2017) calls this the '*Age of Distributed Trust*'; a paradigm shift driven by new technologies that are changing the rules. In order to benefit from this huge transformation, it is important that citizens understand the new mechanics of how trust is built, managed, lost and repaired (Botsman 2017) (Fig. 5).

As a consequence, this shift away from anonymous institutional towards individual trust, is leading towards a rise in trust towards known people, i.e. to friends and family but also to people working in the employing company, which is emerging as a major trusted entity (Edelman 2019). Relationships that are closest to people make them feel more comfortable. People have low confidence that societal institutions will help them navigate a turbulent world, so they are turning to a critical relationship: their employer (Edelman 2019).

Ultimately, the "picture of trust" remains complex: While individual trust is rising, so is trust in business, mainly because of the employer people work for. However, trust in Business as an institution, is declining.

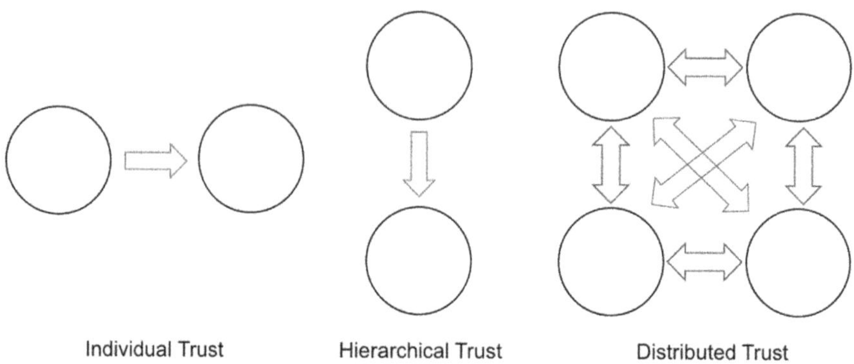

Fig. 5 Concept of digital trust (Botsman 2017, own illustration)

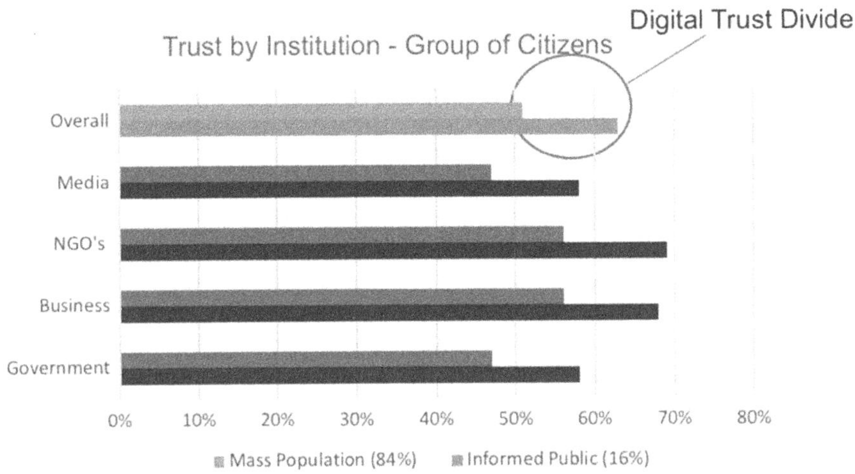

Fig. 6 Trust Levels by Institutions and groups of citizens (Edelman 2019, own illustration)

3.3 *Widening Digital Trust Divide*

Diving deeper into the structure of trust towards institutions, a massive divide among groups of citizens regarding their level of trust can be observed, Edelman (2019) calls this a "mass-class divide". Trust among the informed public (mostly higher income and higher education) reached 65%, while the mass population continues to distrust institutions with only 49% trust levels. This profound ideological divide can provide ample ground for nationalism, protectionism and insurgent grassroots movements (Edelman 2019) (Fig. 6).

3.4 *Focus: Trust in Media*

Media Organizations are an integral part of this world and have to follow similar profitability goals like other companies. As a result, especially in the printed press, we saw budget cuts that have reduced many organizations to skeleton staffs, fast-checking became rare, Twitter, Facebook & Co. started to compete with broadsheet newspapers for scoops (Guess et al. 2018).

Public trust in news reporting is essential for democratic self-governance. However, the media have come under fire from politicians and the public, for the content of their reporting and the journalistic practices they use (Edelman 2019). As trust in Business is at 68%, the Media sector (together with Government) remains the area with the lowest levels of trust at 58%.

Competition with always-on online and Social Media has reduced many news organizations to writing 'he said' stories one day and 'she said' rebuttals the next

(Mitchener 2016). Traditional journalism had tough times, around 2016. There are reasons why people struggle under the weight of fake or worthless content. Every 60 s, 160 million emails are sent, 98,000 tweets are shared on Twitter, 600 videos are uploaded to YouTube, and 1500 blog entries are created. No human being can keep up with it all (Marr 2018). We have never experienced such a time when we have so much information and so many opinions thrown at us from so many angles. In response to our struggles, fact-checking organizations that are dedicated to dissecting and analyze statements made by politicians and public figures now exist and are becoming increasingly visible.

As data continues to explode, the ability to rummage through it to find the truth required in a situation is essential. Consumers won't be patient either. They want to find out anything they seek to know, and they want to know it quickly. Brands will have to respond with truth and transparency if they hope to remain competitive (Barton et al. 2017).

Starting around the time of the U.S. Presidential Election at the end of 2016, the role of Social Media in comparison to traditional press became a topic of societal discussion—mainly in Europe and the U.S. Fake News became a new Buzzword and people started to reflect on their Media behavior (PwC 2017).

Partially due to this higher awareness and media attention by citizens, in 2018 we saw a significant shift in Media consumption. Across the globe, not only was the usage of Media rising, people are increasingly interested in News. Certainly, the ongoing discussion about Fake News and Trust has led to a higher level of interest in what news is coming from what source (Edelman 2019) (Fig. 7).

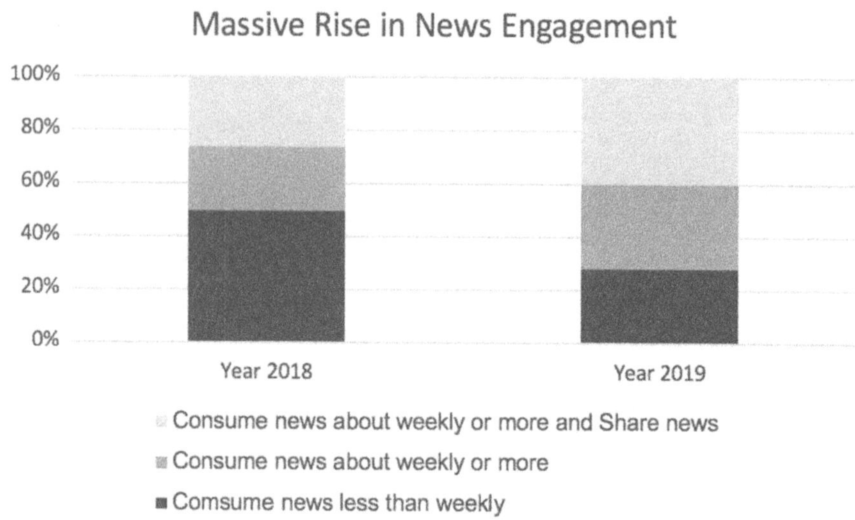

Fig. 7 Rise in news engagement (Edelman 2019, own illustration)

4 Trust in Digital Times

4.1 Challenges Through New Data Usage Models

The digital economy is based on huge streams of data that is created, collected, combined and shared; data for which traditional governance frameworks and risk mitigation strategies are increasingly inadequate.

Commercial usage models derived from data can even introduce entirely new classes of risk. These include the unethical or even illegal use of intelligence, the reinforcement of prejudices that exacerbate social and economic justice issues, and the use of data for purposes that the original disclosures would not have agreed to and without their consent (Banavar 2016).

If companies understand the challenges on ethical data practices and incorporate it in their decision-making processes, such risks can be identified, managed and mitigated. If not, they can permanently damage consumer confidence and trust in a brand (Enkel 2017).

There are also other risks associated with the ethical use of data where current best practices are simply not sufficient to provide guidance to practitioners. These new risk areas require the development of rigid ethical controls across all data supply chains. With such controls, companies can create 'Digital Trust' (Accenture 2016)—a universally accepted belief that a brand is reliable, capable, secure, transparent and truthful—not only in the traditional business but also in its digital practices.

Trust in digital times is more difficult to build, but much easier to lose. That's the main reason, trust is an increasingly more important differentiator in the digital economy (DIVSI 2017). Trust in a brand promotes growth through product development, cooperation with partners and expansion into new markets.

The usage models of Data play a critical role in the perception of trust. The World Economic Forum categorizes the data collected from consumers as "Volunteered Data, Observed Data and Inferred Data" (World Economic Forum 2011). This classification plays a central role in the subsequent discussion on the importance of trust.

- *Volunteered Data*—Voluntary data is deliberately provided by the person concerned when they fill out a form, enter a virtual space that requires authentication, sign a contract, or simply enter the data necessary to provide a particular service. There is usually a concrete awareness of data sharing, even if it is routine.
- *Observed Data*—Observed data is behavioral data collected from a third party that is able to register web surfing behavior, behavioral biometrics, mobility data, browser search history, etc. The data subject is usually unaware that they are being observed and the institution collecting the data may legally claim the data. In contrast to Volunteered Data, observed data does not include name, address or credit card number, but machine-readable behavior that is usually intuitive, unconscious and cannot be measured without computational help.

- *Inferred Data*—Derived data refers to patterns, clusters and correlations that are recognized in databases or streaming services and are often presented as a new type of knowledge. Derived data is created by organizations that categorize databases to identify complex patterns in the data for later matches.

While the increasing collection of Observed and Inferred Data leads to huge amounts of data (Big Data), there is an emerging discussion about the real value of all this data. (Lindstrom 2016) believes that the real value of data, as opposed to derived models, is much more the result of constant consumer observation than the basis for developing the right conclusions. He calls it 'small data' and assumes that two out of three successful innovations come from small data rather than big data.

Furthermore, the area of Volunteered Data will continue to evolve strongly. This is particularly true today for information that is requested when subscribing to newsletters or customer profiles, bonus cards and social networks. Companies will increasingly grant customers who voluntarily provide data considerable advantages (Rosenbach 2016). This gives consumers much more control over the value of their data and enables them to make informed decisions about whether to share or withhold it (De Croo 2015).

4.1.1 Need for New Ethical Data Practices

Until recently, the focus of digital risk concentrated on questions of cyber security threats. These threats are still prevailing, but more and more companies need to identify risks from lack of ethical data practices.

These new risks require a unique framework and best practices at every stage of the project and service lifecycle and should therefore be addressed in all areas and integrated across the whole Value Chain. What is needed is a stronger focus on ethics, which will lead to a radical change in the way companies view data. While the relevance of security and privacy remains high, added instruments and importance of ethical questions and trust become critical. Businesses must begin to consider the ethics of data collection, manipulation and usage (Accenture 2016).

While correct and transparent behavior can help to enable trust, it requires attention at every stage of the data supply chain and collaboration with all stakeholders. By focusing on ethics, companies will improve their customers' trust in them—a mission for those who have gone through digital change and become publishers or participants in digital platforms and ecosystems. This solution is '*Trusted by Design*' (Accenture 2016) across the whole Value Chains (Fig. 8).

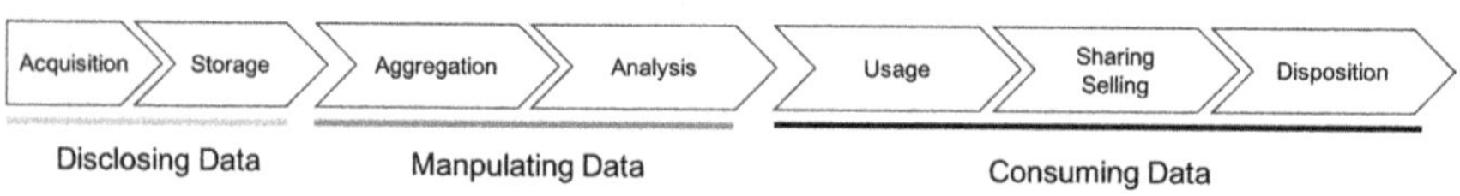

Fig. 8 Data responsibility along the value chain own illustration, based on Accenture (2016)

These seven areas of Data Responsibility can be clustered into three focus segments (Accenture 2016):

Disclosing Data includes *Acquiring Data* and is about collecting data from systems and humans, recording its provenance and consent for later usage, this is followed by *Storing Data*, i.e. the transferring data to a trusted location that is both secure and easily accessible for further proceeding.
Manipulating Data is in the beginning about *Aggregating Data*, which is combining various datasets to create a larger dataset. In a next step, *Analyzing Data* deals with discovering new insights by examining data and transforming it with the purpose of extracting information and discovering new insights.
Consuming Data starts with *Using Data*, concretely applying the insights gained from data analyzes toward making decisions, affecting change, or delivering a product or service. Once the data has proven useful in a first step, the focus shifts to *Sharing and Selling Data*: Providing access to datasets or data insights to new sets of data manipulators or consumers. Finally, *Disposing Data* means removing data from servers to prevent future release or use.

Treating data in an ethical manner throughout its supply chain requires a fundamental change in how data is viewed within organizations. While the perspectives of security (is the confidentiality, integrity, and availability of data adequately protected?) and privacy (do controls on data satisfy regulatory requirements?) remain relevant, added lenses for ethics and trust become critical. Organizations must begin to consider the ethics of data collection, manipulation, and use. This enables trust but requires attention at each stage of the data supply chain and collaboration with every stakeholder.

Today, highly sensitive data exist whose security is subject to an objective protection interest and which must be protected from uncontrolled access by third parties. One could think of sensitive health data or credit card information, account balances or other data that affect one's own financial sphere. If such data falls into the wrong hands, is compromised or misused, considerable damage can be caused to those affected (Ropohl 2010). The personal reputation can also be affected, which in individual cases can have consequences threatening the existence of the operator. This is all the more true in an increasingly digitalized world in which data shapes and represents the identity of people. The frequent cases of identity theft impressively show the importance of a non-manipulated and authentic identity in digital space.

Even though many people today grant a considerable insight into their lives to an often indeterminable number of third parties via social networks, it cannot be concluded that the privacy of certain information is of secondary importance to them. Anyone who writes an e-mail to a good friend in order to report on the results of the last screening will want to trust that nobody, but the friend is reading (Enkel 2017). Those who retrieve their account statements on their bank's online portal will be confident that nobody will intercept and copy the data during transmission—most people will be aware that this data can very easily be misused to the financial disadvantage of the person concerned if it falls into the wrong, i.e. criminal, hands. What's more, the person will trust that after entering the bank's web address in the browser window, they will actually be directed to the bank's website and not to that of a third party, which only looks the same (Chakravorti et al. 2018).

4.2 *Emerging Trust Concepts*

4.2.1 The Trust Stack

The Trust Stack is fast becoming a common term for how people are interacting with companies and individuals online (Botsman 2017). In the first layer of the Trust Stack, people have to trust that a new idea is safe and worth trying. The next layer is trusting the platform or eco-system facilitating the exchange. And the third layer is all about trusting the partner, company and people (Fig. 9).

Trust or faith in eCommerce as a concept, for example, has been well established but if you are involved in ecommerce you need to pay attention to that second layer, "Trusting the platform". When a new customer is contemplating a purchase from your platform they are dealing with uncertainties. Is this the right product? Is that the best price? When will I get it? A good eCommerce website will do everything it can to lower that uncertainty which in turn builds on the trust the customer has in you and your business.

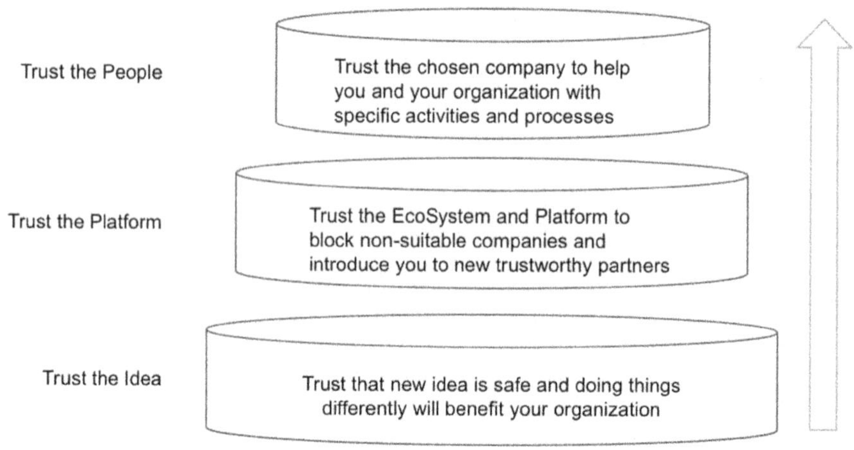

Fig. 9 The new trust stack (own illustration, based on Botsman 2017)

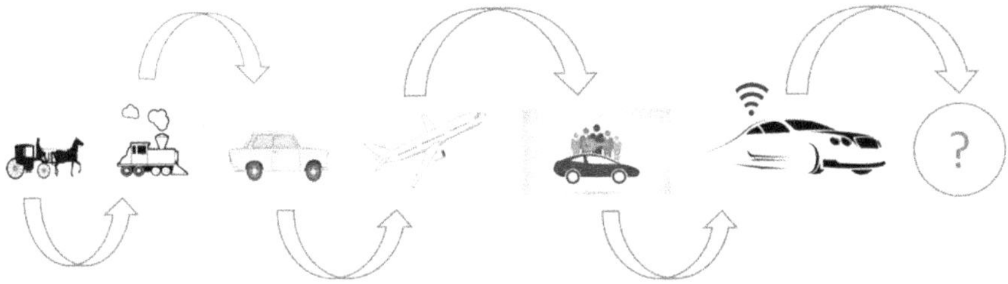

Fig. 10 Trust Leaps (own illustration, based on Botsman 2017)

4.2.2 Digital Trust Leaps

Expanding trust from today's solutions to new concepts is not a new approach. People have always experienced a lack of trust in new technology and thus had to 'perform' a trust leap. Here are some examples (Fig. 10):

What is new, however, is the depth and speed of changes and how people need to somehow transfer their trust to the new environment. People are simply asked to show more trust to more complex and often not understandable solutions that very often touch their lives (Smart Homes, etc.) (Logg et al. 2018).

5 Rebuilding Trust

In order to build or rebuild trust in a world that is dominated by digitalization, there are two main approaches offering significant potential: As individual trust is rising, and as the employers of people also gain in trust, the role of the CEO becomes even more critical (Edelman 2019).The second approach focuses on providing experience and proof points to potential consumers. As digitalization can't always be seen or touched, companies need to show (through innovations) the real benefit and advantage of new solutions to customers and society alike through Trusted Innovations.

5.1 The Role of the CEO

The call for leadership by CEO's is all but new. However, in times of trust vacuum left by government, pressure is on them to do more and faster to create a sense of certainty, reassurance and confidence with employees as well as the general public. CEOs must also consider the significantly heightened expectations on them to be advocates for change in a world that is still confused and uncertain. If the function of trust is to reduce complexity, CEOs are needed at the 'front' to explain benefits (and potential issues) of digitalization to the people (Edelman 2019) (Fig. 11).

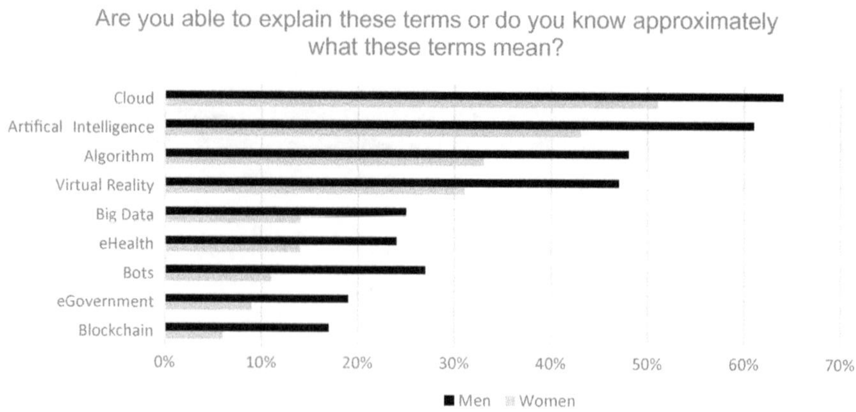

Fig. 11 Knowledge of digital terms in Germany (own illustration, based on Initiative D21 2019)

Second, it's key to note that employees and prospective employees want CEOs to act beyond reproach when it comes to speaking the truth. Candor, honesty and transparency are all powerful trust-building elements, together with high expectations (74%) that CEOs will embody the values and mission of the organization they lead.

5.2 *Trusted Innovations*

The term '*Social Innovation*' can be understood as a focused direction of Innovation (MacGregor and Fontrodona 2008, Osburg 2013). It usually implies a normative approach that something positive is created for the society. In addition to Social Innovation, the concept of '*Trusted Innovation*' includes the overall dimension of Social Sustainability—the Trust that holds societies together. 'Trusted Innovations' are thus a further development of Social Innovation (Osburg 2017). In this chapter, both terms should be used simultaneously.

The EU Commission defines Social Innovation as "… Innovations that are both social in their ends and in their means. Social Innovations are new ideas (products, services and models) that simultaneously meet social needs (more effectively than alternatives) and create new social relationships or collaborations" (EU-Commission 2012). The INSEAD Social Innovation Centre defines Social Innovation as the "… introduction of new business models and market-based mechanisms that deliver sustainable economic, environmental and social prosperity" (INSEAD 2012).

Within this understanding, Trusted Innovation is the applied theory of Innovation where a normative Social component is added. Wanting to do good is not enough. Trusted Innovation needs to be a process that is driven by Innovation and adds a goal and value system to it to create Sustainability.

Trusted Innovation is building on concepts of Creating Shared Value (Porter and Kramer 2011)—for society and business alike. Customers can experience, see or touch these innovations. Those are not just words, but real solutions put in place by companies, adding societal value. This 'proof' of positive potential of innovations is a key component to win back lost trust.

Management buy-in will be critical in order to fully embrace the relevance of Trusted Innovation for the Business as a whole. Because of the strong societal component, leaving Trusted Innovation to the CSR departments is not enough, it must get the needed attention from company leaders. However, to support, CSR Managers need to become Change Agents in leading the company towards transformation.

As the term Trusted Innovations suggests, the function of creating those innovations need to come from the Innovation Department and ultimately be embedded in the DNA of a firm (Osburg 2013). Much will be achieved in order to gain trust in digital worlds, when the majority of innovations will clearly offer societal value at the same time. Trusted Innovation is closer to the core Business of what is generally thought of and the key for companies to achieve Corporate Sustainability and thus meet the needs of triple bottom line reporting.

6 Summary

Trust is nothing new in the relationship between companies and consumers or citizens. Brand Trust is a key marketing concept that will remain and the key trust function (Reduction of Complexity) becomes increasingly relevant. We live in times when only few people (far less than 50% of the population) understand the impacts of Digital Transformation and—in classical terms—need to trust Business and Governments to implement the right solutions.

However, we currently see three global developments—a lack of understanding trends of digitalization among the mass population, a lack of trust towards institutions and companies and a widening gap between an informed public and the mass population with regards to both understand and trusting new solutions. Technology seems to be something for the chosen few. This puts whole societies and the way we live together at risk.

Two potential focus areas arise to overcome these developments: The CEO is critical in acting as a kind of super-ambassador for the societal value of the company's products and service, as well as for the whole business model. CEOs are still trusted as individuals and must assume a stronger role here. The second starting point to regain trust is creating a compelling user experience with the products that people can see and touch, and thrust (Trusted Innovation).

Building trust in Digital Times requires much more than Corporate Governance for Data Security. Companies need to find ways to translate invisible data and algorithms into tangible, valuable and trustworthy solutions for their customers.

References

Accenture (ed) (2016) Building digital trust: the role of data ethics in the digital age. Accenture Labs Mountain View, CA

Banavar G (2016) What it will take for US to trust AI. In: Harvard Business Review https://hbr.org/2016/11/what-it-will-take-for-us-to-trust-ai. Accessed 22 Mar 2019

Barton R, Bender M, Marque F (2017) Trust in the digital age. Publication Accenture Strategy

Botsman R (2017) Who can you trust? How technology brought us together—and why it could drive us apart. Milton Keynes

Bruckner BK (2016) Organisationales Vertrauen initiieren. Determinanten des interorganisationalen Vertrauens von Beschäftigten in Großunternehmen. Springer, Wiesbaden

Chakravorti B, Bhalla A, Chaturvedi RS (2018) The 4 dimensions of digital trust, chartered across 42 countries. In: Harvard business review https://hbr.org/2018/02/the-4-dimensions-of-digital-trust-charted-across-42-countries. Accessed 22 Mar 2019

Cochrane K (2018) To regain consumers' trust marketers need transparent data practices. In: Harvard business review https://hbr.org/2018/06/to-regain-consumers-trust-marketers-need-transparent-data-practices. Accessed 22 Mar 2019

Covey SMR (2009) Schnelligkeit durch Vertrauen: Die unterschätzte ökonomische Macht. Gabal, Offenbach

De Croo A (2015) Why digital is key to sustainable growth. https://www.weforum.org/agenda/2015/03/why-digital-is-key-to-sustainable-growth/. Accessed 12 Oct 2016

DIVSI (Deutsches Institut für Vertrauen und Sicherheit im Internet) (ed) (2017) Vertrauen in Kommunikation im digitalen Zeitalter. Projektbericht, Hamburg

Eccles R, di Piazza S (2003) Vertrauen durch Transparenz. Die Zukunft der Unternehmensberichterstattung. Wiley, Weinheim

Edelman (ed) (2019) Edelman trust barometer 2019. Edelman Trust Barometer, New York

Enkel E (2017) To get consumers to trust AI, show them its benefits. In: Harvard business review https://hbr.org/2017/04/to-get-consumers-to-trust-ai-show-them-its-benefits. Accessed 22 Mar 2019

EU-Commission (ed) (2012) Social innovation http://ec.europa.eu/growth/industry/innovation/policy/social_en. Accessed 13 Jan 2019

Forcepoint (ed) (2019) Cultivating trust to gain competitive advantage. In: HBR analytics series. https://hbr.org/resources/pdfs/comm/forcepoint/HBRASForcepoint3.8.19.pdf. Accessed 22 Mar 2019

GfK Verein (ed) (2017) Global trust report 2017—eine Studie des GfK Vereins. Nürnberg

Giddens A (1991) The consequences of modernity. Stanford University Press, Stanford

Guess A, Nyhan B, Reifler J (2018) All media trust is local? findings from the 2018 Poynter media trust survey. Poynter Institute, https://tinyurl.com/yc8sbtu5. Accessed 29 Jan 2019

Initiative D21 (ed) (2019) D21 digital index 2018/2019. https://initiatived21.de/publikationen/d21-digital-index-2018-2019. Accessed 1 Mar 2019

INSEAD (2012) What is "social innovation". http://www.insead.edu/facultyresearch/centres/isic/home/about_us.cfm. Accessed 9 Dec 2012

Lahmann H, Kreutzer T (2017) Vertrauen in digitale Kommunikation: Eine Bestandsaufnahme. Diskussionspapier im Projekt "Braucht Deutschland einen Digitalen Kodex?" Deutsches Institut für Vertrauen und Sicherheit im Internet (DIVSI). Hamburgs

Lewicki RJ, Bunker BB (1995) Trust in relationships: a model of development and decline. Working paper series, Columbus, OH

Lindstrom M (2016) Small data: the tiny clues that uncover huge trends. St. Martin's Press, New York

Logg JM, Minson JA, Moore DA (2018) Do people trust algorithms more than companies realize? In: Harvard business review, https://hbr.org/2018/10/do-people-trust-algorithms-more-than-companies-realize. Accessed 22 Mar 2019

Luhmann N (2014) Vertrauen, 5th edn. UVK Verlagsgesellschaft mbH, Konstanz und München

MacGregor SP, Fontrodona J (2008) Exploring the fit between CSR and innovation. In: IESE business school. Working paper No. 759, Sep 2008 issue

Marr B (2018) Fake news and how artificial intelligence tools can help. In: Forbes magazine, https://www.forbes.com/sites/bernardmarr/2018/05/16/fake-news-and-how-artificial-intelligence-tools-can-help/#54cc6c98271d. Accessed 19 Dec 2018

Mitchener B (2016) Trust deficit. Of trust, tough love and today's European media. In: Communication Director, Issue 01/2016, pp. 80–83

Osburg Th (2013) Social innovation to drive corporate responsibility. In: Osburg Th, Schmidpeter R (eds) Social innovation—solutions for a sustainable future, pp. 13–22. Heidelberg

Osburg Th (2017)Sustainability in a digital world needs trust. In: Osburg Th, Lohrmann C (ed) (2017) Sustainability in a digital world, pp. 3–19. Springer, Heidelberg

Osterloh M, Weibel A (2006) Investition Vertrauen: Prozesse der Vertrauensentwicklung in Organisationen. SpringerGabler, Wiesbaden

Porter ME; Kramer MR (2011) Creating shared value. In: Harvard business review, Jan–Feb 2011 issue

PwC (ed) (2017) Vertrauen in Medien. Study by PricewaterhouseCoopers, Düsseldorf

Ropohl G (2010) Das Misstrauen in der Technikdebatte. In: Mahring M (ed) Vertrauen—zwischen sozialem Kitt und der Senkung von Transaktionskosten. KTI Scientific Publishing, Karlsruhe, pp 115–132

Rosenbach M (2016) Mit dem Ich bezahlen. Der Spiegel, issue 11/2016, pp 82–83

Shapiro DL, Sheppard BH, Cheraskin L (1992) Business on a handshake. Negot J 8(4):365–377

Stelzig M (2017) Warum wir vertrauen können: Das psychische Urprogramm des Menschen. Ecowin, Salzburg/München

Vollmer A, Clases C, Wehner T (2006) Vertrauen und kooperatives Handeln—Ein arbeits- und organisationspsychologischer Zugang. In: Götz K (ed) (2006) Vertrauen in Organisationen. Hampp, München, pp 169–184

World Economic Forum (WEF) (2011) Personal data: the emergence of a new asset class. World Economic Forum, Cologny

Zenger J, Folkman J (2019) The 3 elements of trust. In: Harvard business review, https://hbr.org/2019/02/the-3-elements-of-trust. Accessed 22 March 2019

Zowislo N, Schulz J (2006) Vertrauen statt Transparenz. In: Bauer HH, Neumann MM, Schüle A (ed) Konsumentenvertrauen. Konzepte und Anwendungen für ein nachhaltiges Kundenbindungsmanagement, pp 27–38. Verlag Vahlen, München

Thomas Osburg is an internationally experienced Professor, Entrepreneur, Advisor and former Executive Director with over 25 years of experience in leadership positions working for global IT companies (i.e. Intel Corp. and Texas Instruments) in the U.S., China, Germany and France. During the last years, Thomas has delivered more than 80 keynote speeches and written over 40 scientific publications, he is teaching Bachelor, Master and MBA classes at leading European Universities and was elected on the Board of Directors at leading European associations. As an Entrepreneur, Thomas recently established a global Research Institute for Urban Live and Future Mobility and a Non-for-Profit NGO for Sustainable Development.

Chapter 3
Socio-historical Contexts of Anti-institutionalist Tendencies in Digital Media Transformation

Jonas Bedford-Strohm

1 Introduction

The Great Digital Transformation is not just a matter of technology. It is a matter of socio-historical change on a foundational level. As the etymological trace of *logos* in "technology" implies, it is a feat of human reason, and therefore a fundamentally social enterprise. Even the most venerated technological geniuses relied on scientific or commercial feats achieved through the complex human knowledge systems before them. Technology, therefore, can only be properly understood through its embeddedness in broader social practices. Hence, the Great Digital Transformation is best approached through socio-technical analysis that can holistically engage technology while retaining attention to human action in the "interplay of society and culture" (Burk et al. 2018, 12). Such analysis does not view technology as a neutral mediator or a set of passive natural objects, but brings socially transformative discourse and normative dimensions of digital practice into focus. This study identifies *participation*, *information*, *consent*, *inclusion* and *accountability* as five key factors for public trust through the socio-historical analysis of anti-institutional tendencies in digital media transformation.

2 Distrusting Media: Fear of Manipulation and Irrelevance

Niklas Luhmann has observed that "what we know about our society, even the whole world in which we live, we know through the mass media."[1] This iconic remark

[1] To provide contextually meaningful translations, German sources are cited in the author's translation.

J. Bedford-Strohm (✉)
Zentrum für Ethik der Medien und der digitalen Gesellschaft (zem::dg), Kaulbachstraße 31a, 80539 Munich, Germany
e-mail: jonas.bedford-strohm@zemdg.de

T. Osburg and S. Heinecke (eds.), *Media Trust in a Digital World*,
https://doi.org/10.1007/978-3-030-30774-5_3

expresses a mediatized version of Ludwig Wittgenstein's linguistic turn: "The limits of my language mean the limits of my world" (Wittgenstein 1963, 5.6). Wittgenstein's intuition is that the linguistic "stuff" of our thought, the verbal content of our knowledge and the propositional material of communication all stem from interactions through language. This paradigm constitutes a communicative transformation of a traditional rationalist paradigm that now also takes the sociality of reason into account.

2.1 *Limits to Linguistic Approaches*

Growing philosophical awareness of mediality and the emergence of theories of mediatization and medialization (cf. Bedford-Strohm and Filipovic 2018), however, make evident that Wittgenstein's early approach lacks the tools to fully grasp the waves of trust and distrust in media communication, and brings only part of issues like populism on social media into focus. One might indeed capture patterns of psychological framing through language, like terming migration movements "a wave of migrants" in "a refugee crisis" (cf. Wehling 2016). So this analytical paradigm can indeed help to understand how trust or distrust, as well as tribal belonging, increases or decreases through conscious and subconscious signals in *verbal* media contributions. But the tool remains limited to the analysis of language games by specific actors, and hence cannot fully grasp the extent of trust or distrust in complex media communication systems.

2.2 *The Tragedy of Trust and Transparency*

This is where Luhmann's remarks offer insight: "What we know about our society, even the whole world in which we live, we know through the media." And then: "But we also know enough about the mass media to *not be able to trust these sources*. We resist it suspecting manipulation, but without consequence, since the knowledge we derive from the mass media, as if by itself, completes itself into a self-reinforcing framework" (Luhmann 2009, 9, emphasis added). This argument offers a unique rendering of a foundational tragedy in modern media societies: The pluralistic media system functions well enough for citizens to know the daily failings of this complex system. Such transparency—a normative ideal of liberal democracy—thereby can tragically erode trust in the vital organizations *creating* transparency, and thereby accountability.

Arguably, this dynamic is inherent to the trends of functional differentiation and increased pluralism in the media system. Increased competition furthers mutual checks and balances, thereby bringing misconduct to the fore. Then, tragically, instead of furthering trust in a functioning democracy, the psychological effect on citizens is the opposite: If news of misconduct is pervasive in one realm, it can emanate distrust in *all* social realms. In other words: Bad news can taint the reputation of the messenger, even if the messenger is the virtuous investigative source for the reported misconduct. This might explain why journalists consistently rank low in German trust rankings (Statista 2018a).[2]

2.3 Trust in Social Versus Traditional Mass Media

As Christian Meier has noted, the general category of "the media" employed by some rankings is problematic, because it lumps together digital social media platforms and traditional journalism. In Germany, but also globally, there is a stark difference in trust between digital platforms like Facebook and Google, and traditional journalism. Impacted by the discourse on "fake news" and "filter bubbles" in the wake of the 2016 U.S. presidential election (cf. Bedford-Strohm 2017), Germans responded with an increase to 61% in trust in traditional journalistic sources, and a decrease to 40% trust in digital platforms (Meier 2018). With Felix Stalder we might call digital platforms "social mass media" (Stalder 2016) and update Luhmann's idea for the platform age: *What we know about our society and life worlds, we know through a mix of mass media, including digital social mass media. But we also know that platforms are never neutral and therefore are never able to trust them blindly.*

This update of Luhmann's analysis of trust in mass media complicates his tracing of distrust to the *lack of interaction* between the producer and the consumer. Key to the dilemma of the mass media, he says, is that "no bodily present interaction is possible between the sending and receiving actors" because of the insertion of technology. One might reject the argument, since social media networks were built precisely to address this lack in the traditional mass media, even though bodily presence continues to be impossible with social mass media. And his following cautioning, arguably, still applies: "Exceptions from this rule are possible (but never with all participants), but they appear staged and are treated as such in the editorial rooms. The exceptions change nothing about the disruption of contact inherent to the technology" (Luhmann 2009, 10).

2.4 Decentralized Production and Distribution of Media Content

Applied to the social mass media of today, Luhmann's challenge adds an interesting twist to the analysis of social media content, as well as of the interests and methods of its producers. Social media was initially heralded as the empowerment of the individual and a means for *authentic self-expression*. Bharat Anand has called its

[2]As indicated by the sources, this analysis is limited to the transatlantic context and makes no claim beyond the region.

rise "the democratization of media" (Anand 2016, xxiii) and concludes that the digital decentralization of content production amounts to the premise that "everyone is a media company today" (ibid, xi). He backs his claim up with numbers: "Nearly 72 hours of video are uploaded to YouTube, 3 million pieces of content shared by Facebook users, and 230,000 new photos posted on Instagram—every minute" around the world (ibid, xxiv).

The vast sum of this content is distributed by empowered individuals who both share and consume content through their personalized media diet with a diverse mix all the way from semi-private vacation photos to political commentary by partisan pundits and comedic media content—the famous "prosumer" consuming what Nicolas Negroponte has termed the "Daily Me" (Negroponte 1995). Since platforms like Twitter and Facebook, and in part Snapchat and Instagram, are at least semi-public, their users have developed strategies to stage their platform-specific content in a way that resembles neither the traditional media content, nor the traditional private sharing. It's a new beast entirely. Hence, it is less professional than a professionally staged enterprise, but also more strategic than the sharing of private photo albums in the family.

2.5 Strategic Social Media Communication by Private Actors

An outgrowth of this strategic component in personal communication on digital platforms are books like Susan Chritton's *Personal Branding for Dummies*, helping you to "distinguish yourself with an authentic personal brand", to "build a strong online identity to showcase your brand" and to "evaluate and evolve your personal brand over time" (Chritton 2014). The increased component of strategic communication and biographical self-management further the *fears of manipulation* in seemingly private spaces and along with the infamous data breach controversies around Cambridge Analytica, might help to explain the dramatic loss of trust in digital media platforms such as Facebook. We can safely conclude that indeed Luhmann's charge that interactive mass media "appear staged" is accurate for much of the individual content production on social mass media.

2.6 Strategic Social Media Communication by Professional Actors

This appears even more accurate for professional actors in social networks. Much of the media content *shared* by the empowered individuals is, in fact, *produced* by (semi-)professional media outlets with explicit strategies to maximize reach through platform-specific content. This goes for partisan outlets like "Democracy Now!" in the U.S. or so-called homeless media outlets like *Now This* (in the U.S.) and *funk* (in Germany), strategically posting their content natively on third-party platforms, hence: “away from home.” But it also goes for traditional media publishers that are striving to translate their content into the language and formats of social media platforms (see, for instance, Al-Jazeera’s approach to social video: AJ Labs 2017). These organizations work hard to present their content as authentic communication with interactive proximity akin to private conversation, but their approach is as professional and strategic as any traditional mass media production. Considering this, Luhmann’s charge that interactive exceptions to the rule that mass media lack interaction always “appear staged and are treated as such in the editorial rooms” indeed holds up.

2.7 *Fear of Manipulation on Digital Platforms*

Since most algorithms steering the curation of content on digital platforms are geared towards the goal of profit maximization through increased attention to advertisement requiring ever-longer time spent on a given platform, these algorithms use interaction as their core signal to determine whether the user should see a given piece of content or not. This adds at least three dynamics feeding the fear of manipulation. (1) The content is selected by an editorial mechanism and therefore resembles the old editorial rooms more than the promised ideals of individual choice, control and empowerment. (2) A platform like Facebook is, after all, a business designed to turn out profits and therefore the rhetoric of empowerment and “giving individuals a voice” appears hollow and farcical. (3) Large digital platforms like Facebook have reached economic maturity by betting heavily on advertisement which constitutes strategic persuasion towards an economic transaction and is, in most cases, legal, but also manipulative by design. Hence, it is no surprise that while Facebook’s revenues went up in recent years (Statista 2018b), its public trust went down (Edelman 2018).

2.8 *Institutions and the Cult of Authenticity*

Part of the social media strategies of professional media outlets is to appear authentic. One might even go so far to call this a new “cult of authenticity” with profound implications for media and politics (Bedford-Strohm 2016). The ideal of authenticity has rendered the traditional approach to bureaucratic institutions counterproductive. Prior to this trend, institutions, organizations, corporations, as well as individuals like C-level managers and heads of state were seen as trustworthy, if they appeared polished, perfect, put together, cared for. That meant they invested in flawless appearance and attempted to hide all failures and insecurities. What used to inspire trust, however, has now turned against these institutions. Nicco Mele calls it “The End of Big" (Mele 2013).[3] The polished, perfect appearance now creates distrust and is suspected of being a strategic way to manipulate the individual and disguise hidden agendas from the active prosumer. Once professional media outlets realized this dynamic, they adapted and began to produce content in a more "authentic" style. The tragedy of it is, that this authenticity is designed through intended flaws that consumers can connect with. The strategy can affirmatively be framed as *user-centric design*, but it can also be critically framed as *strategic manipulation*. The danger in this strategy is, that by staging interaction and human-centric approaches in media content, the user is left with subtle sediments of experienced manipulation. So even if there is no immediate outrage, trust is eroded over time.

2.9 Editorial Decisions Based on Interaction and Engagement

If Anand's conclusion that "everyone is a media company today" is true, then everyone shapes the conditions and practice of media communication. This has already been the case indirectly through the traditional, filtered processes of letters to the editor in newspapers or call-in contributions by listeners on radio programs. But digital media afford a whole new way of tracking engagement and refining content according to user interests. (1) This model is realized as *assistive technology*, that awards the editors insights into which content is clicked, viewed or listened to. This data enables the editors to optimize performance of their news product by adapting content rankings, story framing or topic generation. (2) This model is also implemented through fully *automated curation* systems with a more or less complex algorithm at their core. Facebook's News Feed, for instance, implements such a system, and interprets a variety of signals like type of content posted, language used, location of sharing, location of consumption, previous likes awarded by the user, shares from a user's friend network, time of day, device used to log into the system and degree of interaction between posting party and consuming party. Based on such signals, the algorithm calculates the probability of interaction with a given piece of content and ranks the content accordingly into a seemingly endless stream of content.

Both approaches, the assistive solution and the algorithmic solution, apply user feedback for the creation and curation of content in real-time. This creates at least two potential threats: (1) The more click rates determine creation and curation of news, the more re-affirming the propositional contents of this news becomes. Reinforcing human tendencies of confirmation bias, this disrupts a foundational premise of democratic discourse—the shared base of factual description upon which diverging opinions and solutions can be discussed. (2) The interaction-based editorial approach strengthens enraging and engaging content using neuropsychological manipulation

[3] In his 2013 book, Mele describes the likely ascent of an authoritarian populist in the U.S. exploiting the "End of Big." Drawing the conclusion from his research in 2015, he predicted the electoral victory of Donald Trump (Mele 2015).

to pull emotional triggers and increase the reach of a message. This populist strategy has long been part of the socially accepted toolkit of marketing, but has traditionally been frowned-upon in political discourse. While stigma remains, a solely interaction-based media environment is the perfect tool to mainstream emotionalist strategies of engagement. So while the social mass media, as well as the traditional mass media, are indeed applying a more *interactive* approach to their content creation and curation, trust *decreases* and fear of manipulation *increases* once users realize they are served a specific type of content only to manipulate their political decisions or maximize profits. So does interaction really increase media trust, as Luhmann implies?

2.10 Digital Transformation of Communication Models

Most digital media are based on the internet. The World Wide Web and all other *internet-based* services are *network-based*. Therefore, they are inherently communicative and—despite their *technical* infrastructure—fundamentally *social* in nature. This structural feature makes a degree of interactive communication possible that hitherto existed only on a strictly local scale, where face-to-face communication was ubiquitous, for instance between the editor of a small local newspaper and the limited group of readership. The editor would be regularly confronted with all joys and criticism from readers, since they also shared a social space outside of the strictly professional interactions. With certain limitations, the internet makes such interactive media work possible on a larger scale, and—as I have argued elsewhere (Bedford-Strohm 2017, 88ff)—has been used by media publishers to alter their *one-to-many* communication model into a more *dialogical* model, enhanced by moderated discussion in the form of *many-to-many*. In Horst Pöttker's words, the web has brought "a heavy expansion of the possibility of communication" (Pöttker 2016, 347). This trend has been fueled by the massive expansion of user base on social media platforms, news shared and debated decentrally through messenger applications, enhanced commentary widgets on news sites, and, more recently, conversational journalism with chatbots like Novibot (Tagesschau 2018) and interactive news apps like Quartz (Seward 2016), as well as the rise of voice search and voice assistants (Statista 2018c).

2.11 Brecht's Theory of Interactive Media

In a series of writings around 1930, Bertholt Brecht published one of the first media theories specific to the medium radio. His theory centers around concepts of participation and interaction. With Luhmann, Brecht shared the intuition that participation and interaction could profoundly impact the *degree of trust* that the public had in media institutions. In a letter to the head of the German public radio, Brecht offered advocacy for user-generated content: "In my opinion, you should attempt to turn the radio into a truly democratic enterprise. You would, for instance, already achieve much, if you stopped limiting the range of producers for your wonderful distribution apparatus to yourself" (Brecht 2004, 151). In other words: Engaging users in the creation of content can increase the degree of individual ownership and stake in the collective system.

Brecht sharply phrases his participatory theory of media communication as an explicit critique of the mass media: "Radio has *one* side, where it should have two. It is a mere distribution apparatus. It only allocates content." His solution is to "turn radio from a distribution apparatus into an apparatus for communication." If conceived like this, "radio would be the greatest communication apparatus of public life, an incredible system of channels, meaning: it would be, if it knew how to not only send, but also receive, and would not just make listeners hear, but also speak, and would not isolate, but bring the listener into relationship." Brecht concludes that: "Radio, therefore, should leave the business of delivery, and organize the listener as a supplier" (ibid, 152). Once listeners, Brecht implies, can experience *self-efficacy through content production*, their knowledge of the functional processes of media communication and, hence, their media literacy increases. This increase in literacy and self-efficacy then triggers a positive *spiral of empowerment* and participation, which in turn democratizes the creation and curation of media content on the side of production and distribution.

2.12 Trust and Legitimacy Through Participation

Fittingly, Brecht cites the concept of democracy as a reference point. Inspired by Kantian political theory, the discourse theory of law by Jürgen Habermas contends that the degree of legitimacy for norms increases when those subjected to the norms experience themselves as their authors through an inclusive communicative process of collective deliberation. Leaning on Brecht, we could apply this pattern in a theory of media trust: *The degree of trust in media communication increases when those addressed by media communication experience themselves as its author through an inclusive communicative process of collective participation*. Across studies, we can find this dynamic as a continuous trend: members of elites generally tend to trust more in the institutions of a given society, including the media, since they personally are included in a process of collective participation that governs the generation of norms and institutions of their society. To expand this effect beyond the current elites could be the goal of an explicitly *normative* theory of inclusive media communication.

3 Distrusting Institutions: Fear of Domination and Exclusion

In 2013, the general public in the United States was not debating the advent of a new age of digital populism prominently. There had been general discussions around the Tea Party's political upsets, but the impact of technology on the political system and the coincidence of this great technological revolution with the growing experience of disenfranchisement remained unseen by most pundits in the public spheres. There were, however, several astute observers who—long before the grand successes of Donald Trump and Bernie Sanders—had realized the long-term challenge and were investing in responses. Strategist Doug Sosnik titled one of his famous "big think" memos: *Which side of the barricade are you on?* He noted a decade of "alienation from our political system and its leaders." The prevalent analyses, he criticized, were focusing too heavily on the daily angers and frustration about the economy or dysfunctional law-making. The broader trend, he contended, was an "extended period of dissatisfaction [with] extremely corrosive effect on the nation's social fabric" (Sosnik 2013).

3.1 Long-Term Decline of Trust in Institutions

A causal argument that the digital revolution *itself* is the original cause of corroded social trust is too simplistic (cf. Snyder 2018). While it does have anti-institutional sentiments baked into its origins, *all* sides of the institutional divides have employed technology and expressed pro- or anti-institutional sentiments more prominently through technological media. Both support and attack were empowered by the same source: decentralized, direct and digital distribution of content without filtering by gatekeepers. Technological changes coincided with a long-term historical trend: the general decline of trust in institutions. Analyzing the trust in government in the United States, Pew Research Center found that there has, in fact, been a fairly steady decline since the 77% high in 1964 after JFK's assassination. Nixon's Watergate scandal resulted in a dramatic decline by almost 20 points from 53% trust in 1972 to 34% in 1976. While the Reagan years are marked by a steady incline of trust, the government under George H. Bush loses public trust dramatically again during the first Iraq War in 1991. While Clinton's presidency, like Reagan's, is marked by a steady resurge of trust, George W. Bush's administration is then witness to both the 60% individual poll high after 9/11 in 2001 and the most dramatic loss of public trust during a presidency, resulting in a 17% low in 2008 after the opening of two wars in Iraq and Afghanistan (Pew Research Center 2018). Since then, the public trust in government has remained low throughout the Obama and Trump presidencies, corroborating widespread research of increased partisanship, societal polarization, and the increasing ethnic diversity from a variety of disciplines.

3.2 Linked Trust Levels of Media and Government

While the most dramatic lows of public trust in government in the U.S. indeed coincide with the rise of digital technology and social media, the general trend has been at work ever since the historic highs of post-World-War-II euphoria. Gallup found that following the investigative reporting on Nixon's Watergate scandal 72% of the US population in 1976 expressed trust in the media. The numbers drop to 53% in 1997 and then to 40% in 2015. The numbers continue to drop with Gallup noting a mere 32% before the presidential election in 2016 (Swift 2016). If anything, the data shows that analysis of media trust in digital societies *cannot* be divorced from larger socio-political trends. Any intersubjective category like *trust* in a specific sector of society will be intricately linked to trust in other realms and integrally embedded in larger socio-historical trends. Even if a specific sector like the media manages an extraordinary feat that should, in fact, increase trust, it is unlikely that it alone can turn the tide on a broader cross-sector, socio-historical trend.

3.3 Low Trust in Institutions in Europe

Contemporary political discourse, as well as popular cultural products like the Netflix series *House of Cards* make the distrust in public institutions evident in the United States. But also the European context is showing clear signs of it: While 56% of the German population lean towards trusting parliament, only 39% trust "European institutions." Two thirds lean towards *distrusting* the media, and only 29% trust political parties (SWI 2016). The *Generation What?* study shows that the vast majority of German youth is highly critical of most public institutions. 83% do not trust religious institutions and 71% do not trust political institutions (Sinus 2016).

Doug Sosnik's specific context for the "barricade" analysis is the United States, and should not be applied to the Western European contexts too quickly. But just before Sosnik's memo was published, Germany had seen the founding of a new populist party: *Alternative für Deutschland* (AfD), which would capture many state and national parliament seats across the country in the years to follow. When *Tagesschau* analyzed the Facebook accounts of all major German parties, the AfD was far ahead with close to 350,000 followers, compared to less than 150,000 for the ruling party CDU (Vorndran 2017). Since then, the trend has continued and the AfD reached 410,000 followers in July 2018. Consultant Martin Fuchs, therefore, concludes that "basically, the party does not need any other media anymore to reach their target groups and mobilize them" (ibid).

3.4 Political Echo Chambers on Social Media Platforms

Researchers have found that the AfD has managed to create a strong, tight-knit community in a media setting separate from traditional, independent media, and is now able to share ideological content without any critical framework. Hence, the party can build up a digital universe of ideologically filtered information that finds its social continuation in the form of digital and non-digital echo chambers in which existing opinions become entrenched through repetition and escalation (Heimbach-Steins and Filipovic 2017). This development mirrors the dynamic of President Donald Trump's use of Twitter (cf. Anderson 2017) and the manipulative impact of intentionally aggravating content spread through Russian intelligence agencies in his 2016 election (cf. United States v. Netyksho et al. 2018). Researchers at the MIT Media Lab have found that while many American Twitter users followed both candidates in the 2016 election, there are also many who only followed Clinton or Trump. The interactions with the other side, however, were much more frequent in Clinton-leaning camps than in Trump-leaning camps. The researchers concluded that a "large cluster of Trump supporters on Twitter have little mutual follower overlap with other users and are a remarkably cohesive group. They exist in their own information bubble" (Thompson 2016).

3.5 Theorizing the Filter Bubble Effect

The filter bubble effects were first critiqued by Cass Sunstein as "echo chambers" or "information cocoons" (Sunstein 2007, xi) and theorized by Eli Pariser as "filter bubbles" (Pariser 2011). Both saw them as an assault on the normative foundations of liberal democracy. This assault, arguably, is not a conscious exercise by technology firms. It, rather, is an unintended consequence of the naïve myth of neutrality maintained by many tech executives. As tech entrepreneur Anil Dash has remarked: "We fancy ourselves outlaws while we shape laws, and consider ourselves disruptive without sufficient consideration for the people and institutions we disrupt." (Dash 2017). This disruption becomes broadly destructive, if it lacks mindfulness of the mid- to long-term social implications. The expansive use of neuropsychological "brain hacking" (Cooper 2017) is such a case: "Consuming information that conforms to our ideas of the world is easy and pleasurable; consuming information that challenges us to think in news or question our assumptions is frustrating and difficult." This furthers the dangerous tendency of "partisans of one political stripe […] not to consume the media of another." At its core, the problem is that "an information environment built on click signals will favor content that supports our existing notions about the world over content that challenges them." (Pariser 2011, 88).

3.6 *Sunstein's Democratic Theory of Shared Information*

Cass Sunstein warns, that what looks like a win-win scenario—convenience for the user, profits for the platform—might actually be a lose-lose scenario: "In a democracy, people do not live in echo chambers or information cocoons. They see and hear a wide range of topics and ideas. They do so even if they did not, and would not, choose to see and to hear those topics and those ideas in advance." This raises "serious questions about certain uses of new technologies, above all the Internet, and about the astonishing growth in the power to choose." Adding to Brecht's ideal of *interactive participation*, Sunstein adds the hermeneutic component of *shared information*: "Members of a democratic public will not do well if they are unable to appreciate the views of their fellow citizens" (Sunstein 2007, xi).

3.7 *Personalization's Impact on Trust in Institutions*

Nicco Mele has built on Pariser's and Sunstein's work to study the effect on societal institutions like governing bodies, entertainment corporations, media organizations, political parties and more. The power of digital personalization, he contends, comes with the risk of "becoming trapped in an individual world without shared cultural space." The long-term effect in the United States is dramatic: "the Big Community we once shared as a country is fast disappearing, with implications for democracy and social cohesion" (Mele 2013, 132). Mele suspects that polarization will be the effect, with significant consequences for media communication trust. In this communication environment, evidently false news would not even be necessary to destabilize the democratic process. If media content actively plays into prejudice to earn the trust of a specific target audience: "Everything might technically be true but is manipulated to appeal to the specific person reading it" (ibid).

This brand-managed digital communication with traits of traditional propaganda might in the short-term create legitimacy for a media outlet in this specific target group, but over time it decreases trust by increasing the fear of manipulation, which contaminates the entire eco-system and erodes trust in all media institutions, which in turn becomes a breeding ground for authoritarian or even fascist forms governance. The practice of manipulative brand-managed communication does not only erode the source for generating common *opinions*. In the long run, it also undermines the source for generating common *facts* on which constructive debates of contrasting opinions can be based. While lies, false news and manipulative communication have always been marks of political discourse, the powerful tools delivered by technology companies to hostile actors increase their impact—especially since enraging content tends to create more interaction than positive content. In an opinion piece, historian Timothy Snyder summarized provocatively: "Fascism is back. Blame the Internet" (Snyder 2018).

3.8 Tribal Polarization in Brand-Managed Communication Environments

More recent empirical research corroborates Mele's intuition. The prevalence of brand-managed communication environments results in dramatic erosion of trust in "the other side" and hence means: tribal polarization. A study of "Fear and Loathing across Party Lines" in the U.S. concludes: "When defined in terms of social identity and affect toward copartisans and opposing partisans, the polarization of the American electorate has dramatically increased." The evidence shows "that hostile feelings for the opposing party are ingrained or automatic in voters' minds, and that affective polarization based on party is just as strong as polarization based on race." The effect does not remain limited to politics: "party cues exert powerful effects on nonpolitical judgments and behaviors." Hence: "Partisans discriminate against opposing partisans, doing so to a degree that exceeds discrimination based on race." This daily practice and "increased partisan affect provides an incentive for elites to engage in confrontation rather than cooperation." (Iyengar and Westwood 2015).

3.9 Charges of Election Interference on Social Media

In a blog post for the World Economic Forum, Maelle Gavet agrees with Mele's premise that digital technology profoundly impacts all other spheres of life and contends that "the digital revolution is destroying our democracies" but argues that it need not be that way (Gavet 2017). Like Mele, she demonstrates the impact of the digital platform economy and calls for the reinvention of governing institutions. Confronted with such debates about their impact on the democratic process, platforms like Facebook have changed their tone and policies. Facebook's founder Mark Zuckerberg had still called charges that Facebook was adversely impacting democratic process ahead of the 2016 US election "a pretty crazy idea" (Techonomy 2016), he acknowledged that Facebook had been "making mistakes" (Zuckerberg 2017a) and later apologized for his naïve initial assessment of interference: "Calling that crazy was dismissive and I regret it. This is too important an issue to be dismissive" (Zuckerberg 2017b). In 2018, Zuckerberg acknowledged that Facebook was not simply a neutral network provider and was responsible for the content on its platform, thus ending above-mentioned myth of neutrality for digital platforms. Ahead of a formal hearing in the U.S. Senate, he also expressed openness to governmental regulation, especially to increase transparency of who was paying for what type of micro-targeted content on the platform (CNN 2018).

3.10 Systemic Failures in Computer Science Education

Anil Dash calls for more than acknowledging individual responsibility. There are systemic problems creating and re-creating social problems through naïve adoption and development. Two ideas are brought forward by Dash: a professional society for the tech industry and an ethical curriculum in computer science programs. Every other discipline or sector, Dash notes, has "a professional society that sets standards. And if you don't meet them, you can be disbarred." For instance: "You can lose your medical license." There are clear professional expectations and "in the educational process, there's an extensive ethical curriculum." Dash critiques that this kind of self-reflection is not yet institutionalized in the tech industry. In fact, "there is zero ethical curriculum." A computer science student is currently awarded "the highest credential computer science degree from the most August institutions with essentially having had zero ethics training." With a cynical hint towards the venture capital sector, Dash notes, that a lack of ethics training might even be "the most likely path to getting funded as a successful startup in Silicon Valley" (Dash 2017). When media convergence is turning technology companies into decisive actors in the media industry, the building of a broader consciousness for social impact is indeed necessary in the digital tech sector, for as we noted above with Luhmann: what we know, we know through media. And today, more media than ever are digital an therefore shaped or distributed through digital technology and platforms (cf. Pew Research Center 2018; Koch and Frees 2017).

3.11 Historical Origins of Anti-institutionalism in the Tech Sector

It is no coincidence that the digital products developed by the current technology sector often share an anti-institutional bent: Anti-institutionalism and the digital revolution, in fact, share a long history. Few people exemplify this disposition better than Apple's Steve Jobs. As his biographer Walter Isacsson notes, Jobs's socialization in the San Francisco Bay Area and the Santa Clara Valley came from a peculiar cultural mix: "during the late 1960s, various cultural currents flowed together." The local development of a digital tech sector "began with the growth of military contractors and soon included electronics firms, microchip makers, video game designers, and computer companies." They mixed with "a hacker subculture – filled with wireheads, phreakers, cyberpunks, hoppyists, and just plain geeks – that included engineers who didn't conform to the [big corporation] mold and their kids who weren't attuned to the wavelengths of subdivisions." In addition, there were "quasi-academic groups doing studies on the effects of LSD," as well as "the hippie movement" and "rebellious political activists" in addition to "various self-fulfillment movements pursuing paths to personal enlightenment: Zen and Hinduism, meditation and yoga, primal scream and sensory deprivation, Esalen and est" (Isacsson 2011, 56f).

3.12 *Personal Computers as Individual Versus Institutional Empowerment*

At first, hippies and technologists were opposing subcultures: "the counterculture saw computers as ominous and Orwellian, the province of the Pentagon and the power structure." But in the 1970s this sentiment shifted: "Computing went from being dismissed as a tool of bureaucratic control to being embraced as a symbol of individual expression and liberation" (as cited by ibid, 57). This explains "Job's desire for control and disdain for authority" (ibid, 83). This anti-institutional bent was not kept secret. In 1984, for the product launch of the Macintosh, the ad team was "toying with a tagline that played off the George Orwell novel: 'Why 1984 won't be like *1984*.' Jobs loved it, and asked them to develop it for the Macintosh launch. So they put together a storyboard for a sixty-second ad that would look like a scene from a sci-fi movie. It featured a rebellious young woman outrunning the Orwellian thought police and throwing a sledgehammer into a screen showing a mind-controlling speech by Big Brother" (ibid, 163). "It was a sensation. That evening all three networks and fifty local stations aired news stories about the ad, giving it a viral life unprecedented in the pre-YouTube area." It was eventually selected by key industry publications "as the greatest commercial of all time" (ibid, 165).

4 Relaunching Trusted Inclusive Institutions

This spirit—*us* underdogs versus *them* institutions—has persisted in the Silicon Valley culture for decades. The rhetoric of individual empowerment, playing into the historical trend of distrust against public institutions, still features prominently in Silicon Valley media communication. But as the discourse around the 2016 U.S. election shows, the rhetoric is complicated by the destructive impact that technologies from this anti-institutional environment have had. There is a growing awareness, that dispensing with basic "freedom-ensuring institutions" (Honneth 1992, 11) might constitute a destructive version of "kicking away the ladder" (Chang 2003) that enabled the rough, but steady path to political stability, social peace, democratic discourse, and the rule of law. Historically, these "freedom-ensuring institutions" are at the core of all large-scale development projects that have lifted citizens out of poverty and ensured civic participation—whether in developing, developed, or post-industrial service economies. Asking "why nations fail," economists Daron Acemoglu and James Robinson note: "We have to look at institutions for an answer." The result of their research: "Countries differ in their economic success because of their different *institutions*, the rules influencing how the economy works, and the incentives that motive people" (Acemoglu and Robinson 2012, 73, emphasis added). Corroborating Brecht's intuition about the link of ownership and participation, Acemoglu and Robinson identify inclusivity as the key criterion for successful institutions. Hence we can add *inclusion* as another key factor for trust in media institutions and beyond.

Against the sociohistorical backdrop of Silicon Valley anti-institutionalism and the erosion of trust in public institutions, Maelle Gavet's warning rings true: "As the power of tech companies continues to grow, the corresponding legitimacy of governments starts to leach away. After all, how can a government enjoy the trust of its people if it can no longer fulfill its fundamental obligations? Put even more starkly, if it cannot serve its citizens, or adjust to the hyper speed of the digital economy, then government itself is in danger of slipping into irrelevance" (Gavet 2017). Summarized provocatively: "Our old institutions […] simply aren't up to the task; they're not designed for the networked world" (Mele 2013, 120). With an implicit premise shared by Kant, Habermas and Brecht, Mele states: "Our institutions of government are based on the consent of the governed. If people lose faith in government while relying on emerging technology to provide some alternatives, our existing government will lose its legitimacy" (ibid, 130). To avoid escalation of verbal identity conflicts into full-blown civil war, Mele encourages us to "reimagine our big institutions so that they actually work again" (ibid, 133). How might one go about this ambitious task?

If the current trend continues, Gavet predicts two possible scenarios: (1) "governments, hemorrhaging power, will start to assert their authority in a very aggressive way." (2) "governments will become mere gatekeepers, as they grow increasingly algorithmic, with policy shaped by data and public services outsourced to private business and the slipstream of the marketplace." Citing the United Kingdom and Estonia as positive examples, Gavet recommends to "leverage technology to boost governmental transparency and efficiency, designing all interactions with the state around the user." Gavet, in fact, interprets the crisis fueled by digital technology as a unique opportunity: "As Western governmental systems fray at the edges and their budgets creak under the strain, the digital revolution offers a once-in-a-century opportunity for renewal. Handled correctly, technology-powered reform can refresh democracies – and reenergize their populations in the process" (Gavet 2017).

This "surge of activity could fuel reform of other key aspects of government" like "streamline processes, strip out duplication, reduce bureaucracy, drive decentralization, and most importantly overhaul existing laws to ensure they're fit for purpose in the digital age." Beyond increasing efficiency, however, civic tech might also "enable a tide of participatory democracy, where citizens play a far greater role in local decision-making." To Brecht's element of *participation*, Sunstein's element of *information*, Mele's element of *consent*, and Acemoglu's and Robinson's element of *inclusion*, Gavet adds the element of *accountability* as a means to regain legitimacy and trust: "Greater accountability will only reinforce democracy, granting it a new lease of life" (ibid).

References

Acemoglu D, Robinson J (2012) Why nations fail. The origins of power, prosperity, and poverty. Crown Business, New York

AJ Labs (2017) We grew monthly Facebook video views 200% to 100 M in six months. Here's what we learned. Published on 8 Apr 2017. https://medium.com/@ajlabs/we-grew-monthly-facebook-video-views-500-to-100m-in-six-months-heres-what-we-learned-20a557e7d96c. Accessed 18 July 2018

Anand B (2016) The content trap: a strategist's guide to digital change. Random House, New York

Anderson B (2017) Tweeter-in-chief: a content analysis of president Trump's tweeting habits. Elon J Undergraduate Res Commun 8:2

Bedford-Strohm J (2016) The emerging cult of authenticity. Re-published on 18 July 2018. https://bedfordstrohm.weebly.com/blog.html. Accessed 22 July 2018

Bedford-Strohm J (2017) Beyond the bubble: the digital transformation of the public sphere and the future of public institutions. zem::dg, München

Bedford-Strohm J, Filipović A (2019) Mediengesellschaft im Wandel – Theorien, Themen, ethische Herausforderungen. In: Ulshöfer G, Wilhelm M (eds) Theologische Medienethik im digitalen Zeitalter (Ethik – Grundlagen und Handlungsfelder 14). Kohlhammer, Stuttgart

Brecht B (2004) Radio – eine vorsintflutliche Erfindung? Vorschläge für den Intendanten des Rundfunks. Über Verwertungen. Der Rundfunk als Kommunikationsapparat. In: Helmes G, Köster W (eds) Texte zur Medientheorie. Reclam, Stuttgart

Burk S et al (eds) (2018) Privatheit in der digitalen Gesellschaft. Dunker & Humblot, Berlin

Chang H (2003) Kicking away the ladder: development strategy in historical perspective. Anthem Press, London/New York

Chritton S (2014) Personal branding for dummies. Wiley, Hoboken

CNN (2018) Mark Zuckerberg in his own words. Published by CNN on 21 Mar 2018. http://money.cnn.com/2018/03/21/technology/mark-zuckerberg-cnn-interview-transcript/index.html. Accessed 2 Apr 2018

Cooper A (2017) What is 'brain hacking'? Tech insiders on why you should care. Published by CBS on 9 Apr 2017. www.cbsnews.com/news/brain-hacking-tech-insiders-60-minutes/. Accessed 16 July 2017

Dash A (2017) Tech's moral reckoning. Published by on being on 12 Jan 2017 at https://www.onbeing.org/programs/anil-dash-techs-moral-reckoning/. Accessed 16 July 2017

Edelman (2018) 2018 Edelman trust barometer global report. https://cms.edelman.com/sites/default/files/2018-01/2018%20Edelman%20Trust%20Barometer%20Global%20Report.pdf. Accessed 18 July 2018

Gavet M (2017) The digital revolution is destroying our democracies—it doesn't have to be that way. Published by world economic forum on 7 Feb 2017. https://www.weforum.org/agenda/2017/02/the-digital-revolution-is-destroying-our-democracies-it-doesn-t-have-to-be-that-way/. Accessed 21 July 2018

Heimbach-Steins M, Filipovic A et al (2017) Grundpositionen der "Alternative für Deutschland" und der Katholischen Soziallehre im Vergleich. Published by ICS in July 2017. https://www.uni-muenster.de/FB2/aktuelles/ics/ankuendigungAP8.html. Accessed 21 July 2018

Honneth A (1992) Kampf um Anerkennung: Zur moralischen Grammatik sozialer Konflikte. Suhrkamp, Frankfurt am Main

Isacsson W (2011) Steve Jobs. Little, Brown, London

Iyengar S, Westwood S (2015) Fear and loathing across party lines: new evidence on group polarization. Am J Polit Sci 59:3

Koch W, Frees B (2017) ARD/ZDF-Onlinestudie 2017: Neun von zehn Deutschen online. Media Perspektiven 6/2017. http://www.ard-zdf-onlinestudie.de/files/2017/Artikel/917_Koch_Frees.pdf. Accessed 24 July 2018

Luhmann N (2009) Die Realität der Massenmedien, 4th edn. VS Verlag, Wiesbaden

Meier C (2018) Warum das Vertrauen in den Journalismus wieder steigt. Published by WELT on 31 Jan 2018. https://www.welt.de/kultur/medien/article173027687/Medien-Vertrauen-Sie-Journalisten-Hier-steht-warum.html. Accessed 18 July 2018

Mele N (2013) The end of big. How the internet makes David the new Goliath. St. Martin's Press, New York

Mele N (2015) 7 reasons why Trump will win. Published by Soapbox on 30 Nov 2015. https://medium.com/soapbox-dc/7-reasons-why-trump-will-win-be76b33de2df. Accessed 21 July 2018

Negroponte N (1995) Being digital. Knopf, New York

Pariser E (2011) The filter bubble: what the internet is hiding from you. Penguin Books, London

Pew Research Center (2017) Public trust in government 1958–2017. Published on 14 Dec 2017. http://www.people-press.org/2017/12/14/public-trust-in-government-1958-2017/. Accessed 24 July 2018

Pew Research Center (2018) Digital news fact sheet. Published on 6 June 2018. http://www.journalism.org/fact-sheet/digital-news/. Accessed 24 July 2018

Pöttker H (2016) Kommunikationsfreiheit im digitalen Zeitalter. Zwölf Thesen. Communicatio Socialis 49:4

Rohgalf J (2016) Coding populism? Populismus und Soziale Medien. Published by Theorieblog on 6 May 2016. https://www.theorieblog.de/index.php/2016/05/coding-populism-populismus-und-soziale-medien/. Accessed 21 July 2018

Seward Z (2016) It's here. Quartz's first news app for iPhone. Published by Quartz on 11 Feb 2016. https://qz.com/613700/its-here-quartzs-first-news-app-for-iphone/. Accessed 20 July 2018

Sinus Institute (2016) Generation what? 2016: Abschlussbericht Deutschland. Published by Bayerischer Rundfunk on 11 Nov 2016. http://www.br.de/presse/inhalt/pressedossiers/generation-what/generation-whatendergebnisse-102.html. Accessed 15 Dec 2016

Snyder T (2018) Fascism is back. Blame the internet. Published by Washington Post on 21 May 2018. https://www.washingtonpost.com/news/posteverything/wp/2018/05/21/fascism-is-back-blame-the-internet/?noredirect=on&utm_term=.b1240770db7f. Accessed 21 July 2018

Sosnik D (2013) Which side of the barricade are you on? Published by POLITICO Magazine on 25 Nov 2013. https://www.politico.com/magazine/story/2013/11/which-side-of-the-barricade-are-you-on-100302. Accessed 21 July 2018

Sozialwissenschaftliches Institut der EKD (2016) Solidarität in Europa. Published on 7 Nov 2016. https://www.ekd.de/ekd_de/ds_doc/solidaritaet_in_europa_si_studie_ekd_2016.pdf. Accessed 15 Dec 2016

Stalder F (2016) Kultur der Digitalität. Suhrkamp, Berlin

Statista (2018a) Umfrage zum Vertrauen in verschiedenen Berufsgruppen in Deutschland 2017. https://de.statista.com/statistik/daten/studie/1470/umfrage/vertrauen-in-verschiedene-berufsgruppen/. Accessed 18 July 2018

Statista (2018b) Facebook's annual revenue and net income from 2007 to 2017. https://www.statista.com/statistics/277229/facebooks-annual-revenue-and-net-income/. Accessed 19 July 2018

Statista (2018c) Smart speaker market revenue worldwide in 2017 and 2022 (in billion U.S. dollars). https://www.statista.com/statistics/822511/worldwide-smart-speaker-market-revenue/. Accessed 20 July 2018

Sunstein C (2007) Republic.com 2.0. Univ. Press, Princeton

Swift A (2016) Americans' trust in mass media sinks to new low. Published by Gallup on 14 Sept 2016. https://news.gallup.com/poll/195542/americans-trust-mass-media-sinks-new-low.aspx. Accessed 24 July 2018

Tagesschau (2018) Novi – Nachrichten im Chatformat. Published by Tagesschau on 25 June 2018. https://www.tagesschau.de/inland/novi-103.html. Accessed 20 July 2018

Techonomy (2016) In conversation with Mark Zuckerberg. Published on 17 Nov 2016. https://techonomy.com/conf/te16/videos-conversations-with-2/in-conversation-with-mark-zuckerberg/. Accessed 3 Apr 2018

Thompson A (2016) Parallel narratives. Published by VICE NEWS on 8 Dec 2016. https://news.vice.com/en_us/article/d3xamx/journalists-and-trump-voters-live-in-separate-online-bubbles-mit-analysis-shows. Accessed 21 July 2018

United States of America v. Netyksho et al, No 18 U.S.C. §§ 2, 371, 1030, 1028A, 1956, and 3551 et seq., United States District Court for the District of Columbia, 13 July 2018. https://www.justice.gov/file/1080281/download. Accessed 24 July 2018

Vorndran M (2017) Fans sind nicht automatisch Wähler. Published by Tagesschau on 8 Sept 2017. https://www.tagesschau.de/inland/btw17/parteien-facebook-101.html. Accessed 21 July 2018

Wehling E (2016) Politisches Framing: Wie eine Nation sich ihr Denken einredet – und daraus Politik macht. Halem, Köln

Wittgenstein L (1963) Tractatus logico-philosophicus/Logisch-philosophische Abhandlung. Suhrkamp, Frankfurt am Main

Zuckerberg M (2017a) Building global community. Published on Facebook on 16 Feb 2017. https://www.facebook.com/notes/mark-zuckerberg/building-global-community/10103508221158471. Accessed 3 Apr 2018

Zuckerberg M (2017b) Post on Facebook. Published on 27 Sept 2017 https://www.facebook.com/zuck/posts/10104067130714241. Accessed 3 Apr 2018

Jonas Bedford-Strohm is a research fellow at the Center for Media Ethics and Digital Society (zem::dg) at Munich School of Philosophy and studies the digital transformation of public communication. He built the voice assistant team at the German Public Broadcaster *Bayerischer Rundfunk* and now manages artificial intelligence project in its news division. He recently co-founded the European media startup Forum.eu and serves as its Chief Evangelist. Having studied theology, philosophy and political theory at Stellenbosch (South Africa) and Yale (US), he holds B.A. and M.A. degrees from Heidelberg University (Germany). A co-founder of the non-profit Wikwiheba, he co-authored a conversation book on religion and translated a series of children's books on global issues. His recent academic publications include the edited volume of essays *Digitaler Strukturwandel der Öffentlichkeit: Interdisziplinäre Perspektiven auf politische Partizipation im Wandel* (2019).

Chapter 4
Financial Value of Trust in the Media Business

Harald Watzek

1 Introduction

We live in a time where the term "fake news" has become a household term and has even entered the German dictionary Duden. However, it is not just plain lies that are an issue as Jami (2012) correctly points out: "Just because something isn't a lie does not mean that it isn't deceptive".

It is therefore no surprise that various research papers report a record low polling in media trust such as Edelman (2018) or Gallup (2016). According to the Gallup (2016) poll, trust in mass media in the United States "is lower than it has ever been since the organization started asking that question in 1972".

Trust in the Media Business is a concept with multiple dimensions such as social, political, personal or journalistic. This article aims at elaborating a particular dimension, namely the Financial Value of Trust in the Media Business for individual businesses.

In the next chapter of this text a definition of Trust, Media and Financial Value for the purposes of this article will be provided. In the third chapter, the relationship between Trust and Financial value will be established. In the fourth chapter, this relationship will be examined according to three fundamentally different strategic approaches that Media Businesses can pursue. Then, social media will be brought into the picture as it is a high growth and special kind of media. Finally, the article tries to provide answers for the hypotheses/assumptions that are presented below and will outline future fields of research.

The key assumptions underlying this article which are to be "tested" here are:

A1: Trust has significant Financial Value for Media Businesses in general.
A2: This Financial Value is constant across various strategic approaches within the media business.

H. Watzek (✉)
Hochschule Fresenius, Infanteriestr. 11a, 80797 Munich, Germany
e-mail: harald.watzek@hs-fresenius.de

T. Osburg and S. Heinecke (eds.), *Media Trust in a Digital World*,
https://doi.org/10.1007/978-3-030-30774-5_4

A3: [Due to the recent developments in Data Protection and Privacy] Trust has become more important for the Financial Value of specific Media Business models, in particular social media.

This specific concept has not been intensively researched yet. Therefore I will aim to develop and build it up in this article. The testing of the above assumptions will take place in an entirely conceptual way. The assessment will consequently NOT happen in an empirical way here, but this may be done in future efforts or future articles. In summary, in order to fill the academic void the methodological approach in this article is to establish and develop the concept of Financial Value of Trust in the Media Business in an explorative way.

2 Key Definitions and Development of the Concept

Trust is an important Success Driver in the Media Business. In some papers, however, Trust is not explicitly mentioned in this context, such as in Giesecke and Immonen (2016), or in a PWC study (PWC 2017) where future growth drivers are presented that include "Professional Journalism" or "Content Strategy". However, these two drivers are closely linked to the concept of Trust. Both drivers can only be successfully employed, if a media business uses experienced and knowledgeable journalists in order to produce serious and reliable online or offline content. This concept is strongly related to my definition of Trust which is:

Trust (in Media) in this article means the amount of reliance the reader, client or user attributes to the facts and opinions presented in the Media as well as their professional analysis and evaluation. A client is then considered to be either a reader/user/partaker/member/subscriber or similar of a media or platform. Especially regarding social media, Trust also refers to how much you trust a social media platform with your personal data.
Media in general is defined as "the means of communication that reach large numbers of people, such as television, newspapers, and radio" (Collins 2016). This is now complemented by all digital ways of communications such as websites, blogs as well as social media platforms.
Media Business for the purposes of this article is defined as a business publishing *written* digital news or other time-sensitive information such as online newspapers and magazines, websites, blogs (traditional digital media) as well as social media platforms (new digital media). This definition of a *news source* is selected in order to be able to distinguish between strategies that differentiate by their timing of news publication. Consequently, "long-term" media such as e-books or scientific articles are not to be treated under this article. This applies despite the fact that those "long-term" media items can certainly also win or lose Trust with users or clients.
Financial value is defined here as the effect of Trust (or other parameters not treated here) on financial parameters of individual Media Businesses. Financial parameters include i.a. revenues and prices claimed for a product or service, or incurred cost for

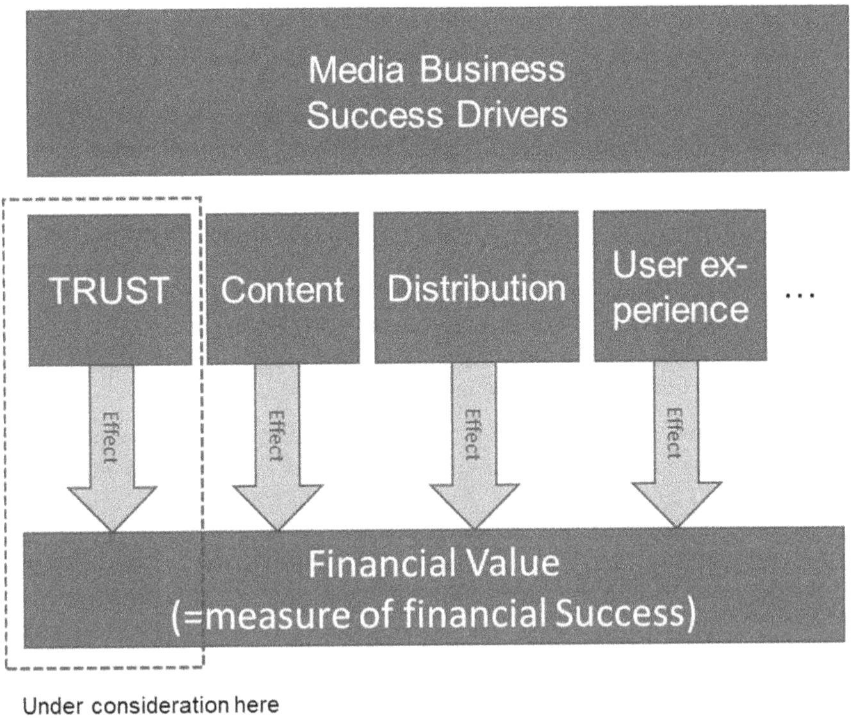

Fig. 1 Media Business Success Drivers and their (potential) effect or contribution on Financial Value, own creation, partly based on Giesecke and Immonen (2016) and PWC (2017)

a litigation. In summary, Financial Value in this paper refers to current or future net income of a media business.

Figure 1 depicts a couple of the main success drivers including Trust and their potential effects on Financial Value. Financial value is considered an overall measurement of the level of financial success of a business.

3 How Trust and Financial Value Are Linked

After having established the key definitions, we will now examine the nature and extent of the relationship between Trust and Financial Value. As per the hypothesis A1 (see above), we assume that there is a significant link between them and we will now analyse the background of this relationship. This should help establish the level of correlation.

The economic or Financial Value of trust has been analysed in various settings, such as in bilateral supplier-buyer or seller-clients constellations or the effect on brand equity (Briggeman and Newman 2016; Dyer and Chu 1997; Ambler 1997).

The Financial Value of Trust in the media business has not been analysed yet, at least not in a published way. Therefore, this chapter will try to establish the concept of link between Trust and Financial value.

In general, the effect that Trust has on Financial Value can have both a positive as well as negative sign/dimension: A **positive effect on Financial Value** occurs if Trust can be maintained or increased. Examples are:

- Articles or posts that are well investigated, fact and source checked as well as properly corroborated
- Articles utilising a high quality journalistic approach
- Short factual news that are timely, precise and also corroborated
- Information (facts or ads) that the recipient have been sent is relevant or tailor-made for and is considered an added value by the recipient.

Each of the above could lead to an increased usage (including increased payments) of this media. Users could also be motivated to continue or start paying for the used services. The perceived quality and—if applicable—uniqueness of the services could be correlated to the prices that are asked and paid. Such prices then translate into higher revenues leading to higher net income ceteris paribus. Higher income would then mean generally higher Financial Value of the particular media business.

Even if higher revenues directly by the users cannot be achieved, a higher usage or traffic of the site (criteria such as unique visitors or clicks can be used) could lead to higher revenues from advertising by third parties. Higher usage could therefore increase the attractiveness of the website to various advertisers as well as online marketing in general. The decision and steering of the split of these two income streams (users revenues and third party revenues) is a strategic decision for each Media Business. This decision is also driven i.a. by the target client group for the Media and/or the partner businesses that wish to cooperate with this Media Business.

It should be obvious but still be noted that high quality corroboration mentioned in the examples above requires time, cost and expertise. This also weighs negatively on the financial parameters. When a high-quality strategy with the corresponding cost is chosen, this should be considered a conscious decision and investment.

A **negative effect on financial value** happens, if Trust is or could be lost (passive consequence) or if litigation cost or other cost increase (active consequence). Examples are:

- News that are not well investigated, or that lack some of the most basic information in order to fully understand the full contents and background of the article.
- News presented or broadcast that are fake and/or prove to be incorrect after their publication.
- Information, that you are sent is either irrelevant for you or is considered an intrusion into your privacy as it contains information that you did not think was available to the sender of the information.

Each of the mentioned examples could lead to a reduced usage by users (including payments) of this media. This counts as a passive or indirect consequence. There can also be active or direct negative consequences in case an information leads to a private

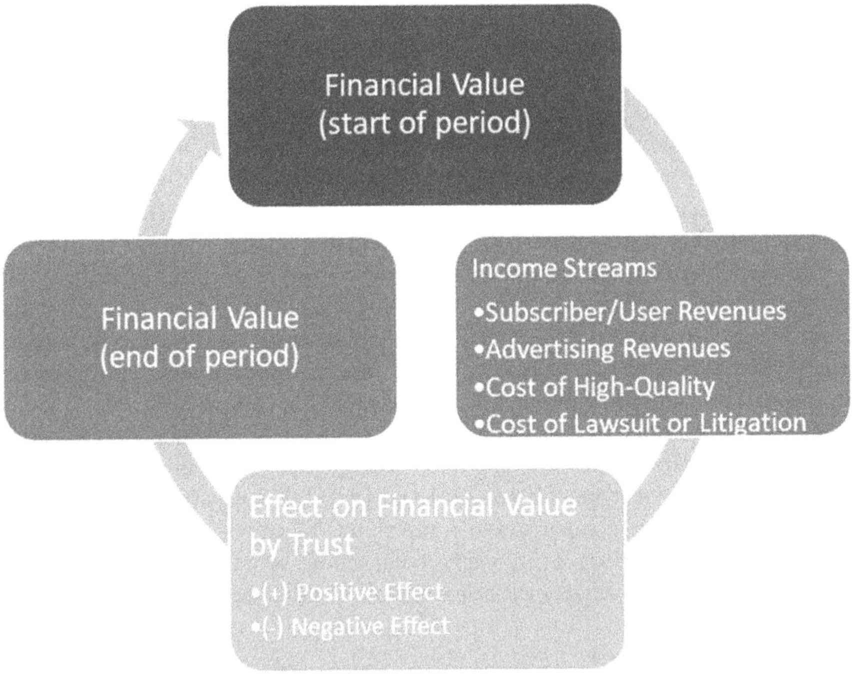

Fig. 2 Concept of effects on Financial Value (own considerations)

or public law suit or litigation. Such a lawsuit can result in significant penalties or charges, that translate into the additional cost and therefore into a negative effect on Financial Value of a media business. Figure 2 illustrates the concept explained above.

4 Does Strategy Matter (For the Importance of Trust)?

The thoughts in the last chapter can lead to strategic decisions by media businesses. The question as per Assumption 2 (A2) is, whether the link between Trust and Financial Value is constant across all types of media. We will first distinguish media by their strategic approaches. Then we will deliberate, whether the impact of Trust is different for the various strategic approaches.

Which are the strategic approaches Media Business can take in this context? Porter (1985) stipulates three generic distinct strategies to differentiate a company in comparison to competitors and gain competitive advantage. His main strategies (those which target the entire market and not only part of it) suggest to position a business either as (i) quality leader or (ii) price leader. Alternatively, a business can try to become leader in a (iii) focus area or specialisation in a special segment of the market and lead in that niche. Due to the current nature and evolution of the media industry, the chosen focus area will be *speed* as the third dimension of differentiation. Why speed? Formerly the time slots for news dissemination were rigid and less flexible, e.g. newspapers had to be printed once or twice a day, TV programs were scheduled long before the emergence of particular news etc. Today, news dissemination happens flexibly and, in many cases, instantly after the news have been received or researched. In addition, the clients expect to receive the news much quicker than was the case 10 or 20 years ago.

These three dimensions are put into a strategic triangle. It is shown as a triangle with the different leaders at its corners. This shape indicates that you can only reach one corner at a time and that each strategy cannot be easily optimised to be a leader in more than one area. Consequently, there is the need for a trade-off between the various strategic approaches, which is visualised by Fig. 3.

According to Porter's general concept, any business, which does not manage to compete for leadership in one of the three strategies, is "stuck in the middle" and should aim to leave that spot for one of the corners. Taken negatively, they have no clear differentiation in comparison to competitors. Taken positively, they combine various benefits to provide a reasonable compromise or middle-of-the-road offer. How are these three strategic approaches characterised in the media business?

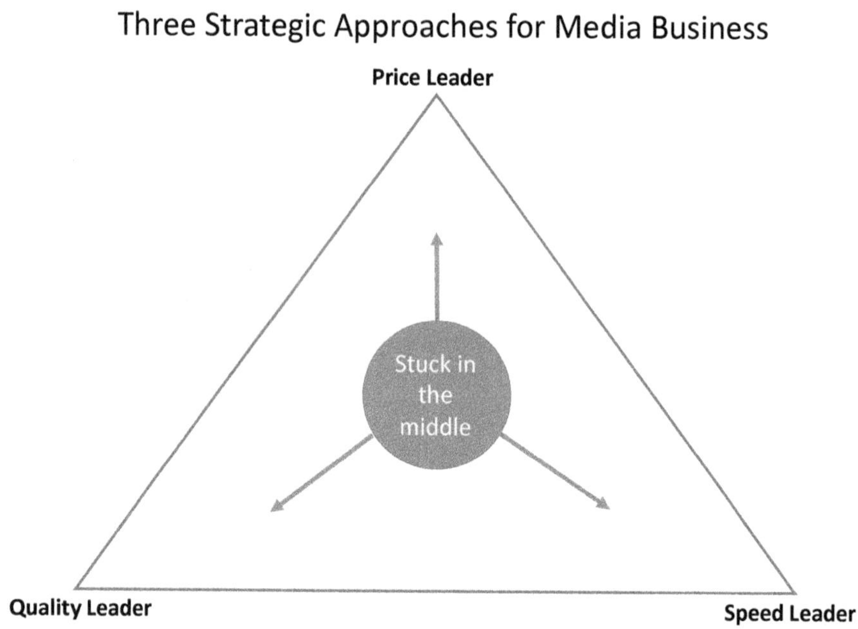

Fig. 3 Three strategic approaches for Media Businesses. Adapted from Porter (1985)

4.1 Quality Leader

A quality leader should consider and strive i.a. for the following aspects:

- High quality journalism including well researched articles. If facts prove to be incorrect in the article after publishing, a transparent "correction" of the mistakes or misunderstandings should be given and be visible for the readers.
- High added value of the journalistic efforts or journalistic analysis, which goes beyond stating the mere well researched fact.
- Facts are put into perspective, analysed and the reader can either form his own opinion or follow the opinion of the author, which is clearly recognisable as an opinion. Any bias is therefore transparent.
- High level of knowledge and experience about the industry sector the news are about.
- High fit of personal information, news and advertising towards its clients, without overburdening or annoying them.

The overall aim is to produce and provide high quality services. In return, a quality leader strives to receive a justified and satisfactory remuneration, either by user fees or subscriptions or by the generated advertising revenues. In general, the amount of revenues generated directly by clients is higher in comparison to the two other strategies.

Examples of such high-quality media are in the U.S. New York Times, Washington Post, in Germany: Frankfurter Allgemeine Zeitung, Süddeutsche Zeitung or Spiegel Online. A Social Media example is Linked-In, which strives to corroborate the information provided.

What are the criteria to identify a Quality leader: There are various studies trying to identify the categories, that differentiate a high-quality news source from a low-quality one. The suggested criteria below are compiled from Lacy and Rosenstiel (2015) and Bogart (1989) and include own additions (Table 1).

As an additional and simplified rule of thumb indicated above, many quality leaders charge their clients directly at least for some or premium services. Premium

Table 1 Criteria for high-quality media (Lacy and Rosenstiel 2015; Bogart 1989)

1. Number of words per article
2. Pricing
3. Ratio of text to pictures
4. Depth and breadth of information
5. Trustworthiness
6. Total amount of non-advertising content
7. Ratio of news interpretation and backgrounders to spotty news reports
8. Presence of news summary
9. Ratio of cultural news, reviews and features to total news coverage

online services are often more expensive that competing offers. This helps to pay their highly professional staff and should enhance their independency in producing the news from third parties such as advertisers.

4.2 Price Leader

A **price leader** on the other side, should aim to provide reasonable news and information for a low or even no (direct) price paid by the readers. Consequently, the amount of revenues generated by third parties is comparatively high. In some cases, a price leader often is in line with the concept of being a very large or even the largest player (e.g. Facebook). This enables the implementation and use of economies of scale, which in turn reduce the general cost and thus facilitate low prices. Examples of such media are in the U.S.: USA Today, in Germany: Bild Zeitung or Facebook in Social Media.

Criteria to identify a Price leader: The price charged for their minimum offers, as well as mid and total level of access to the information.

In summary, in contrast to quality leaders, price leaders get their revenues to a higher extent from third parties. Facebook is the classic example. User do not pay Facebook to use their services directly. Instead you could say they pay with their personal data and information. Based on this, Facebook lets third parties advertise to the platform's users. Those third parties aim to find and address their target group very successfully, as they have much more data on them. Consequently, the vast majority of Facebook's revenues of the first quarter of 2018 of $14 billion stem from advertising (Kuchler 2018).

4.3 Speed Leader

A speed leader focuses on getting information to the clients as quick as possible and quicker than its competitors. This has also the secondary effect, that many aggregating sites will quote the speed leader and not necessarily those sites that posted the same information later. This can also be regarded as "the winner takes it all" concept when the media, who first publishes information may be quoted by other media sources and therefore increase its reach further and sometimes exponentially.

Criteria of a Speed Leader: examples are

- Point in Time that news or post is actually published
- Length of Time it takes to create post
- Length of Time it takes to read post
- Responsiveness to answers, comments or questions to the posts
- Levels of internal corroboration (if any) before information is disseminated.

A typical example is the social Media Platform Twitter, which is mostly geared towards getting out news to the public quickly. Initially limited to only 140 characters per news message (=tweet), each message can now contain up to 240 characters. This still favors a quick and non-complex writing style over a more differentiated and complex analysis. Therefore, Twitter facilitates both sides of the news dissemination in terms of speed: the creation of the news and the distribution including the short time it takes to read the news. Media Examples in the U.S. are CNN, striving to be first in producing breaking news and cover that via a liveticker, in Germany Focus Online who reports breaking news swiftly.

Potential examples of Media Businesses positioned in the strategic triangle are presented in Fig. 4.

How can you measure the concept and the extent of the various strategic approaches of the various Media Businesses in reality? Please be aware that this is a conceptual model and categorization. Any empiric test, would need to be undertaken by an empiric study, the details of which would need to be set up.

How do these three strategic approaches feed into the concept of Trust and which strategic approach strives for which level of Trust? Figure 5 tries to answer that question.

In reference to meaning of Fig. 5, I suggest that Trust has a much higher importance (and consequently effect on Financial Value) to quality leaders, than it has to speed or price leaders. This also means that the concept of Trust is much more linked and related to the quality aspect of media business's and their strategies. In summary, trust is most important for Quality Leaders, when optimizing their Financial Value.

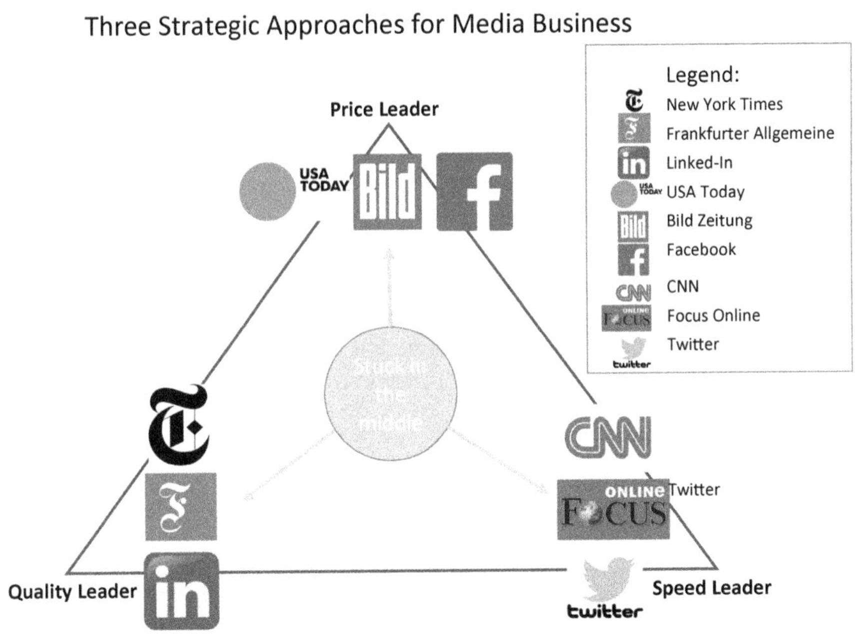

Fig. 4 Exemplary categorization of various Media Businesses

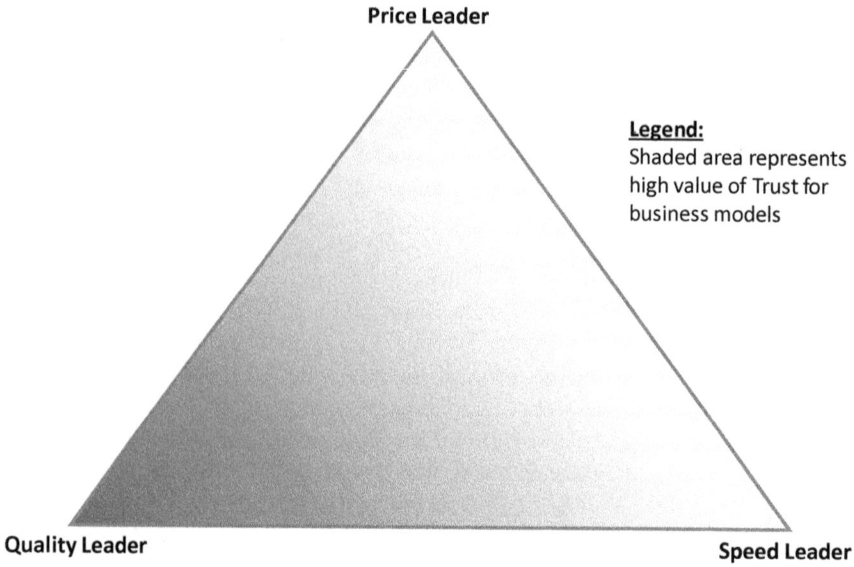

Fig. 5 Relationship between strategy and the Financial Value of Trust (except social media)

Example for traditional digital media: a quality leader has an audience that relies on their facts and analysis. Any negative deviation from their high quality standards would result in a significant uproar and loss of trust. Some of the loyal readers may change for another perceived quality leader. On the other hand for a tabloid price leading type media information, it may well be that the main purpose of the articles is to entertain, to surprise and to confirm their readers opinions, without being too complex and difficult. It may also well be that a less reliable information is still accepted as it is either tolerated or even expected. Therefore Trust is less important than the other mentioned characteristics such as entertainment or spectacular effects. In addition, any bias may coincide with the preferences of the clients.

If information is consumed from a speed leader, it may well be the most important point to broadcast it quicker than anyone else. The consumers then discuss it, share it on social media, but do not necessarily rely fully on the trustworthiness of the information and should not build material decisions on them.

This may be the reason that social media has its challenges to produce quality leaders, or as Laurenson (2017) puts it: "There is no New York Times in social media (yet)".

5 Social Media as a Special Category?

Social Media is a strange animal in the context of this paper. For the purposes of this article social media encompasses platforms such as Facebook, LinkedIn Twitter, Youtube or Instagram. On the one hand their business model is partly built on the concept of distributing private and public information. On the other hand, they tend to insist that they are not media businesses at all but rather platforms for the *interaction and distribution of news and information provided by others*. Their argument for not being a media business is likely that they want to avoid the responsibility for the media's or information's contents. The term "social networks" may be the preferred term from the perspective of social media platforms. In a recent Reuters study, even if the majority of people do not trust the mainstream news media, social media is trusted even less in its ability to separate fact from fiction (Newman and Fletcher 2017).

Social media is changing the way and the speed by which our digital absorption of information/news influences our lives and our way of communication. Social media has also changed the way Financial Value for such services is established. The mostly *free* model of Facebook means that those platforms do not earn any or no significant amount of money directly from their clients. The revenues come from indirect sources such as advertising or online marketing or other firms using the data about the clients derived from the platform. Not surprisingly, businesses are restricted by the rules of the platform regarding the extent by which they use these platforms for advertising themselves through their own "profiles" or sending out advertising. They need, however, to go through the platforms to reach their target clients. Alternatively, they can use influencers, who are individuals who use their own profiles to disseminate information. These influencers then report about their products and market them e.g. through product placement. In many cases, the influencers as individuals are more trusted by the users than the companies whose products they present.

How does Trust affect which information you allow a social media platform to use, assuming you get the choice? Either you completely trust the platform that it will use the data only for themselves and for the right purposes. Alternatively, if you do not have full trust in a platform, you may not mind, either (i) because the results you get are so outstanding or (ii) because you are indifferent with what happens with your personal data (see Vanhonacker 2016, p. 1). If all of the above does not apply, a user will withdraw current or future important personal data from the platform.

Recent data scandals such as the one involving the now defunct firm Cambridge Analytica in connection with Facebook user data have triggered an intensive discussion about data protection and the use of clients' data in general. Some firms such as Tesla, Commerzbank or Mozilla Firefox publicly announced to stop or consider stopping their online marketing via Facebook after the scandal broke. The Trust of users that "Facebook is committed to protect the personal information of users" dropped from 80% in 2017 to below 30% in mid-2018 (Kuchler and Jopson 2018). These discussions and development have the potential to disrupt the Trust in the platforms and their owners and their business models. The loss of Trust eventually could lead to a long term destruction of Financial Value as the business models of social media platforms are put into question.

6 Conclusions/Recommendations

This paper is written to establish the general concept and inspire more discussion, not provide definitive conclusions beyond some general insights. The questions raised and discussed above deserve more thought and research, given the rapid and intense changes in the media landscape.

In this paper the concept of Trust with respect to its Financial Value for the Media Business has been established. It shall provide general guidance what the various strategic approaches of media business are and how important Trust is for each of these approaches. Some practical examples aim to illustrate the concept and the relationships.

The summary of findings in relations to the three main Assumptions are:

A1: Trust has a significant Financial Value for Media/businesses in general.
According to this article, the definite answer is true.
A2: This Financial Value is constant across various strategic approaches within the media business.

This is not true. If you follow the three strategic approaches for the media that have been presented in this article only a quality leader in traditional digital media urgently needs a high level of trust. A speed leader as well as price leader relies more on other facts, even if Trust may still be an important factor. A deviating result occurs for social media, especially when private data is provided or can be collected. In this case even a price leader such as Facebook heavily relies on Trust, which is the basis for their business models and the quality and quantity of data they can use.

A3: [Due to the recent developments in Data Protection and Privacy] Trust has become more important for the Financial Value of specific business models, in particular social media.
In line with this article and the explanations for A2, this is true.

A future field of research or empirical analysis could expand on what level of trust clients actually expect from each of the media they use. The results could then be linked with the individual preferences of the clients such as price, quality or speed.

References

Ambler T (1997) How much brand equity is explained by Trust. Manage Decis 25(4):283–293

Bogart L (1989) Press and the public: who reads what, when, where and why in American newspapers. Lawrence Erlbaum Associates, Hillsdale, NJ

Briggeman B, Newman C (2016) The economic value of Trust. Conference paper presented in the 2016 NCERA-210 cooperatives annual meeting, Nov 2, Minneapolis, Minnesota. http://ageconsearch.umn.edu/record/265452/files/EconomicValueofTrust_Briggeman.pdf. Accessed 25 Nov 2018

Collins (2016) Collins-dictionary of the English language. https://www.collinsdictionary.com/de/worterbuch/englisch/media. Accessed 26 June 2018

Dyer J, Chu W (1997) The economic value of trust in supplier-buyer relationships. Paper for the Wharton School, University of Pennsylvania. http://hdl.handle.net/1721.1/1439. Accessed on 25 Nov 2018

Edelman (2018) Edelman trust barometer. Annual global study 2018. https://www.edelman.com/sites/g/files/aatuss191/files/2018-10/2018_Edelman_Trust_Barometer_Global_Report_FEB.pdf. Accessed on 25 Nov 2018

Gallup (2016) Americans trust in mass media sinks to new low. https://news.gallup.com/poll/195542/americans-trust-mass-media-sinks-new-low.aspx. Accessed 30 June 2018

Giesecke R, Immonen S (2016) Media sector business drivers in 2020. Paper produced for the Aalto University School of Science and Technology, Espoo Finland. https://pdfs.semanticscholar.org/84f1/d72f86fbf1d6be4a6a6c41ec71edb672ba5f.pdf. Accessed 25 Nov 2018

Jami C (2012) Venus in arms. CreateSpace International Publishing Platform, United States

Kuchler H (2018) Facebook blows through Wall Street's ad revenue expectations. Financial Times, 26 Apr 2018. https://www.ft.com/content/50eaff86-48b6-11e8-8ae9-4b5ddcca99b3. Accessed 10 July 2018

Kuchler H, Jopson B (2018) Facebook faces an uphill struggle to regain trust. Financial Times, 6 June 2018. https://www.ft.com/content/c2a243c6-699c-11e8-8cf3-0c230fa67aec. Accessed 10 July 2018

Lacy S, Rosenstiel T (2015) Defining and measuring quality journalism. Paper for Rutgers School of Communication, New Jersey. http://mpii.rutgers.edu/wp-content/uploads/sites/129/2015/04/Defining-and-Measuring-Quality-Journalism.pdf. Accessed 25 Nov 2018

Laurenson L (2017) Social media platforms can be built around quality, not scale. Harv Bus Rev. https://hbr.org/2017/04/imagining-a-social-media-platform-built-around-quality-not-scale. Accessed 03 July 2018

Newman N, Fletcher R (2017) Bias, bullshit and lies audience perspectives on low trust in the media. Reuters Institute digital news report 2017. Reuters Institute for the Study of Journalism, Oxford. http://mpii.rutgers.edu/wp-content/uploads/sites/129/2015/04/Defining-and-Measuring-Quality-Journalism.pdf. Accessed 25 Nov 2018

Porter M (1985) Competitive advantage. The Free Press, New York

Price Waterhouse Coopers (2017) Perspectives from the global entertainment and media outlook 2017–2021. https://www.pwc.com/gx/en/entertainment-media/pdf/outlook-2017-curtain-up.pdf. Accessed on 15 Nov 2018

Vanhonacker W (2016) Social media and the business of trust. Published on The European Business Review website, 12 July 2016. http://www.europeanbusinessreview.com/social-media-and-the-business-of-trust/. Accessed 25 Nov 2018

Harald Watzek has been working in the finance industry for more than 20 years. He started at Austria Wirtschaftsservice GmbH in Vienna and then switched to HypoVereinsbank in Germany, now UniCredit Bank. Working in project finance, he acquired, negotiated and financed large international infrastructure projects. Harald was then promoted to head the sales team of Bavaria South for trade finance and cash management products. In order to understand and support the inner workings of a large international bank, Harald then led various strategic projects directly reporting to the board. Projects included Basel III and SREP—the new evaluation process of banks by the ECB. Harald is now Professor for finance and marketing at Fresenius University of Applied Sciences in Munich. Harald studied Business at the University of Economics and Business in Vienna, Austria as well as at the University of British Columbia in Vancouver, Canada.

Chapter 5
Corporate Social Responsibility Competences and Value Cocreation Through Corporate Communication

Zhanna Belyaeva

1 Introduction

The purpose of this paper is to examine the development of competences that force stronger CSR in western and eastern cultures. It has been previously studied by international scholars that there are different models of CSR in various countries. This research investigates the systems and processes involved in developing and implementing CSR supporting competences in various institutional, business, historical and cross-cultural environments. It is suggested that the institutional contour of a country's CSR model could be predefined by the historical preconditions of the formation and development of the CSR model in the respective country, the current state of the CSR level in business-state-society relationship, and the analysis of the stakeholders' core concerns and their perceptions of related risks (Belyaeva 2010). Visser (2010) suggested that we have entered into the new era of strategic, so called "glocal" CSR 2.0, while Porter and Kramer (2006, 2011) pointed to the tendency of moving from reactive CSR to creating shared value. Although this research stream is still based very much on the development of Stakeholder Theory (Freeman 1984, 2005), nowadays, we can clearly see that external factors change the business attitude towards nurturing sustainable mindsets. Among critical factors one would name the implications of the global financial crisis and the ability derived from it to influence the broader circles of stakeholders and avoid standard mechanisms to develop organizations on a short term basis. A socially responsible corporate entity takes cognizance of the impact of its actions on its communities, stakeholders and the environment when formulating its corporate objectives and making its corporate decisions. One of the salient issues is to differentiate that being socially responsible is not just very 'trendy' but also good for business, society and personal growth. The aim of this

Z. Belyaeva (✉)
Graduate School of Economics and Management, Ural Federal University, GSEM-UrFU, Yekaterinburg, Russia
e-mail: zh.s.belyaeva@urfu.ru

T. Osburg and S. Heinecke (eds.), *Media Trust in a Digital World*,
https://doi.org/10.1007/978-3-030-30774-5_5

research is to formalise the acceptance, perception and actual implementation of this attitude in different environments.

2 Global Approach to Corporate Responsibility Competence

Modern Corporate Communications focusing on reputation related to social responsibility and legitimacy (Czinkota et al. 2014) are linking businesses, governments and society in understanding the signals to further co-develop in a sustainable way (Belyaeva 2016). This kind of communication embraces a variety of cross-functional and multidisciplinary concepts and goes beyond marketing theory aiming to advance both internal and external multi-stakeholder dialogue. In the broader context, CSR:

- is often associated with philanthropy in the USA, India;
- has more sophisticated institutionalized models in the EU, while still has differences at a country level, depending on a history and business attitude;
- works as a window-dressing technique for some Asian companies entering the global market as an entry strategy (China, Malaysia, Indonesia);
- in some countries, e.g. Australia, NGOs try to police different aspects of corporate and governmental behaviors in both, the developed and less developed countries of the world in order to ensure that these behaviors do not fall short of acceptable standards;
- develops better internal stakeholder relationships for some business cultures or only external stakeholder relationship for the others;
- interrelates to so called "curative marketing" (Czinkota et al. 2014; Kaufmann et al. 2015).

Often, however, transparency and accountability of corporate communications are questionable if they do not reflect standards of business ethics and responsible and authentic leadership. This paper aims to analyze the changing tactics of corporate communications in terms of aspects on social responsibility. Pursuing a phenomenological research philosophy, we have attempted to compare international ways to communicate the businesses development. The paper aims to fill the gap on how socially responsible corporate communications contribute to value co-creation. Through presenting a multilevel framework, this study allocates reviews of competences that can be assumed by individuals, organizations, movements and institutions and illustrates them through examples in the development of corporate social responsibility as an empirical phenomenon.

Observing an actor's competence within systems is especially fruitful when considering complex global unregulated or under-regulated phenomena that are typically constantly in flux or take place unexpectedly and where no one legitimate solution exists. Such phenomena include for instance large-scale natural disasters and the related relief, rehabilitation and development efforts, the debate and approaches related to addressing climate change, and global poverty and the development of market activity at the base of the income pyramid. The lively debate over defining the competence of companies in society, namely the CSR debate, can also be considered such an empirical phenomenon with a huge number of relevant actors, perspectives, and approaches.

Based on mainstream literature, a number of approaches to define Corporate Communication tackles its several key objectives:

First stream addresses key stakeholder groups to build, develop and shape corporate reputation (Cornelissen 2008, 2014). It is suggested that the increasing knowledge public transfer neglects the public relations efforts of multinational organisations if they seem to exaggerate. In contrast to this particular focus on shaping company performance, Corporate Communication's objectives are originally twofold: to "communicate with different stakeholders for both moral (legitimacy) and instrumental (profit) reasons (Cornelissen 2008)." The question arises if there should be certain limitations to apply Corporate Communication or as Czinkota et al. (2014) and Kaufmann et al. (2015) suggest to differentiate within Corporate Communications between a corporate reputation and legitimacy orientated mindset and behavior underpinning this statement by a synthesis of multidisciplinary concepts such as identity, thermodynamics, system or complexity theory.

Second general approach is described as "an instrument of management" to integrate internal and external communications in one strategy (van Riel and Fombrun 2007), "to create a favourable basis for relationships with groups upon which the company is dependent" (van Riel and Balmer 1997) By using different kinds of communicative materials (positive storytelling, reports, memos, events, campaigns, debates) companies are trying to transmit diversified messages to different groups of stakeholders as outlined by Dowling (2006).

One of the minor tools is to downsize negative effects from financial and corporate scandals, and also to neutralize critical perceptions as stakeholders ask "fundamental questions about the moral compass of all companies (Dowling 2006)."

Some researchers note the CSR communication as a "source of competitiveness". Gray and Balmer stated that "an increasing number of astute executives recognizes [corporate communication] as a critical corporate asset directly linked to competitive success." The corporate identity, defined as "the dynamic interplay amongst the company's business strategy, the philosophy of its key executives, its corporate cultures, and its organizational design" (Gray and Balmer 1998) is transmitted and formed into an external corporate image or reputation through the channels of CC. In contrast to Dowling's model, Gray and Balmer stress that corporate communication might directly be influenced by the external image and the perception of a company with the goal of creating a competitive advantage rather than being purely based on the existing identity and culture (feedback of corporate image influences communication).

One of the major research streams concludes that it is an integral part of business strategy to share insights into their culture and disseminate the value system. One core benefit of CC is the control that an organization possesses regarding the information it reveals to the public. Scholars agree that companies are trying to show "a particular positive image of the organization" (Cornelissen 2008) when communicating to their external stakeholders. In addition, other scholars such as Gray and Balmer (1998) have seen the creation of a favourable corporate image only as one of two core objectives in increasingly using CC. In their opinion, an increase in the general awareness of a company's brand name is the primary motive. Again, the aspect of legitimacy in this context as mentioned earlier is suggested to be explicitly integrated into this equation.

This customization of communication materials further emphasizes the strategic position that professional communication has for an organisation. Within academic literature a variety of models and theories further illuminate the business strategy behind corporate communications, but to our knowledge no research, so far, has discovered the value co-creation in terms of social responsibility of the organizations communicating their strategies.

The second part of the paper outlines corporate communications as well as classifies some strategies to perform communications in accordance with the five customized objectives of strategic and responsible communication to define corporate social responsibility for value cocreation.

A company's culture, values and actions are directly influencing the way a corporate story is communicated to all stakeholders, which, in turn, influences their understanding of and belief in the organization. This increased corporate reputation and/or legitimacy might lead to improved business outcomes and represents therefore the economic motivation for companies to publicly share insight into their operations, values and beliefs. While defusing the direct link between communication, corporate reputation, legitimacy and performance (or in the case of Gray and Balmer competitive advantage), the usage of corporate communication has a potential power to increase both Corporate and Social Performance to co- create shared values with an extended circle of stakeholders. According to a stream of research within competence theory, competences are heterogeneous positions that form the division of labor within society.

Observing an actor's competence within systems is especially fruitful when considering complex global unregulated or under-regulated phenomena that are typically constantly in flux or take place unexpectedly and where no one legitimate solution exists. Such phenomena include for instance large-scale natural disasters and the related relief, rehabilitation and development efforts, the debate and approaches related to addressing climate change, and global poverty and the development of market activity at the base of the income pyramid. The lively debate over defining the competence of companies in society, namely the CSR debate, can also be considered such an empirical phenomenon with a huge number of relevant actors, perspectives, and approaches.

Guided by the seminal work of Freeman (1984), the importance of stakeholders has been emphasized by many scholars (O'Riordan and Fairbrass 2014; Preston and Sapienza 1990; Donaldson and Preston 1995) and promoted in many reports. This has been associated with the emergence of the corresponding research stream relating to stakeholder theory of the firm (Wheeler and Sillanpaa 1997; Clarke and Clegg 1998). Implicit in this paradigm is the idea that survival depends on the firm's relationships with the external world.

In the BRICS countries, along with «the advanced» socially responsible group of companies, evidence exists of a negatively minded group of businessmen and local residents (Belyaeva 2010). In addition, many companies in China consider CSR as an unnecessary western concept and as a trading barrier (Belyaeva and Kazakov 2015).

CSR is not only a tool to manage social problems in the region. Rather, the advanced companies consider CSR as a part of negotiations, a tool to increase of competitiveness of the company, as a possibility to enter new markets, and also to strengthen mutual relations with suppliers, investors, and buyers. This pragmatism and economic benefit expectation 'force' the companies to put huge investments into social and ecological spheres, but unreasonably fewer in personal development.

Hence, a sample of business representatives and students from western and eastern countries has been studied to categorize so called stages of CSR related competences and maturity. We are defining the competences in risk management, project management, cross-cultural management, strategic envisioning, building trust and knowledge transfer. To accomplish this task, a comprehensive body of literature focusing on CSR and its implementation, as well as on the, so called VUCA (Volatility, Uncertainty, Complexity and Ambiguity) approach, as an analytical framework for understanding CSR in its broader context was reviewed. In this section, five generic competences that different actors have adopted within the development of corporate social responsibility are described: inventing, expanding, integrating, translating, and contesting. These competences emerge from both existing academic and practitioner literature on CSR as well as practical experiences working within this field.

The first generic competence related to the development of CSR in practice is inventing. An important function within this inventing competence is the creation of new practices, tools, and approaches, which necessitates capabilities related to specialized technical, managerial, or practical know-how about CSR. Since these practices, tools and approaches are commonly created in cooperation with other actors, partnership skills are typically needed. Within CSR, innovative companies are constantly creating new more responsible and sustainable products and services, consultancies such as Account Ability are developing new tools and software to manage CSR, social entrepreneurs are redefining the possibilities of businesses to engage with global challenges, universities are developing new approaches for CSR, radical innovations from nongovernmental organizations and social movements are being transferred to the corporate sector, and new types of partnerships between the private, public and third sector are expanding the responsibilities of business enterprises.

Another function within the inventing competence is sponsoring or providing capital for CSR innovations to take place. Actors such as government agencies and foundations are important contributors to the development of these innovations. All in all, this inventing competence can be adopted by any type of actor within the multilevel context.

A second generic competence, expanding, involves propagating and transferring CSR practices either horizontally within a level from one actor to another or top-down or bottom-up between levels. Various functions within this expanding competence can be identified. National governments, professional associations, international events such as the World Economic Forum, and influential company CEOs play an important function when promoting CSR, thus providing the concept legitimacy through their own reputation and seal of approval. Business schools and networked consulting firms use their pedagogical resources to teach courses on CSR or offer training on best practices. However, the perception of the same core theories and implications seem to be different in various cultures (Belyaeva et al. 2018). Consulting and accounting companies are commercializing CSR and creating new industries around sustainability reporting and auditing these reports by developing business models. Finally, a great number of companies are participating in the expansion of CSR by adopting it into their discourse, policies and practices. This requires know-how about practical implementation of these approaches as well as a willingness, typically at the top management level, to happen. A third generic integrating competence emerges, within which the various individuals, organizations, national and transnational actors create and undertake positions, functions or responsibilities relationships in relation to each other. The key driver for the interaction is understood to be linked to the need to operate within a common, shared environment. Consolidating involves gathering available knowledge through research and offering it publicly. Within CSR, the European Union has done important work in researching existing organization, tools and approaches and offering them publicly through a web portal. Globally CSR is less codified and the meaning for multistakeholders varies, so the communication. The codification of CSR is a standout amongst the most focal capacities. It has customarily been finished by governments through the administrative procedure—national law and control is the most required source characterizing the skills and obligations of partnerships inside social orders. The legislative practices shape the CSR standards. Ongoing multi-partner activities have created thorough definitions and measurements for CSR. The most respectful ones incorporate the Global Reporting Initiative, the ISO 26000, a Global Compact standard that characterizes what is incorporated into CSR and what isn't. Every one of these on-screen characters embracing a systematizing capacity get their authenticity through participatory procedures, regardless of whether they are parliamentary or wide multi-partner arrangements in nature. A last integrative capacity is planning and integrative ability. The focal point of the circle can be believed to speak to the inception of the integrative action. A fourth competence relates to the sense-making needs that exist between actors that operate on varying levels, and between actors of varying nature. This translating competence enables actors to engage in transmission (of e.g. knowledge) between levels and within different actors. Unlike the case of expansion, translating involves a transformation of CSR. Since CSR is a complex phenomenon involving a huge number of concepts, approaches and tools, translation is sometimes needed to advance adoption. Within translation, an important function is the contextualization of CSR. National CSR associations and ministries typically attempt to understand the global CSR field and transform it to be appropriate to a specific context. For instance, small and medium sized enterprises do not have the resources to research all the available CSR practices (typically developed for large multinational enterprises) and are often supported by national level actors to adjust CSR to fit their needs and operations. While CSR emphasizes the responsibilities of business enterprises, many CSR approaches are appropriate to examine any type of organization's responsibility. Indeed, within the translation competence, an adapting function can be recognized. Public sector organizations and nongovernmental organizations have adapted practices and tools originally developed for CSR, such as sustainability reporting, life-cycle thinking, and reputation management, to fit their own organizational contexts.

The translating competence has an epicenter (or multiple ones), in terms of the lead agency within the particular circumstance. The hollow circle represents the origin of the translating function; the space within which the transformation takes place that is inherent in the process. The arrows imply both a direction and potentially a weight (possible demonstrated by line thicknesses) of the translations taking place.

A final competence of contesting has received significant attention in CSR literature and is also constantly present in the press. Within the contesting competence, the function of challenging is an central one. Watchdog nongovernmental organizations (NGO) such as Corporate Watch and Greenpeace commonly criticize CSR initiatives for being "too little, too late" and trade unions have been very critical of CSR as providing corporations opportunities to self-govern. The business press and most notably the magazine Economist has presented critical perspectives on CSR through special issues on the topic area. All these organizations gain the legitimacy to challenge CSR through representative means, the NGOs describe themselves as representing the general public or nature and they commonly have a large number of members, trade unions promote the rights of their members, and the business press, with its many readers, can be seen to represent the business community as a whole.

Another way of contesting CSR is attempting to replace it with an alternative solution. Fair Trade and other social movements attempt to put in practice viable options to multinational corporations, and the meeting of the World Social Forum develops alternative approaches to what the participants see as corporate power and dominance. Nobel Laureate Professor Milton Friedman viewed that the only responsibility of companies is to increase their profits. As an alternative to CSR, he offered a libertarian conception of society and the economy. A final function, which could be seen as part of contestation, is silent disapproval (or possibly lack of knowledge of CSR)—companies can ignore CSR altogether. The literature review helped to discover and update some fundamental gaps of CSR forming competences as a part of a "curative" strategy for business and society of today (some of them are presented in Fig. 1).

It should be noted that in many (if not most) cases the competences are concurrent and exist in the same space and within the same actors. The five competences described above are by no means exhaustive, and it is assumed that others remain to be identified. The results were designed as a "Complexity-volatility, ambiguity, uncertainty" matrix. All in all, CSR competences mentioned above are summarized

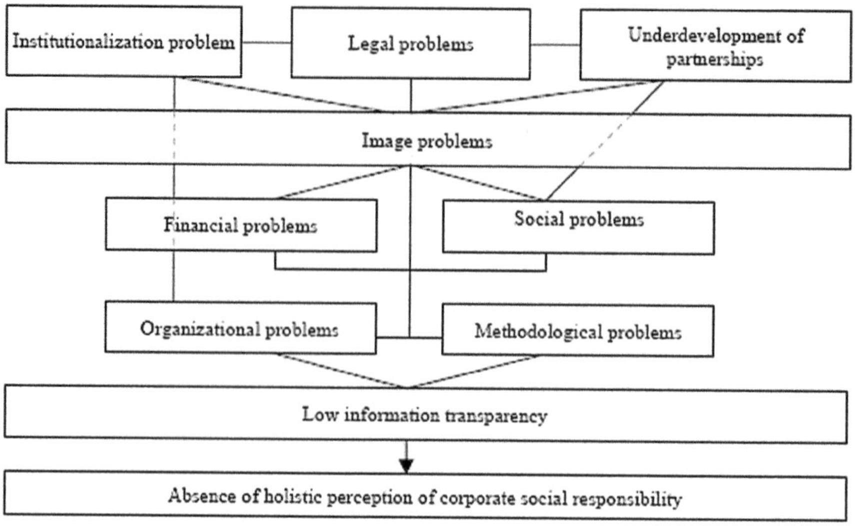

Fig. 1 Sources for gaps in holistic approach to CSR (Belyaeva and Canen 2015)

in a Table 1 and each of them is illustrated with an example referring to social corporate responsibility in the world.

The socially responsible communication has to ensure that all of the stakeholders, whether internal or external, can voice their opinions or grievances with the values that the organizations claim to uphold. To this effect, companies have to ensure that they are using the right kind of communication method. Morsing and Schultz (2006) have identified three common communication strategies used by organisations: the stakeholder information strategy, the stakeholder response strategy and the stakeholder involvement strategy.

As a prevalidation attempt of the literature study above, we have performed a comparative documentary analysis (websites and other sources of public communications of 20 public organizations embracing companies, universities and municipalities in Russia and Germany). It is interesting to see that our results show differences between perceiving the corporate communications role in shared value co-creation between different types of organizations, but not between the two countries. One of the important takeaways is that the number and volume of CSR spending is increasing in Germany and decreasing in Russia in 2014–2018, while the prevailing means of communication varies (see Fig. 2).

The research is limited by the sample size, but shows some novel interesting facts, which could be used to develop a better integrated CSR and communication strategy for all types of organisations in order to stimulate its sustainability, harmonization with multistakeholder groups and advancing business and social values.

The need for a flexible model and fast changing adoptive strategy in a transboundary context based on the stakeholder management and developing the communication towards raising competences for CSR. The value cocreation is based on the

Table 1 Generic competences of CSR

Competence	Function	Capability	Illustration	Environment
Inventing	Creating	Specialized technical, managerial or practical know-how abd partnership skills	Companies, consultancies, social entrepreneurs, universities, social movements	Ambiguity, uncertainty
	Sponsoring	Capital	Governmental agencies, foundations	Uncertainty
Expanding	Promoting	Legitimacy or reputation	Governments, professional associations, individuals such as CEOs	Complexity-volatility
	Teaching	Pedagogical resources	Business schools	Ambiguity, complexity-volatility
	Commercializing	Business model	Consulting and accounting firms	Volatility, uncertainty, complexity-ambiguity
	Adopting	Specialized know-how and strategic intent	Corporations	Volatility, uncertainty
Integrating	Consolidating	Information and communications technology	EU	Volatility, uncertainty, complexity, ambiguity
	Codifying	Legitimacy through participatory process	Government	Complexity
	Coordinating	Legitimacy through broad stakeholder base	United Nations Global Compact	Complexity
Translating	Contextualizing	Local knowledge	National CSR association	Complexity
	Adapting	Managerial know-how	Public sector organizations	Ambiguity, complexity-volatility
Contesting	Challenging	Representative legitimacy	Greenpeace, trade unions	Ambiguity, uncertainty, complexity-volatility
	Replacing	Specialized know-how about alternative solutions	Fair Trade	Uncertainty, ambiguity
	Ignoring	None	Companies	Ambiguity, complexity-volatility

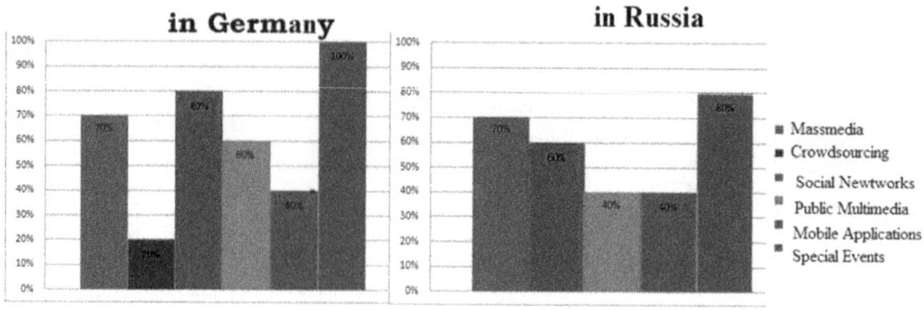

Fig. 2 CSR communication channels in Germany and Russia. *Source* Author calculation

human competences building new holistic principles incorporating social responsibility, leadership and ability to re-conceptualize the nature of the business largely depend on institutional and cross-cultural environment projected in digital media.

3 Conclusions

National governments and businesses are still lacking sustainable social efficiency towards local and global communities, especially in the emerging markets. The defining frames of such a partnership should be based on a, so far, missing systematic approach to social responsibility which is substantially defined by institutional norms, economic culture and personal motivation and mentality. This research calls for the new conceptualizations based on the novel structure of stakeholder's engagement and compliance to both international and domestic standards and also cultures.

The paper identifies very different levels of CSR penetration in various environments. The increase in competition among the multinational and national companies to gain the first mover advantage for economically advanced countries with developed sustainable mindset by establishing sustainable relationships with both the government and the civil society is essential to stimulation of a strategic CSR application. The author finds that firms which operate internationally are more likely to engage in CSR and to institutionalize it through various domestic codes, suggesting that glocalization (and not westernization) is a key CSR driver for emerging markets. Interesting is the finding that the companies in countries with a stronger Governmental CSR regulation appear to be less creative in social responsibility and rarely go beyond the suggested frameworks, then those with business activated by a bottom-up approach: the latter achieve more in sustainable solutions. Today the government policy sets the boundaries and motives of the social investment business in both emerging and advanced countries, and the business obviously determines the vectors of transformation of the landmarks in the social, environmental and corporate governance. It is interesting to note that multinational companies adapt their socially responsible strategies in each country, using the glocalization approach.

Thus, the globalization of standards is gradually changing with local strategies. Who is the initiator and executor of the introduction of such changes?

The internationalization and globalization has led to an interesting effect of enhancing the visibility of the socially responsible behavior of corporations. However, this is not limited to the publication of non-financial reports on the GRI standard, support for principled initiatives that strategically contribute to improving the reputation of companies, supporting the global treaty and the goals of sustainable development of the United Nations. The globalization of such social strategies has led to an actual increase in CSR of companies' activities, including for the sake of guidance from "above" (Li et al. 2010).

The government is called upon to stimulate and support companies with an integrated nationally oriented CSR strategy, since the main task of enhancing CSR communications and competences is to develop a mechanism for a tripartite dialogue between government, business and society that will promote the implementation of the basic principles, norms and best practices of socially responsible behavior. This mechanism will also help to effectively solve the problems of territorial development. Measuring the total contribution of companies and the government to the socio-economic development of society is still an unsolved problem.

In the emerging economies countries, along with "the advanced" socially responsible group of companies, evidence exists of a negatively minded group of businessmen and local residents. CSR is not only a tool to manage social problems in the region. The companies in many countries today consider CSR as a part of negotiations, a tool to increase of competitiveness of the company, as a possibility to enter new markets, and also to strengthen mutual relations with suppliers, investors, and buyers. This pragmatism and economic benefit expectation 'force' the companies to invest into social and ecological spheres, but unreasonably fewer in personal developments. A systematic government policy is needed to popularize CSR ideas, to introduce a social and economic ideology, according to which social responsibility will be considered both by business and society as one of the tools for building a harmonious society.

In most of the emerging markets, the government still holds the key to business success because of the existence of trade and business regulations restricting the freedom of multinational companies to incorporate their previously successful business doctrines which have been tried and tested in the developed nations.

In particular, it is possible to refer to a creation of a new model of the global interests' management and balance which is based on creation of neo-corporate values to that, directed on a sustainable development through creation of digital trust. Economic imperatives of socialization of business differ on regions of world economy that is caused by the cross-cultural distinctions, different legal and economic systems, and also the historical line of corporate development. Such distinctions cause higher levels of complexity for empirical research on the efficiency of social responsibility on a corporate level, and, furthermore, subjects relating to world economy. Available tools of an assessment illustrate the various directions of socially responsible behavior of the companies, using different indicators and representing non-comparable information.

The presented research is eliciting personal competences that help to cover the possible gaps in corporate responsible relations in the lenses of media.

References

Belyaeva ZS (2010) Models of socially responsible business in world economy. IE RAN, Yekaterinburg (in Russian)

Belyaeva Z (2016) Entrepreneurial innovation and stakeholder relationship management. In: Kaufmann HR, Riad Shams SM (eds) Entrepreneurial challenges in the 21st century: creating stakeholder value co-creation. Palgrave M, Basingstoke, pp 120–132

Belyaeva Z, Kazakov A (2015) Integrated approach to social responsibility: a model of stakeholders interaction in Russia and China. Syst Res Behav Sci 32(2):240–246

Belyaeva Zh, Canen A (2015) Socially responsible business in the "Brics" economies: the way to a sustainable future. Social responsibility—range of perspectives per topics and countries. In: Matjaž Mulej, Robert G. Dyck (eds) Social responsibility beyond neoliberalism, vol 4. Bentham Publishers, UAE, pp 221–240

Belyaeva Z, Scagnelli SD, Thomas M, Cisi M (2018) Student perceptions of university social responsibility: implications from an empirical study in France, Italy and Russia. World Rev Entrepreneurship Manage Sustain Dev 14(1–2):23–42

Clarke T, Clegg T (1998) Changing paradigms: the transformation of management knowledge for the 21st century. HarperCollinsBusiness, London

Cornelissen J (2008) Corporate communication. SAGE, Los Angeles

Cornelissen J (2014) Corporate communication: a guide to theory and practice, 4th edn. SAGE, Los Angeles

Czinkota M, Kaufmann HR, Basile G (2014) The relationship between legitimacy, reputation, sustainability and branding for companies and their supply chains. Ind Mark Manage 43(1):91–101

Donaldson T, Preston LE (1995) The stakeholder theory of the corporation: concepts, evidence, and implications. Acad Manage Rev 20:65–91

Dowling G (2006) Communicating corporate reputation through stories. Calif Manage Rev 49(1):82–100

Freeman RE (1984) Strategic management: a stakeholder approach. Prentice-Hall, Englewood Cliffs, NJ

Freeman RE (2005) A stakeholder theory of modern corporation. In: Hartmann LP (ed) Perspectives in business ethics, 3rd edn. New York, pp 112–122

Gray E, Balmer J (1998) Managing corporate image and corporate reputation. Long Range Plan 31(5):695–702

Kaufmann HR, Czinkota M, Zakrzewski M (2015) B2B and internal relationships and curative international marketing: a Polish case study. Ind Mark Manage 51:69–78

Li S, Fetscherin M, Alon I, Lattemann C, Yeh K (2010) Corporate social responsibility in emerging markets—The importance of the governance environment. Manag Int Rev 50:635–654

Morsing M, Schultz M (2006) Corporate social responsibility communication: stakeholder information, response and involvement strategies. Bus Ethics Eur Rev 15(4):323–338

O'Riordan L, Fairbrass J (2014) Managing CSR stakeholder engagement: a new conceptual framework. J Bus Ethics 125:121–145

Porter ME, Kramer MR (2006) Strategy & society, the link between competitive advantage and corporate social responsibility. Harvard Bus Rev 84(12):78–92

Porter ME, Kramer MR (2011) Creating shared value. Harvard Bus Rev 89(1):2–17

Preston LE, Sapienza HJ (1990) Stakeholder management and corporate performance. J Behav Econ 19(4):361–375. http://EconPapers.repec.org/RePEc:eee:beheco:v:19:y:1990:i:4:p:361-375

van Riel C, Balmer J (1997) Corporate identity: the concept, its measurement and management. Eur J Mark 31(5):340–355

van Riel C, Fombrun C (2007) Essentials of corporate communication: implementing practices for effective reputation management. Routledge, Abingdon

Visser W (2010) CSR 2.0 and the new DNA of business. J Bus Syst Gov Ethics 5(3):7

Wheeler D, Sillanpaa M (1997) The stakeholder corporation. Pitman, London

Chapter 6
Communication and Trust: A Linguistic Analysis

Anna-Maria Meck

1 Introduction

In times of shifting media, communication shifts as well. With these changes, today we observe a fundamental change in trust attribution away from formerly established systems. Institutions and the classic media have been sources of trust for a long time but recipients nowadays would rather trust their family, friends, and even strangers with Rachel Botsman having shaped the term "Distributed Trust" to refer to this phenomenon (Botsman 2018). If it is no longer institutions people trust in, they trust individuals which bears the danger of arbitrariness as these individuals are not backed and monitored by any institutional tradition, reputation, or control. This becomes even more critical as (social) media paves the way for a tremendous amount of individuals to position themselves quickly and effortlessly on numerous channels 24/7. Whilst being exposed to this kind of sensory overload, people do not only have to consider whom to trust and whom not to multiple times a day, they furthermore have to decide at once. What does it take to assign or deny trust though?

Trust is an essential building block of society and acts as "social glue" (Bakir and Barlow 2007). The study of trust and its components, therefore, is far-reaching and rightly a deeply researched topic as it carries many implications and derivations for our day-to-day life. Communication and trust thereby are two highly interlinked concepts, for language works as a trust enabler and a means to build trust:

> (…) human language offers an endless repertoire of significant symbols to convey one's perspective to others. It is the most important medium of communication in the development of trust and for the successful constitution of a trust relation. (Rompf 2015)[1]

[1] Speech and Communication will be used as synonyms throughout this article as communication contains speech in its verbal and nonverbal form.

A.-M. Meck (✉)
VUI.agency, Agnes-Pockels-Bogen 1, 80992 Munich, Germany
e-mail: anna.meck@googlemail.com

T. Osburg and S. Heinecke (eds.), *Media Trust in a Digital World*,
https://doi.org/10.1007/978-3-030-30774-5_6

This article is concerned with the *how* exactly trust and communication are intertwined: Is it the voice itself which demands for trust or rather the content? If so, how does that content have to be structured to evoke trust? How is trust transported linguistically? And what role does the listener hold? As the established question is multi-layered, it is crucial to first define trust and the character traits that form it. Hereinafter—and only focussing on spoken language—paraverbal, nonverbal as well as content-related features leading to a development of trust on the listener's side are compiled and described to answer the question "How can communication be utilized to build trust?".

2 What Is Trust?

Based on a multidisciplinary analysis by Rousseau et al. merging economical, psychological, and sociological views, trust can be defined as "a psychological state comprising the intention to accept vulnerability based upon positive expectations of the intentions or behavior of another" (Rousseau et al. 1998). It is however a delicate concept to define as it has many contrasting manifestations and is highly subjective. To nevertheless get to a clear-cut understanding of trust, a definite distinction from related terms trust partly consists of—namely persuasion, confidence, and credibility—needs to be established.

Persuasion is classified as one of the major components in creating trust. It can be defined as speaker-dependent emotional and rational strategies to encourage opinion changes (Renn and Levine 1991). In using persuasive strategies, a speaker/message will succeed in generating trust in a given audience. Studies moreover show that persuasion and credibility correlate significantly (Burgoon et al. 1990).

A confident source is one which proves to be trustworthy over an extended period of time. It achieves and holds its status by positive reinforcement (Renn and Levine 1991). Credibility finally is accomplished by adding up confidence and trust on a social scale, as it has a distinctively social dimension and is agreed upon by collective perception. Credibility "is a major medium of power control and social influence" (Renn and Levine 1991).

Based on these distinctions, the following streamlined value chain of trust can be put in place (Fig. 1).

With persuasion being the basic building block in trust development, following chapters will especially focus on this character trait's content related and linguistic expressions.

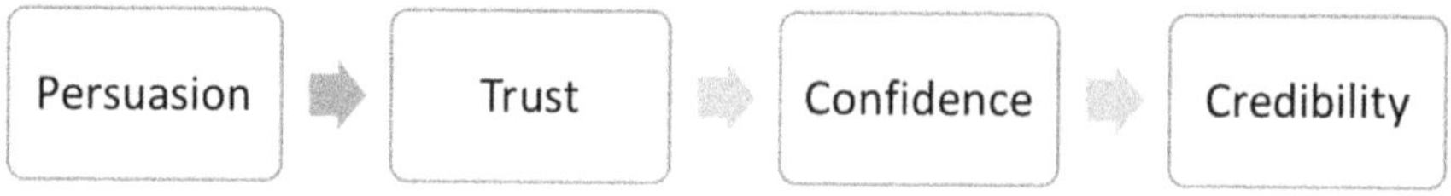

Fig. 1 The value-chain of trust building

From a neurobiological view, trust results from oxytocin being produced and released in the brain, as evidenced in studies by Kosfeld et al. (2005). When infused with the neuropeptide, people in interpersonal interactions (note that communication falls into that category) showed a substantial increase in trust towards their vis-à-vis in comparison with a control group given a placebo (Kosfeld et al. 2005). Trust therefore is a measurable and influenceable hormonal variable, not only a theoretical concept which people can apply at will. As the oxytocin release in the brain still has to be triggered by something perceived and/or experienced—be it physical or psychological—the question remains, how trust is built? To answer this, the following paragraph elaborates on the characteristics trust consists of. Researchers propose a scheme that clusters five attributes which, when taken together, form trust (Renn and Levine 1991). If a source (be it message and/or speaker) succeeds in integrating these characteristics, their message and demeanour will eventually evoke trust in a given recipient:

1. Competence: expertise in a certain field
2. Objectivity: absence of bias or partiality
3. Fairness: multilateral presentation of facts
4. Consistency: in comparison to previous utterances/behaviour
5. Faith: faith in the source's good intentions (Renn and Levine 1991).

There is no comprehensive formula stating how these five have to be distributed, nor do they have to be weighted equally to achieve a positive outcome. At first glance, none of these attributes is of a linguistic nature. They nevertheless do have verbal manifestations by means of which they are transported which will be elaborated on this research paper. A competent person simply *sounds* different than an incompetent one.

Aiming at a full understanding further on, trust has to be looked at from three perspectives, as source, distributor, and message are part of every interaction comprising trust and mutually dependent.[2]

1. The source is the background of every distributor or message and can take various shapes, e.g. an institution (with the message being a newspaper article) or the education and qualification of a distributor (in a public address); to be trusted, a source needs to be true and reliable (Renn and Levine 1991).
2. The distributor is the messenger of a given message and will consistently be assessed in regard to the source and their background; competence and honesty are a distributor's key properties in evoking trust (Renn and Levine 1991).
3. Besides the actual text, every message carries assumptions about its source and distributor; its trustworthiness is dependent on accuracy, objectivity, and versatility (Renn and Levine 1991) (Fig. 2).

Renn and Levine's characteristics for building trust can, once more, be clustered into three categories, namely credibility, emotionality, and rationality (Renn and Levine 1991) (Table 1).

---

[2]This figure does not display the recipient of a given message despite their great importance because it is, for now, only concerned with building trust on the speaker's side.

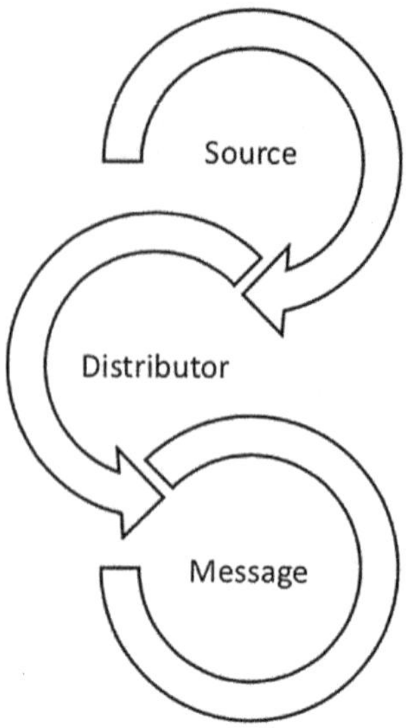

Fig. 2 The threefold composition of trust

These findings partially stem from and are consistent with Aristotle's Rhetoric, in which he debates how an audience can be convinced of something by means of Ethos, Pathos, and Logos, or following the classification above, credible (Ethos), emotional (Pathos), and rational (Logos) means (Braet 1992). With this knowledge about trust and the characteristics which form it in mind, the bridge between trust and communication becomes yet again clearer. The voice is considered as the means of expression and reflects a person's personality traits (Hammer and Teufel-Dietrich 2017). Since the above-mentioned features are such personality traits (especially the Pathos ones), they can be transported linguistically. The voice as a means of communication therefore is a crucial part of any attempt to build trust.

3 Communication and Speech as Trust Enablers

The preceding chapter provided a definition of trust as well as neurobiological explanations for its development. It was stated that trust is a psychological state and, as a result, is impressionable to speech. However, this assertion has not yet been fully

Table 1 Trust-building categories

Credibility	Emotionality	Rationality
Objectivity, fairness, reliability, and versatility	Faith, honesty, and truthfulness	Competence, accuracy, and consistency

grounded. Trust as a psychological state is very much impressionable by speech, to the extent that Vygotsky—a main voice in the field of linguistics—even calls this "an indisputable fact of great importance" (Vygotsky 1994). "Thought development is determined by language" (Vygotsky 1994) and intellectual growth is crucially linked to thinking which is arrived upon by speaking (Vygotsky 1994). Without language, there would be no thought; without thought there would be no thinking; without thinking there would be no psyche. With trust being a psychological state as established earlier, it is at least influenced by language, more likely even initiated by it. Furthermore, the aforementioned positive expectations for intention and/or behaviour associated with trust are arrived upon by listening to someone speaking and assessing the used language. "Whenever agreement or assent is arrived at in human affairs (…), THIS AGREEMENT IS REACHED BY LINGUISTIC PROCESSES, OR ELSE IT IS NOT REACHED (emphasis in original)" (Whorf 1940). Correspondingly, trust must be regarded an agreement between trustor and trustee and is hence only reached by communication and communicative means in a linguistic process.

Regarding the addressed neurobiological cause of trust, oxytocin, findings indicate cerebral links between communication and trust (Kosfeld et al. 2005). The remaining question however is how the hormone release is triggered when not induced synthetically. As previously established, oxytocin is mainly produced in interpersonal interactions (Seltzer et al. 2010). These interactions are comprised of different channels, with one channel being the voice as a means to communicate. Studies with mother-daughter dyads which put the respective child in a stressful situation showed that the mother's vocalisation caused the release of nearly as much oxytocin to fight the induced stress in the child as the mother's physical contact with her child (Seltzer et al. 2010). The neuropeptide is essential in setting up social attachments, including trust, and is empirically shown to be directed by speech, more accurately prosodic and linguistic vocal cues (Seltzer et al. 2012). Further studies showed that it is in fact the voice itself, thus the auditory and not the content-related information, which causes the release of oxytocin in the listener's brain as written communication did not elicit the same effect as spoken communication (Seltzer et al. 2012).

This leads to the conclusion that, at least on a neurobiological scale, the communicated content is unimportant or not as important in building trust as linguistic information. Therefore, at least Pathos—with Faith, Honesty, and Truthfulness building trust emotionally—is directed by hormonal signals which are orchestrated by a speaker's voice. Regarding the issue as a whole, one cannot jump to conclusions yet, as building trust might still be dyadic with Ethos and Logos being rationally comprehensible and possibly content dependent. Building on the discussion of a dyadic formation of trust, the following chapters will provide further insights into different strategies in building trust with the aid of communication: first, the only just displayed emotional, also called affect-based, trust-building by means of the voice; and second what is referred to in this paper as the rational, also known as cognition-based, opportunities in trust-building, namely content related measures (Rompf 2015).

3.1 *The Voice as Emotional Trust Builder: Paraverbal and Nonverbal Cues*

Communication not only means speech, but rather a multimodal conglomerate consisting of verbal, nonverbal, and paraverbal linguistic cues (Beattie and Ellis 2017). This means listeners use more than one channel to split the speech flow they are exposed to into convenient sections before they ultimately interpret it. Hence, more than one channel is used and needed to build trust on the speaker's side and experience trust on the listener's side. A given listener assesses speech from various standpoints and might not even focus on what is said exactly. The content only functions as auxiliaries, it is "behaviours which accompany speech [that] may emphasize it, contradict it or even substitute for it" (Beattie and Ellis 2017). An audience therefore finds itself in a perpetual interplay between what it hears and what it perceives. The same goes for trust. A person may seem trustworthy and utter supposedly trustworthy statements, but an audience may still not put trust in them. This is because the audience reads linguistic cues, consisting of paraverbal and nonverbal information which potentially contradict the aforementioned impressions.

One of the building blocks responsible for creating trust is persuasion, a very well-studied character trait in regard to its linguistic manifestations. The following section illustrates how persuasion—and hence trust—is expressed paraverbally and nonverbally.

Paraverbal Trust-Building Cues

Paraverbal communication is concerned with how someone talks which e.g. includes speech rate, volume, and tone of voice. Vocal characteristics have been shown to have a significant impact on how a speaker is perceived, including in regards to persuasiveness and therefore trust (Jackob et al. 2011). Vocal intensity, dynamic speaking style, and vocal pleasantness are all parameters which contribute to a speaker's trustworthiness. Since they partly overlap, the different subchapters will vary in detail.

(a) **Vocal intensity** refers to speaker specific variations in amplitude (which means loudness), intonation (meaning perceptible pitch changes), fluency, and tempo. To be assessed as trustworthy, a relatively high speaking volume (loudness being the technical term) needs to be aimed at. Speakers with a more intense and/or powerful voice tend to be viewed as more persuasive than people with a softer and more quiet voice (Shim et al. 2015). The average loudness of a normal conversation is gender dependent, at 58.84 dB(A) for female and 59.84 dB(A) for male speakers. Transferred in hertz, values amount in 166 Hz for female and 110.6 Hz for male speakers. During a lecture or a talk, the loudness increases and stabilises at 66.79 dB(A) for women and 67.82 dB(A) for men (respectively 196.7 Hz for women and 128.9 Hz for men) (Berger et al. 2014). In order to increase one's persuasiveness through loudness, these respective values should in no case be undercut, at least be matched, and at best slightly exceeded.

Variations in intonation and amplitude allow a speaker to be perceived as more trustworthy due to more liveliness and less monotony in their message (Shim et al.

2015). Hence, engaging in perceptible pitch (intonation) and amplitude changes over the course of a communicative attempt will increase a speaker's trustworthiness. Variations in pitch and amplitude can be achieved by following linguistic principles like rising intonation when asking a question and dropping intonation when making a point. Emphasising a phrase will automatically lead to a change in amplitude and as such in loudness. These cues furthermore organise the speech flow and emphasise a message's most essential parts. Here, intonation as well as amplitude may result in a content-related simplification, transported by linguistic cues, that result in a listener's better understanding of a topic. It will be established later on that this type of simplification culminates in ascribing trust.

Fluency is one of the most straightforward and relatively effortless ways of generating trust. On the listener's side, it allows them to easily follow the red thread; on the speaker's side, a message can be prepared in advance to be flawless in this regard. A fluent speaking style means one which lacks the use of pause fillers, lengthy pauses, halting speech, stuttering, hesitations, repetitions, sentence changes, and interrupted vocalisations (Burgoon et al. 1990; Shim et al. 2015). Non-hesitant speech is perceived as dynamic and competent and it is because of these attributes that an audience assigns trust to a speaker who masters fluent speech. As fluency is correlated with competence, it holds not only an emotional, but also a rational dimension and is hence of some importance.

The last parameter contributing to vocal intensity is tempo, also referred to as speaking rate. Speaking rate was empirically found to enable trust when being "somewhat quickened" (Burgoon et al. 1990). A speaker producing less than 50 words per minute is considered very slow, slow when uttering 50–90 words/minute and normal when articulating more than 90 words/minute (Franke 2016).[3] In evaluating "Tagesschau"-newscasters, anchors were found to have a significantly increased average speaking rate of 129.6 words per minute (2.16 words per second) (Gebhard 2012), making them persuasive and trustworthy through confidence.

(b) **Dynamic speaking** style A dynamic speaking style can be obtained by considering loudness, pitch and its emphasis, and variety as well as tempo. All these cues are parameters that fall under both dynamic speaking style and vocal intensity. These parameters and related findings on their status as trust enablers were established earlier in this paper. It should be noted that they create trust in both their function as dynamic and intensity criteria (Burgoon et al. 1990; Shim et al. 2015), and that a dynamic speaking style enhances a speaker's perceived trustworthiness.

(c) **Vocal pleasantness** is marked by fluency, pitch variety, and voice quality. As fluency and pitch variety were covered under vocal intensity, this paragraph is only concerned with voice quality. The clearer the voice quality, the more persuasive the obtained effect (Burgoon et al. 1990). In the research field of linguistics, different vocal qualities are distinguished: breathy, flat, thin, throaty, and orotund. A *breathy voice* sounds quite aspirated, resulting in an airy, sighing-like, and

[3]Note: speaking rate is language-dependent, values may therefore change in comparison; the here listed numbers are representative for German.

intensity-low sound (Pompino-Marschall 2009). The *flat voice* is marked by a more monotonous and repetitive audible impression; whereas an *orotund voice* reflects expressiveness, robustness, and full soundness. A *thin voice* resembles a flat voice and is described as reedy and unsupported (Montrey 2005). The *throaty voice* finally is defined as hoarse and rather rough or husky (Montrey 2005). Studies concerned with vocal pleasantness find gender specific differences in a voice's perception.

While the highest degree of persuasion in both men and women can be achieved with an orotund voice, women with breathy, thin, and throaty speaking styles are judged less persuasive while a female flat voice did not lead to significant results. In concordance, a male breathy voice is judged as least persuasive, with flat, thin, and throaty voices assessed as only mildly better (Montrey 2005). An orotund voice is perceived as authoritarian and charismatic, which again attributes credibility and persuasion to a speaker (Rosenberg and Hirschberg 2005). Interestingly, findings propose that a "female speaker was afforded greater latitude to violate expectations of normal vocal characteristics" than a male speaker. This can be interpreted knowing that a female speaker's voice is generally judged in regard to her social behaviour whereas a male voice is linked to his social status, with him being potentially powerful (Montrey 2005). A non-orotund speaking man may therefore be perceived as less authoritative while a woman will be evaluated more leniently as she may react to her specific time- and socially-dependent surroundings.

3.2 *Nonverbal Trust-Building Cues*

Nonverbal communication means a speaker's communicative signals, which are not of a spoken nature, namely body language, facial expressions (including [a degree of] eye contact), and gestures.

(a) **Gestures** Many studies emphasise the importance of nonverbal cues, particularly gestures, for both speech production and speech perception, and even regard them as mutually dependent (Peters and Hoetjes 2017). This interdependence becomes more apparent when learning that speech and gestures are collectively obtained during language acquisition. In their capacity as structuring elements, gestures are a vital part of every communicative attempt and help listeners to more effectively organise the speech flow to which they are exposed. Being well understandable helps a speaker to create trust amongst their audience, hence the use of gestures is an effective means of acquiring trust. A study was conducted which evaluated the effect of gestures on persuasiveness (Peters and Hoetjes 2017). When asked about a speaker's performance and characteristics, the study found a significant effect of gestures on perceived persuasiveness by the listener. Taking a closer look at those characteristics, there was also a main effect of gestures on the perceived sincerity and interestingness of a given speaker. There was however no effect on factual accuracy. This again shows the meaningfulness of a dyadic approach regarding the research of trust: sincerity and interestingness are both subjective, hence emotional impressions, whereas factual accuracy is of an objective and rational nature (Peters and Hoetjes 2017). An earlier passage in this contribution stated that linguistic information, not the content per se, can be a means to create trust on an emotional scale. Peters' and Hoetjes' results undermine these findings.

(b) **Kinesic/proxemic behaviour** Likewise nonverbal, kinesic/proxemic behaviour refers to building or reducing both physical and physiological distance between communicating parties (Comadena et al. 2007) by applying different strategies from actual movement to more subtle facial expressions or engaging in either self-adaptors (e.g. playing with one's hair) or object-adaptors (e.g. playing with notes). Smiling, agreeing mimic behaviour, eye contact, and touch e.g. are subsumed under the term kinesic/proxemic immediacy, and are found to have a positive impact on persuasiveness. The more approachable a speaker appears, the more trustworthy they become to an audience. Despite a great deal of subjectivity involved in such an assessment, findings nevertheless were significant (Burgoon et al. 1990). The same study by Burgoon et al. also demonstrated that both kinetic dominance and kinetic relaxation are linked to persuasiveness. Although this may seem incompatible prima facie, it ultimately shows that listeners are not compelled by specific kinds of movements, but rather more by random movement itself (Burgoon et al. 1990). Conversely, the use of above explained object-adaptors is negatively correlated with persuasiveness, and hence trustworthiness (Burgoon et al. 1990). In sum, potent kinesic and proxemic behaviour establish a speaker as approachable, pleasant, and candid. This leads to them being perceived as trustworthy. As a substantial correlation between nonverbal behaviour and persuasiveness is evidenced in various studies, it can be regarded as probable secure that nonverbal performance enhances the creation of trust—on a subjective and emotional scale maybe, but verifiably nonetheless (Burgoon et al. 1990; Comadena et al. 2007; Peters and Hoetjes 2017).

This section provided an overview of paraverbal and nonverbal, and hence linguistic, cues which are a means for appearing trustworthy through persuasion. In applying some of the listed features, one may succeed in building trust through communication. There is, however, a fine line: exaggeration in any of the described parameters—besides maybe fluency—will result in a loss of trust as the speaker will come across as artificial and excessive. Illustrative loudness: a person with a soft voice may try to sound more persuasive by speaking up. This person may eventually end up talking too loudly to meet or exceed the indicated ~68 dB(A) and will not only not inspire trust, but rather the disapproval of the audience. After thoroughly outlining linguistic parameters resulting in trust, the next section will engage in clearing up the role of a message's content in building trust in order to meet the criteria of a dyadic approach to trust analysis.

3.3 *The Content as Rational Trust Builder*

Linguistic information on a paraverbal and nonverbal level were found to have an impact on persuasiveness and trust. These cues can nonetheless not be evaluated thoroughly without their framework: the content of a message which in the end transports and supports the linguistic dimension. One of the more obvious characteristics of a trustworthy message is the utilisation of technical terms instead of colloquial language—not surprisingly, swear words do not encourage trust-building (Mika 1981). Depending on the general assessment of a speaker, accelerated and intensive vocabulary supports the development of trust when the respective speaker is already perceived as trustworthy, though evokes the opposite effect when judged as non-trustworthy (Hamilton et al. 1990). Predominantly passive sentence structures were found to trigger trustworthiness as they create the impression of neutrality/objectivity and distance, characteristics positively attributed with trust (Hurwitz et al. 1992).

A more personal speaking style with high occurrence of "I", "We", and "You" (as in the German polite form "Sie") on the other hand also led to research subjects ascribing more trust to a respective speaker (Carbone 1975). These studies illustrate the high speaker-dependent dimension of persuasion, as both findings contradict one another. A positive correlation between distance to an audience and trust was also found by Ostermeier who established that self-references lead to an identification between speaker and audience and hence an increase in trust (Ostermeier 1967). Another finding concerning the sentence structure was identified when studying its complexity: the more complex a sentence, the more unlikely its rating as trustworthy—most likely due to comprehension challenges for the listener (the vocabulary on the other hand should be varied and complex, but lack abstraction to evoke trust) (Carbone 1975). Furthermore, metaphors and comparisons are said to lead to an increase in trustworthiness, though existing sources reveal somewhat inconsistent results on this matter. Additionally, images need to be particularly vivid, forceful, repeated, and varied frequently to be persuasive (Reinsch 1974).

A study by DeLemos et al. found a strong link between communication and trust and developed an acronym for this phenomenon: HICCC—meaning Honest, Inclusive, Compassionate, Clear and Comprehensive, and Coordinated (DeLemos et al. 2010).[4] In applying a HICCC speaking style, a speaker will succeed in building trust. Earlier mentioned findings mirror the importance of both emotional (Honest, Inclusive, and Compassionate) and rational (Clear and Comprehensive, Coordinated) trust-building parameters and hence support these results.

These insights into the possibilities of building trust through rational parameters by focussing on the content show that listeners do indeed use the rational level to assign or deny trust. Surprisingly, rationality is ostensibly much more difficult

---

[4]The study was conducted in a clinical environment with patient's parents in the PICU. Findings can nonetheless be seen as being generally valid even outside this setting as the communicative behaviour resembles crisis communication and is therefore an exemplary extreme case of building trust by means of communication.

to successfully operate than emotion, as findings regarding the content are often inconsistent and much more speaker-dependent than linguistic parameters. At this point, the following conclusion can be drawn: emotional trust-building parameters may be subjective, but they are stable and speaker-independent whereas rational parameters are indeed more objective, but simultaneously unstable and speaker-dependent.

Looking into "ideal methods of persuasion" (Adler et al. 2015), Adler's research group also confirmed that emotional positive strategies of trust-building were most effective compared to emotional negative, rational positive, and rational negative ones (Adler et al. 2015). These findings serve as justification to reconsider or rather expand the matched conceptual pairs *emotional–subjective* and *rational–objective* as it became clear that emotional trust-building measures are (1) in fact more objective than rational ones; and (2) more effective and reliable in building trust. A new composition can therefore be proposed as follows:

1. Emotional trust-building—Subjective (in terms of perception)—Objective (in terms of processing).
2. Rational trust-building—Objective (in terms of perception)—Subjective (in terms of processing).

4 The Listener's Role in the Process of Building Trust

Trust is built rather subjectively. This leads to huge differences in people's perception of trust (Rosenberg and Hirschberg 2005). Accordingly, trust is an interpersonal factor. The preceding chapters aimed at a broad explanation of how trust can be built and expressed linguistically, but did not yet take into account one further factor. Despite the speaker's pivotal position in establishing trust, the listeners themselves play a role of some importance in a trust-building scenario. In fact, it all comes down to the audience and their respective engagement in a certain topic for a listener can take one of two so-called "routes". First, the central route and second, the peripheral route (Peters and Hoetjes 2017).

These routes are contingent on the listener's level of involvement in the speaker's topic and are discussed extensively in recent and former studies as the "Elaboration Likelihood Model" or the "Heuristic Systematic Model" (Peters and Hoetjes 2017). Both models assume that there are two divergent ways a given listener can be persuaded by a message. If a listener takes the so-called central route, it means they use a more rational approach in assigning trustworthiness to a given speaker. This route is normally unconsciously selected if a listener has knowledge about the respective topic and is hence more involved. Listeners "engage in systematic thinking, they elaborate the arguments carefully and focus on the quality of communication content" (Jackob et al. 2011) before trusting a speaker. The peripheral route, conversely, is used by listeners in a more emotional manner, whilst focussing on superficial information with the content being incidental (Peters and Hoetjes 2017).

Via the peripheral route, a speaker will be assessed to a lesser extent by the quality of the given arguments, but rather by objective and emotional characteristics assigned to it. This peripheral approach will also succeed in persuading someone who is not paying particularly attention. In choosing the central route of persuasion, a listener will evaluate the content of an argument rather than the linguistic cues provided by a speaker. Hence, paraverbal as well as nonverbal information will not—or at least not to the same extent—be a means of persuasion and thus of building trust. A listener on the peripheral route will, on the contrary, be persuaded by exactly this kind of emotional information, namely linguistic cues and a speaker's characteristics. The content will only be assessed superficially; the underlying mechanisms are past judgements, experiences, and observations.

5 Summary

This contribution showed that and how it is very possible to build trust through means of communication. It is potentially achievable for a speaker to appear trustworthy when projecting one's voice and respecting linguistic, but also content-related rules and stipulations on both an emotional as well as on a rational level. Interestingly, emotional possibilities in building trust are in fact to a greater extent objective than initially thought; and on the contrary rational possibilities are subject to fluctuations in the attribution of trustworthiness.

Listeners themselves hold an essential role in the procedure of trust-building and should not be taken for being at a speaker's mercy, as the more informed they are, the less they can be manipulated into trusting someone. Still, communication exercises a great deal of influence, despite the fact that one must keep in mind that it is a fine line between being a speaker creating trust and being an overachiever who ends up undermining trust. In appearing too artificial, one will hardly be perceived as trustworthy as this impedes the building of trust.

Now to come back to the five attributes building trust which were listed early in this contribution: Competence, Objectivity, Fairness, Consistency, and Faith (Renn and Levine 1991). Consistency and faith were the only characteristics not to have shown distinctive linguistic manifestations (although it cannot be ruled out that further research may obtain complementary results). Consistency may not have proven to be a considerable factor in creating trust since it requires listeners to take the central route of persuasion and focus on a speaker's arguments. Faith, on the other hand, may just be overridden by persuasiveness per se. Intending to extend and modify Renn and Levine's attributes (Renn and Levine 1991) tailored to a linguistic explanatory model of trust, the following adjusted scheme is proposed:

1. Competence: expertise in a certain field
2. Objectivity: absence of bias or partiality
3. Fairness: multilateral presentation of facts

4. Consistency: in comparison to previous utterances/behaviour (only relevant for central route users)
5. Persuasiveness: speaker-dependent emotional and rational strategies to encourage opinion changes.

By being competent, objective, fair, consistent, and persuasive, a speaker will succeed in building trust. How these character traits are expressed through communication is depicted in the following table, which shows all linguistic features for building trust included in this research paper. These features are to be understood as cautious recommendations for action (Table 2).

Though verified by scientific research, trust-building mechanisms such as the listed ones only convince listeners who use the so-called peripheral route of persuasion. In an ideal environment, rational and objective persuasive strategies would outdo emotional and subjective ones, but these scenarios rarely occur. The following figure mirrors this observation and shows the weighting of the *logos*-dimension, which reflects the central route of persuasion, and the *ethos and pathos*-dimension, displaying the peripheral route of persuasion. The less "ideal" a situation, the more ethos and pathos come into play (Fig. 3).

This is, in fact, problematic as it means that it is mainly listeners with less access to education and limited information on a certain topic who are at risk of putting their trust in someone they potentially should not. It is crucial to eliminate this risk factor by investing in information procurement and information flow to guarantee media literacy throughout education classes. In doing so, the *logos*- dimension is

Table 2 Recommended actions for building trust

(a) Emotional trust-building				
Paraverbal				
Feature	*Loudness*	*Variations in pitch and loudness*	*Fluency*	*Tempo*
Recommended "action"	<66.79 dB(A)/196.7 Hz for female speakers <67.82 dB(A)/128.9 Hz for male speakers *Attribute*: Persuasiveness	Alternate in rising and dropping pitch by emphasising important parts of a message by following logical intonation structures like questions/statements *Attribute*: Persuasiveness	Refrain from: long pauses, pause fillers, halting speech, stuttering, hesitations, repetitions, sentence changes, interrupted vocalisations *Attribute*: Competence	Approximately 120–130 words per minute *Attribute*: Persuasiveness

(continued)

Table 2 (continued)

Paraverbal		Nonverbal	
Feature	*Vocal pleasantness*	*Gestures*	*Kinesic/proxemic behaviour*
Recommended "action"	Orotund speaking style, meaning expressiveness, robustness, and full soundness *Attribute*: Persuasiveness	Normal to increased use of gestures, greater random movement *Attribute*: Persuasiveness	Smiling, agreeing mimic behaviour (head-nodding), eye contact, touch (if applicable), greater random movement, close distance to audience, no engaging in adaptor behaviours (self- and object-adaptors) *Attribute*: Persuasiveness

(b) Rational trust-building				
Content-related				
Feature	*Utilisation of technical terms*	*Accelerate and intense vocabulary*[a]	*Passive sentence structure*	*Personal speaking style*
Recommended "action"	Use of technical terms to show expertness *Attribute*: Competence	Use of accelerate vocabulary to captivate the audience *Attribute*: Persuasiveness	Use of passive sentence structure to show neutrality/objectivity *Attribute*: Objectivity	Use of personal pronouns like "I", "We", and "You" *Attribute*: Persuasiveness
Feature	*Complexity*	*Metaphors and comparisons*	*HICCC*	
Recommended "action"	Straightforward sentence structure *Attribute*: Persuasiveness	Creation of vivid and forceful images[b] which need to be repeated and varied frequently *Attribute*: Persuasiveness	Apply a speaking style characterised by honesty, compassion, clarity and comprehensiveness, and coordination *Attribute*: Fairness, objectivity, persuasiveness, and competence	

[a]Only when already being perceived as trustworthy.
[b]However, sources are inconsistent in this matter and some scientific opinions suggest just the opposite effect.

strengthened and users are empowered to adopt the central route of persuasion to impartially evaluate a speaker's trustworthiness and avert the potential misuse of communicative power.

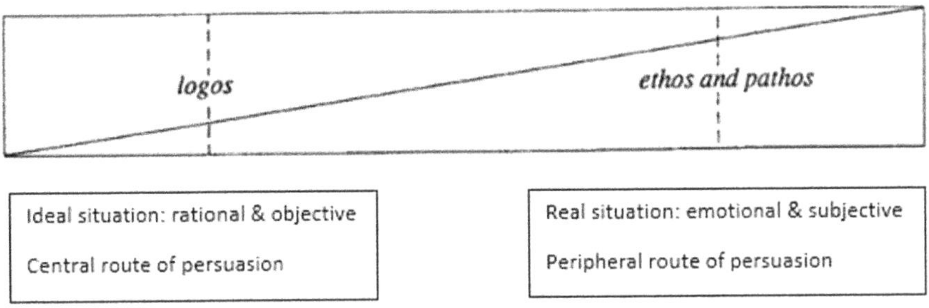

Fig. 3 The weighting of *logos*, *ethos*, and *pathos* Adapted from Braet (1992)

References

Adler RF, Iacobelli F, Gutstein Y (2015) Are you convinced? A Wizard of Oz study to test emotional vs. rational persuasion strategies in dialogues. Comput Hum Behav 57(April 2016):75–81

Bakir V, Barlow DM (2007) The age of suspicion. In: Bakir V, Barlow DM (eds) Communication in the age of suspicion. Trust and the media. Palgrave Macmillan, Basingstoke, pp 3–8

Beattie G, Ellis AW (2017) The psychology of language and communication. Routledge, London

Berger T, Engel C, Meuret S, Fuchs M (2014) Alters- und geschlechtsspezifische Normwerte für Sprechstimmprofile in der Allgemeinbevölkerung: Erste Ergebnisse aus der Leipziger LIFE-Adult-Studie, 31. Wissenschaftliche Jahrestagung der Deutschen Gesellschaft für Phoniatrie und Pädaudiologie (DGPP) zusammen mit dem 5. Pädakustiker-Symposium der Akademie für Hörgeräte-Akustik. Viewed 21 Mar 2018, from http://www.egms.de/static/en/meetings/dgpp2014/14dgpp24.shtml

Botsman R (2018) Q&A: Rachel Botsman on the third trust revolution. Digit Bus Lawyer 20(2):10–11

Braet AC (1992) Ethos, pathos and logos in Aristotle's Rhetoric: a re-examination. Argumentation 6(3):307–320

Burgoon J, Birk T, Pfau M (1990) Nonverbal behaviors, persuasion, and credibility. Hum Commun Res 17(1):140–169

Carbone T (1975) Stylistic variables as related to source credibility: a content analysis approach. Speech Monogr 42(1975):99–106

Comadena ME, Hunt SK, Simonds CJ (2007) The effects of teacher clarity, nonverbal immediacy, and caring on student motivation, affective and cognitive learning. Commun Res Rep 24(3):241–248

DeLemos D, Chen M, Romer A, Brydon K, Kastner K (2010) Building trust through communication in the intensive care unit: HICCC*. Pediatr Crit Care Med 11(3):378–384

Franke U (2016) Logopädisches Handlexikon. UTB, Stuttgart

Gebhard C (2012) Sprechtempo im Sprachvergleich: Eine Untersuchung phonologischer und kultureller Aspekte anhand von Nachrichtensendungen. Ph.D. thesis, Humboldt-Universität zu Berlin

Hamilton MA, Hunter JE, Burgoon M (1990) An empirical test of an axiomatic model of the relationship between language intensity and persuasion. J Lang Soc Psychol 9(1990):235–255

Hammer SS, Teufel-Dietrich A (2017) Stimmtherapie mit Erwachsenen: Was Stimmtherapeuten wissen sollten. Springer, Berlin

Hurwitz SD, Miron MS, Johnson BT (1992) Source credibility and the language of expert testimony. J Appl Soc Psychol 22(1992):1909–1939

Jackob N, Roessing T, Petersen T (2011) The effects of verbal and nonverbal elements in persuasive communication: findings from two multi-method experiments. Communications 36(2011):245–271

Kosfeld M, Heinrichs M, Zak PJ, Fischbacher U, Fehr E (2005) Oxytocin increases trust in humans. Nature 435(2005):673–676

Mika S (1981) Some determinants of source credibility. Pol Psychol Bull 12(1981):79–86

Montrey J (2005) An investigation of the effects of speakers' vocal characteristics on ratings of confidence and persuasion. Ph.D. thesis, University of Central Florida

Ostermeier H (1967) Effects of type and frequency of reference upon perceived source credibility and attitude change. Speech Monogr 34(1967):137–144

Peters J, Hoetjes M (2017) The effect of gesture on persuasive speech. Proc Interspeech 2017:659–663

Pompino-Marschall B (2009) Einführung in die Phonetik. De Gruyter, Berlin

Reinsch NL Jr (1974) Figurative language and source credibility: a preliminary investigation and reconceptualization. Hum Commun Res 1(1974):75–80

Renn O, Levine D (1991) Credibility and trust in risk communication. In: Kasperson RE, Stallen PJ (eds) Communicating risks to the public. Springer, Dordrecht, pp 175–217

Rompf SA (2015) Trust and rationality. An integrative framework for trust research. Springer, Wiesbaden

Rosenberg A, Hirschberg J (2005) Acoustic/prosodic and lexical correlates of charismatic speech. INTERSPEECH-2005, pp 513–516

Rousseau DM, Sitkin SB, Burt RS, Camerer C (1998) Not so different after all: a cross-discipline view of trust. Acad Manage Rev 23(3):393–404

Seltzer LJ, Ziegler TE, Pollak SD (2010) Social vocalizations can release oxytocin in humans. Proc R Soc B 277:2661–2666

Seltzer LJ, Prososki AR, Ziegler TE, Pollak SD (2012) Instant messages vs. speech: hormones and why we still need to hear each other. Evol Hum Behav 33(1):42–45

Shim HS, Park S, Chatterjee M, Scherer S, Sagae K, Morency L-P (2015) Acoustic and paraverbal indicators of persuasiveness in social multimedia. In: 2015 IEEE international conference on acoustics, speech and signal processing (ICASSP), pp 2239–2243

Vygotsky LS (1994) Extracts from thought and language and mind in society. In: Stierer B, Maybin J (eds) Language, literacy, and learning in educational practice: a reader. Multilingual Matters, Bristol, pp 45–58

Whorf B (1940) Science and linguistics. Technol Rev 42(6):229–231, 247–248, 207–219

Anna-Maria Meck is a research assistant at Hochschule Fresenius in Munich. She studied in Innsbruck and Munich and holds a bachelor's as well as a master's degree in Phonetics and Speech Processing from Ludwig Maximilians University of Munich.

Chapter 7
Shifts in Communication and Ego-Identity in the Digital World

Anke Werani

1 Introduction

Nowadays, *communication* is recognized as being the most important skill in everyday life. Communication is generally understood to mean all cooperative processes between two or more individuals, especially to coordinate action (Messing 2014). Communication is a subject of research in a lot of scientific disciplines, not just in psychological and linguistic fields but also, e.g., in media studies, economics and technology. On the one hand, social systems like the family, working teams or social groups are analyzed; on the other hand, medial communication is investigated. Communicative skills are important for all occupational fields, they are engaged in business and public life as well as private life. In order to identify previously neglected aspects of communication, the psycholinguistic focus is on the interface of communication in social and medial systems.

The main focus of cultural-historical psycholinguistics is the examination of the use of language activity in human individuals. Language activity comprises oral, inner and written speech. In communication, oral speech is expressed verbally, paraverbally and nonverbally. Inner speech is speech-for-oneself; it is the richest, most common and most intimate form of speech, because a lot of language activity is left unsaid. Inner speech, the most regulating and censoring form of speech, assumes the role of a mediator of thinking, speaking, and acting. Therefore, it is a kind of centre for self-regulation and cooperation (Werani 2014). The written form of speech is more complex given the requirement of a much more elaborate and developed linguistic shape. This is why writing is considered to be the most elaborate form of speech (cf. Vygotsky 1934/1987).

A further step in this direction requires a short introduction to the way language, cognition, and identity are connected from the point of view of cultural-historical

A. Werani (✉)
LMU München, Schellingstr. 3, 80799 Munich, Germany
e-mail: anke.werani@lmu.de

T. Osburg and S. Heinecke (eds.), *Media Trust in a Digital World*,
https://doi.org/10.1007/978-3-030-30774-5_7

psycholinguistics. The main tenet of cultural-historical psycholinguistics is that all cognitive processes—including speech—as well as constructions of identity have a social genesis (Vygotsky 1931/1997; Werani 2011a, b). It is a fact that human existence is socially embedded. The individual process of socialization is of particular interest. The formation of personality is influenced, for example, by the environment, the education, the material world, the interaction with caregivers and peer groups. The most striking aspect is: human beings exist in language. The basis of common action is built on language activity. Through language activity, individuals are in a position to share perceptions and experiences. This also applies to social media.

With regard to the functions of language activity, Vygotsky (1934/1987) has identified communication as the first and original function of speech. It enables individuals to cooperate. This cooperation takes place in societal, cultural and historical contexts. An important circumstance in language activity is that it never exists in isolation but always in social contexts. Human individuals develop in social settings filled with language activity and gradually become enriched individuals. The second function of language activity focuses on the fact that individuals are in a position to direct language toward themselves. By speaking-to-myself, the mediating function of language activity becomes a formative power which builds cognitive processes and especially identity. The ability to use mediating processes of language activity is therefore remarkable: language activity enables individuals to form *spaces of communication* as well as *spaces of cognition*. Both of these aspects are further involved in constructing *spaces of identity*. Identity contains the reflections of the other in the environment. A metaphor used by Vygotskij (1935) to explain the perception of experience is a prism. The development of identity can be seen as a prism refracting the social influences and depicting them inside the individual, where they are connected with the personal disposition of the individual. Therefore, the same influence, for example on siblings in a family, is quite different even though they grow up in the same environment. The functions of language activity are intricately interwoven because, finally, "speech is not only a means to understand others, but also a means to understand oneself" (Vygotsky 1930/1997: 95).

In developing an identity, the clear face-to-face picture of the other covers the track of identity-construction and of the construction of reality. The face-to-face situation and the vivid presence of the other leads to a maximum of symptoms to be related to (Berger and Luckmann 1966). As mentioned by Frühwald (1996), digitalization is a sign of the shift from an industrial to a knowledge company.

It can be assumed that the development of the World Wide Web and the Internet since the 1980s and its increasing use by consumers since the 1990s influence communication processes. In particular, this applies to social media in different forms. It is important to study the Internet (Newhagen and Rafaeli 1996), especially the shift from oral communication to written communication. Traditionally, writing skills have predominantly been used to preserve knowledge. Now, they are increasingly being used as a daily means of communication. Both oral communication skills as well as writing skills are changing their forms and functions. The oral medium is sometimes replaced and sometimes supplemented by the written medium. An obvious change is the corporeal presence: face-to-face situations shift to telecopresence situations (Zhao 2005).

The present paper aims to investigate how digital media change communication, and, furthermore, how this change of communication leads to a change in cognitive processes and in identity.

2 Shifts in Communication

There is no final definition what communication is. Krauss and Fussell (1996) proposed a kind of taxonomy to cover all theories of communication. This quite classical point of view includes four types of models: (1) the encoder/decoder model, (2) intentionalist models, (3) perspective-taking models, and (4) dialogic models. In summary, in encoder/decoder models it is assumed that in verbal communication a message passed between individuals. An internal representation of a speaker is encoded into a code and transmitted over a channel. The addressee decodes the code as a representation. Important is that the meaning is a property of the messages. A well-known example is the model by Shannon and Weaver (1949). In intentionalist models the communicative intention is focused and the message in-between individuals is seen as a vehicle to exchange these intentions. Of course, the message has to be decoded by the hearer but a further and more important aspect is the process of inference which derives the underlying communicated intention. The meaning is not supposed to be in the message, but it is socially shared. Models belonging to intentionalist models are, e.g., Grice's (1975) cooperative principle and Austin's (1962) and Searle's (1969) theory of speech acts. Perspective-taking models suppose that comprehension depends on the vantage points. Real comprehension is possible if it is achievable to experience, for example, a situation from the vantage point of the other individual. Communication is a process which is continuously expanded and refined while participants alternate between their own perspective and the perspective of the other. The interaction situation is of fundamental interest in dialogic models. From this vantage point, meaning is socially situated; meaning is constructed and can only be understood in the context of each situation. Thus, the conversational aspect is emphasized which is characterized by the features real-time constraints and responsiveness between the interacting individuals. Examples of how speakers tailor speech to their hearers can be found in Bakhtin (1981) or Rommetveit (1974).

By conflating these theories, Anselm and Werani (2017) propose a new approach. The point of entry is the idea that individuals construct a specific *space of communication* in each interaction. Language activity is the dynamic means to an end which allows the interacting individuals to construct reality cooperatively as some reciprocal, intermediate process. Furthermore, by constructing a space of communication, language activity can also be aimed at oneself, even though both inter- and intramental processes are enhanced in the construction process. Intermental speech is directed and addressed to the other, intramental speech is directed and addressed to oneself.

In both cases, language activity has the function of communication and of building higher mental functions. This highlights that the dynamic and reciprocal process of communication is a selective event as well as a dynamic process. Linell (1998: 81) underlines that a comprehension process is a kind of “doing understanding”. Thus, verbal interaction processes in a space of communication can be called *doing communication*. The relationship between the individuals is a basic issue of doing communication to construct a space of communication. This stresses the importance of the here and now in the sense of the I-origo introduced by Bühler (1934/1990). The quality of the relationship is the baseline for the emotional quality of the space of communication. In the space of communication, reality is constructed by language activity via both communication and cognition. The latter includes attention, valuating, memory, and problem solving. The construction of reality also includes embodiment with all nonverbal aspects like gestures or mimic in communication. Communication, cognitive processes and embodiment lead to the construction of identity. In spaces of communication, attribution processes shape identity, directly and indirectly. Every instance of communication is an actualization of the personality through the prism of social relationships.

With respect to social media, there is a shift from face-to-face-interaction to computer-mediated communication (Bubaš and Spitzberg 2008; Zhao 2005). Computer-mediated communication is defined by Spitzberg (2006) as referring to all text-based interactions through any kind of digitally-based technologies. Walther (2011) gives a brief overview of theories focussing on computer-mediated communication. A main change in written language is that written language is now used for short written communication and no longer only to store knowledge. In describing the difference between communication spaces, three main aspects will be referred to: orality and literacy, embodiment as well as simultaneity of spaces (Fig. 1).

The first shift outlines the topic *orality and literacy*. As mentioned by Koch und Oesterreicher (1994), different genres of texts can be classified between the poles of orality and literacy. The two dimensions of the fundamental distinction are the medial realisation (spoken or written) and the conceptional character (spoken-informal or written-formal) of the planned language activity. Any text can be classified on the continuum communicative immediacy vs. distance by this medial-conceptual distinction. For instance, a face-to-face-interaction is both conceptually and medially oral. A lecture in a classical sense is realized in an oral medium, but conceptually it is literal. Texts which are conceptually and medially oral are closer between individuals than conceptually and medially written forms of texts. The first shift therefore is that written forms in social media like SMS messages, chat, and WhatsApp are conceptually oral but medially in the written form. Thus, even though there theoretically is a distance brought about by the medium, but textual changes underline the oral character of speech and create more communicative immediacy. For example, in written chat-speech emoticons, sound words or acronyms are used to stress an oral character of speech (Dürscheid and Siever 2017). Beck (2010) describes this new form as oraliteracy.

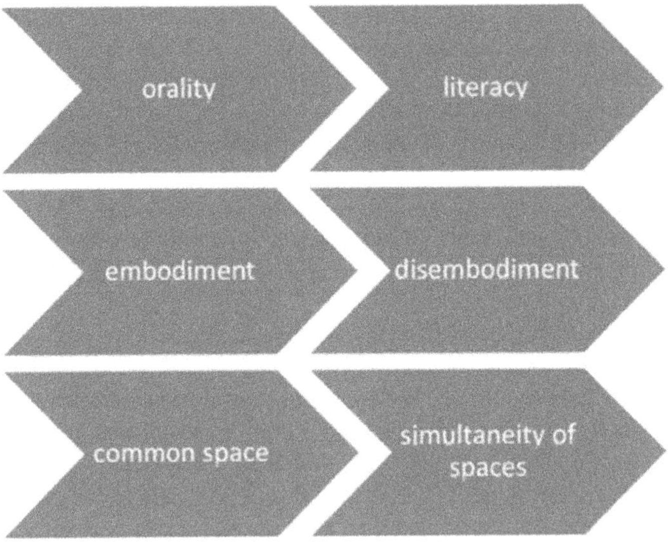

Fig. 1 Summarizing the aspects of the shift of communication

The second shift is defined by the term *embodiment*. In real face-to-face-interactions, the whole body is involved in communication. There are, for example, tone of voice, proxemics, facial expression, gesture, and eye contact. The first impression of an individual determines how the communication will proceed. A case in point is that nonverbal communication has a decisive influence on the valuation of sympathy (Mehrabian and Ferris 1967; Mehrabian 1972). The modality of the voice influences whether a person is experienced as attractive, dominant or serious (e.g. Borkowska and Pawlowski 2011; Rezlescu et al. 2015). Also, Bubaš and Spitzberg (2008) compare face-to-face communication and computer-mediated communication and mention the loss of nonverbal cues in text-based computer-mediated communication, which may lead to a lower quality of social interaction. Döring (2000) gives a brief overview of nine different theories of communication in the Internet. She uses terms like less emotional, less spatial, less timing, less contextual and less real to describe the shift of communication using the Internet. Therefore, the body carries a lot of information used in the construction of a space of communication. In social media, disembodiment without being physically copresent is involved in the creation of an avatar or the construction of oneself as another person which is not real. In an early investigation of telecommunication with regard to intimacy, Short et al. (1976) introduced the theory of social presence. Media richness is an important fact in the discussion of computer-mediated communication (Daft and Lengel 1986). There is evidence that individuals change their individuality when they describe another body or other personality traits they want to have.

The third shift, finally, analyses the *simultaneity of spaces*. In a face-to-face-communication the individuals involved are at the same place at the same time.

Therefore, both the physical location and the participants of the communication are obvious. In social media, this kind of I-origo is given up, the common location of the individuals is lost. This also applies to the exclusive face-to-face situation, because in social media more than one conversation can be realized at the same time. Furthermore, before starting a social media communication it is possible to choose the medium with respect to the desired medial richness, whether, for example, it is better to use the phone, to text or to email (Schmitz and Fulk 1991). Nowadays medial richness is re-generated by visual aspects like photos or videos and especially in video-telephony it is interesting that an appointment is also needed as in face-to-face situations.

To sum up, there obviously is a shift in communication processes. But there is doubt whether the shift is only negative. A field of research founded some years ago by Walther and Burgoon (1992) focusses on social information processing. In an extreme but unrealistic view, individuals are victims of social media. In fact, they are active designers of communication. Therefore, individuals acquire the new forms of social media and adapt them. As described above, a new form of oraliteracy in social media can be interpreted as an indicator of adaption. Especially with regard to finding new signs for emotions, individuals show up with new social skills. Importantly, the shift which has actually occurred does not exclusively favour written text-messages and disembodied spaces. New technologies in social media enable multimedia presentations such as photos and videos, as well as voice-mails and video telephony. To conclude, social media have to be accepted as a new social space embedded in sociality.

3 Communication and Identity-Construction

As mentioned above, the functions of language activity serve communication and cognition as well as the construction of identity and perspectives on the world.

The notion of constructing identity involves three kinds of terms in the disciplines sociology and psychology: identity, self and personality. Identity is the term mostly used in sociology, self in social psychology and personality in psychology. Each term is connected to the same entity with a different focus. In the following, the term identity is used to underline the social character of the ego. It is supposed that all these terms have a common root in James' (1890) theory.

Following James (1890), the *self* emerges with the duality of *I* and *me*. The *I* refers to the individual being a thinking subject. James stresses the stream of consciousness and the notion that the *I* is the point of entry to become self-aware and to focus on oneself as an object. This ability to focus on oneself leads to the fact than the *I* shifts to a *me*. In other words, one can look at oneself like an object, this object is called the *me*. Individuals are able to "make themselves the object of their own thinking" (Zhao 2014: 201). There is a difference, though, between the *self* as an active part and the *self-as-an-object* enriched by knowledge about oneself. The self as an object entails beliefs and feelings about oneself, and it is the baseline for all self-concepts (Mummendey 1995). Following Mummendey (2006) it is difficult to speak of a *self* itself, because the important aspects are the processes constructing the self which are all attributing and valuating processes concerning the individual. Some examples of the investigation of self-concepts are aspects such as self-awareness, self-representation or self-regulation (ibid.). Nowadays, the phenomenon of tracking the body has become fashionable. This trend to perceive the body as an object has been intensified by this perspective.

The idea of the self proposed by James lends support to findings in the literature. A well-known theoretical claim is outlined by Goffman (1963). He shifted from the terminology of *self* to that of *identity*, differentiating *ego-identity* from *personal identity* and *social identity*. Personal identity summarizes all traits that make the individual unique. This is a development task of the individual to become singular. Social identity involves specific roles in the role-play system in a specific context. In particular, the social identity is constructed by normative expectations of the others. The development task for the individual in this case is to become a group member who fits in and is like the others. The challenge is to find a balance between personal and social identity and to develop and to form a well-balanced ego-identity. Ego-identity is an interactive and reflexive process depending on the personal structure and the social expectations. The development of ego-identity is an open process and especially in postmodern age Keupp et al. (1999) emphasize that having an identity is the concatenation of perspectives of time (past, present, future), perspectives of specific contexts of the own life (peers, parents, teacher), and all associations. Important aspects in the construction of identity are different feelings. Keupp et al. mention the feeling of identity, the feeling of coherence and the feeling of the self. The interesting point is that identity is not a collection of experiences but rather a large bundle of valuations of all relationships to others and the world, and valuations are related to language.

To connect the construction of ego-identity and language activity it is important to understand Vygotsky's (1931/1997) general genetic law of cultural development. He proposes that all individual consciousness and all higher mental processes have a social genesis, and Vygotsky was convinced that they are structured by language. His general genetic law of cultural development states that every mental process appears twice: first, in social interaction interwoven in language; second, as higher mental process after interiorizing social interaction and language activity. Pursuing this notion of the genesis of higher mental processes by analogy with the construction process of ego-identity it is essential that ego-identity is an *intermediate* between social and personal aspects and depends on language activity. Thus, the way we interact with others influences the development of higher mental processes as well as the view of ourselves. To sum it up, it is supposed that language activity is central for the construction of our reality as well as our identity (Werlen 2002; Anan'ev 1963). Language activity is an intermental process for the purpose of communication and an intramental process for the purpose of cognition and identity construction. Therefore, every speech act reveals, by varying language expressions, an ego-identity. For example, traits or attributions both in personal and social identity are expressed through language. As a case in point, the testing of personal traits is closely linked to adjectives (Allport and Odbert 1936). The view we have on ourselves is influenced by others and how they respond to us (Goffman 1963).

Thus, it is claimed that all language activity is an expression of ego-identity. It is like an expression of the habitus as kind of lifestyle (Bourdieu 1993; Miosga 2006). In this notion, corporeal presence is involved, including all verbal, paraverbal and nonverbal aspects of language activity. Ego-identity shows something about the way the individuals feel, perceive, think, value and act; in ego-identity, all habits are put together and emerge connected to a person. It is supposed that language activity also expresses ways of living, for example nonverbal behaviour determined by the physical appearance, emotional states by the quality of the voice and attitude by the use of words (Anselm and Werani 2017). It is postulated that language activity is an expression of ego-identity and therefore interwoven with it. In other words, the construction of identity-concepts develops out of verbal interaction. Especially language activity in communication is very important for the presentation of the *self-as-an-object* like self-concepts and/or self-feelings (James 1890; Mummendey 2006; Keupp et al. 1999). The language use in dynamic, communicative interactions constructs inner structures of language as well as identity-concepts. Therefore, it is supposed that all these identity-aspects represented as self-as-object employ parts of language. In this view, language is not a kind of by-product of cognitive processes, language activity is the most important process for human individuals constructing their cognitive processes and identity. The corporeal presence of others in a face-to-face situation provides us with a maximum of symptoms that enable us to see a clear picture of ourselves in others' appraisals of our performances (Berger and Luckmann 1966).

The next issue leads to the question whether ego-identity exists in an essentialist way without language or whether the ego-identity is constructed by language. Ricœur (1985) claimed that telling stories creates identity. In his view, individuals possess narrative identities.

> Just why is the act of telling close to the heart of our experience? Perhaps it is because our own existence cannot be separated from the account we can give of ourselves. It is in telling our own stories that we give ourselves an identity. We recognize ourselves in the stories we tell about ourselves. It makes little difference whether these stories are true or false, fiction as well as verifiable history provides us with an identity (Ricœur 1985: 214).

Interestingly, Ricœur (1985) relates to telling stories, regardless whether they are true or false, real or fiction. Identity is, from this point of view, constructed by stories we tell each other.

This is an important fact with regard to social media, where stories are more important than common actions. The baseline of social media are the narratives we use to connect to other individuals.

To sum up, language activity and ego-identity are interwoven and language activity is needed for both constructing and expressing ego-identity. At this point, the interesting question arises how construction processes change because of the use of digital media.

4 Communication and Ego-Identity in Social Media

Shifting to social media leads to a different view of both language activity and ego-identity. Initially, the term social media was used as an umbrella term and refers to all software and applications that enable individuals to communicate with each other using internet or other mobile devices (Von Muhlen and Ohno-Machado 2012). Several authors contend that social media affect the construction of the ego-identity. For example, Zhao (2005) is convinced that the Internet produces a *digital self* that differs from the self being formed in face-to-face-interactions, especially in adolescence. These differences between online and offline self-representations were also observed by DeAndrea and Walther (2011). Furthermore, Voirol (2010) justified a concept of the digital self which focusses on a theory of intersubjectivity.

Early studies by Turkle (1995) reported the observation that cyberspace offers a lot of opportunities to individuals to play with their identity. Here, it is an obvious shift typical for postmodern society from the notion of a unitary identity to multiple identities. In a way, Turkle introduced the issue of thinking about online identities.

In the discussion of social media today, there is a debate about whether adolescents already develop *digital selves* (e.g. Zhao 2005; DeAndrea and Walther 2011; Voirol 2010). Communication technology has radically changed all social interactions (Barth 2015). Digitization has become an integral part of everyday life. Voirol (2010) reported on two perspectives of research. The first perspective outlines the difference between offline- and online-interactions and highlights the opportunity to expand identity in an optimistic manner. The second perspective focuses on negative consequences and leads to the conclusion that identity is negatively affected by technology.

There is no doubt that new technologies change the world. With regard to the current state of communication technology, it is nearly inconceivable that the introduction of the telephone at the beginning of the last century was a comparable situation. Communication changed because the telephone was the first step to telecopresence (Zhao 2005) and the first step to virtual aspects. Aspects of digital intersubjectivity are outlined by Voirol (2010) who mentions a concept of the digital self which focuses on a theory of intersubjectivity. There is a considerable overlap between this concept and some of the areas of interest investigated by cultural-historical psycholinguistics. In short, the three levels of digital intersubjectivity are: first, the relationship of the subject with a digital interface (Turkle 1995; Zhao 2006); second, the digital relationship with other users; third, the relationship to the whole digital world (Voirol 2010).

With regard to communication and identity-construction, intersubjectivity is also present in social media. The digital interface is a kind of medium that is used to get in contact with other individuals. The connections in social media are also between individuals. But where are the differences between online- and offline communication and what are the influences on constructing identity? The shift in communication affecting the conceptual pairs orality and literacy, embodiment and disembodiment,

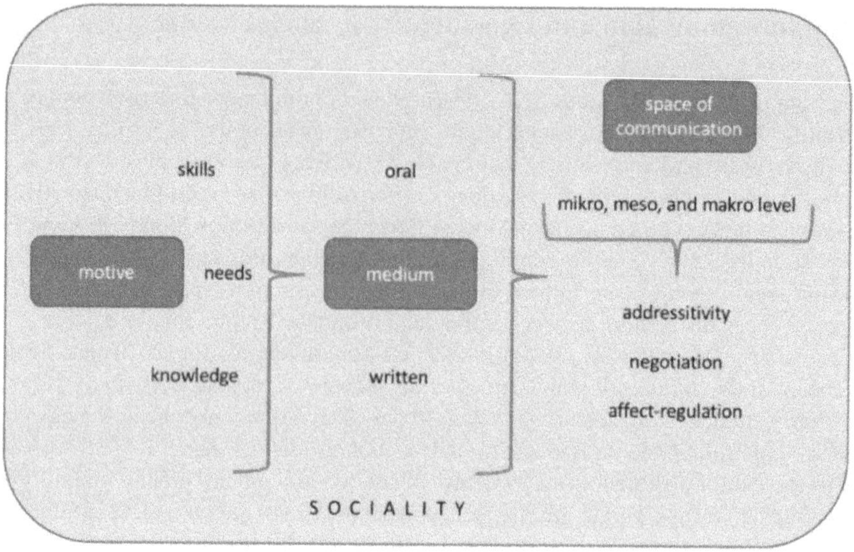

Fig. 2 A perspective of communication and constructing ego-identity within social media

together with common space and simultaneity of space, is now discussed regarding identity-construction processes in social media. The combination of the facts already mentioned results in the following model: motive, medium, and space of communication. This is summarized in Fig. 2.

(1) *Motive*. The motive is the source behind every activity. Close to the motive are needs, skills, and knowledge (Spitzberg 2006). Max-Neef (1991) reported on nine basic and universal needs that are identity, freedom, participation, idleness, creativity, subsistence, understanding, protection, and affection. Great importance is attached to the personal sense as a fundamental baseline for human behaviour (Leont'ev 1984, 2012). Therefore, the motive lies behind thought. "Thought has its origins in the motivating sphere of consciousness, a sphere that includes our inclinations and needs, our interests and impulses, and our affect and emotion" (Vygotsky 1934/1987: 282). This means that affect and volitional tendencies are behind thought. The motive is driven by skills, needs and knowledge (Spitzberg 2006) and depends on social influences. The motive is the starting point in all activities, both in face-to-face interaction and in social media.

(2) *Medium*. Focusing on the medium which is used in social media, oral and written utterances can be chosen. Depending on the motive it is possible to adapt the medium directly. For example, a decision can be made between using text, email, phone, photo, video. An interesting combination has arisen towards the new form *oraliteracy* in social media, which is an obvious change in the medial formation (Beck 2010). Written language is enriched by emoticons or other written symbols to underline oral aspects of language activity. Furthermore, in

social media asynchrony in communication is possible, and therefore utterances are editable.

(3) *Space of Communication*. The main aspects of changes in communication and ego-identity in social media are summarized with respect to the phenomenon of space of communication. Spaces of communication are constructed on micro, meso and macro levels (Bronfenbrenner and Morris 2006). Three aspects will be discussed in the following: addressitivity, the aspect of negotiation, and self-regulation as well as self-ascertainment.

   (a) Addressitivity. In face-to-face interaction addressitivity is obvious. The two-way interaction is enriched by verbal, paraverbal and nonverbal language activity. All interaction within social media end at a kind of screen and the virtual reality exists beyond the screen. First of all, there is a lack of symptoms (Berger and Luckmann 1966) and second, not in all interactions the addressee is known. Some preliminary work has been carried out which shows that a main aspect is the anonymity and often the lack of a known addressee (Zhao 2005). Anonymity changes the interaction process. As mentioned above, to develop an identity an addressee—someone other—is needed to act like a mirror and reflect attributes and behaviour back on myself. Behind the screen, it is mostly unknown who gives feedback to postings or pictures published online. Zhao (2005) investigated the influence of others on the self-conception in the online world by asking how people conceive their self in contact with disembodied and anonymous others. Zhao is convinced that individuals are less affected by people they do not know well, and more influenced by people they respect and value. It is easier to hide feelings and attitudes in telecopresence. This is not only the fact of anonymity but further the possibility of diachronic interaction. The reaction in-between interactions in social media need not take place immediately in real time, any kind of reaction can be thought about before reacting, also self-representations, e.g. on homepages, can be well thought out. Following Goffman (1963), ego-identity is always a construction resulting from social feedbacks. Walther et al. (2011) investigated the role of feedback on identity shift in computer-mediated communication. They are convinced that feedback plays an important role for identity shift in social media systems. In this theory, feedback resulting from copresence is mentioned, and it is obvious that a lot of work has to be done to get an insight into the effect of feedback. Walther (2011) underlines the fact that we do not know whose recommendation can be trusted in social media; an interesting fact is that contact has priority because a lot of messages sent via social media are quite trivial. A new perspective on communication and ego-identity has to consider the aspects anonymity, diachroneity and expansion of social interaction.
   (b) Negotiation. The influence of social media leads to new forms of constructing communicative spaces. Therefore, face-to-face interactions have other forms of negotiation than interactions in social media. For example,

Koutamanis et al. (2013) are interested in the development of social competence and especially the process of maintaining close and meaningful relationships. They investigate adolescence and observe the influence of instant messaging on the ability to have offline relationships. In fact, the long-term study shows that instant messaging has a positive effect on the ability to have offline relationships. It seems as if the diversity of communication partners provides a training ground which improves face-to-face interactions and therefore develops social skills. These results conform to the theory of Vygotsky that social experiences lead to higher mental skills. Vygotsky (1931/1997) supposes that, in the development of higher mental processes, the relation to caregivers is important for interiorizing language activity. Individuation depends on negotiation and attachment to others. The fact that the quality of attachment is important for individuation processes is outlined in attachment theory (e.g. Bowlby 1969, 1988). The idea is that a healthy attachment leads to a healthy individuation; Barth (2015) calls this attachment-individuation. A main development task is the individuation within attachment and separation, in other words the individual has to find a balance between connection to and independence from others. Social media afford the opportunity to be anyone or everyone in the virtual world (Barth 2015). Regarding social media the kind and quality of attachment is important. On the one hand social media are a possibility to keep in touch with, e.g., friends, parents, and colleagues and to have positive relationships (Wood et al. 2016); on the other hand, studies show that social media can reinforce feelings of loneliness (Barth 2015; Spitzberg 2006). It would be wrong to conclude that social media cause loneliness. As outlined in cultural-historical psycholinguistics, even in social media, negotiation has a social origin.

The most remarkable observation in social media is the fact that negotiations depend on language activity, even though negotiation can be more obvious than in face-to-face interactions. Strictly speaking, there are narrative identities in social media. As Zhao (2005: 388, italics original) pointed out: "*as others cannot see who we really are, we are free to claim to be whoever we want to be*.".

(c) Self-regulation and self-ascertainment. Following Vygotsky (1934/1987), the main functions of language activity are, first, communication in regulating social interaction, and, second, developing and coordinating higher mental processes (for an overview see Werani 2014). Concerning self-regulation Barth (2015) also mentions a change in affect-regulation by the influence of social media in adolescence. Barth describes a difference between the emotional and intellectual development, and she observes that young people are able to name their feelings, but they cannot actually describe what they feel in their bodies. One thesis to explain this change is that social media lead to feelings like loneliness, another thesis focuses on the fact that computer-mediated communication improves the ability to interact emotionally in face-to-face-interactions as well.

Nevertheless, there are also negative effects in social media like cyberbullying and online harassment (Valkenburg and Peter 2011). This is the potential downside of social media and Valkenburg and Peter are convinced that cyberbullying is enhanced by anonymity, asynchronicity, and accessibility in social media. A main difference to face-to-face interaction is that you cannot leave the space of communication. Via social media you stay in the space of communication—also at home.

(4) *Consequences for communication and construction of ego-identity*. The everyday use of social media leads to a change in communication and in identity construction (Walther et al. 2011). In cultural-historical psycholinguistics we propose that the individual mind is related to forms of social activity in common practice, and language activity is always in its relationships to social and individual processes (Bertau and Werani 2011; Werani 2011a). Interestingly, *doing language* has to be focused, though in social media, too. In doing language there are changes in addressitivity causing other registers and formats of communication.

Affect and volitional tendencies are behind thought and therefore behind speech in the origin but language activity is shaping our consciousness, which is closely connected with the development of volitional acts and of identity (Luria 1982; Anan'ev 1963). This wide interaction between motive and language activity enables consciousness and shows that consciousness has a social origin. The individual mind cannot be separated from the study of society. Therefore, the study of social media and their influences on individuals is very important and cannot be separated from societal processes. Language activity has a smooth transition from social relationships to inner processes. Thus, language activity is involved in all higher mental functions, particularly consciousness and the development of identity. In a way, social media have also become an important instrument of thinking. The specific environment leads to different experiences, valuations and attributions. All these aspects are reflected in language activity, and especially the quality of language is important in how individuals acquire a positive or negative self-assessment. Identity arises by the interiorization of social relationships. Both the interiorization of language activity and the interiorization of social norms and values exert an influence on the development of identity (Werani 2014).

A fundamental question is how identity and reality are constructed in the real and the virtual world. There is a new continuum of contact from individuals with a body towards virtual bodies. In fact, reality is not constructed outside the individual, e.g. in the internet, reality is constructed inside the individual influenced by sociality. Therefore, all self-representation (Mummendey 1995) is constructed in the individual's mind. In the same vein, what is called the *digital self* is a construction of the individual and related to it. Voirol (2010) proposes to distinguish between a digital self and a practical self. The practical self is bound to the body and refers to practical experiences whereas the digital self lacks a body and a continuum of experiences. Gonzales and Hancock (2008) found an effect in their study about identity shift in computer-mediated environments and have interpreted this effect as evidence of identity shift. In their two conditions—public and private—they observed that the public online-condition presenting the self caused a shift in identity. At this point it could be asked if there is a difference between social media interaction and face-to-face interaction because shifts in self-presentation are also observable in public or private presentations. Keupp et al. (1999) are convinced that the identity process is a kind of patchwork, and therefore it could be possible to construct an identity via social media. In all cases the feeling of identity, the feeling of coherence and the feeling of the self are important for the construction of ego-identity. The digital self is nothing more than another piece of patchwork within the framework of identity-construction. Interestingly, Ginzburg (1991: 11) noticed: "As early as the end of the nineteenth century, James (1890/1950) was maintaining that in practice everyone 'has as many different social selves as there are distinct *groups* of persons about whose opinion he cares'". Strikingly, users of social media will thus have a lot of social selves. Furthermore, the focus on verbal communication is especially high. Therefore, the point of entry in reflection processes about the self is more obvious than in face-to-face interaction.

However, in social media there is the opportunity to play with multiple identities—but that is only possible in a state of mental health. It is not clearly defined where this borders on the psychopathological (Turkle 1995). In creating an avatar, the change of, e.g., sex, age or character, it is possible to construct someone with attributions that have nothing in common with the person in the real world. Referring to theories of embodiment (Gallagher 2008), it is doubtful if it is possible to construct very different identities belonging to one body. It is a question concerning construction processes of ego-identity if one identity is connected to one body. Whitty and Young (2017: 15) for example asked: "Can people completely separate themselves from their physical bodies to create a utopian self?".

All varieties of the identity have to be constructed in a convenient context to be aware of oneself as one or the same individual. Vygotsky (1930/1997: 95) is convinced that "speech is not only a means to understand others, but also a means to understand oneself". Now, the processes of understanding ourselves occur under different conditions (Joinson 2001).

5 Summary and Perspectives

This paper looks at communication and ego-identity concerning the shift from face-to-face interaction to interaction in social media. A main aspect is that language activity is not only a vehicle for interaction. Rather, language activity also mediates and forms a space of communication, higher mental processes and, ultimately, ego-identity. In both face-to-face interaction as well as in social media, language activity is a means of communication and a mediator of higher mental processes, highlighting its social nature and its formative power.

A main problem is the speed of technology and the change of communication processes nearly every day. To keep up with fast moving new technologies, we need theoretical models which can deal with them (Walther 2011; Scott 2009).

So, in sum, the main priority is not to judge whether social media are to be seen positively or negatively—many of their questionable aspects occur in face-to-face interaction as well—but to recognize that this kind of communication and construction of ego-identity also needs its own kind of proficiency.

> If new technologies translate into new effects on society and human relationships, then the competence with which any given person utilizes these new technologies is likely to affect whether this person views the technology as utopian or dystopian (Spitzberg 2006: 629).

Here, the argument has come full circle: as maintained in cultural-historical psycholinguistics, all higher mental process—here language activity and the construction of ego-identity—appear twice: first outside, second inside. Thus, the way we want to construct our reality is the way we need to construct social life in social media.

References

Allport G, Odbert HS (1936) Trait-names. A psycho-lexical study. In: Peterson J (ed) Psychological monographs. Psychological review publications, 211, vol XLVII, no 1

[Anan'ev, Boris G.] Ananjew BG (1963) Psychologie der sinnlichen Erkenntnis. VEB Deutscher Verlag der Wissenschaften, Berlin

Anselm S, Werani A (2017) Kommunikation in Lehr-Lernkontexten. Klinkhardt utb, Bad Heilbrunn

Austin JL (1962) How to do things with words. Oxford University Press, Oxford

Bakhtin MM (1981) In: Holquist M (ed) The dialogic imagination: four essays. University of Texas Press, Austin & London

Barth DF (2015) Social media and adolescent development: hazards, pitfalls and opportunities for growth. Clin Soc Work J 43(2):201–208

Beck K (2010) Soziologie der Online-Kommunikation. In: Schweiger W, Beck K (Hrsg) Handbuch der Online-Kommunikation. VS Verlag, Wiesbaden, S. 15–35

Berger PL, Luckmann T (1966) The social construction of reality: a treatise in the sociology of knowledge. Doubleday, New York

Bertau M-C, Werani A (2011) Contributions to cultural-historical psycholinguistics. J Act Theor Res Ger 5(Special Issue). http://psyjournals.ru/en/tatigkeitstheorie/index.shtml

Borkowska B, Pawlowski B (2011) Female voice frequency in the context of dominance and attractiveness perception. Anim Behav 82(1):55–59

Bourdieu P (1993) Sozialer Sinn. Kritik der theoretischen Vernunft. Suhrkamp, Frankfurt a. M.

Bowlby J (1969) Attachment. Attachment and loss. Loss, vol 1. Basic Books, New York

Bowlby J (1988) A secure base: clinical applications of attachment theory. Routledge, London

Bubaš G, Spitzberg B (2008) The relations of communication skills in face-to-face and computer-mediated communication. In: 2nd European Communication Research and Education Association (ECREA) conference, Barcelona, Spain, 25–28 Nov 2008

Bühler K (1934/1990) The theory of language. John Benjamin's Publishing Company, Amsterdam

Bronfenbrenner U, Morris PA (2006) The bioecological model of human development. In: Damon W, Lerner RM (eds) Handbook of child psychology: theoretical models of human development, vol 1. Wiley, New York and others, pp 793–828

Daft RL, Lengel RH (1986) Organizational information requirements, media richness and structural design. Manage Sci 32(5):554–571

DeAndrea DC, Walther JB (2011) Attributions for inconsistencies between online and offline self-presentations. Commun Res 38(6):805–825
Döring N (2000) Kommunikation im Internet: Neun theoretische Ansätze. In: Batinic B (Hrsg) Internet für Psychologen. Hogrefe, Göttingen u.a., pp 345–378
Dürscheid C, Siever CM (2017) Jenseits des Alphabets – Kommunikation mit Emojis. ZGL 45(2):256–285
Frühwald W (1996) Die Informatisierung des Wissens. Zur Entstehung der Wissensgesellschaft, in Deutschland. In: Stiftungsreihe der Alcatel-SEL-Stiftung für Technische und Wirtschaftliche Kommunikationsforschung, Bd 12. Alcatel SEL Stiftung, Stuttgart, pp 5–14
Gallagher S (2008) Understanding others: embodied social cognition. In: Calvo P, Gomila A (eds) Handbook of cognitive science: an embodied approach. Elsevier Ltd., San Diego, pp 439–452
Ginzburg L (1991) On psychological prose. Princeton UP, Princeton
Goffman E (1963) Stigma: notes on the management of spoiled identity. ORT: Englewood Cliffs
Gonzales AL, Hancock JT (2008) Identity shift in computer-mediated environments. Media Psychol 11(2):167–185
Grice HP (1975) Logic and conversation. In: Cole P, Morgan JL (eds) Syntax and semantics: speech acts. Academic Press, New York, pp 41–58
James W (1890) The principles of psychology. Holt, New York
Joinson AN (2001) Knowing me, knowing you: reciprocal self-disclosure in internet-based surveys. Cyberpsychol Behav 4:587–591
Keupp H, Ahbe T, Gmür W, Höfer R, Mitzscherlich B, Kraus W, Sraus F (1999) Identitätskonstruktionen: Das Patchwork der Identitäten in der Spätmodern. Rowohlt, Hamburg
Koch P, Oesterreicher W (1994) Schriftlichkeit und Sprache. In: Günther H, Ludwig O (Hrsg) Schrift und Schriftlichkeit. de Gruyter, Berlin, New York, pp 587–604
Koutamanis M, Vossen HGM, Peter J, Valkenburg PM (2013) Practice makes perfect: the longitudinal effect of adolescents' instant messaging on their ability to initiate offline friendships. Comput Hum Behav 29(6):2265–2272
Krauss RM, Fussell SR (1996) Social psychological models of interpersonal communication. In: Tory Higgins E, Kruglanski AW (eds) Social psychology. Handbook of basic principles. Guilford Press, New York, pp 655–701
[Leont'ev, AA.] Leontjew AA (1984) Sprachliche Tätigkeit. In: Leontjew AN, Leontjew AA, Judin EG (Hrsg) Grundlagen einer Theorie der sprachlichen Tätigkeit. Akademie, Berlin, pp 31–44
Leont'ev AN (2012) Tätigkeit, Bewusstsein, Persönlichkeit. Lehmanns, Berlin
Linell P (1998) Approaching dialogue. Talk, interaction and context in dialogical perspectives. Benjamins, Amsterdam/Philadelphia
Luria AR (1982) Language and cognition. Wiley, New York u.a.
Max-Neef M (1991) Human scale development: conception, application and further reflections. Apex Press, New York
Mehrabian A (1972) Nonverbal communication. Aldine-Atherton, Chicago
Mehrabian A, Ferris SR (1967) Inference of attitudes from nonverbal communication in two channels. J Consult Psychol 31(3):48–258
Messing J (2014) Communication. In: Teo T (ed) Encyclopedia of critical psychology. Springer, New York, pp 271–275
Miosga C (2006) Habitus der Prosodie. Die Bedeutung der Rekonstruktion von personalen Sprechstilen in pädagogischen Handlungsfeldern. Peter Lang, Frankfurt am Main u.a.
Mummendey HD (1995) Selbstdarstellungsverhalten und Persönlichkeit. In: Pawlik K (Hrsg) Bericht über den 39. Kongress der Deutschen Gesellschaft für Psychologie in Hamburg. Hogrefe, Göttingen, pp 378–382
Mummendey HD (2006) Psychologie des "Selbst". Theorien, Methoden und Ergebnisse der Selbstkonzeptforschung. Hogrefe, Göttingen
Newhagen JE, Rafaeli S (1996) Why communication researchers should study the internet: a dialogue. J Comput Mediated Commun 1(4)

Rezlescu C, Penton T, Walsh V, Tsujimura H, Scott SK, Banissy MJ (2015) Dominant voices and attractive faces: the contribution of visual and auditory information to integrated person impressions. J Nonverbal Behav 39(4):355–370

Ricœur P (1985) History as narrative and practice. Philos Today 29(3):213–222

Rommetveit R (1974) On message structure: a framework for the study of language and communication. Wiley, New York

Schmitz J, Fulk J (1991) Organizational colleagues, media richness, and electronic mail. A test of the social influence model of technology use. Commun Res 18:487–523. https://doi.org/10.1177/009365091018004003

Scott CR (2009) A whole-hearted effort to get it half right: predicting the future of communication technology scholarship. J Comput Mediated Commun 14:753–757

Searle J (1969) Speech acts: an essay in the philosophy of language. Cambridge University Press, Cambridge

Shannon CE, Weaver W (1949) The mathematical theory of communication. University of Illinois Press, Urbana, IL

Short J, Williams E, Christie B (1976) The social psychology of telecommunications. Wiley, London

Spitzberg BH (2006) Preliminary development of a model and measure of computer mediated communication (CMC) competence. J Comput Mediated Commun 11(2):629–666

Turkle S (1995) Life on the screen: internet in the age of the internet. Weidenfeld & Nicolson, London, UK

Valkenburg PM, Peter J (2011) Online communication among adolescents: an integrated model of its attraction, opportunities, and risks. J Adolesc Health 48:121–127

Voirol O (2010) Digitales Selbst: Anerkennung und Entfremdung. WestEnd. Neue Zeitschrift für Sozialforschung 7(2):106–120

Von Muhlen M, Ohno-Machado L (2012) Reviewing social media use by clinicians. J Am Med Inform Assoc 19(5):777–781

Vygotskij LS (1935) Die Bedeutung der Umwelt für die Entwicklung des Kindes. http://www.ich-sciences.de/pages/de/texte/uebersicht/

Vygotsky LS (1934/1987) Thinking and speech. In: Rieber RW, Carton AS (eds) The collected works of L.S. Vygotsky. Problems of general psychology, vol 1. Plenum Press, New York and London

Vygotsky LS (1931/1997) The collected works of L. S. Vygotsky. The history of the development of higher mental functions, vol 4. Plenum Press, New York

Vygotsky LS (1930/1997) On psychological systems. In: Rieber RW, Wollock J (ed) The collected works of L.S. Vygotsky. Problems of the theory and history of psychology, vol 3. Plenum Press, New York and London, pp 91–107

Walther JB (2011) Theories of computer-mediated communication and interpersonal relations. In: The handbook of interpersonal communication, vol 4, pp 443–479

Walther JB, Burgoon JK (1992) Relational communication in computer mediated interaction. Hum Commun Res 19:50–88

Walther JB, Liang YJ, DeAndrea DC, Tong ST, Carr CT, Spottswood EL, Amichai-Hamburger Y (2011) The effect of feedback on identity shift in computer-mediated communication. Media Psychol 14(1):1–26

Werani A (2011a) Inneres Sprechen – Ergebnisse einer Indiziensuche. [Inner speech – results of research]. Lehmanns Media, Berlin

Werani A (2011b) Investigating inner speech and higher psychological functions through speech profiles. J Act Theor Res Ger 5(Special Issue). http://psyjournals.ru/en/tatigkeitstheorie/index.shtml

Werani A (2014) A review of inner speech in cultural-historical tradition. In: Yasnitsky A, van der Veer R, Ferrari M (eds) The Cambridge handbook of cultural-historical psychology. Cambridge University Press, Cambridge, pp 272–294

Werlen I (2002) Sprachliche Relativität. Francke, Tübingen und Basel

Whitty MT, Young G (2017) Cyberpsychology. The study of individuals, society and digital technologies. Wiley, Chichester, West Sussex

Wood MA, Bukowski WM, Lis E (2016) The digital self: how social media serves as a setting that shapes youth's emotional experiences. Adolesc Res Rev 1:163–173

Zhao S (2005) The digital self. Through the looking glass of telecopresent others. Symbolic Interact 28(3):387–405

Zhao S (2006) Humanoid social robots as a medium of communication. New Media Soc 8(3):401–419

Zhao S (2014) Self as an emic object: a re-reading of William James on self. Theor Psychol 24(2):199–216

Anke Werani (Prof Dr.) is a professor for psycholinguistics in the Institute of Phonetics and Speech Processing at the LMU Munich (Germany). Qualified in psycholinguistics, psychology, philosophy and phonetics, she explores the links between experimental and socio-hermeneutical approaches to language as psychological phenomena. Her research interests include constructing cultural-historical psycholinguistics and investigating the relation between speaking and thinking, especially the role of inner speech on the basis of speech profiles. Her investigations focus on such speech profiles taking into account processes in thinking, communication and identity. Her current project focuses on speech style and identity, especially digital speech style and identity.

Part II
Journalism and Social Media

Chapter 8
From Trusted Friend to Trusted Brand? Influencer Marketing Between Trust and Mistrust

Julia Merz

1 Introduction

Dude Perfect, Julien Bam and Bibis Beauty Palace—they all reach millions of young people, are idolized by teenagers and not understood by most adults. But they are more than teen idols: They turn market mechanisms upside down and change media communications profoundly with their ability to combine entertaining, authentic content with trustworthiness. But how does trust in Influencer build up and what is needed to keep it the long term? How can Influencer Marketing be embellished responsibly for young audiences? This article discusses opportunities and risks concerning gain and loss of trust in Content Creators especially on YouTube and asks for solution approaches regarding ethical standards of a whole new industry.

Do you remember? MySpace started the Social Game in 2003. Facebook, YouTube and Twitter followed up in 2004, 2005 and 2006. Especially YouTube has gained an existential importance to media use of Millenials and Postmillenials. A representative study recently showed: More than two thirds (66%) of young Germans between 14 and 24 watch videos on YouTube daily, nearly two thirds of this generation (58%) cannot imagine a life without YouTube anymore (Appinio 2018). This marks a shift between generations: 30–40 year olds still live—medially spoken—in an analog *and* a digital world, although media usage clearly transforms in any generation (Brix 2018). And this marks a general shift in using media and reacting to media driven advertisement: Especially teenagers and increasingly young adults have plenty of options to consume information digitally. What sounds like an opportunity for even more touchpoints on the costumer journey is an actual challenge as young people increasingly avoid classic advertisement and install adblockers exceptionally often (YouGov 2016).

J. Merz (✉)
Hochschule Fresenius, Infanteriestr. 11a, 80797 Munich, Germany
e-mail: julia.merz@hs-fresenius.de

T. Osburg and S. Heinecke (eds.), *Media Trust in a Digital World*,
https://doi.org/10.1007/978-3-030-30774-5_8

New, innovative ways of persuasive communication in social media are needed, to regain influence on young audiences. Influencer Marketing therefore is not a new phenomenon: Almost 60% of European companies already have identified Influencer Marketing as a suitable instrument and more than 40% developed strategies and concrete actions to address Influencers (Zerfass et al. 2016). But is Influencer Marketing only a temporary hype or a long-term matter for companies? It at least seems to be a successful gain for the marketing mix: Every sixth internet user between 14 and 29 years of age already has bought a product advertised by an Influencer (BVWD and Influry 2017). Industries like beauty, fashion, food and gaming mark special possibilities to profit from digital opinion leaders (ibit.). But what exactly determines an Influencer and why do people trust in what Influencers say and promote?

2 Who Is an Influencer? The Pyramid of Influence

Influencers reach millions of people. This is not a new phenomenon as research regarding the social influence of opinion leaders can be traced back to the 1940s (Lazarsfeld et al. 1944). About ten years after the first research was conducted, Katz and Lazarsfeld were able to proof the multi-staged diffusion process of media driven information and the concept of personal influence of opinion leaders in different spheres of life, which is known as the two-step-flow model (1955) and displayed in Fig. 1.

Today, certain people become more influential in advertisement even though they are not necessarily promoted by classical media. YouTube idol LeFloid (aka Florian Mundt) for example reaches several millions of followers on YouTube, which makes him an interesting brand ambassador (Jahnke 2018). Besides cooperating

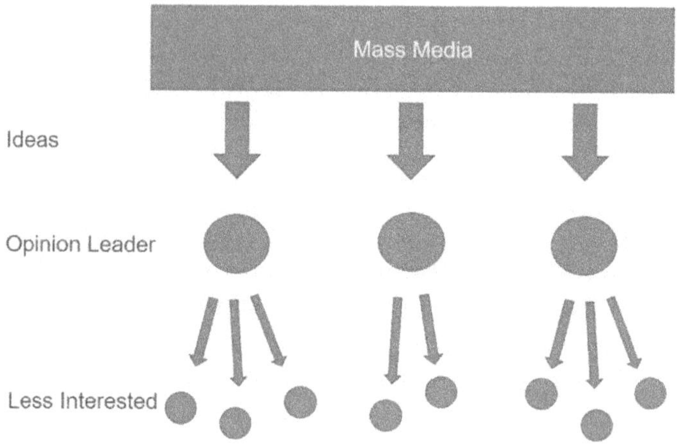

Fig. 1 Two-step-flow model. *Source* Own illustration based on Schenk (2007, p. 352)

with brands, he interviewed the German chancellor Angela Merkel in 2015—over five million people watched his video #netzfragtmerkel, which shows that Influencers can even play a key role in forming political opinions (ibit.).

Influencers can be categorized in different ways such as how they communicate and reach their community. The Pyramid of Influence, illustrated in Fig. 2, describes four levels of Influencers and the respectively attached consumer behavior. It shows, that not only the reach of an Influencer determines the success of an Influencer, but also *who* is reached. Using the example of fashion Influencers, the lowest level of involvement for fashion are persons with a broad range of topics, like for example Taylor Swift, who addresses other mainstream topics to her community besides fashion (Influencer DB 2017). This also marks a mainstream approach to Influencer Marketing: High reachability is possible but also a quite broad and therefore heterogenic target group is reached. In turn, absolute experts in fashion like Italian style icon Anna dello Russo are found on the highest level of the Influence Pyramid, who address a certain clientele of fans: "These are consumers whose life and identity consists of this vertical and who define themselves completely by the topic" (ibit.). This marks the opposite category of opinion leaders: a very homogenous target group is addressed by a specialist on this field.

As has been shown, Influencer are multipliers, that spread products, messages and brands over particular digital channels. As the term Influencer involves digital media, a strong and communicative personality and a certain thematic competence the term can be defined as

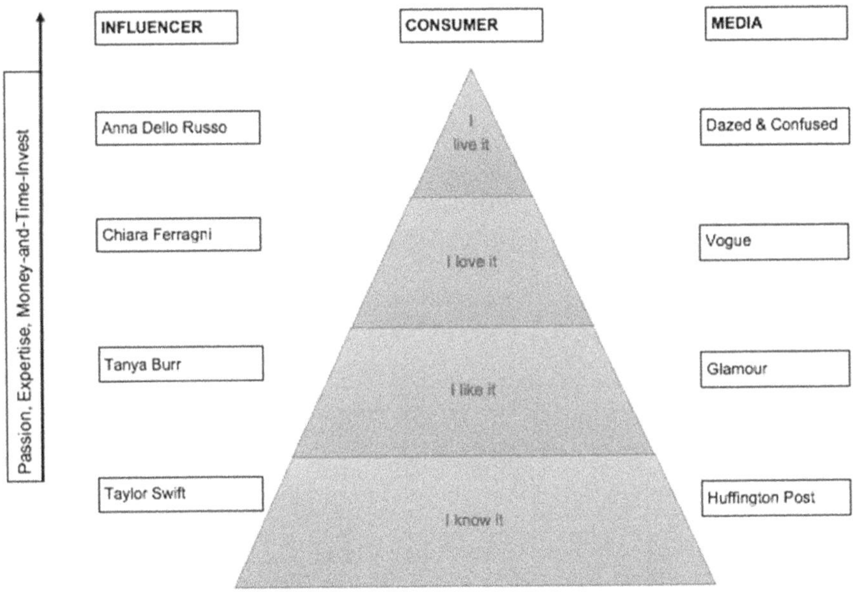

Fig. 2 Pyramid of influence. *Source* Own illustration based on Influencer DB (2017)

> persons, who, on the basis of their digital network, use their strength of personality a specific thematic competence, communicative activity own credibility for certain topics and make them accessible via digital channels for a broad group of people. (Schach 2018, p. 31)

3 Four Steps of Building Trust in Influencers

Digital transformation processes changed something significant in contrast to early research on opinion leaders: Modern opinion leaders—especially in Social Media—do not use single-way but mutual interactions as an opportunity to build parasocial relationships, which lead to new possible ways of building trust in digital media. Parasocial relationships describe seemingly interpersonal connections between humans, evoked by repeated contacts and interactions (Döring 2013). Parasocial opinion leaders (a) inform and reduce complexity, which means, that they prepare content in a comprehensible way (b) give orientation regarding values, conventions and political opinions and (c) arouse interest for new and motivate dealing with so far not pursued topics (Rösler et al. 2014, p. 248).

But what is the difference between personal and parasocial relationships? How are personal and based on that parasocial relationships e.g. Influencer Relations built? "Social penetration processes proceed from superficial to intimate levels of exchange" (Altman and Taylor 1973, p. 39). Altman and Taylor in this regard defined four stages in which personal relationships are built (ibit., p. 136 ff.), which are shown in Fig. 3. In the following, the findings of Altman and Taylor are applied to parasocial relationships with Influencers.

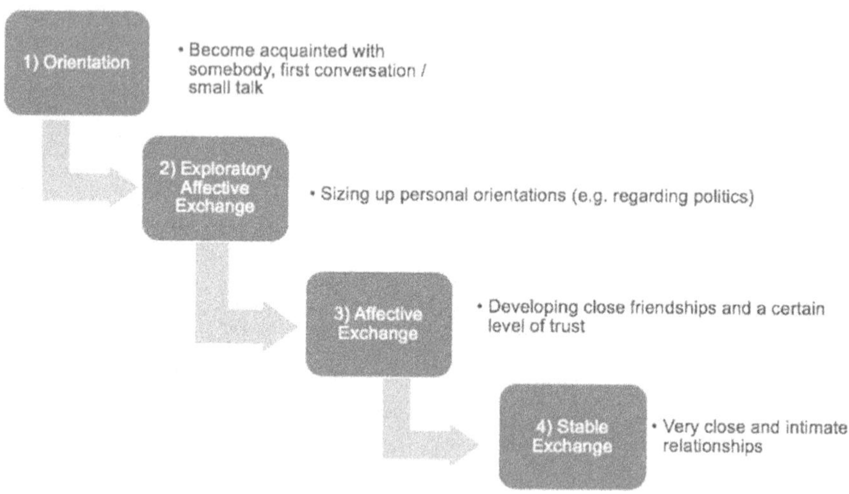

Fig. 3 Stages of the social penetration process. *Source* Own illustration based on Altman and Taylor (1973, p. 136 ff.)

Stage one addresses *orientation* and corresponds to small talk and other rather superficial conversation as part of social conventions and standards. In this stage on a parasocial level, recipients search for interesting Influencers on Social Networks, but in a rather superficial way. Stage two describes the *exploratory affective exchange*, a level of sizing up each other's personal orientation of relevant topics (e.g. politics), which still is predominantly at a periphere level of personality. In this stage, first relevant views by digital opinion leaders are sounded out and recipients try to identify, if a specific Influencer fits their own views and values. This changes at stage three, the *affective exchange,* in which people become close friends and share private and personal conversation topics with each other. Interaction between Influencers and recipients take place in the form of commenting content by sharing own experiences concerning discussed topics. This is a level in a social relationship, that is already distinguished by trust and can only be exceeded by stage four, *a stable exchange*. Stable exchange means the reciprocity of deep feelings, opinions and social norms. Recipients then see digital opinion leaders as complete confidants and feel motivated to entrust their deepest feelings to Influencers of their choice by comment or personal message. In this stage it is even usual that Influencers take issues up, that are on the minds of their recipients and maintain the close bond between them and their community.

These intense levels of personal involvement and trust are a key to new forms of Marketing, as brands are still having trouble to build true brand relationships in other ways (Edelman 2016). But at the same time, consumers acknowledge the willingness, to engage with brands and to shift their engagement to a committed level, which needs dialogue oriented communication (ibit.). Peer to peer communication therefore is the most reliable source of media communications, as consumers network with like-minded people and especially Influencers, who in their eyes are trustworthy and authentic (Nguyen 2018). This means that "a person like yourself (60%) is now just as credible a source of information about a company as is a technical (60%) or academic (60%) expert" (Edelman 2017). Furthermore, trust in business (52%) dropped in 18 countries, which makes external trustworthy opinion leaders necessary to regain reliance in business organisations (ibit.).

Using an Influencer to build the in this case parasocial relationship, moves people like "you and me" in the front of marketing campaigns in order to gain trustworthiness and authentic approaches to brands and products. The advertising impact on Influencer based promotion can be affected by specific characteristics of the Influencer: especially *credibility* and *attractiveness* are the two key indicators for an impact on consumers (Scheunert et al. 2018). As Carl Hovland already described in the context of his Source-Credibility-Models (Hovland et al. 1953), credibility can be divided into the two dimensions *competence* and *trustworthiness* as central character traits in order to gain the widest possible ability to persuade consumers. Both competence and trustworthiness are key character traits that can be attributed to successful influencers.

Parasocial relationships are primarily based on persons, not on brands—Influencers make brands personal. But where trust in persons is built up, the loss of trust is also taken personally. This leads to a possible new level of disappointed trust, as editorial and promotional content is approaching one another, which makes it more difficult to precisely identify advertisement. This hybrid form of advertising often includes product placement, which needs to be marked in order to be identified by consumers (Mallick 2009).

4 From Trust to Mistrust?

Trust is a high value, that constantly needs to be manifested. Recent warnings against well-known influencers made headlines. But the media not only reported on the warned ones themselves. They increasingly criticize the methods of Influencer Marketing as well as the very young target group. To create promotion via Influencer Marketing is, beyond that, especially sensitive, as those forms of advertising (especially product placements) usually address a young audience.

Different authors describe different age groups to classify the development of advertising competence at a young age: Effertz and Teichert (2010) state that advertising competence is gained between eleven and fourteen years, Bogus confirmed in general that younger viewers recognize product placements more infrequent than older viewers (2018). However, in terms of young recipients this must not be seen as a problem, as trust in advice and personal recommendations is one of the leading components of the relationship between an Influencer and his recipient. As young persons grow older, studies show that the older recipients get the more negative they evaluate unmarked product placements by Influencers (ibit.). This shows that there is not only a legal but also a moral commitment of influencers to their recipients, as Influencer Marketing often involves promotional content for children and young adults.

Recent examples show that first judgements by courts or fines by competent regulatory authorities also gain public interest. The legal requirement of labeling follows is based on the so-called separation requirement. This is written e.g. in provisions of the Broadcasting Treaty, the Telemedia Act, various national press laws and the law against unfair ones Competition (UWG) (Meinen and Gerecke 2018). In 2017, the media council of Hamburg's competent regulatory authority decided on a 10.500 Euro fine for YouTube Star "Flying Uwe", who repeatedly integrated unmarked product placement in his YouTube videos. Despite several warnings by the authorities, "Flying Uwe" did not adjust his approach to create promotional content. Lothar Hay, chairman of the media council said: "The internet is not a legal vacuum. Anyone who works professionally on YouTube or similar platforms must comply with the applicable advertising regulations" (Medienanstalt Hamburg/Schleswig Holstein 2017). Other recent judgements are indicating the further legal development of Influencer Marketing, also on Instagram. With its judgment against the Instagram post of Rossmann, the Higher Regional Court Celle has put the young industry under pressure. The drugstore chain has already responded to the precedent and tightened their own labeling rules significantly (Campillo-Lundbeck 2017). The lawsuit between the association of social competition (VSW) and Cathy Hummels has ended with in a defeat for the Influencer, after Hummels dropped a formal objection regarding the verdict (Wille 2018). What looks like serious image losses for the whole industry of Influencer Marketing is indispensable: Tangible judgements are needed to improve promotional content creation regarding legal aspects. The warnings and judgements of legal institutions like the association of social competition (VSW) bring the subject of labeling not only to a legal and therefore public interest, but also to the political agenda. Dorothee Bär, newly appointed German Parliamentary Secretary of State for Transport and Digital Infrastructure, announced a roundtable to discuss possible adjustments concerning the identification of promotional content (Brecht 2018).

Instagram Influencer Vreni Frost, herself being warned for posting corporate links to products that she purchased herself, says: "In my opinion, the topic of advertising labeling has to be discussed publicly. It cannot be right that bloggers are treated differently from magazines and journalists" (Brecht 2018). She and various colleagues especially demand transparency analogical to content publisher in other disciplines to gain transparency not only in an Influencer related context but in a greater connection of all publishers (ibit.).

5 Professionalisation of a Whole New Industry

More and more influencers demand clear, consistent, international rules that make no difference between bloggers and publishers, what editorial content is and what needs to be labeled as advertising. Initiatives like the newly established federal association Influencer Marketing (BVIM) get involved in the public discussion not only on a regional level, but as a nationwide union of marketers, companies and content creators. The board of BVIM emphasizes to depict versatility in a heterogeneous new industry:

> As the representative and voice of the influencer marketing sector in Germany, we are committed to a creative, sustainable and future-oriented discipline. In dialogue with decision-makers in politics, society and the economy, we develop proposals and recommendations for action that promote the professionalization of the industry. As a network, we connect content creators, bloggers, influencers, companies and their friends and prospects with each other. (BVIM 2018)

Several aspects need to be discussed in order to put the industry permanently on professional footing. Transparent labeling of advertising content is certainly the top priority, not least to protect young target groups. A uniform code is needed that goes beyond legal aspects and takes into account ethical and moral aspects. There are several possibilities to implement this: Such as introducing uniform guidelines for the labeling of advertising or product placement or the marking of #noadvertising for strict transparency reasons to gain and regain trust in recommendations of Influencers (cp. Meinen and Gerecke 2018).

However, transparency should also be the maxim in pricing and reporting for companies that want to work with influencers. Technical advantages of platforms come to fruition regarding transparent reports, which can be recorded live via interfaces. All

KPIs such as reach, interactions and their development are thus completely visible and transparent for the customers. This allows companies to evaluate campaigns in depth, providing real value compared to other relatively subtle promotions and to build confidence in working with influencers.

Another component of the professionalization is targeting education and training at universities and educational institutions. In this way, the job profile of the content creator, but also of the marketer and producer of Influencers can be upgraded. Media literacy must also be built up early in this field. Platforms, but also public institutions, education providers and media institutions are required to prepare teaching materials and events for pupils and teachers to sensitize for this topic.

A professionalization of the scene must not only be linked to duties for Influencer, but should also bring along rights for those who create content. It needs to be discussed, if professional Influencers—usually engaged in self-employment—meet the requirements to be included to Social Insurance for Artists equally to e.g. self-employed authors, media artists or journalists. The Artists' Social Insurance protects artistic and journalistic working people in regards to legal health, long-term care and further benefits (Kuenstlersozialkasse 2018).

Influencer Marketing brings together the human search for interaction—not only on a personal base, but also media-related. In a digital world, opinion achieve high reachability because they manage to connect trust in their person with a business model. Brands can benefit enormously from this, however, mere trust in people as a basis for sales decisions at this point should not be too present. New regulations should restore balance—whether a lasting success succeeds here is still questionable.

References

Altman I, Taylor DA (1973) Social penetration: the development of interpersonal relationships. Holt, Rinehart and Winston, New York

Appinio (ed) (2018) Zwei Drittel der jungen Deutschen können nicht mehr auf YouTube verzichten: Repräsentative Befragung der Generation Z zur Videoplattform YouTube. https://www.appinio.com/de/blog/youtube-video-repraesentative-umfrage. Accessed 04 Jul 2018

Brecht K (2018) Influencer Marketing: Das steckt hinter der Abmahnwelle des Verbands Sozialer Wettbewerb. https://www.horizont.net/marketing/nachrichten/influencer-marketing-das-steckt-hinter-der-abmahnwelle-des-verbands-sozialer-wettbewerb-168472. Accessed 05 Aug 2018

Brix R (2018) Wie sieht das Marketing im Influencer-Zeitalter aus? In: Jahnke M (ed) Influencer Marketing. Für Unternehmen und Influencer: Strategien, Plattformen, Instrumente, rechtlicher Rahmen. Mit vielen Beispielen. Springer Gabler, Wiesbaden.

Bundesverband Digitale Wirtschaft (BVDW) e.V., Influry GmbH (eds) (2017) Bedeutung von Influencer Marketing in Deutschland 2017. Eine Studie im Auftrag von BVDW und Influry. https://www.bvdw.org/fileadmin/bvdw/upload/studien/171128_IM-Studie_final-draft-bvdw_low.pdf. Accessed 05 Jul 2018

Bundesverband Influencer Marketing (BVIM) (ed) (2018) Ziele und Aufgaben. https://bvim.info/ziele-und-aufgaben/. Accessed 06 Aug 2018

Campillo-Lundbeck S (2017) Influencer Marketing: So reagiert Rossmann auf das Schleichserbe-Urteil von Celle. https://www.horizont.net/marketing/nachrichten/Influencer-Marketing-So-reagiert-Rossmann-auf-das-Schleichwerbe-Urteil-von-Celle-160673. Accessed 03 Aug 2018

Döring N (2013) Wie Medienpersonen Emotion und Selbstkonzept der Mediennutzer beeinflussen. Empathie, sozialer Vergleich, parasoziale Beziehung und Identifikation. In: Schweiger W, Fahr A (eds) Handbuch Medienwirkungsforschung. Springer, Wiesbaden

Edelman (ed) (2016) Earned Brand 2016: Edelman Earned Brand Markenstudie 2016. http://www.edelmanergo.com/newsroom/studien-insights/earned-brand-2016-von-respekt-zu-commitment. Accessed 24 Jul 2018

Edelman (ed) (2017) 2017 Edelman trust barometer reveals global implosion of trust. https://www.edelman.com/news/2017-edelman-trust-barometer-reveals-global-implosion/. Accessed 24 Jul 2018

Effertz T, Teichert T (2010) Kindermarketing aus neurologischer Sicht: Empfehlungen für ethisch korrekte Gestaltungen des Marketing-Mix. Journal für Betriebswirtschaft 60(3):203–236

Hovland CI, Janis IL, Kelley HH (1953) Communication and persuasion, psychological studies of opinion change. Yale University Press, New Haven

Influencer DB (2017) The pyramid of influence in influencer marketing. https://www.influencerdb.net/blog/pyramid-of-influence-influencer-marketing/. Accessed 16 Jul 2018

Jahnke M (2018) Ist Influencer-Marketing wirklich neu? In: Jahnke M (ed) Influencer Marketing. Für Unternehmen und Influencer: Strategien, Plattformen, Instrumente, rechtlicher Rahmen. Mit vielen Beispielen. Springer Gabler, Wiesbaden

Katz E, Lazarsfeld PF (1955) Personal influence: the part played by people in the flow of mass communications. Free Press, New York

Kuenstlersozialkasse (ed) (2018) Fragebogen zur Prüfung der Versicherungspflicht nach dem Künstlersozialversicherungsgesetz. http://www.kuenstlersozialkasse.de/fileadmin/Dokumente/Mediencenter_Künstler_Publizisten/Allg._Infos_u._Anmeldeunterlagen/Anmeldeunterlagen-Fragebogen-Ausfuellhinweise-Infoschrift-Aktuelle_Werte_in_der_SV.pdf. Accessed 06 Aug 2018

Landesmedienanstalt Hamburg/Schleswig-Holstein (ed) (2017) Medienrat der MA HSH beschließt Geldbuße in Höhe von 10.500 Euro gegen YouTuber "Flying Uwe" wegen fehlender Werbekennzeichnungen. https://www.ma-hsh.de/infothek/pressemitteilung/medienrat-der-ma-hsh-beschliesst-geldbusse-in-hoehe-von-10-500-euro-gegen-youtuber-flying-uwe-wegen-fehlender-werbekennzeichnung.html. Accessed 03 Aug 2018

Lazarsfeld PF, Berelson B, Gaudet H (1944) The people's choice: how the voter makes up his mind in a presidential campaign. Duell, Sloan and Pearce, New York

Mallick R (2009) Product-Placement in den Massenmedien. Rechtstatsachen und Rechtsgrundlagen. Nomos, Baden-Baden

Meinen D, Gerecke M (2018) Kennzeichnung und Transparenz in der Zusammenarbeit mit Influencern. In: Schach A, Lommatzsch T (ed) Influencer Relations. Marketing und PR mit digitalen Meinungsführern. Springer Gabler, Wiesbaden

Nguyen LA (2018) Influencer Relations: Der neue King of Content. Springer, Wiesbaden

Rösler P et al (2014) Parasoziale Meinungsführerschaft. Beeinflussung durch Medienpersonen im Rahmen parasozialer Beziehungen: Theoretische Konzeption und erste empirische Befunde. Publizistik 59:247–267

Schach A (2018) Botschafter, Blogger, Influencer: Eine definitorische Einordnung aus der Perspektive der Public Relations. In: Schach A, Lommatzsch T (ed) Influencer Relations. Marketing und PR mit digitalen Meinungsführern. Springer Gabler, Wiesbaden

Schenk M (2007) Medienwirkungsforschung. Mohr Siebeck, Tübingen

Scheunert L, Schlütz D, Link E, Emde-Lachmund K (2018) Inspiration oder Störung? Ein Experiment zur Wirkung von Influencer-Werbung auf Instagram. In: Schach A, Lommatzsch T (eds) Influencer Relations. Marketing und PR mit digitalen Meinungsführern. Springer Gabler, Wiesbaden

Wille, A (2018) Schleichwerbung: Cathy Hummels akzeptiert Abmahnung. https://www.lead-digital.de/bis-zur-letzten-instanz/. Accessed 05 Aug 2018

YouGov (ed) (2016) Jeder Dritte blendet Online-Werbung aus. https://yougov.de/news/2016/07/05/jeder-dritte-blendet-online-werbung-aus/. Accessed 16 Sep 2019

Zerfass A, Verhoeven P, Moreno A, Tench R, Verčič D (2016) European Communication Monitor 2016. Exploring trends in big data, stakeholder engagement and strategic communication. Results of a survey in 43 Countries. EACD & EUPRERA, Brussels

Julia Merz (née Kirn) is professor for corporate and culture communication at the University of Applied Sciences Hochschule Fresenius in Munich. She studied communication science at the Ludwig-Maximilians-Universität in Munich, as well as violin at the Munich University of Music and Performing Arts (master class diploma). In parallel to her subsequent doctoral studies in musicology she worked as a freelance writer for the radio station BR-Klassik and played in orchestras such as the Munich Radio Orchestra and the Bavarian State Orchestra, and was awarded with the European Culture Award. At the beginning of 2013, Julia became spokesperson and head of public relations for the concert hall Tonhalle Düsseldorf and their Düsseldorf Symphonic Orchestra, broadening their marketing activities by building collaborations with influencers.

Chapter 9
Truth and Trust: Credibility Secures the Sustainability of Journalism

Thomas Mrazek

1 Introduction

There are warnings and signs that the public doesn't trust journalism any longer in abundance. Instead of ennumerating all of these, I will cite journalism professor Stephan Ruß-Mohl here at the beginning: "[We are] in this moment gambling away the credibility of our media and therefore the essence of our democracy – as an unplanned side effect of the digital age, but also as a consequence of a long term power shift between journalism and public relations as well as the pubertal (sic!) hybris of global internet companies" (Ruß-Mohl 2017).

If, in fact, technological inventions, emissarys or profiteers advance this negative trend, I can't say. But I believe that given the circumstances, journalists themselves as the main players in this must act.

The trust in the acceptance of journalism have declined steadily in the past years. This may have diverse reasons, that the relationship between journalism and public is not always at its best was already stated pointedly in 1969 by Glotz and Langenbucher with their fictive character of the "disregarded reader". There is no need to dramatize the current situation, though: "Save journalism" is not yet on the agenda, it would be a headline too brash, too impertinent. Still, the stakes are high for journalists and the principle of journalism itself. The difficulty of their position is startling clear to some journalists and media representatives, and so there are attempts and efforts to improve the relationship between journalism and public. We will discuss some of these.

In an ideal world, one would say that every journalist, every day, tries to do the best for her or his recipients, nonregarding over which channel she or he is publishing.

But business as usual doesn't seem enough to contribute to the social discourse.

T. Mrazek (✉)
Bavarian Association of Journalists, St.-Martin-Str. 64, 81541 Munich, Germany
e-mail: kontakt@thomas-mrazek.de

T. Osburg and S. Heinecke (eds.), *Media Trust in a Digital World*,
https://doi.org/10.1007/978-3-030-30774-5_9

2 "Serious, Reliable, Credible"—Campaign for More Credibility at the Mittelbayerische Zeitung

German media have been increasingly confronted with critical calls and letters as well as hate posting in social networks since the so called "refugee crisis" in autumn 2015. Above all, reporting on refugees did not seem balanced to many media users. The study published in July 2017 by Michael Haller "The 'refugee crisis' in the media" confirmed that: Something goes wrong in journalism (Haller 2017). It is understandably difficult for responsible media makers to publicly admit and react appropriately to these developments within journalism.

The german newspaper landscape is quite diverse, there are about 200 regional daily editions. For those newspapers a good relationship with their readers is vital, because their public is well informed on the topics reported, and often journalists and readers know each other personally.

Here I want to describe the initiative of a Bavarian regional newspaper in response to "the crisis". At the Mittelbayerische Zeitung (MZ) in Regensburg (which has a circulation of about 110.000 copies), they noticed a growing dissatisfaction of their readers. In addition, after the US election in autumn 2016, phenomena such as "fake news" or "alternative truths" unsettled the audience: who could one still believe? If not someone from the newspaper could speak plain text, some readers explicitly demanded a reaction from the journalists. The wake up call was heard. "In this atmosphere, we were forced to stop, to take a critical look at ourselves and to think about whether and which mistakes we had made and what we could do better in the future", reports Claudia Bockholt, Head of Newsroom at MZ.

"We had almost only positive reports about refugees, negative aspects were hidden", she thinks back critically. In the editorial office, they had to realize they were not in an ivory tower. Bockholt, who has been working at MZ for 25 years, and her colleagues designed a credibility initiative for the newspaper in April 2017 with the slogan "Serious, Reliable, Credible". With this campaign, the media house wants to show "good reasons why we deserve your trust", it says on the website. The MZ designed its own logo, celebrities were won as supporters and testimonials for the newspaper; articles that have been particularly successful in the opinion of the editorial team have been awarded the logo as a "quality stamp"—a measure on which meaning you can certainly argue, Bockholt also admits.

It was enormously important, however, to involve the readers, she says: "To show them that some of their criticism has reached us." The critics admonished not only the refugee reporting, but also the environment, taxes and pensions were frequently mentioned topics. The newspaper introduced a new format: "One topic – two opinions". But is that really something new? Not by itself, says Bockholt, but it's new in their newspaper to let two opinions clash so drastically. It sometimes goes to the "pain threshold" to discuss topics such as "age determination of refugees" or the "Fortress Europe". The readers have to be shown that "the mainstream or even the supposed, from the 'top decreed' opinion" in the newspaper does not exist. In a newspaper in which publishing area there is a county where the right-wing populist AfD is the second strongest force, there is still also the fear of serving “the wrong people” with the reporting, explains Bockholt (Mrazek 2018).

In May, the newspaper invited its readers to a conference in the media house. Here they were able to talk openly with the editors about “sensitive topics, mistakes and credibility”. 75 guests took part and “a critical but thoroughly constructive debate emerged”, remembers Bockholt. She herself had been personally attacked in 2015/2016 for her reporting on refugees, an experience she describes as “borderline”. However, the readers’ conference also showed her that opinions expressed in social networks are “not representative of our readership”.

More closeness between reader and editorial staff, that is a central goal for the future of the MZ, and this had been initiated with the campaign. Also, the editor was once more shown that “one must be grateful for every reader who interacts.” The campaign will soon conclude with another readers’ conference. Bockholt is convinced that the intense reflection on their own work and the daily approach towards the readers have strengthened the credibility of their newspaper.

The news magazine Der Spiegel also reported on the actions of the Regensburg newspaper (Hülsen 2018). Whether this newspaper’s approximately one-year initiative has really changed the credibility ratings of the audience is difficult or impossible to prove empirically, and that was probably not the urgent intention of the newspaper makers. The dialogue between the journalists and their readers was intensified, the readers were able to present their criticism of the reporting, and at the same time some gained more insights into journalistic work and action. The journalists themselves gained new insights on their own actions and their readers through this dialogue, summarizes Bockholt, this had been immensely important and also motivating.

However, anyone who deals so transparently with their own content must also accept that external critics rate the newspaper very strictly. One of these critics is the editor of the blog Regensburg Digital, Stefan Aigner. For example, in March 2018, he proves that the Mittelbayerische Zeitung quoted from an article published in his blog—although of course without naming him as the author, another article from the blog was not transparently rewritten for the readers. Aigner often points to craft errors of the newspaper, mentioning the slogan “Serious, Credible, Reliable”. This may seem to the outsider as maybe childish criticism of a competing media entrepreneur, but such public scolding—in a moderate form—I think can be constructive and important, especially in that it refutes the common view within the audience that “hawks will not pick out hawks’ eyes”, according to which journalists rarely criticize each other.

The blogger Stefan Aigner has earned a very good reputation with his investigative journalism as a “lone fighter”. Media like Bayerischer Rundfunk or the Süddeutsche Zeitung are increasingly involving Aigner and his blog in their research. However, the undoubtedly good reputation for the blog founded in 2008 pays not yet off financially, as Aigner concedes in his self-description: “Independent, courageous, underfunded”. Although the blog generates advertising revenue and has a support association with 150–200 supporters, a sustainable financing is not guaranteed, admits Aigner. It is visibly difficult for the lone blogger to adequately market his journalistic work.

Better chances and possibilities to solidify their efforts towards their credibility with their readers have larger media such as Der Spiegel or the Süddeutsche Zeitung. All media categories suffer from a loss of credibility with their public. Some publishing houses openly address these problems and the solutions they try to apply. As an example, several actions shall be briefly presented here. Der Spiegel, founded in 1947, invited in the spring of 2018 for the first time to a "readers' conference" into its house. Editor-in-chief Klaus Brinkbäumer reported on this issue on two pages and did not mince his words: "But it would be wrong if I said: Oh God, these are just some few individuals. There are not a few angry readers. The criticism is allegedly towards all media, but the SPIEGEL, as the strongest brands in any industry stay in the brightest light, is attacked certainly no less than the others." (Brinkbäumer 2018) The editor concluded: "It follows from all that, we will have to review our self-assessment, we will continue to work on language, on thematic and intellectual diversity". On top of that, the dialogue should be consolidated: "We will continue to invite readers to conferences (…). This also belongs to successful communication: At some point, it has to start somewhere. Then it can grow. Hopefully, both of us will then be smarter, senders and receivers."

The Süddeutsche Zeitung is also trying to intensify the dialogue with readers. After an editorial tour in 2017, editors, product- and community-managers of the Munich newspaper met with selected users in 2018 to speak personally about the offer on SZ.de. "We do not just want to be virtually connected to our readers, but also ask them about the beer, what's on their nails," says online editor-in-chief Julia Bönisch in a press release.

While only selected readers were able to take part in the above-mentioned campaign, the Süddeutsche Zeitung offered its readers the opportunity to discuss their wishes and concerns for three weeks with a public pop-up office in a container in the summer of 2018. According to the press release, the program included topics such as "Living in Munich, Security in the City or Insights into Everyday Editorial Work" (SWMH—Südwestdeutsche Medienholding (2018a, b), press release: The Süddeutsche Zeitung moves back into the container).

In addition to the intensive dialogue with the readers, the goal of those—ultimately very expensive—marketing measures is to strenghten image of the newspaper should. "Many journalists still trust today (…) that journalistic quality prevails on its own. This view is honorable (…). In a world in which advertising and PR gain in importance and experts minutely plan entire communication campaigns, media companies and their editors can not help but worry about their appearance in public", writes Russ-Mohl, but at the same time he also admonishes: "On the other hand, it is also important not to overdo in self-expression. Because this too can lead to credibility losses in the audience." (Ruß-Mohl 2016).

The editorial team of Zeit Online opted for a different approach. In December 2016, they launched a transparency blog called "Glashaus" (literally, glass house). The blog should be a place "where we can occasionally carry the internal debates about our work to the outside," said editor-in-chief Jochen Wegner at the blogs start. "In the glass house, we now also collect our mistakes: all cases in which we had to correct ourselves seriously – so far, corrections are made only in the articles themselves."

In addition to listing up errors the blog also tries to explain unclear or controversial editorial practices to the readers. Among the first contributions were topics such as "When do we name the home country of a suspect", "Why we almost never report on crimes" or "How our rubric 'What we know' developes." Readers can comment on these posts or suggest topics that interest them. "With the growing criticism of the work of journalists, we also note the sincere interest in it has increased," says Wegner. With persons who represent views like "Journalists are all controlled by Chancellor Merkel" there is probably no arguing with even with those efforts. But in fact one often hears from conversations with readers, listeners or spectators that they know little about the working methods of editorial staff and journalists and would like to know more about it. Journalism is not a rocket science, and online channels in particular offer good opportunities to get closer to the audience and to make editorial work transparent. As with the aforementioned example of the Mittelbayerische Zeitung, there were also criticisms from journalist colleagues regarding the "Glass House" blog. So Frederic Servatius complained in February 2018 in the media blog Übermedien that the balance of the "Transparency Blog" is altogether sobering. His criticism is based mainly on the small number of posts in this blog: "Only ten contributions have been published after the first in the 'Glasshouse'. Altogether so only eleven contributions in well 14 months". Editor-in-chief Jochen Wegner vowed to improve after the publication of this critical article. In mid-May, the Übermedien editors again checked the "Glass House" blog, within four months, just one other contribution had been published.

3 Transparency and Media Criticism

Transparency has meanwhile become an increasingly important quality criterion of journalism, as emphasizes i.a. Claudia Mast in her basic work "ABC of journalism". The fact that to gain that transparency journalists criticize each other as in the aforementioned case, is in my opinion by no means to be classified as persnicketiness. No, here media criticism is conducted in a constructive manner, which in turn can steadily improve the quality and credibility of journalism. The correction of errors is still not very prominent in German journalism, Ruß-Mohl even speaks explicitly of a "missing corrective culture" and "ignored search for errors" (Ruß-Mohl 2016). The media professor also complains of significant shortcomings in media journalism: this has been "greatly reduced in the recent past, yes almost completely unwound." So not only the audience lacks "a reliable guide in the media jungle, but also journalism and the media industry miss a seismograph – a visible continuous introspection, suffice to professional journalistic standards." While there are some media blogs as the already mentioned Übermedien or the watchblog Bildblog, also relevant media services such as turi2, Meedia, DWDL and others have continuously and sometimes very critical written about their colleagues, but to the general public these offers apparently have not yet the big impact. However, this would not be unimportant, because these offers ultimately work at a high level to reduce the widespread distrust in the media about self-criticism.

Also on a somewhat lost post as far as the resonance of the audience is concerned, are the so-called ombudsmen. Such positions, which occur between the audience and the editorship as a "reader's lawyer", are currently available in about a dozen German media. "But we are still very few", admits Anton Sahlender of the Würzburg Main-Post (Prinzing et al. 2015). Those intermediaries might very well contribute to greater credibility for journalists: "Just that too few people know how journalism works and what tasks they have, vandalize the reputation of journalism", Sahlender claims. The basic teaching of media literacy even in elementary school would certainly have further potential to strengthen the credibility of journalism.

4 Summary

The examples given here demonstrate that journalists and the media engage in a variety of activities designed to strengthen their credibility in the long term, and sometimes even achieve success with it. Of course, one shouldn't exaggerate the danger dwindling credibility raises to journalism. But on the other hand, journalism in an ever-changing ecosystem of media—through sometimes unpredictable actors such as social networks, IT and communications companies but also increasingly volatile users—will not be harmed if its actors, its stakeholders, preserve and expand democratic and professional ethical virtues together with their audience. The efforts for credibility presented here are a good approach for this. Such confidence-building measures are one of the most important investments in the future of journalism. Credibility becomes an essential asset of future journalism.

References

Aigner S (2018) Aus dem Redaktionstagebuch (8/18). https://www.regensburg-digital.de/aus-dem-redaktionstagebuch-8-18/07032018/. Accessed 11 Aug 2018

Brinkbäumer K (2018) Wut und Wahrheit. Der Spiegel, issue 23(2018):72–73

Glotz P, Langenbucher WR (1969) Der missachtete Leser. Zur Kritik der deutschen Presse. Kiepenheuer & Witsch, Köln

Haller M (2017) Otto Brenner Stiftung: Die "Flüchtlingskrise" in den Medien—Tagesaktueller Journalismus zwischen Meinung und Information. https://www.otto-brenner-stiftung.de/wissenschaftsportal/informationsseiten-zu-studien/studien-2017/die-fluechtlingskrise-in-den-medien/ Accessed 11 Aug 2018

Hülsen I (2018) Die Wut der klugen Köpfe. Der Spiegel 9:68–73

Mrazek T (2018) Beziehungsarbeit am Leser. BJVreport, issue 2(2018):26

Prinzing M, Rath M, Schicha C, Stapf I (eds) (2015) Neuvermessung der Medienethik. Bilanz, Themen und Herausforderungen seit 2000. Beltz, Weinheim Basel

Ruß-Mohl S (2016) Journalismus. Das Lehr- und Handbuch. Frankfurter Allgemeine Buch, Frankfurt

Ruß-Mohl S (2017) Die informierte Gesellschaft und ihre Feinde. Warum die Digitalisierung unsere Demokratie gefährdet. Herbert von Halem, Köln

Servatius F (2018) Wer im "Glashaus" bloggt, sollte mit Beiträgen werfen. https://uebermedien.de/25425/wer-im-glashaus-bloggt-sollte-mit-beitraegen-werfen/ Accessed 11 Aug 2018

SWMH—Südwestdeutsche Medienholding (2018a) Die Süddeutsche Zeitung baut persönlichen Kontakt zu Lesern aus. Pressemitteilung. https://www.swmh.de/presse/die-sueddeutsche-zeitung-baut-persoenlichen-kontakt-zu-lesern-aus/ Accessed 11 Aug 2018

SWMH—Südwestdeutsche Medienholding (2018b) Die Süddeutsche Zeitung zieht wieder in den Container. Pressemitteilung. https://www.swmh.de/presse/die-sueddeutsche-zeitung-zieht-wieder-in-den-container/ Accessed 11 Aug 2018

Thomas Mrazek works as a press officer for the Bayerischer Journalisten-Verband (BJV, bavarian journalists union) and as freelancer in media journalism. The BJV is—with around 7.000 members—one of the biggest regional journalist unions in Europe. In addition, Thomas works as a freelance media journalist and lecturer at various universities and further education institutions. In his master's thesis in communication science (Ludwig-Maximilians-University Munich) Thomas dealt with the topic "Internet and Journalism—Impact of a new medium on journalism" (1998). He heads the non-profit portal onlinejournalismus.de with which he won the Grimme Online Award in the media journalism category in 2003, among other awards. For some years now he publishes the bookmark collection Medien-Journalismus.de, which with approximately 50,000 predominantly German-language entries is likely to be one of the largest indexed databases on journalism and media.

Chapter 10
Journalists, Meet Your New Colleague Algorithm: The Impact of Automation on Content Distribution and Content Creation in the Newsroom

Jessica Kunert

1 Introduction

Not only academia, but also daily life has been affected by the arrival of automation and algorithms with many applications.

Algorithms for example determine the type of recommendations shown on e-shopping sites, or the status updates appearing in social media feeds. In general, an algorithm is defined as "a sequence of computational steps that transform the input into output" (Cormen et al. 2009: 5). In the case of e-shopping, the input might be previous browsing behaviour on the respective e-shopping website, such as Amazon.com, or items put on an e-shopping website's wish list (Ricci et al. 2011). The algorithm then transforms this input into personalised recommendations. Algorithms are also used to determine the distribution of content on social media platforms, such as on the Facebook newsfeed, in which information is prioritised according to the popularity of a post, or the contact frequency with a Facebook friend (Facebook Help Center 2019).

The use of algorithms in these domains is criticised. Relevant information might be lost to the user as some types of content are prioritised over others. As a case in point, in early 2018, Facebook has updated its news feed algorithm to prioritise posts from friends and family over posts from news outlets and advertisers. This turn to more user-friendliness, as Facebook put it (Mosseri 2018), has led to criticism from news outlets, which fear that their click rates will decline if they are not featured as much in users' news feeds as before (Vanian 2018).

To analyse the status and uses of algorithms in the newsroom, the nascent field of computational journalism studies "the combination of algorithms, data, and knowledge from the social sciences to supplement the accountability function of journalism" (Hamilton and Turner 2009: 2; see also Cohen et al. 2011). In practice,

J. Kunert (✉)
Universität Hamburg, Allende-Platz 1, 20146 Hamburg, Germany
e-mail: Jessica.Kunert@uni-hamburg.de

T. Osburg and S. Heinecke (eds.), *Media Trust in a Digital World*,
https://doi.org/10.1007/978-3-030-30774-5_10

computational journalism examines how journalism employs data sources that were previously unavailable, also in combination with highly powered data-mining and other kinds of software (Flew et al. 2012: 161). Moreover, Coddington (2014: 335) emphasises the techniques computational journalism offers to journalism, such as the "application of computational methods and thinking to the practices of information gathering, sense-making, and information presentation". While these computational techniques go beyond the use of algorithms and also, for example, include the use of crowd-sourcing for gathering material (see Daniel and Flew 2010), this chapter focuses on the use of algorithms in journalism.

While the definitions given above regard computational tools as a mere means to an end, the field is also concerned with wider changes in journalism through the rising relevance of algorithms. How the arrival of algorithms has changed journalism and continues to do so has been under debate, from optimistic claims that journalists will adapt (van Dalen 2012), to wide-reaching statements that algorithms change the cultural practice of writing news (Anderson 2013). The claim of profound change because of algorithms might even constitute a "technological drama" (Pfaffenberger 1992), as a new social and economic relationship between technology and journalism develops. In sum, to assess the impact of algorithms to journalism, also surrounding factors like politics and culture have to be considered (Anderson 2013; Flew et al. 2012).

This chapter sets out two prominent examples for the use of algorithms in the newsroom. Starting with how algorithms are employed for content distribution, news personalisation is discussed. For content creation through algorithms, the chapter evaluates the state of automated journalism in newsrooms.

2 Algorithms for Content Distribution: News Personalisation

The intention to employ algorithms in news reporting is not new (see Manber et al. 2000), but algorithms have only increasingly been used by news outlets for the past few years (Thurman and Schifferes 2012; Kunert and Thurman 2019). One functionality frequently made use of is news personalisation, which tailors the distribution of content to the individual user. In this section, news personalisation is defined as well as discussed regarding to its challenges and potential.

2.1 Explicit and Implicit News Personalisation

Even though news outlets do not use algorithms to emulate Negroponte's (1995) vision of the "Daily Me", a fully personalised digital newspaper for every single reader, they still employ them to shape the distribution of news according to users' interests. News personalisation features aim to provide readers with content that is relevant to them, hereby for example making use of the reader's help by asking them which kind of content they would like to receive more of. Thus, in terms of explicity influencing how their content is personalised, users may choose topics on the news outlets' websites or in the respective news apps, such as sports, politics, or even fine-grained keywords, so that the outlet prioritises such news over others (Montaner et al. 2003). Other explicit personalisation measures are asking the user to set up a personal profile, or to subscribe to RSS feeds or e-mail newsletters. Apart from explicit personalisation, also implicit personalisation may be used (see Thurman and Schifferes 2012). Implicit measures analyse the user's behaviour by using data analytics tools, so that articles are chosen by an algorithm based on previous articles read or on the location of the user.

A combination of both explicit and implicit personalisation measures has been found to yield the most accurate picture of the user's preferences. As Kamba et al. (1997) and De Pessemier et al. (2015) demonstrate, both types of measures have their advantages: implicit personalisation is not reliant on the user and thus easier to employ, but explicit personalisation measures fill gaps that arise when only relying on the user's previous reading and browsing behaviour.

As both types of personalisation increasingly find their way into news outlets' strategies, algorithms are generally viewed favourably by users. When online news users were asked how they would like to get their news selected for them on social media or on news websites, more people were inclined to let algorithms choose their content than an editor or a journalist (Newman et al. 2016: 12). In the same study, a participant emphasised that "with social media, you are your own editor" (Newman et al. 2016: 12), showing that the help of algorithms for choosing articles is becoming more popular for users.

2.2 *Challenges and Potential of News Personalisation Through Algorithms*

However, while algorithms seem to be a trusted forms of news distribution, also challenges arise. With explicit personalisation measures, users are often found to skip the process of setting up a profile, or not maintaining it, leading to interests being catered to that are long out of date (Gauch et al. 2007). Moreover, users may see the mere act of setting up a profile as a hassle (Groot Kormelink and Costera Meijer 2014) and might withhold information because they are ashamed of stating certain interests (Sela et al. 2015: 2).

Concerns are also voiced whether personalisation catches the user in a "filter bubble" (Pariser 2011; Sunstein 2001). Thus, it is feared that the user is continuously presented with content they agree with, shutting out other views of the world. While the amount of empirical evidence for this is small (see Flaxman et al. 2016; Zuiderveen Borgesius et al. 2016), especially public service providers have been found to be wary of personalisation (Sørensen 2013), fearing a "limited or damaged worldview" (Groot Kormelink and Costera Meijer 2014: 635). Here, it is indicated that the user may only be fully informed if they are exposed to all kinds of news, and that news outlets should make use of their agenda-setting power, a process which personalisation is believed to hinder.

Groot Kormelink and Costera Meijer (2014) present similar findings, as their respondents noted that they were anxious that that they would miss information that let them connect to their family and friends (see also Newman et al. 2016: 12). Thus, the value of news does not only lie in articles that directly address the interests of the reader, but also in an overview of what is going on in the world, emphasising that there is a set of news that people ought to know about. These findings contradict Newman et al.'s (2016) study, which shows that users trusted content selected by algorithms based on their own behaviour more than content selected by friends or editors. This demonstrates that user opinion may be divided on personalisation.

In contrast, the use of algorithms and personalisation of news distribution also has potential advantages. While many public service providers are highly critical of personalisation, some have readily embraced such features (Sørensen 2013). BBC News, for example, focuses on the potential of personalisation to segment content to make it more relevant to underserved groups, such as young people and women (Kunert and Thurman 2019). As content is tailored to underserved audiences, it becomes more relevant to them, which, in turn, fosters brand loyalty (personal communication, 14.12.2016, Head of Product at BBC News). This approach is also viable for international outlets, which may use IP locators to specifically tailor their website to visitors from abroad.

All in all, while personalisation is in principle a tool which helps readers to shape their own news experience, it comes with quite a few challenges. Apart from users feeling hassled to set up a profile or dealing with inaccurate personalisation efforts, data protection is also an issue that has to be discussed. Making transparent which personal data is used and to what end is crucial for both users and news outlets (Helberger 2016). Apart from the use of data, there are also calls for "algorithmic accountability", which means that news outlets should be transparent about the workings of their algorithms, for example how these prioritise and filter information (Diakopoulos 2015).

3 Algorithms for Content Creation: Automated Journalism

While the personalisation technology makes use of content that has already been produced and delivers it according to the taste of the user, algorithms may also generate whole articles from scratch in both textual and video form.

Several terms have been put forward to describe this technology, such as "algorithmic journalism" (Dörr 2016), "robot journalism" (van Dalen 2012), and "automated journalism" (Carlson 2015), which are mostly used interchangeably. In this chapter, "automated journalism" is used to refer to algorithms creating news content, defined as "algorithmic processes that convert data into narrative news texts with limited to no human intervention beyond the initial programming" (Carlson 2015: 417). The workings, the perception of the articles and the challenges to automated journalism are laid out in the following section.

3.1 Workings of Automated Journalism

Automatically generated articles are created through natural language generation software (see Dörr 2016), which produces text based on pre-defined data. All datasets that deliver information in a structured manner may be used for this process, such as data on sports game statistics, crime rates or financial matters. In order to put the data into a coherent text, most software needs a template to be defined after which the articles are then modeled. Using the software Wordsmith[1] as an example, in a first step, placeholders for data points are put into this template, such as for the number of goals or yellow cards in a football game. Second, not unlike a fill-in-the-blank text, different narratives are produced for different data points, such as the different football matches. To do so, the algorithm has to be trained so that it can account for different outcomes, such as gains and losses of different football teams, or, in the case of crime reporting, for falling and rising crime rates, so that the text changes according to the data given. This training has to be complex in order to account for all possible events, for example by employing an if-then-else structure.

In a stylistic manner, there are also ways to make sure that not all produced articles use the same expressions, for example through defining synonyms for the text. When the template is complete, the algorithm automatically accesses the relevant information from the dataset, and generates articles instantly. Once the template is written, it can in principle be used repeatedly. While it is possible to publish these articles as they are, some newsrooms prefer to use automatically created texts as a base for their reporting, meaning that they rewrite parts of the story and add quotes and other facts that are not featured in the dataset (Johannes Sommer, CEO of Retresco, personal communication, 13.07.2018).

For automated video, the process is different from the natural language generation process. In the case of the automated video provider Wibbitz,[2] an already existing text is summarised by the algorithm, and then this summary is used for automatically creating captions for the video. Appropriate pictures and video sequences to illustrate the topic are taken from a database and music and further graphic elements are added. Similar to editing an automatically created article, there are many settings that can be manipulated by a journalist, such as the choice of music or of the pictures, but also elements like the length of the video and each picture frame.

---

[1]Wordsmith is distributed by Automated Insights, see https://automatedinsights.com/wordsmith (last accessed March 8, 2019).

[2]See http://www.wibbitz.com/ (last accessed March 8, 2019).

3.2 Use of Automated Journalism in Newsrooms

Automated journalism is now used in a plethora of journalistic beats (Dörr 2016). One of the first notable applications using automatically produced text was QuakeBot, which has generated articles on earthquakes in the Los Angeles area since 2014, and is still in use (Oremus 2014). Statsheet, another early application, reported on sports games and has since become Automated Insights, a company offering automated journalism for many journalistic beats (Schonfeld 2010; Wauters 2011).

Finance, crime, and sports are especially viable for the use of automated journalism due to their richness in structured data. For example, automated text generation is used by the Associated Press for reports on corporate earnings (Automated Insights 2019), and by the German football portal Reviersport for local sports coverage (Gizinski 2017). Automated news production also plays a big role at the Washington Post, where the software "Heliograf" was programmed in-house to report on a plethora of topics (WashPostPR 2016). In 2016 and 2018, "Heliograf" was used for reporting on the Olympics in Rio and Pyeongchang, [3] for which it automatically posted medal counts and the results of Olympic events on Twitter. Beyond sports, "Heliograf" is also used for other Twitter bots that for example cover local events such as high school sports (Moses 2017).

Going further on the potential of automated news for local or hyperlocal news, events that might not have gotten any or only very limited media attention can be reported on with this technology (Lokot and Diakopoulos 2015). One example are targeted weather reports, or, in the case of sports, reports which may emphasise the achievements of one team over the other, depending on where the article is distributed. Jeremy Gilbert, the Washington Posts's director of strategic initiatives, emphasises the potential of their software "Heliograf" for local reporting: "In the past, it would not have been possible for The Post to staff more than a handful of the most significant games each week. Now, we'll be able to cover any game that we have data for, giving the teams and fans near-instant coverage to read and share" (WashPostPR 2017).

3.3 What Journalists Think About Automated Journalism

Journalists are generally wary of these developments. As Thurman et al. (2017) show, journalists generally found the creative side of the process lacking, and the software not quite intuitive. Apart from these general observations, they were anxious to deal with large volumes of data, and feared that the many data points obscure the actual story behind them. However, they also saw potential in using natural language generation software, as they were inclined to use it to make sense of the data as a starting point, for example by having it generate simple texts out of the data provided.

[3] The Washington Post Medal Bot for the 2018 Olympics can be found here: https://twitter.com/wpolybot (last accessed March 8, 2019). The Twitter account for the 2016 Rio Olympics has since been deleted.

Representatives of Reuters also saw the software as a way to speed up their reporting, as they envisioned that they could send out breaking news to their customers, and then, in a second step, write a full article with further analysis and context. Flew et al. (2012: 160f.) expand on these advantages in a more theoretical sense, saying that the use of computational tools has the potential to free journalists up to do more investigative reporting.

Supporting this view, van Dalen (2012) found in his analysis of opinions on the sports portal Statsheet that journalists did not dismiss the notion of automated journalism, but rather saw it as an opportunity to be freed up from routine work, and as a chance to adapt their skills. In contrast to van Dalen's (2012) findings, Bucher's (2016) interviews with key executives of Scandinavian news organisations revealed that algorithms are regarded as mere assistants to journalists, as her sceptical interviewees emphasised the importance of experience and journalistic instincts which an algorithm cannot emulate. Supporting this assessment of an overall rather negative view on automated journalism, van der Kaa and Krahmer (2014) found that journalists perceived an article that was supposedly written by a human as more trustworthy, even though the article shown to their respondents had actually been written by an algorithm.

It has to be noted that these findings are at least in part contingent on the state of the available technology and the respondents' experience with it. In the case of van Dalen's (2012) study, Statsheet was used only for sports reporting and not for other beats, and opinions might be different on Statsheet's successor Automated Insights and other applications. In the case of Thurman et al.'s (2017) research, journalists were trained on the software and wrote their own templates before being interviewed, which could also have influenced their responses.

3.4 *What the Audience Thinks About Automated Journalism*

The quality of automated news is also assessed by the audience. The dimensions along which evaluations are made are generally the quality, credibility, readability, expertise, and trustworthiness of content (Clerwall 2014; Graefe et al. 2017, 2018; Jung et al. 2017; van der Kaa and Krahmer 2014; Haim and Graefe 2017; Waddell 2018). Up to now, only the perception of text articles has been studied, with automatically created videos not taken into consideration.

Research on the perception of automated content is still in its infancy, with studies using a large array of different respondents, dimensions, and stimulus material. However, overall, it has been found that when presented with human-written articles and those written by an algorithm, the audience is often not able to differentiate between human-written and automatically generated content on a significant level if they do not know which is which (see Clerwall 2014; van der Kaa and Krahmer 2014). However, when respondents knew which article they were asked to evaluate, human-written articles were rated righter for readability than those written by an algorithm, whereas automatically generated news were favoured in terms of credibility (Haim and Graefe 2017).

When not considering the whole article, but the effect of the byline, which identifies the author as either a human or an algorithm, results are inconclusive. Whereas Graefe et al. (2018) found that computer-written articles were rated more favourably in terms of credibility and journalistic expertise, Graefe et al. (2017) results show that computer-written articles were evaluated as less credible the more detailed the description of how the article created was (see also Waddell 2018). The latter finding is a counterpoint to calls for algorithmic accountability (Diakopoulos 2015).

In contrast, Jung et al.'s (2017) study of South Korean news consumers and journalists reveals surprising results. Both journalists and the general audience rated the quality of the shown article as higher if it was attributed to an algorithm and not to a human journalist. These results correlate with media trust in South Korea (see Newman et al. 2017: 20), which is very low, giving insight to why algorithms are trusted more than humans in this case. Moreover, South Korea also exhibits a very high level of acceptance of technology (see Kim 2017), and thus, as it might be, of algorithms.

In sum, while the differences between the studies' results are indeed surprising, they can partly be explained with differing methodological setups. Challenges lie in the selection of the stimulus material, which may be in the country's native language and on a familiar topic (e.g. van der Kaa and Krahmer 2014) or in a language foreign to the respondents (e.g. Clerwall 2014); in the article topic, for an effect might be found (e.g. van der Kaa and Krahmer 2014), whereas in other studies, these effects have been insignificant (e.g. Graefe et al. 2018); or in the sample selected and its size, which varies from small samples of university students (e.g. Clerwall 2014) to larger sizes from commercial national panels (e.g. Haim and Graefe 2017). Apart from methodological differences, the study by Jung et al. (2017) demonstrates that the country's culture also plays a role when algorithmic content is evaluated. In line with the theme of this book, media trust is a decisive variable here. Thus, instead of only taking the shown articles and bylines at face value, intervening variables have to be taken into consideration. Apart from macro level variables such as the media system, also micro level variables can be tested, such as Graefe et al. (2018) did as they asked their respondents for their media usage patterns, their journalistic experience, and also their interest in different topics. While these had no impact in Graefe et al.'s (2018) study conducted with German respondents, they might have in another country.

3.5 Challenges to Automated Journalism

As it is for the personalised distribution of content, the filter bubble is also a concern for automated journalism. While it is possible to cover events no reporter could report on before, may it be due to time constraints or to the small relevance of the event, a heavily localised service may also lead to shutting out national or international news in favour of the local news. The same argument applies to very specific news, such as automatically created weather reports for a single neighbourhood, which may either been seen as either a service to the people in the region, or as a threat to the perception of wider issues. By focusing on many small events, the big picture may get lost (see Thurman et al. 2017). While providing an automated medal count and very short sentences on wins on the Olympics on Twitter may be a helpful tool, it also shuts out other reporting on the Olympics by focusing on only very narrow aspects, whereas how the medal was won might have been the actual story.

Up to now, automatically created articles only include the information that can be found in the data. Events that may have also taken place, such as the surrounding events of a medal win, cannot be taken into consideration. Moreover, if the dataset is prone to errors in the first place, articles will also be faulty if there is no form of quality and data control (Flew et al. 2012: 167). What happens when the data feed delivers incorrect information can be seen in an incident from June 2017 in which the Los Angeles Times Quakebot reported an earthquake that happened in 1925 as current news, which was due to a software error and an erroneously sent e-mail, out of which the Quakebot gathered its data (Lin II 2017). Even though there was no harm, this example vividly shows automated journalism's dependency on correct data.

Another question comes with authorship auf automatically created articles. Who does the reader actually trust when reading such content? It has been discussed whether or not to use a byline identifying the text as computer-written, and, going beyond that, how this can be done so that this byline is comprehensible to readers (see Montal and Reich 2016). This issue addresses the question of the original authorship of an article. It is discussed whether a journalist the author of automatically created text because they wrote the template or because they edited the automatically created video, or whether it is the algorithm that wrote an article or constructed a video. In any case, assessing who the "moral agent" is—meaning, who is responsible for the content—is a question media corporations have to ask, for example by developing ethical guidelines for the usage of automated journalism (Dörr and Hollnbuchner 2017: 414). The discussion of the "moral agent" is not only of normative nature, but also related to business since algorithms may also produce libellous content (Lewis et al. 2019). Following from that and as already mentioned in the case of news personalisation, algorithmic accountability and transparency has been found crucial for automated journalism (Diakopoulos and Koliska 2017), and accountability is demanded for the workings and the limits of the algorithm (Diakopoulos 2015).

4 Conclusions

Algorithms have found their way into news reporting, whether it be for content distribution or content creation. While these technologies are continuously developed further, they are also subject to quite a few challenges and concerns.

For news distribution via personalisation, concerns mainly revolve around questions of whether users miss information due to algorithmic news personalisation, and what the quality, and thus the value of automated journalism is for news reporting. Moreover, what does it mean for media trust if people feel that they do not get the full picture of what is going on in the world? Research has shown that readers and news outlets prefer a middle ground, in which crucial stories are still shown to everyone, but other content that might be especially relevant to the individual user is still prioritised (Kunert and Thurman 2019). This setup has the potential to strengthen trust in the media, as media outlets stay relevant to the user's daily life.

Automated journalism also has the potential to enhance media trust, because as it fills a gap in publishing by being able to report on previously dismissed topics, media coverage may become more relevant to the individual reader. However, as studies show, the devil is in the details, and even naming the phenomenon "robot journalism" may have a negative effect on how the technology is perceived, regardless of the actual content (e.g. Waddell 2018).

The potential of algorithms in journalism depends on their functionalities and, in the end, on the actual utility to newsrooms and users alike, especially since the future of the capabilities of the software is wide open for both the use of algorithms on news websites and apps and automated journalism. For automated journalism, initial criticism was that the automatically generated articles are rather boring (see Thurman et al. 2017), and some people not even considered such content to be journalism (Rebecca Greenfield, quoted in Carlson 2015: 428). Models that address this issue—and further challenges, such as filling data gaps—have already been tested, even if only in prototype stage (Caswell and Dörr 2017). Moreover, automated reporting is getting adopted more and more by newsrooms. Whereas news agencies were previously found to be reluctant to embrace automated journalism (Fanta 2017), the Press Association, which won a grant from Google, developed an automated local news service together with startup Urbs Media, which generates about 8,000 local articles a month for the UK market (Diakopoulos 2019; Gregory 2017).

In the end, are algorithms threatening to replace human journalists? The answer is no, as human journalists rather work with algorithms side by side, almost as colleagues. In terms of using algorithms for news personalisation, algorithms help human journalists to segment content, and deliver relevant information to the users, but do not replace them. In addition, as research shows, there is not a linear development for the employment of personalisation features—while some features were popular a few years ago, such as RSS feeds, they were be replaced by other technological means, or even scrapped completely (Kunert and Thurman 2019; Thurman and Schifferes 2012). Judging from that, news outlets use a try-and-error strategy for making the most of using algorithms, with concepts continuously changing.

A similar assessment has to be applied to automated journalism. As of now, automated journalism is only used by relatively few news outlets. But even if automated journalism becomes more and more popular, the human journalist won't become obsolete because of automatically generated content entering the newsroom. The journalist is still needed to explore leads further, to gather opinions, and to get the story out of the data. The algorithm can support them in their work by extracting an initial narrative out of a large dataset, or free them up to take on special-interest topics. Thus, for now, the aim is for journalists and algorithms to work side by side for a product that has the potential to be of high relevance to the user. While doing so, journalists have the opportunity to re-examine their own skills in light of this new partnership with 'colleague' algorithm (van Dalen 2012; Linden 2016).

References

Anderson CW (2013) Towards a sociology of computational and algorithmic journalism. New Media & Society 15(7):1005–1021

Automated Insights (2019) Associated Press. https://automatedinsights.com/case-studies/associated-press. Accessed 08 Mar 2019

Bucher T (2016) 'Machines don't have instincts': articulating the computational in journalism. New Media & Society

Carlson M (2015) The robotic reporter. Digit J 3(3):416–431

Caswell D, Dörr K (2017) Automated journalism 2.0: event-driven narratives: from simple descriptions to real stories. J Pract 7(15):1–20

Clerwall C (2014) Enter the robot journalist. J Pract 8(5):519–531

Coddington M (2014) Clarifying journalism's quantitative turn: a typology for evaluating data journalism, computational journalism, and computer-assisted reporting. Digit J 3(3):331–348

Cohen S, Hamilton JT, Turner F (2011) Computational journalism. Commun ACM 54(10):66–71

Cormen TH, Leiserson CE, Rivest RL, Stein C (2009) Introduction to algorithms, 3rd edn. The MIT Press, Cambridge Mass

Daniel A, Flew T (2010) The guardian reportage of the UK MP expenses scandal: a case study of computational journalism. Sydney, November 15. http://eprints.qut.edu.au/39358/1/39358.pdf. Accessed 08 Mar 2019

De Pessemier T, Leroux S, Vanhecke K, Martens L (2015) Combining collaborative filtering and search engine into hybrid news recommendations. In: Proceedings of the 3rd international workshop on news recommendation and analytics, in conjunction with the 9th ACM conference on recommender systems, pp 13–18

Diakopoulos N (2015) Algorithmic accountability. Digit J 3(3):398–415

Diakopoulos N, Koliska M (2017) Algorithmic transparency in the news media. Digit J 5(7):809–828

Diakopoulos N (2019) Boosting local news with data journalism and automation. Columbia Journalism Review, 31 Jan 2019. https://www.cjr.org/tow_center/diakopoulos-automation-local.php. Accessed 08 Mar 2019

Dörr KN (2016) Mapping the field of algorithmic journalism. Digit J 4(6):700–722

Dörr KN, Hollnbuchner K (2017) Ethical challenges of algorithmic journalism. Digit J 5(4):404–419

Facebook Help Center (2019) How news feed works. https://www.facebook.com/help/327131014036297. Accessed 08 Mar 2019

Fanta A (2017) Putting Europe's robots on the map: automated journalism in news agencies: Reuters Institute Fellowship Paper. University of Oxford. http://reutersinstitute.politics.ox.ac.uk/our-research/putting-europes-robots-map-automated-journalism-news-agencies. Accessed 08 Mar 2019

Flaxman S, Goel S, Rao JM (2016) Filter bubbles, echo chambers, and online news consumption. Public Opin Q 80(S1):298–320

Flew T, Spurgeon C, Daniel A, Swift A (2012) The promise of computational journalism. J Pract 6(2):157–171

Gauch S, Speretta M, Chandramouli A, Micarelli A (2007) User profiles for personalized information access. In: Brusilovsky P, Kobsa A, Nejdl W (eds) The adaptive web: methods and strategies of web personalization. Springer, Berlin, pp 54–89

Gizinksi M (2017) Die Schreib-Maschine, die aus Daten Fußballberichte macht. Übermedien, 19 Aug 2017. https://uebermedien.de/19028/die-schreib-maschine-die-aus-daten-fussballberichte-macht/. Accessed 08 Mar 2019

Graefe A, Haim M, Diakopoulos N (2017) Should news outlets let their readers know that they are reading automated content? Effects of algorithmic transparency on perceptions of automated news. Poster at ICA 2017, San Diego

Graefe A, Haim M, Haarmann B, Brosius HB (2018) Readers' perception of computer-generated news: credibility, expertise, and readability. Journalism 19(5):595–610

Gregory J (2017) Press Association wins Google grant to run news service written by computers. The Guardian, 06 Jul 2017. https://www.theguardian.com/technology/2017/jul/06/press-association-wins-google-grant-to-run-news-service-written-by-computers. Accessed 08 Mar 2019

Groot Kormelink T, Costera Meijer I (2014) Tailor-made news: meeting the demands of news users on mobile and social media. J Stud 15(5):632–641

Haim M, Graefe A (2017) Automated news: better than expected? Digit J 5(8):1044–1059

Hamilton JT, Turner F (2009) Accountability through algorithm: developing the field of computational journalism. 27 July 2009. https://web.stanford.edu/~fturner/Hamilton%20Turner%20Acc%20by%20Alg%20Final.pdf. Accessed 08 Mar 2019

Helberger N (2016) Policy implications from algorithmic profiling and the changing relationship between newsreaders and the media. Javnost—The Public 23(2):188–203

Jung J, Song H, Kim Y, Im H, Oh S (2017) Intrusion of software robots into journalism: the public's and journalists' perceptions of news written by algorithms and human journalists. Comput Hum Behav 71:291–298

Kamba T, Sakagami H, Koseki Y (1997) Anatagonomy: a personalized newspaper on the World Wide Web. Int J Hum Comput Stud 46(6):789–803

Kim S (2017) South Korea. In: Newman N, Fletcher R, Kalogeropoulos A, Levy D, Nielsen RK (eds) Reuters institute digital news report 2017, pp 126–27

Kunert J, Thurman N (2019) The form of content personalisation at mainstream, transatlantic news outlets: 2010–2016. J Pract 13(7):759–780

Lewis SC, Sanders AK, Carmody C (2019) Libel by algorithm? Automated journalism and the threat of legal liability. J Mass Commun Q 96(1):60–81

Lin II R-G (2017) Revenge of Y2K? A software bug might have caused false alert for big (and very old) earthquake. Los Angeles Times, 22 Jun 2017. https://www.latimes.com/local/lanow/la-me-earthquakesa-earthquake-68-quake-strikes-near-isla-vista-calif-jyhw-htmlstory.html. Accessed 08 Mar 2019

Linden C-G (2016) Decades of automation in the newsroom: why are there still so many jobs in journalism? Digit J 5(2):123–140

Lokot T, Diakopoulos N (2016) News bots: automating news and information dissemination on Twitter. Digit J 4(6):682–699

Manber U, Patel A, Robison J (2000) Experience with personalization on Yahoo! Commun ACM 43(8):35–39

Montal T, Reich Z (2016) I, Robot. You, Journalist. Who is the Author? In: Digit J 5 (7): 829–49

Montaner M, López B, de La Rosa JL (2003) A taxonomy of recommender agents on the internet. Artif Intell Rev 19(4):285–330

Moses L (2017) The Washington Post's robot reporter has published 850 articles in the past year. Digiday UK, 14 Sept 2017. https://digiday.com/media/washington-posts-robot-reporter-published-500-articles-last-year/. Accessed 08 Mar 2019

Mosseri A (2018) News feed FYI: bringing people closer together: 11.01.2018. https://newsroom.fb.com/news/2018/01/news-feed-fyi-bringing-people-closer-together/. Accessed 08 Mar 2019

Negroponte N (1995) Being digital. Knopf, New York

Newman N, Fletcher R, Kalogeropoulos A, Levy DAL, Nielsen RK (eds) (2017) Reuters institute digital news report 2017. https://reutersinstitute.politics.ox.ac.uk/sites/default/files/Digital%20News%20Report%202017%20web_0.pdf?utm_source=digitalnewsreport.org&utm_medium=referral. Accessed 08 Mar 2019

Newman N, Fletcher R, Levy DAL, Nielsen RK (eds) (2016) Reuters institute digital news report 2016. https://reutersinstitute.politics.ox.ac.uk/sites/default/files/research/files/Digital%2520News%2520Report%25202016.pdf. Accessed 08 Mar 2019

Oremus W (2014) The first news report on the L.A. earthquake was written by a robot. Slate, 17 Mar 2014. http://www.slate.com/blogs/future_tense/2014/03/17/quakebot_los_angeles_times_robot_journalist_writes_article_on_la_earthquake.html. Accessed 08 Mar 2019

Pariser E (2011) The filter bubble: what the internet is hiding from you. Viking, London

Pfaffenberger B (1992) Technological dramas. Sci Technol Human Values 17(3):282–312

Ricci F, Rokach L, Shapira B (2011) Introduction to recommender systems handbook. In: Ricci Francesco, Rokach Lior, Shapira Bracha, Kantor Paul B (eds) Recommender systems handbook. Springer, New York, pp 1–35

Schonfeld E (2010) Automated news comes to sports coverage via statsheet. TechCrunch, 12 Nov 2010. https://techcrunch.com/2010/11/12/automated-news-sports-statsheet/. Accessed 08 Mar 2019

Sela M, Lavie T, Inbar O, Oppenheim I, Meyer J (2015) Personalizing news content: an experimental study. J Assoc Inf Sci Technol 66(1):1–12

Sørensen JK (2013) PSB goes personal: the failure of personalised PSB web pages. MedieKultur: J Media Commun Res 29(55):43–71

Sunstein CR (2001) Republic.com. Princeton University Press, Princeton

Thurman N, Dörr K, Kunert J (2017) When reporters get hands-on with robo-writing. Professionals consider automated journalism's capabilities and consequences. Digit J 5(10):1240–1259

Thurman N, Schifferes S (2012) The future of personalisation at news websites: lessons from a longitudinal study. J Stud 13(5–6):775–790

van Dalen A (2012) The algorithms behind the headlines: how machine-written news redefines the core skills of human journalists. J Pract 6(5–6):648–658

van der Kaa H, Krahmer E (2014) Journalist versus news consumer: the perceived credibility of machine written news. In: Proceedings of the computation + journalism conference., New York. https://pure.uvt.nl/portal/files/4314960/c. Accessed 08 Mar 2019

Vanian J (2018) Everything to know about facebook's big news feed change. Fortune, 12 Jan 2018. http://fortune.com/2018/01/12/facebook-news-feed-change/. Accessed 08 Mar 2019

Waddell TF (2018) A robot wrote this? How perceived machine authorship affects news credibility. Digit J 6(2):236–255

WashPostPR (2016) The Washington Post experiments with automated storytelling to help power 2016 Rio Olympics coverage. 05 Aug 2016. https://www.washingtonpost.com/pr/wp/2016/08/05/the-washington-post-experiments-with-automated-storytelling-to-help-power-2016-rio-olympics-coverage/. Accessed 08 Mar 2019

WashPostPR (2017) The Washington Post leverages automated storytelling to cover high school football. 01 Sep 2017. https://www.washingtonpost.com/pr/wp/2017/09/01/the-washington-post-leverages-heliograf-to-cover-high-school-football/?utm_term=.66b4f75f3805. Accessed 08 Mar 2019

Wauters R (2011) StatSheet changes name to automated insights, scores $4 million. TechCrunch, 12 Sep 2011 https://techcrunch.com/2011/09/12/statsheet-changes-name-to-automated-insights-lands-4-million/. Accessed 08 Mar 2019

Zuiderveen Borgesius FJ, Trilling D, Möller J, Bodó B, Vreese CHD, Helberger N (2016) Should we worry about filter bubbles? Internet Policy Rev 5 (1)

Jessica Kunert is a Postdoctoral Research Fellow at the Institute for Journalism and Communication Studies at the University of Hamburg. Prior to her work in Hamburg, she held a position as Postdoctoral Research Fellow at the Department of Communication Studies and Media Research at Ludwig Maximilian University of Munich. She received her doctorate in political science from Leuphana University Lüneburg, and attained her master's degree in Politics and Government in the European Union from the London School of Economics and Political Science. Her research focuses on the impact of algorithms and automation on news production and distribution, such as how algorithms are employed in newsrooms for automatic creation of text and video. She also studies communication patterns and networks in professional and amateur sports. She is on Twitter: @jessicakunert.

Chapter 11
Like a Phoenix from the Pixel: Local TV and Its Special Story of Trust

Uwe Brückner

1 Introduction

Why actually has nobody complained at that time? More than 20 years I worked as a reporter for national TV stations in Germany: Unlawful deliveries of arms during the Iran/Iraq wars, dubious machinations of the intelligence services, scoops about the German concrete mafia. There was never a complaint, a reply or even a fair comment/personal critique on the part of the viewer. Not because these reports have been perfect … No! Simply the viewers were not touched personally. The national scandals took place far from the own doorstep. And the protagonists of the stories were unknown to them.

The situation changed abruptly when I founded a small regional window for Greater Munich in 1993. For the biggest German private TV channel. Daily half an hour of news from the neighborhood. Already in the first broadcasting week I had a visit from two older men. They came undeclared to my office. They were really mad about our new programme. I also were very much surprised, were horrified. What had happened? Well, we reported about a demonstration in the very traditional "Schwanthaler Street" on the day before. Particular emphasis should be put on the letter "h". However, we spelled the street wrong in the Chyrons: "Schwahntaler Street".

Why do I tell this story? It points exemplarily out what the citizens expect from a local medium, from their home medium: Regional competence, common language, personal responsibility and reachability. And of course, local knowledge, right into the saucepans and drinking habits. Somebody who does not know the first name of his neighbor is out. Someone, who can not even spell his place of residence does not belong to it. This was the first lesson which I learnt in the matter of expectations

U. Brückner (✉)
muenchen.tv, Raiffeisenstraße 3, 85293 Reichertshausen, Germany
e-mail: brueckner@tvbayernlive.de

T. Osburg and S. Heinecke (eds.), *Media Trust in a Digital World*,
https://doi.org/10.1007/978-3-030-30774-5_11

and sympathy of local viewers. Till this day I use a formula for it. "Referring to the episode described above, I call it the "H factor".

Viewers are very demanding, when it comes to local media. Actual journalism takes up a close range of the viewers part of their real life. The scenes of our news and stories are well known by them. The Presenters as well. The usage becomes a habit and creates a base for trust. The broadcasts come with firm program places and daily recurring airtime. The viewer takes this reliability and discoverability as a sign of reliability. The certainty that many thousand citizens see at the same time the local programme, which makes the viewer the imaginary participant of a public debate. The invitation to own position regulation resonates always implicitly. An effect which does not appear by using video portals and local media centers. Many voices made their opinion known in surveys about the local TV. The identity of the region becomes visible, the public opinion takes shape on the local television. This involvement makes the channel special.

In addition of all these factors the viewer is ready to give his "Golden Gift" to this source of information: It is Credibility. In addition, one could also say confidence, trustworthiness or truthfulness, likelihood or simply trust. But that should be handled with kind gloves, the gold is only one loan. Trust is the main factor for usage, popularity and effect. And the key to long viewing times, to positive mind set and lasting screen relationship.

2 Which "Golden" Qualities Does a Local Journalist, a Medium Need in the Neighborhood?

Credibility

The users of regional media can understand the subjects mostly by themselves and check the quality of the facts. Quite often they are directly or indirectly affected by these regional subjects of the reporting or are personal touched by it. Not seldom do readers know it "better" and contribute infos and other material by post. Local report concerning legality, professionalism and common identity is expected to be in a high degree. The local media should pronounce this, "what everybody thinks about". The most important effect is "Credibility". In the close range it is more effective than actuality, relevance, professionalism or entertainment (Bentele, Kuebler, Volpers e.a.). Almost all local media are used regularly, if not daily. Local news is a part of the informal basic care. In South Africa the slogan for that is "Local is Lekker", (which means something like "Local is delicious".).

Common Base

Local journalists must know language and traditions. They must be accompanying plausible without writing from "us". Regional competence is also shown in dealing with the common past. A colleague spoke of the "visual memory" of a region. He meant local television. In addition, the work with archive material strengthens the connection to the local transmitter. It is a special sign of the regional media. It's taken for granted that a local medium reports from the broadcasting area (transmitter location). Already a foreign phone number of a local journalist leads to necessity of explanation during the investigations.

And at this point we as regional journalists very often have problems. We hardly take part in the public life, where we live and work. Certainly, it has something to do with the special working hours. Certainly, the professional overkill plays a role, also by phone, appointment calendar, shootings and interview series. At home, that is the Cocoon: "Don't disturb!". And if we sometimes go for a beer in the pub after work, it would be with colleagues. And in the bar it is again only about our job and about our stories. To be a "speech tube of the small people", means knowing what a 1/2 lb of butter costs. And also, as a member of the voluntary fire brigade (in Germany this is an honorary task) one gets to know a lot about his fellow citizens.

A honorable old colleague of mine found his stories on the street: "The story is, where I am." And these were good stories. "Why does it drip there?", he asked himself, for example, when he went for a walk in the shade under the "Donnersberger Bridge". By a closer examination cracks were also found in the pre-stressed concrete. The journalist did further research. The result of his work were six reports and a 4-year-lasting renovation of this Munich bridge. It is till this day the most busy bridge in Europe. Now even in the rain it is dry under it.

Connected Home

Of course the local transmitter will accompany all traditions: Parties and manners, peculiarities and specific traditions. Ancient music and young new culture. The TV channel reflects and offers stage. Often it is even an organizer. And the ones left at home can count on the fact that on the local television many impressions and voices of the event are to be seen. It is, so to speak, the visual "walking stick" and the look outward for many which could not be present. Problem only, when a regional transmitter shoots nothing and reports nothing on the weekend. This can really happen and these transmitters have a hard time benefiting of the love of one's native region or of the location solidarity of the advertising customers. Just politics, VIPs, economy, sport and blue light is not enough. Native country is there where the people come together. The local transmitter illustrates native country. The local viewers mostly given motive: "I want to know what's going on at home".

Distance

Trust in regional media which was formed by the donation of credibility and reliability also needs time. The number of viewers grows with the rooting in the space of communication. A new citizen becomes a subscriber of his local newspaper after having lived there for 5–6 years. Local TV is moving ahead more quickly. But the trust is fast gambled away by a lack of neutrality and objectivity. This is necessary: "Distance in the neighborhood". Of course local reporters are important factors in the struggle about highness of interpretation and in the process of public opinion. They get paid court to and are a welcome guest at the birthday party of the mayor. However, there is a distance. She is invisible, but everyone should notice her.

Emotion

Regional reporting is not always for the victory of the home team. But almost always.

Space

The origin of the term communication was called "co-municare". It describes (after Jacques Derrida) common and protected ("municare", lat.) contact. Together and in a space the citizens discussed their future. There, in a sort of covered court, the stands assembled and formed the permanent meeting and constitutional-giving House of Representatives. The concept "Communication" was used for the first time. The "Tennis Court Oath" gave not only the semantic origin of the concept of "Communication" to us. It also gives unequivocal instructions for the future of the communication culture.

Circularity

Even then in 1789 communication was no one-way street. One discussed within the scope of an equal community: "One man, one vote". Every participant had that right to talk. Every speaker had the obligation to listen. And also the silent participants got very close to who had said something to whom. The information came from a personified source. The reaction was not anonymous, it was rather coram publico. Fake news fell on the author own feet. It is nowadays that local and regional media turn into a "Tennis Courts". They become stages for debates and many-voiced forums for common subjects.

Dialogue

How low it is shows the power of communication of the traditional mass media, for example radio, TV or newspaper, appears in the transmitter—receiver-model: The TV transmitter sends—the viewer is quiet. The radio sounds—the listener hears. The reader reads and remains still dumb. This one-way communication already provided in the early 19th century, has been responsible for the bad call of the first mass media. Which turned the public opinion to a so-called "general opinion". Contradiction, complement or second opinion on a topic was and remains nearly impossible till this day. However, a transmitter in the neighborhood integrates his viewers: In camera surveys and public talks or with the help of a "glass studio" on the marketplace. The station is visible in the town, it implements suggestions in the programme. Someone even makes programme with a citizen: Civil reporters, user generated contents or even viewers as everyday presenter.

We achieved overriding success with "Didi, der Obsthändler". The nature boy was cheerful and suntanned. He sold his fruit in the Munich subway station "University". "Didi" became our everyday weatherman. 13 years long we sent a everyday weather forecasts by Didi, the man on the street. In a short period of time he was voted "most popular inhabitant of Munich". Turnover rose, even though he quite often got the weather forecast wrong. On the local television credibility is not always equivalent to precision. It is about the person and about empathy. The same in the local election campaign: Person before programme. Our viewers loved "Didi" in almost all cases they left their umbrellas at home.

Even today Didi stands at his fruit stand in the sun. And the regional transmitter merged once with a big broadcaster. No room left anymore for Didis weather forecast, which used to be in 2008. The TV ratings fell, even though the new meteorological forecast is much more precise. And our old fruit seller has found a lucrative part-time job: Didi gives big industrial enterprises advise on "authentic marketing".

Cooperative

To communicate with each other means consideration of sensitivities and expectations of the person opposite. Virtue has been internalized by headquarters and Marcom departments. The customer is recently become a partner at eye level. This discovery of the customer or supplier is new, as well as his integration with product development and market activities. On top of that stakeholder expect: inward- and outward-oriented transparency, instead of an isolation. For a long time, the media partnership in regional economic areas functions at eye level and with mutual respect. Of course: Until a few years one was depended on each other. Meanwhile many examples of regional owned media platforms are in the web. Domestic companies or associations send a corporate program on their own responsibility. However, as a service provider, studio renter, program supplier or media trainer the local TV transmitter is likely to be used as such.

Moderative

The participants in local communication stand for their theses. It is clear who says what. An ideal condition in the matter of the search of sources. And a toxic environment for Fake News. Indeed, it is also the opportunities for many different perspectives and aspects. Such controversies are the chance for the media in the neighborhood. They initiate debates, organize public hearings and forums. And they report on that. Recently Harvard professor Daniel Ziblatt stamped a new dimension of decision-making with public matters: "We don't need coalitions of like-minded people, what we need is coalitions of political opponents to save the democratic system" (Levitsky and Ziblatt 2018).

Consensus instead of confrontation: A new job for the national mass media which delights themselves no longer in loud-mouthed outbreaks, instead using the chance to work it out/fathom it out together. Local media has already lived for a long time on this multiperspective imaging performance. The public opinion ("The Folk's Way") is dynamic and multi-layered and is not formed by market criers. Local media positions itself in the service of public wealth if they take over the function of "Public Eye" and the presentation of discourses.

Constructive

A platform organized out of enthusiasts from the public interest delivers in the "running tape" news, arguments, problem consciousness and also results, solution proposals and motivation. For the last 150 years, local media has not been like this. For a while local media took a side, promoted political trends or faded out positions. They joined with the decision makers in politics and business in so called "Medien-Poly-Monopole" (Röper 1984), particulary in Bavaria. Nowadays the regional journalism is solution-oriented, does not celebrate scandals and looks out for the local backgrounds at blue-light-stories. They don't need a press conferences to pick up subjects which formulate out themselves from the local "Public spirit" and whose time has come.

Under Deco

Local media doesn't have to deliver bright luster broadcastings from a news temple with high altar. But it has to be authentic and "with the people": Surveys without a tie, more listening than being smart aleck. And judgement should be handled with a grain of salt. Basically, local reporting has almost a documentary reverence for the events. Often radio analyses and viewer's questionings of the past 20 years show that the expectation of the local transmitter is: "to show people whom one knows" and: "is megaphone of the small people". A very successful transmitter in Greater Boston (many media prices) found the concept "Under Deco". This continues in Europe among other things, the new transmitter chain in Middle England and Wales "MADE.TV".

Economic

When have you last seen an interesting report from a company, from a production hall or a developing lab on TV? You will be hard pressed to remember. Most big transmitters don't report from the world of the work. Instead it is swarming with "stock market news", with scandal reports on "Rivets in Pinstripes", from insolvencies of big companies or with strikes that immobilize the public life. This is the picture of the business from the point of view of the big national TV transmitters. The reality of the viewers in the matter of business looks different: Two thirds of the European population spend more than two third of their life in any job. There you sweat, construct, optimize, plan, market and sell. The subjects are: Research, development, energy relation, supply of raw material, working hour models, location protection, qualification of employees, equal payments, health at work et cetera. These topics are a goldmine for the local transmitters. Finally, the broadcasting area is also an economic location. And, finally, the viewers are also employees and female employees with their families. Attentive accompaniment of the home business does not happen during the show of a balanced press conference. But, for example, in the companies' kindergarten.

And, "yes", it is right that many big enterprises are paying advertiser or being sponsors for infomercials at the regional transmitter. In some places the transmitter is even elementary depending on the money and from the goodwill of the economy in the location. However, bought reporting will be seen: No criticism, no errors in formulation, no comparisons. But praise hymns about boards of directors and product lines. Badly—for the transmitter. Because the viewers reverse their golden present to themselves. "Reaktanz" is the cruel word which uses the social science for it. Former trust becomes mistrust. Reaktanz is a virus which turns a cold, empty coffee cup into a fragrant home medium.

Live

Local TV stations cannot afford a professional "live programme" with big technique. Of course not. In times of high definition, SNG carriage and transponder cost more than the local advertising customer allows. Moreover, 20 tons on three axes flattens even the nicest rose festival. However, the moment of "Live Reporting" linked with the raw reporting has turned from a hygiene factor to a momentum necessary for survival for the locals. Sounds like a dilemma.

Nevertheless, we found a solution which works: It is called "ROL". The Workshop is called "Reporter On Location" and indicates a sort of Road Movie. In Bavaria our up-and-coming young reporters are off the hinges and favor to work with this format.

Extract from the training programme: "The reporter is an identification figure and ceremony master. As One take conceived he leads the spectator through great situations, like fairs, festivals or misfortunes. He gets spontaneous civil statements, shows details and works with requisite. He delivers background and lets the senses speak. An authentic road movie with a co-creative camera which explores curiously the scenery. Unexpectedly, however, not furious!"

These short, approximately 90 s reporter's raids are not being cut. But send directly from the smartphone or the camera via WLAN to the broadcasting direction. Spontaneously told and with eye contacts to the viewer. This very personal presented—quasi live—event, functions as kind of campfire story. And: It functions excellent in the net. Also, the live button on fb, YouTube and somewhere else is used daily by many local stations to fuel the community. No: Our outdoor reporters don't do film yet on end like 9:16.

Two Step

Already in 1944 Paul Lazarsfeld and Elihu Katz formulated the mighty effect of the so-called "Two Step Flow", as shown in Fig. 1: The growing importance of the news as an outcome of opinion leaders, who confirm in the circle of friends of the recipient their opinion. These leaders are known for special expertise concerning the subject.

Lazarsfeld distinguishes interpersonal communication between opinion leader and opinion follower as "less active sections". The main distinguishing features of opinion leaders are above-average media use and interest in political, social subjects. They were normally not in social or economic prestige positions and on top of that they didn't differ substantially sozio-economically from other people influenced by them. Besides, due to the narrow sphere of activity and the commonly high penetration of a broadcasting in the local TV, the Involvement of the recipients increases, as well as the quality of the penetration of this Two Step-communication. The group of the opinion leader don't only come from the circle of acquaintances of the recipients. Experts on science and research, presenters, reporters and newscaster increasingly act as an opinion leader. Circumstances which regional media benefits from. Also in regional viewer's circle countless experts can be found, experts who have own access and special additional information on the varying subjects ready. These are the affected persons of a regional subject: Local resident, employee, civil representative, club members or friends of a protagonist. The intensity of a subsequent

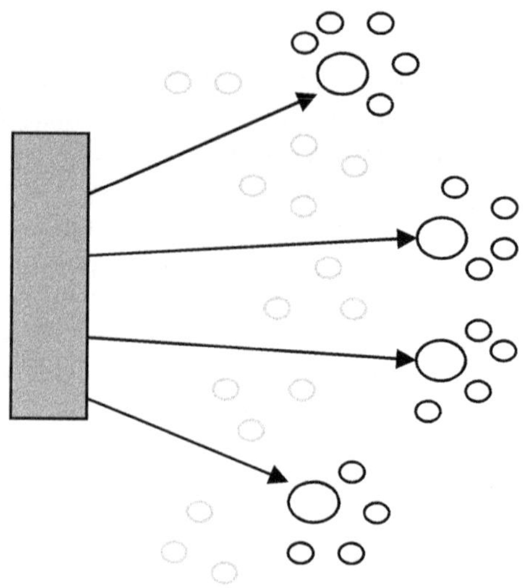

Fig. 1 Two—step—communications model by Lazarsfeld/Katz (own illustration based on Bonfadelli 1999). The transmitters message hits opinion leaders among the audience. And there a second discussion starts

discussion in the personal sphere of a regional viewer is far higher, than a national program offers.

Me Too

Home subjects concern the inhabitants of a broadcasting area equally: "What's going on at home?" regional TV-top news become the daily conversation. "Have you also seen this?" The shares of the market of the local main newscasts, for example, of 16 Bavarian regional TV stations (first radiation of the regional news from 6 p.m.) average shares of the market reach more than 17%. On comparison: The big national Networks must be content in this time slot with one-digit ratings. This aspect in particular is of the utmost importance for the marketers work of the regional media. The especially high credibility of regional media feeds itself not only from accountability, the resemblance, the authenticity and uniqueness, but also quite profane from the reach success.

Paleo

A friendly journalist commented on my idea of founding an institute of "Paleo publicism" with a comparison. This sounds like "cave painting"! Really many active principles of old times can be found in the modern reporting of regional media. Telling the news by stories! Be yourself! Be true! The most important Paleo quality of the media in the neighborhood is the surgical accountability of sources, informants, suppliers or tip givers. Experiences can flow into the journalistic assessment from long-standing company of actors, from background information from spheres, in addition there are the interesting, long-standing statements from the local archive. "Where does this information come from?"—This easy question brings click baiter from the hasty online news business to start stuttering. Published by drag and drop. The mouse as new opinion leader? That doesn't lead all of us to the journalistic match point in the competition for successful communication.

"Where does this information come from?" The viewers of local media and regional videomain entrances know this. Because they themselves have seen who has said it: In the local TV.

3 Outlook

How trustworthy does the future of the local media looks like? Without doubt the primate of the visualisation will become even stronger. B2B or B2C, civil forums, press offices even regional radios and local newspapers make their online appearances more attractive with videos. Besides, the language of pictures or the art of the assembly or even dramaturgy is not of importance. In case of doubt, mobile phones help with clip programme. Especially people, who turn to the general public, want to be new, modern and authentic work: Blurred and pictures out of focus are welcome. Who turns to the general public, does not want to bore: Everything over 60 s is injurious. Analyses or background comments are absolutely fatal.

Young and occasional customers will soon forgo the sound with these video clips. Short phrases are already put as a striking written insertion. Local videos as snack. At least they provide the feeling, that one took part and missed nothing.

And this is the triplet's hook with which the local TV stations pull their viewers ashore: "The worm must be tasty for the fish and not for the angler", said the Austrian inventor of the new private television in Germany, RTL manager Helmut Thoma. He didn't say anything about a hook though.#

- Of course the local transmitters post their best day-topical pics on Instagram. However, the great Tv story will be viewed a short time after it in the local news.
- Of course this functions quite excellent on fb as well. During the day reporters make a very personal and brief comment, by Selfie.
- And our professional media partners and press offices are vaccinated via Twitter.

It needs countless personal contacts and teaser, hints and treats to draw the attention to local TV offer. A few years ago, there was a basic rule, when it came to the shape of TV programmes. It is: Not the thrilling and great moments of a telecast determine the/set the tone for success. It is rather the absence of boredom and the lack of switching off moments. However, in future the following will apply: It needs many thrilling and great moments to move a viewer to turn on of a television.

We are almost at the end of this short story about the credibility of regional media.

If there hasn't been this blizzard: In the winter of 2013, 13 pioneers of the very first German private TV project met again for the first time, after more than 30 years. At that time the pilot project was called "tele newspaper Munich" and in 1980 it daily sent 30 min of topical local programme for Munich. The Munich press club was full of guests who celebrated this "big bang of the private television" in Germany: Analyses and old film contributions, proud reviews and also many disappointed hopes of the doers of that time. The new private television in Germany would not have seized the opportunities to a later point: Controlling instead of creativity and lawyers instead of editorial staff. And almost the evening would have come to an end without a technical leader of the "tele newspaper". He was detained on the highway because of the snow and had given a video course at school. And then he was there and said:

> "Big bang of the television? The big bang was not 30 years ago!" And then he lifted his smartphone upwards: "Do you know what this is?" And it became very quiet in the hall: "Here this is the big bang of the television!" Icy fright seconds in the audience. And then blustering applause. "From now on your viewer sends back!"
>
> The last sentence got lost in the hustle.
>
> But I have noticed it.

References

Bonfadelli H (1999) Medienwirkungsforschung I. Grundlagen und theoretische Perspektiven. UVK, Konstanz

Levitsky S, Ziblatt D (2018) How democracies die. Crown, New York

Röper H (1984) Statt Vielfalt Poly-Monopole. Konzentrationstendenzen auf dem Markt der Neuen Medien. In: Media Perspektiven, 1985/1, pp 24–31

Uwe Brückner studied Documentary and Television Journalism at HFF in Munich. After directing and producing of several documentaries, he joined the very first German private TV, named "Tele-Zeitung München". Afterwards he startet as editor and reporter for RTL in Munich, founded the regional programme "RTL MÜNCHEN live" and the production unit "news and stories" with many hunderts of reports for national and international broadcasters. With "Oberfranken TV", he startetd another regional channel as founding member and Chair of the Advisory Board. He pitched the license of the new "münchen.tv" and founded as program manager the Bavarian window "TV BAYERN live", wich works together with the 16 Bavarian local stations. At least he started with "plenum.tv" a programm for politics and citizen partizipation. He is Deputy Chairman of the oldest German "Int. PresseClub München" and speaker for "TV Journalism" at German Academy of Television/DAFF. Lecturer at universities and academies. In 2018 he got Ph.D. for media studies at Filmuniversity Babelsberg "Konrad Wolf" with dissertation about "Credibility of Business-TV".

Chapter 12
The Filter Bubble in Social Media Communication: How Users Evaluate Personalized Information in the *Facebook* Newsfeed

Katharina Klug and Charlotte Strang

1 Introduction

In the digital age, more and more often an algorithm decides what we get to see (Bozdag 2013; Stalder and Mayer 2009). Hence, online companies such as *Amazon, Facebook*, and *Google* continuously collect data about their users clicking and buying behavior. Systematically analyzing this **(big) data** sheds light into individual user preferences and enables companies offering targeted products and services. The consequences of those analyzing based market research results in target marketing activities (e.g., Aaker et al. 2000) focusing on highly individualized marketing communications (Smith and Cooper-Martin 1997). In this context, a phenomenon called filter bubble is discussed more and more often in practice and science context (Emmer and Strippel 2015). A filter bubble is a highly individual personalized web environment representing information provided by filter algorithms based on individual user preferences (Pariser 2011). In that way, users are mainly confronted with information from within their fields of interest automatically eliminating information from "outside".

Even if an intensive and critical discussion about this practice is visible from a societal perspective (Behrens 2016), companies extend the algorithm and databased approach to get consumers' attention (Emmer and Strippel 2015). In marketing and communication practice, this selective information is used quite often, especially in social media. From the scientific perspective, more and more studies focus on filter bubble effects from various disciplines such as informatics (e.g., Eslami et al. 2015; Gottron and Schwagereit 2016; Bakshy et al. 2015) or communication science

K. Klug (✉)
Fresenius University of Applied Science, Infanteriestr. 11a/E2, 80797 Munich, Germany
e-mail: katharina.klug@mail.de

C. Strang
University of Leipzig, Raimundstraße 7, 01477 Leipzig, Germany
e-mail: charlotte_strang@web.de

T. Osburg and S. Heinecke (eds.), *Media Trust in a Digital World*,
https://doi.org/10.1007/978-3-030-30774-5_12

(e.g., Emmer and Strippel 2015; Ovens 2017). Concerning the enormous spread of social media and its rising importance as information channel, deeper insights into filter bubble effects from the user perspective are necessary. Especially, to what extant a filter bubble is perceived by social media users and how far do personalized information influence the users **trust** in social media as communication channel.

This study investigates the effects of filter bubble examining the social media platform *Facebook*. First, societal and technical determinants of filter bubble effects are discussed and technical options are explained. Second, a systematic literature review leads to a research model covering the whole chain of effects from users' perception to behavioral reactions. Third, an empirical study among 120 *Facebook* users shows how far respondents are aware of the filter bubble. The results reveal users' evaluation of the filter bubble and its consequences.

2 Theoretical Background of Filter Bubble Effect

2.1 Drivers of Filter Bubble Effect

Basically, considering the societal and the technical perspective four drivers are identifiable promoting the filter bubble effect. From the **societal perspective**, an increasing individualization leads to highly differentiated lifestyles and individual communication (Klug 2018; Sontos et al. 2017; Schwertler 2006). Moreover, surfing in the internet effects the consumption behavior (e.g., Pagel 2017; Gadatsch 2016). Especially the growing usage of mobile devices paired with an increasing relevance of social media fosters the (digital) connectivity and makes a continuous data transfer as a matter of course for all participants. From the **technical perspective**, in a digital transformation companies command information to identify user behavior and preferences (Schackmann and Schü 2001; Piller and Zanner 2001). As generating and saving data has become easy, data analytics gets highly relevant (Wirtz 2016). Various existing business models (e.g., *Amazon, Facebook, Google*) base on analyzing (user) data and offering relevant information (e.g., Shahd et al. 2016). This content based personalization is categorized into two types (e.g., Schackmann and Schü 2001; Mertens and Höhl 1999; Fridgen et al. 2000).

Push personalization indicates customized information provided by companies based on user preferences driven from user data (e.g., click and search profiles). *Pull* personalization contains individual information requested by users. Companies use a combination from push and pull personalization to precisely offering additional benefits to consumers (e.g., product recommendations and individual user interfaces). In the long run, objectives of personalized proposals are customer retention and loyalty (e.g., reuse) by making users trust the (algorithm filtered) personalized information (Heinzmann 2002).

Digital personalization assumes an expansive knowledge of the target group. For instance, server log files provide information about a persons' surfed content as well as clicking and buying behavior (Wirtz 2016). Next to **cookies**, companies use content based or collaborative filter methods as a technical tool to personalize content. Cookies automatically save tracking files on the users' computer tracing personal profiles and clicking processes (Wirtz 2016; Bliemel and Theobald 2002). According to Angwin (2010) companies (e.g., *Yahoo*) save up to 60 cookies per user session. Basically, it is not allowed to save personalized data (e.g., login details) via cookies. However, numerous websites require users' agreement. **Content based filtering** forecasts user preferences based on previous behavior (e.g., queries, visited sites). Accordingly, the algorithm identifies products and services from similar user profiles providing relevant recommendations (Schackmann and Schü 2001; Kollmann 2016). While content based filtering drives recommendations by identifying affinities among content, **collaborative filtering** categorizes user profiles based on similarities. Therefore, the algorithm assumes homogeneous user profiles with similar characteristics and heterogeneous user profiles to distinguish user categories. Accordingly, implicit or explicit recommendations are provided such as "*Customers who bought this item, also bought this…*" (Kollmann 2016; Wirtz 2016).

Additional to previous buying behavior algorithms apply sociodemographic and psychographic user characteristics to distinguish categories (Reichwald and Piller 2002). Companies usually combine content bases and collaborative filtering to overcome weaknesses of a single method usage. For instance, collaborative filtering is limited in case little data is available (Kollmann 2016). Using those hybrid filtering means integrating the strength of both filter methods such as *Amazon* does. Stated on the website (Amazon, no year), *Amazon* analyzes products users buy, users already own and users like. Moreover, filters compare user activities with other user profiles to cluster user characteristics. Based on those information *Amazon* provides user interest based recommendations.

2.2 *Relevant Terms and Consequences of Filter Bubble Effect*

In 2011 the internet activist Eli Pariser addressed the phenomenon of filter bubble (also called *echo chamber* or *echo room*) first in his book "The Filter Bubble—What the Internet is Hiding from You" (Pariser 2011). Accordingly, a **filter bubble** is an algorithm-based selection of information in digital environment using behavioral data (e.g., click tracking) of individual users or user clusters to illustrate preferences, to predict behavior and to provide personalized recommendations. Pariser critically refers to the ego-centered effect created by the filter bubble ("You Loop", Pariser 2011, 9) as the algorithm allows only particular information to reach the user. Novel and different information are filtered out by the algorithm in favor of personalize content. On the one hand, personalization might help users to better handle the information overload caused by an overwhelming amount of information. On the other hand, personalization at the same time means a simplification and limitation made by an algorithm.

For instance, *Amazon* provides "convenient" sales opportunities or *Facebook* supplies user "relevant" news in its newsfeed (Weiber and Krämer 2002). Thus, extensively personalized information takes users' chance to explore the wide range of products, arguments and opinions. Consequently, we are more and more prisoned in a filter bubble making it even harder in the long run to leave it for getting objective information. Especially, young or less critical users preferring social media information are caught in a restricted world with a filter algorithm as **gate keeper** (Newman et al. 2017; Mitchell et al. 2016). These users assume information of a peer group (e.g., from friends in social media platforms) as relevant and reliable by implicitly or explicitly trusting in a filter algorithm.

Users publish, share and like posts in social media platforms such as *Facebook*. Accordingly, the *Facebook* content is user-generated. In 2006, *Facebook* established the newsfeed chronologically presenting news from *Facebook* friends to a user. However, a raising number of *Facebook* members (and friends) make the newsfeed too complex and confusing. For this reason, in 2010 *Facebook* introduces an algorithm named **EdgeRank**. The algorithm filters and sorts about 1,500 posts per user representing the posts due to their relevance (Birkbak and Carlsen 2016; Ovens 2017). *Facebook* does not talk about the filter algorithms criteria in public. However, it is visible that factors as intensity of interaction between users (e.g., *Facebook* friends) and up-to-dateness of posts effect the newsfeed presentation (Bucher 2012). Accordingly, EdgeRank prefers new and highly relevant posts and gives news from good (often liked, shared or commented) friends a more visible position. From its beginning, EdgeRank has been adapted continuously. Presumably, the algorithm nowadays respects about 100,000 factors in its filtering process (Budde 2013). This close mashed filtering determines user preferences enabling both, commercial and uncommercial personalized content. By intensively using filtering algorithms *Facebook* knows its users in a remarkable way. Hence, the company occurs as **trustee** or curator, watching and deciding about the content a user receives (Bakshy et al. 2015). While an uncommercial curator (e.g., for expeditions) guards the relevant situation entirely, *Facebooks* content has to be considered as commercial (Pariser 2011) and thus, its roll of trustee might be interpreted in a different way.

2.3 State-of-the-Art of Filter Bubble Research

Even if first papers about filter bubble effects appeared earlier (e.g., Bozdag and Timmermans 2001) Pariser's book (2011) marks a pivotal public perception of the phenomenon. Since that time, scholars—especially from computer science—focus their attention to technical aspects of filter bubble effects (e.g., Eslami et al. 2015;

Hannak et al. 2013; Rader and Gray 2015). Additionally, scholars from communication and media studies consider methodical and communicational consequences of the filter bubble (e.g., Bucher 2017; Emmer and Strippel 2015; Jürgens et al. 2015) and economists shed light into consumers' reaction (e.g., Ovens 2017). Not least, further disciplines such as education studies (e.g., Allyson and Wukovitz 2013) as well as library and information studies (e.g., Davis 2011) come up to the phenomenon of filter bubble. Appendix-Table 4 provides a holistic overview of scientific papers considering the filter bubble. Most of the 25 conceptual and **empirical studies** have been presented at scientific conferences—a common form especially in the discipline of computer science to distribute scientific knowledge. Moreover, most articles have been published in scientific journals (e.g., *Science, Ethics and Information Technology*) between 2013 und 2016 (e.g., Bakshy et al. 2015; Bozdag 2013; Flaxman et al. 2016) intensifying the scientific awareness of the filter bubble. While prior studies are rather conceptual in nature (e.g., Bozdag and Timmermans 2001; Davis 2011; Maccatrozzo 2012), information scientist from the US more and more often use empirical approaches investigating the filter bubble (e.g., Hannak et al. 2013; Liao and Fu 2013; Nagulendra and Vassileva 2014; Nguyen et al. 2014). Scholars bridging the disciplines information systems and communication studies (e.g. Bucher 2017; Bozdag 2013; Bozdag et al. 2014; Bozdag and van den Hoven 2015; Bozdag and Timmermans 2001; Emmer and Strippel 2015; Mahrt 2014) mostly contribute conceptual papers. In economics, there are few papers available presenting a wide range of various empirical research methods (e.g., Flaxman et al. 2016; Matt et al. 2014; Ovens 2017).

Overall, so far there are hardly empirical papers representing the highly relevant topic of filter bubble effect. This might be due to the short period of about one decade the filter bubble is existing yet. Additionally, measuring the filter bubble is quite difficult (Bakshy et al. 2015). The **literature review** identifies in total 15 empirical studies focusing on filter bubble effects (see Fig. 1) starting from the year 2011 when Pariser published his book "*The Filter Bubble—What the Internet is Hiding from You*"). Information scientists contribute most of those studies focusing on technical aspects. Delayed in time, scientists from further disciplines consider the user perspective. A deeper view reveals that five out of the 15 studies are qualitative in nature (Bucher 2017; Emmer and Strippel 2015; Jürgens et al. 2015; Ovens 2017; Rader and Gray 2015), four studies use a qualitative-quantitative mixed method approach (Bozdag et al. 2014; Eslami et al. 2015; Flaxman et al. 2016; Nagulendra and Vassileva 2014) and six studies are quantitative oriented (Bakshy et al. 2015; Gottron and Schwagereit 2016; Hannak et al. 2013; Liao and Fu 2013; Matt et al. 2014; Nguyen et al. 2014).

As filter algorithms may prioritize, classify, screen and connect data, they powerfully control the user experience (Eslami et al. 2015). Filtering concerns continuously updated information like a newsfeed or a search engine environment. This is highly visible in the studies' objects of investigation: 12 studies focus on **social media** platforms (e.g., *Facebook, Twitter*) and search engines (e.g., *Google, Bing*). Existing filter bubble research centers the social media network *Facebook* reflecting its high relevance in the literature review. 70% of all internet user have a *Facebook* account

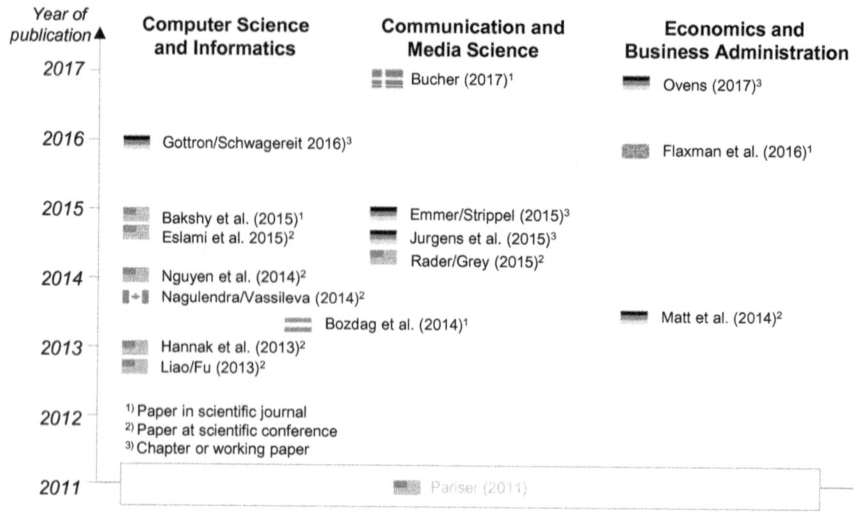

Fig. 1 Empirical studies about filter bubble effects

and 78% of those people use *Facebook* daily (Vor dem Esche and Henning-Thurau 2014). With about two billion users *Facebook* commands the biggest social network worldwide.

Summing up, the literature review reveals filter bubble investigations mostly from a technical perspective (e.g., Bozdag et al. 2014; Gottron and Schwagereit 2016). Additionally, the perception and knowledge about the phenomenon has been focused. However, further reactions considering the chain of effects (e.g., attitudes towards the filter bubble and behavioral issues) from a user perspective has not been issued so far. Existing studies are mainly qualitative in nature (e.g., Bucher 2017; Emmer and Strippel 2015; Ovens 2017; Rader and Gray 2015) using an explorative approach. Furthermore, studies considering the context of *Facebook* usually use data from the US (e.g., Eslami et al. 2015; Rader and Gray 2015). Considering different conditions in European countries (e.g., privacy, trust in data based business models) empirical studies using non-US data are needed (Ovens 2017). Based on quantitative studies focusing on social media communication (e.g., Eslami et al. 2015; Gottron and Schwagereit 2016) statistical relevant effects are available for technical aspects (e.g., content-based vs. collaborative filtering) and for user aspects (e.g., number of *Facebook* friends, duration of *Facebook* membership as well as frequency and intensity of *Facebook* usage) excluding further variables (e.g. attitudes towards the filter bubble). Accordingly, a **research gap** calls for quantitative investigations considering the filter bubble effects in a holistic research model going beyond the users' perception to the points of attitudes and behaviors.

2.4 Model of Filter Bubble Effects in Social Media Communication

For empirically testing the impact of filter bubble perception and user reactions a model and relevant hypotheses (H1–H3) has been developed (see Fig. 2). Next to sociodemographic influences also online media usage and *Facebook* usage are integrated as independent variables. Main objective of this model is to show a holistic view of the filter bubble phenomenon from user perspective considering the whole **chain of effects** on cognitive, affective and behavioral outcomes.

Filter bubble effects are not limited to social media. Users intensively engaged in online media presumably are more experienced in handling information in the internet. Applying various devices (e.g., mobile phone, tablet, laptop) and continuously surfing the internet might foster the awareness of the filter bubble (Eslami et al. 2015; Rader and Gray 2015).

H1a: Users intensively being engages in online media rather perceive the filter bubble than users less intensively using online media.

It can be assumed that users intensively being engages in social media such as *Facebook* realize filter bubble effects. Using the *Facebook* newsfeed extensively and interacting with numerous friends enables the filter algorithm to collect behavioral data additionally fostering the filter bubble effect (Bucher 2017; Eslami et al. 2015; Gottron and Schwagereit 2016).

H1b: Users intensively being engaged in Facebook *rather perceive the filter bubble than users less intensively using* Facebook.

Presumably, sociodemographic characteristics (e.g., age, education) influence the filter bubble perception. Especially, user born from the 1980s (= digital natives) grew up using digital media and content (ARD/ZDF-Onlinestudie 2016). Contrarily to digital immigrants, digital natives experienced a livelong presence of digital technologies intuitively using it (Oh/Reeves 2014). Nevertheless, there is a controversial discussion how basic knowledge about information technology leads to a deep understanding of complex phenomena such as filter bubble (e.g., Caruso and Kvavik 2005). Accordingly, the education level might influence the capability of knowledge transfer.

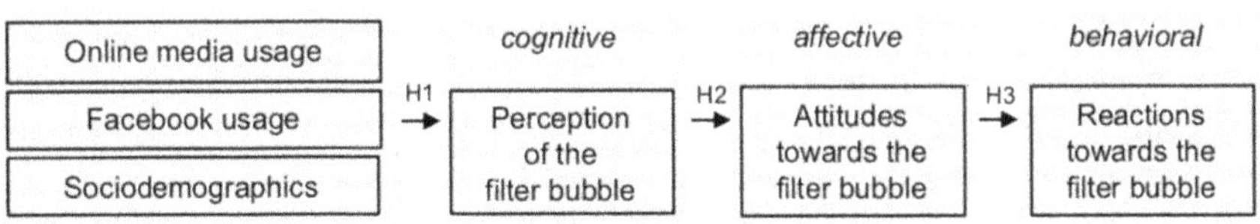

Fig. 2 Model of filter bubble effects

H1c: Sociodemographics have an impact on the perception of the filter bubble.

According to Eslami et al. (2015), the knowledge about filtering influences the users' attitude toward the filtering effects. Bucher (2017) demonstrates various emotional reactions towards the filter bubble. In accordance with the theory of planned behavior (Ajzen 1985) it is supposed that attitude towards the filter bubble influences users' behavior.

H2: Perception has an impact on the users' attitude towards the filter bubble.

H3*: Attitude towards the filter bubble has an impact on the users' behavior.*

3 Empirical Study

3.1 Objectives and Measures

The main objective of the empirical study is to investigate the effects of filter bubble in the *Facebook* newsfeed. Concretely, attitudes and behavioral reactions of *Facebook* users are explored. Concerning the online context, an **online questionnaire** appears appropriate for data collection. The data was collected in May 2017. First, the respondents are briefly informed about voluntarily and anonymity of answers. Second, ensuring relevant data a filter question sorts out non-*Facebook*-users at the beginning. Third, respondents actively using a *Facebook* account answer several questions about personalized information in the *Facebook* newsfeed and about their online media usage, their *Facebook* usage and sociodemographics (see Table 1). Perception of filter bubble, attitude towards the filter bubble and behavioral reactions (adapted from Eslami et al. 2015; Ovens 2017) are measured with a 5-point likert scale ranging from 1 (= "I completely disagree.") to 5 (= "I completely agree."). Additionally, emotional reactions towards data storage have been measured by three negative and three positive emotions.

3.2 Sample

Respondents were randomly recruited from a pool of **consumers** who agreed to take part in market surveys. In total, 125 respondents filled out the online-questionnaire. Five datasets had to be eliminated due to missing values. Hence, 120 questionnaires took part in the analysis. The average age of the respondents is 28.8 years (SD 9.0). The age groups share of respondents (see Table 2) corresponds with the actual shares of *Facebook* users (Hootsuite 2017). As the sample is somewhat skewed to female users (82%), a test of gender differences was performed showing no group differences.

Table 1 Questionnaire

	Item
Perception of fiber bubble	I have got the impression to usually get posts about similar topics in my *Facebook* newsfeed
	I have got the impression to usually get posts from similar friends in my *Facebook* newsfeed
Attitude towards filter bubble	I am bored by my *Facebook* newsfeed because the posts are usually about similar topics
	I am bored by my *Facebook* newsfeed because the posts are usually from the same friends
	It bothers me when *Facebook* decides about what is relevant information for me
Behavioral reactions to-ward filler bubble	I deliberately subscribe for news of selected *Facebook* friends
Emotional reactions towards data storage	(Online) companies collecting data about me makes me… alert/angry/nervous/curious/calm/content
	(Online) companies tracking and profiling my user behavior to provide personalized content makes me… alert/angry/nervous/curious/calm/content
Online media usage	
Internet usage	How long do you use the internet per day on average?
Devices usage	How many devices (e.g. mobile phone, tablet, laptop) do you use to surf the internet?
Social media usage	How many different social media platforms {e.g., *Facebook, Twitter)* do you use daily?
***Facebook* usage**	
Facebook relevance	How long do you use *Facebook* per day?
Facebook networking	How many *Facebook* friends do you have approximately?
Facebook interaction	With how may *Facebook* friends do you interact frequently (e.g., once per week)?
Sociodemographies	
Age	When were you born?
Gender	You are male or female?
Education	Which is your highest education so far?

Table 2 Sample structure

	Absolute	Percental (%)
Age		
18–24 years	6	38
25–34 years	53	44
35–44 years	10	8
45–54 years	9	7
55–64 years	1	1
≥65 years	1	1
Total	120	100
Gender		
Male	22	18
Female	98	82
Education		
School leaving certificate	45	38
First educational degree[a]	55	46
Further educational degree[b]	20	17
Total	120	100

[a]Professional training/bachelor degree
[b]Master degree/state examination

3.3 *Findings*

Description Analysis

Personalized information implies storage of data. Descriptive analysis show that this fact is interpreted twofold. While for 50% (n = 60) negative emotions (e.g., anger) where triggered by tracking online behavior, for 30% (n = 37) positive feeling (e.g., curiosity) occur and 20% stated both, positive and negative emotions simultaneously (see Fig. 3). Most respondents feel alert by filtering methods, which might be an indicator for **lacking trust** in (algorithm based) technologies.

Figure 4 shows the usage of online media in general. Accordingly, moderate internet usage is quite common for 60% of the respondents. About one third of the sample might be categorized as **heavy user** (surfing the internet for longer than four hours per day), while weak user (surfing the internet for less than one hour per day) is an exception. Considering the number of devices 50% use two devices and a remarkable percentage of 43% surfs with three or more devices, first of all the mobile phone. Social media usage shows that most respondents use three or four social media platforms per day (e.g., *Facebook, Instagram, Google+* , *Twitter*). One out of five users abstains from using social media platforms daily.

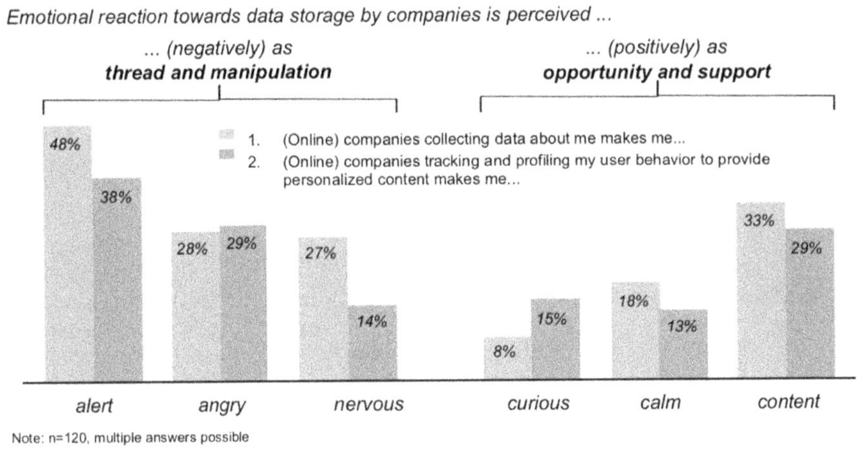

Fig. 3 Emotional reaction towards data storage

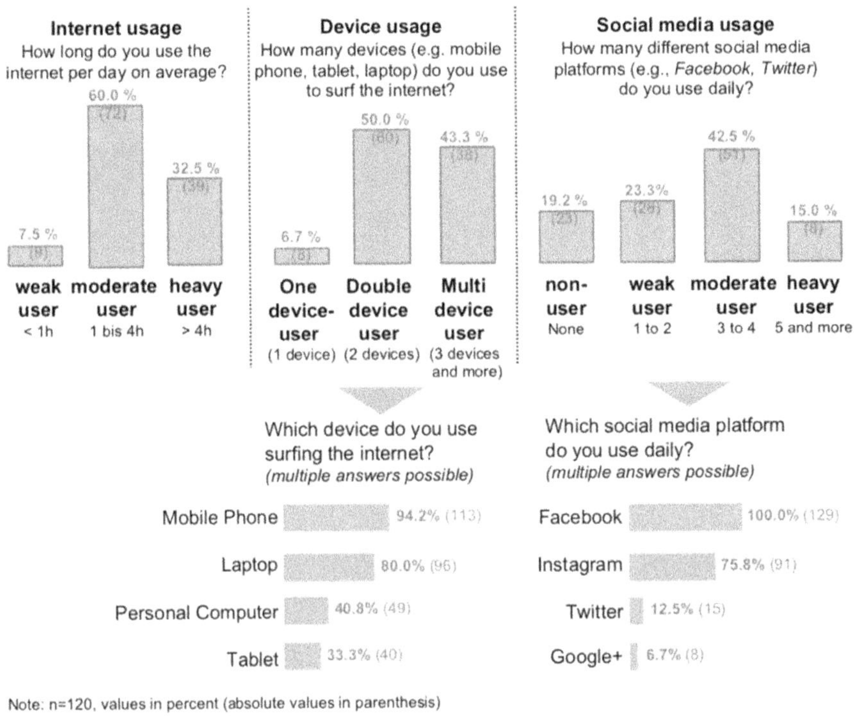

Fig. 4 Online media usage

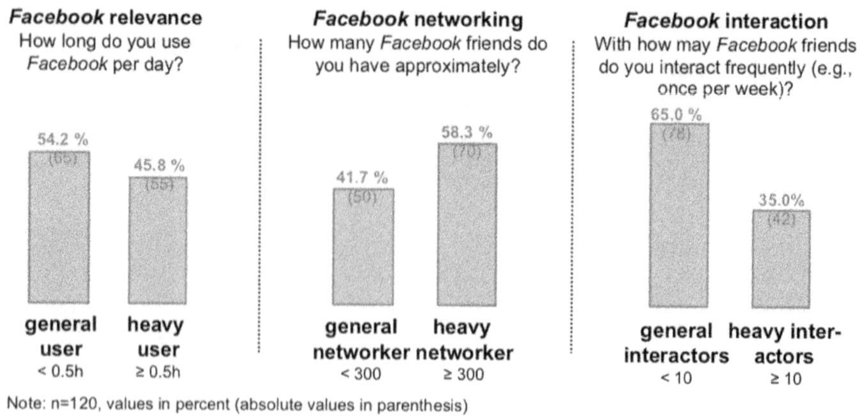

Fig. 5 Facebook usage

Figure 5 indicates the *Facebook* usage. The relevance of *Facebook* divides the respondents in normal user (54.2%) and heavy user (45.8%). Moreover, about 60% of the sample networks quite intensively at the social media platform being connected to 300 friends or even more. Considering the *Facebook* **interaction**, about two-thirds out of the sample frequently are connected to less than ten friends (=general interactors) and one-third of respondents might be classified as heavy interactors frequently interacting with ten or more friends.

Model testing

Factor analytics show acceptable **internal consistency** for all multi item constructs (perception of the filter bubble, attitude towards the filter bubble, reaction towards the filter bubble). All factor loading exceed ≥ 0.7 and cronbach's alpha value is ≥ 0.6. Moreover, the average explained variance (AEV) of each factor is $\geq 50\%$. Hence, the index of the variable is able to be used for statistically testing the assumed filter bubble model.

Multiple **ANOVA analysis** indicate the influence of online media usage, *Facebook* usage and sociodemographic characteristics on the perception of the filter bubble (Hypotheses H1a-c, see Table 3) showing that social media usage statistically significant influences the filter bubble perception ($F(3, 116) = 3.053$, $p = 0.03$). Means show that users handling one or two social media platforms per day notice the filter bubble effect less often than other users ($M_{\text{non-users}} = 3.65$; $M_{\text{weak users}} = 3.39$; $M_{\text{moderate users}} = 3.70$; $M_{\text{heavy users}} = 3,63$). Surprisingly, non-daily users are more aware of the filter bubble effects than weak users. As the internet usage and the device usage does not have an impact on the perception hypothesis H1a has been confirmed partly. Neither *Facebook* relevance nor *Facebook* networking or *Facebook* interaction statistically influences the perception of the filter bubble. Thus, hypothesis H1b has not been confirmed . While different age or gender groups does not have

Table 3 Main effects of online media usage, *Facebook* usage and sociodemographics

	df	F	P	Hypotheses	
Online media usage					
– Internet usage	2	0.758	0.40 NS	Hl_a	Partially confirmed
– Device usage	2	1.222	0.30 NS		
– Social media usage	3	3.053	0.03 **		
***Facebook* usage**					
– *Facebook* relevance	1	1.314	0.25 NS	Hl_b	Not confirmed
– *Facebook* networking	1	1.913	0.17 NS		
– *Facebook* interaction	1	0.085	0.77 NS		
Sozitidemografika					
– Gender	1	1.036	0.31 NS	Hl_c	Partially confirmed
– Age	5	0.317	0.92 NS		
– Education	2	2.334	0.10*		

Note df = degree of freedom, F = F value, p = p value/level of significance
$*p \leq 0.1$; $**p \leq 0.05$; NS not significant

an impact on the filter bubble perception, the education level influences the awareness of the filter bubble very well ($F(2, 117) = 2.334, p = 0.10$). User having a lower educational level are statistically significant less aware of the filtering effects ($M_{\text{school leaving certificate}} = 3.41$; $M_{\text{first educational degree}} = 3.72$; $M_{\text{further educational degree}} = 3.77$). Accordingly, hypothesis H1c has been confirmed partly.

While *Facebook* usage shows no main effect on filter bubble perception, there is a statistically significant **interaction effect** of *Facebook* relevance and *Facebook* interaction ($F(1, 116) = 3.607$, $p = 0.06$). According to Fig. 6, users engaged in

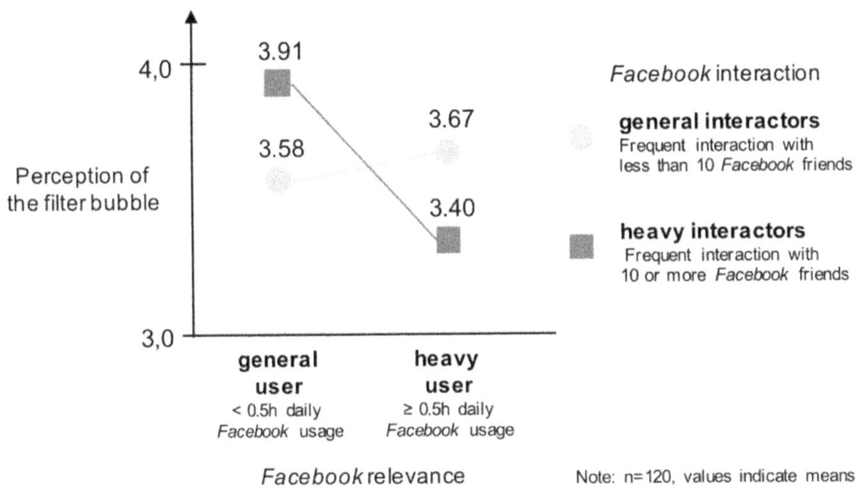

Fig. 6 Interaction effect on the perception of filter bubble

Facebook for less than 30 min per day (=general user) but interacting with many friends during this period of time (=heavy interactors) notice the filter bubble statistically significant stronger ($M = 3.91$) than users spending more time at *Facebook* (=heavy user) but interacting less intensively (=general interactors) ($M = 3.40$).

A linear **regression analysis** proves a statistically significant effect from filter bubble perception on attitude towards the filter bubble ($b = 0.26$, $p = 0.04$). Accordingly, H2 has been confirmed. In contrast, there is no evidence for an impact of attitude towards the filter bubble on behavioral reactions towards the filter bubble ($b = -0{,}03$, $p = 0{,}75$). Thus, H3 has not been confirmed.

4 Summary and Implications

This study contributes to the field of social media communication by shedding light into the filter bubble effect. First, existing literature has been reviewed providing an overview over the **young research topic**. It has been shown that the discipline of computer science and informatics is engaged from a technical perspective and further disciplines such as communication and media science and economics more and more often consider a user-centered approach. Second, the present study empirically proves that the perception of the filter bubble is determined by various factors (e.g., social media usage, education level) in the context of *Facebook* newsfeed. Accordingly, users daily spending time in one or two social networks and users having a lower educational level are less aware of the filtering effect. Moreover, an interaction effect indicates that the individual *Facebook* relevance reveals an effect on the filter bubble perception only when additionally considering the *Facebook* intensity. While timely restricted heavy integrators know about the filter bubble effect, expanded *Facebook* sessions with few interactions hardly lead to appropriate knowledge about the filter bubble. Finally, it has been proved that the perception of the filter bubble significantly effects (negative) attitude towards the filter bubble (e.g., being alert due to **distrust**).

This article introduces an empirical approach investigating the filter bubble phenomenon from. Nevertheless, the study is not free of limitations. For further research, some implications might be deduced. To generalize the findings the adoption of the model to further environments of filter bubble effects (e.g., search engines) might be relevant. Considering the **secrecy of filtering** algorithm, user awareness and perceived knowledge about the phenomenon become important. Thus, speculations about filter methods are part of the chain of effects (Bucher 2017; Rader and Gray

2015). For instance, Eslami et al. (2015) report users believing to manipulate the *Facebook* algorithm by tagging private photographs with brand names to boost the pictures visibility within the *Facebook* community. Those user assumptions might be part of further research models. Moreover, a deeper view into existing behavioral reactions might be highly relevant using multi method approaches. In any case, scholars should be also aware of filter bubble effects influencing their research design itself. For instance, Emmer and Strippel (2015) demonstrate relevant effects on using an online sampling procedure.

Considering users **distrusting** filter algorithms, a technical solution shielding filter bubble effects appears far from reality (Emmer and Strippel 2015). However, beside filter algorithm online behavior is also traced by crawling, indexing and further identification processes. Given the huge amount of information in the world wide web abstaining from those processed would simultaneously limit numerous advantages of the technology (e.g., crawling available information platforms). Filter algorithms are one of the most secret issues of the business, enabling just a few insiders to influence its process.

Appendix

See Table 4.

Table 4 Overview of filter bubble studies

Author(s)	Year	Discipline[a]	Country	Scientific journal	Conference	Working paper	Chapter	Published in	Ranking[b]	Conceptual paper	Empirical paper
Allyson/Wukovitz	2013	Edu	USA	x				*Pennsylvania Libraries*	-	x	
Bakshy et al.	2015	In	USA	x				*Science*	A+		x
Bozdag	2013	Co/In	NL	x				*Ethics and Information Technology*	-	x	
Bozdag/Hoven	2015	Co/In	NL	x				*Ethics and Information Technology*	-	x	
Bozdag/Trimmermanns	2001	Co/In	NL		x			*International Workshop on Values in Design*	-	x	
Bozdag et al.	2014	Co/In	NL	x				*Computers in Human Behavior*	-		x

(continued)

Table 4 (continued)

Author(s)	Year	Discipline[a]	Country	Scientific journal	Conference	Working paper	Chapter	Published in	Ranking[b]	Conceptual paper	Empirical paper
Bucher	2017	Co	DK	x				*Information, Communication & Society*	-		x
Davis	2011	Li	CA		x			*Library Conference*	-	x	
Emmer/Strippel	2015	Ko	DE				x	*Digitale Methoden in der Komm.-wissenschaft*	-		x
Eslami et al.	2015	In	USA		x			*ACM*	*B*		x
Flaxman et al.	2016	Eco	UK/USA	x				*Public Opinion Quarterly*	-		x
Gottron/Schwagereit	2016	In	DE			x		-	-		x
Hannak et al.	2013	In	USA		x			*WWW*	-		x
Holone	2016	In	CRO	x				*Croatian Medical Journal*	-	x	

(continued)

Table 4 (continued)

Author(s)	Year	Discipline[a]	Country	Scientific journal	Conference	Working paper	Chapter	Published in	Ranking[b]	Conceptual paper	Empirical paper
Liao/Fu	2013	In	USA		x			*CHI*	-		x
Jürgens et al.	2015	Co	DE				x	*Digitale Methoden in der Komm.-wissenschaft*	-		x
Maccatrozzo	2012	In	NL		x			*ISWC*	-	x	
Mahrt	2014	Co	DE				x	*Medienkonvergenz und Medienkomplementarität*	-	x	
Matt et al.	2014	Eco	DE		x			*ICIS*	*A*		x
Nagulendra/Vassileva	2014	In	CA		x			*ACM*	*B*		x
Nguyen et al.	2014	In	USA		x			*WWW*	-		x
Ovens	2017	Eco	DE				x	*kommunikation@gesellschaft*	-		x
Rader/Gray	2015	Co	USA		x			*ACM*	*B*		x
Resnick et al.	2013	Eco	USA		x			*CSCW*	*C*	x	

Note Studies in alphabetical order of authors; [a]Co: Communication & media studies; Eco: Economics; Edu: Education studies; In: Informatics & computer science; Li: Library & information studies; [b]VHB-JOURQUAL3

References

Aaker JL, Brumbaugh AM, Grier SA (2000) Nontarget markets and viewer distinctiveness: The impact of target marketing on advertising attitudes. J Consum Psychol 9(3):127–140

Ajzen I (1985) From intentions to actions: a theory of planned behavior. In: Kuhl J, Beckman J (eds) Action-control: from cognition to behaviour. Springer, Berlin Heidelberg New York Tokyo

Allyson V, Wukovitz L (2013) Using the filter bubble to create a teachable moment: a case study utilizing online personalization to engage students in information literacy instruction. Pennsylvania Libraries 1(1):24–34

Amazon (no year): Über Empfehlungen, https://www.amazon.de/gp/help/customer/display.html/ref=hp_left_v4_sib?ie=UTF8&nodeId=201483710, [download 26. Mai 2017]

Angwin J (2010) The web's new gold mine: your secrets, via https://www.wsj.com/articles/SB10001424052748703940904575395073512989404, [download 18 Mai 2017]

ARD-/ZDF-Onlinestudie (2016): Onlinenutzung, via http://www.ard-zdf-onlinestudie.de/index.php?id=560 (28 Sept 2017)

Bakshy E, Messing S, Adamic LA (2015) Exposure to ideologically diverse news and opinion on Facebook. Science 348(6239):1130–1132

Behrens C (2016) Der Mythos von der Filterblase, Süddeutsche Zeitung online, via http://www.sueddeutsche.de/wissen/erkenntnistheorieder-mythos-von-der-filterblase-1.3254772 (download 17 Juli 2017)

Birkbak A, Carlsen HB (2016) The World of Edgerank: Rhetorical Justifications of Facebook's News Feed Algorithm, Computational Culture (5), Special Issue on Rhetoric and Computation, no pages

Bliemel F, Theobald A (2002): Marktforschung im Internet. In: Weiber R (Hrsg.) Handbuch Electronic Business. Informationstechnologien—Electronic Commerce—Geschäftsprozesse, 2. Aufl., Wiesbaden: Gabler, pp 283–304

Bozdag E (2013) Bias in algorithmic filtering and personalization. Ethics Inf Technol 15(3):209–227

Bozdag E, Timmermans JFC (2001) Values in the filter bubble Ethics of Personalization Algorithms in Cloud Computing. In: Proceedings 1st International Workshop on Values in Design—Building Bridges between RE, HCI and Ethics, Lisbon, Portugal, 6 Sept 2011

Bozdag E, Gao Q, Houben GJ, Warnier M (2014) Does Offline Political Segregation Affect the Filter Bubble? An Empirical Analysis of Information Diversity for Dutch and Turkish Twitter Users, Computers in Human Behavior 41:405–415

Bozdag E, van den Hoven J (2015) Breaking the filter bubble: democracy and design. Ethics Inf Technol 17(4):249–265

Bucher T (2012) Want to be in the top? The algorithmic power and the threat of invisibility on facebook. New Media Soc 14(7):1164–1180

Bucher T (2017) The algorithmic imaginary: exploring the ordinary affects of facebook algorithm. Inf Commun Soc 20(1):30–40

Budde L (2013) Der Tod des EdgeRank: Facebook integriert 100.000 neue Rankingfaktoren, via http://t3n.de/news/facebook-edgerank-nachfolger-488185/ (download 28 Mai 2017)

Caruso JB, Kvavik RB (2005) ECAR study of students and information technology, 2005: convenience, connection, control, and learning. EDUCAUSE Center for Applied Research, via https://net.educause.edu/ir/library/pdf/ERS0506/ecm0506.pdf (download 22 Juni 2017)

Davis D (2011) Relevancy redacted: web-scale discovery and the "filter bubble". In: Proceedings of the Charleston Library Conference, pp 556–562

Emmer M, Strippel C (2015) Stichprobenziehung für Online-Inhaltsanalysen: Suchmaschinen und Filter Bubbles. In: Maireder A, Ausserhofer J, Schumann C, Taddicken M (Hrsg.) Digitale Methoden in der Kommunikationswissenschaft, Bd. 2, Berlin: ohne Verlag, pp 274–300

Eslami M, Rickman A, Vaccaro K, Aleyasen A, Vuong A, Karahalios K, Hamilton K, Sandvig C (2015) I always assumed that I wasn't really that close to [her]: Reasoning about Invisible Algorithms in News Feeds. In: Proceedings of the 33rd Annual ACM Conference on Human Factors in Computing Systems, Seoul: ACM, S. pp 153–162

Flaxman S, Goel S, Rao JM (2016) Filter bubble, echo chambers, and online news consumption. Public Opin Q 80:298–320

Fridgen M, Schackmann J, Volkert S (2000) Preference based customer models for electronic banking. In: Hansen HR, Bichler M, Mahrer H (Hrsg.) Proceedings of the 8th european conference on information systems ECIS 2000, Bd. 2, Wien: Wirtschaftsuniversität, pp 819–825

Gadatsch A (2016) Einfluss der Digitalisierung auf die Zukunft der Arbeit. In: Gadatsch A, Krupp A, Wiesehahn A (Hrsg.) Controlling und Leadership—Konzepte, Erfahrungen, Entwicklungen. Springer, Wiesbaden, pp 193–213

Gottron T, Schwagereit F (2016) The impact of the filter bubble—a simulation based framework for measuring personalisation macro effects in online communities. arXiv preprint aXiv:1612.06551. https://pdfs.semanticscholar.org/5308/b193f5097ac491852d65d8391b7af5cbc0a0.pdf (download 10 Apr 2017)

Hannak A, Sapiezynski P, Kakhki AM, Krishnamurthy B, Lazer D, Mislove A, Wilson C (2013) Measuring personalization of web search. In: WWW 2013, proceedings of the 22nd international conference on world wide web, international world wide web conferences steering committee, pp 527–538

Heinzmann P (2002) Internet—Die Kommunikationsplattform des 21. Jahrhunderts. In: Weiber R (Hrsg.) Handbuch Electronic Business. Informationstechnologien—Electronic Commerce—Geschäftsprozesse, 2. Aufl., Wiesbaden, Gabler Verlag, pp 1–40

Holone H (2016) The filter bubble and its effect on online personal health information. Croatian Med J 57(3):298–301

Hootsuite (2017) Digital in 2017, Profile of Facebook-users, slide 49, via https://wearesocial.com/special-reports/digital-in-2017-global—overview (download 28. September 2017)

Jürgens P, Stark B, Magin M (2015) Messung von Personalisierung in computervermittelter Kommunikation. In: Maireder A, Ausser-hofer J, Schumann C, Taddicken M (Hrsg.) Digitale Methoden in der Kommunikationswissenschaft, Bd. 2, Berlin: ohne Verlag, pp 251– 270

Kollmann T (2016) E-Business. Grundlagen elektronischer Geschäftsprozesse in der Digitalen Wirtschaft, 6. Aufl., Wiesbaden, Gabler Verlag

Klug K (2018) Vom Nischentrend zum Lebensstil: Der Einfluss des Lebensgefühls auf das Konsumentenverhalten. Wies- baden, SpringerGabler

Liao QV, Fu WT (2013) Beyond the filter bubble: interactive effects of perceived threat and topic involvement on selective exposure to information. In: CHI 2013 proceedings of the 2013 SIGCHI conference on human factors in computing systems, pp 2359–2368

Maccatrozzo V (2012) Burst the filter bubble: using semantic web to enable serendipity. In: ISWC 2012 proceedings of the semantic web, pp 391–398

Mahrt M (2014) Vom Lagerfeuer zur filter bubble—Konsequenzen der Nutzung digitaler Medien für die Integrationsfunktion von Medien. In: Kleinen-von Königslöw K, Förster K (Hrsg.) Medienkonvergenz und Medienkomplementarität aus Rezeptions- und Wirkungsperspek- tive, nomos pp 127–146

Matt C, Benlian A, Hess T, Weiß C (2014) Escaping from the filter bubble? The effects of novelty and serendipity on users' evaluations of online recommendations. In: ICIS 2014 proceedings of the 35th international conference on information systems, Auckland, New Zealand, pp 1503–1520

Mertens P, Höhl M (1999) Wie lernt der Computer den Menschen kennen?. Bestandsaufnahme und Experimente zur Benutzermodellie- rung in der Wirtschaftsinformatik. In: Scheer AW, Nüttgens M (Hrsg.) Electronic Business Engineering. Proceedings zur 4. Internatio- nale Tagung Wirtschaftsinformatik 1999, Heidelberg: Physica-Verlag Heidelberg, pp 25–49

Mitchell A, Gottfried J, Berthel M, Shearer E (2016) The modern news consumer. News attitudes and practices in the digital era, via http://www.journalism.org/2016/07/07/the-modern-news-consumer/ (download 21 Mai 2017)

Nagulendra S, Vassileva J (2014) Understanding and controlling the filter bubble through interactive visualization: a user study. In: HT 2014 Proceedings of the 25th ACM conference on hypertext and social media, pp 107–115

Newman N, Fletcher R, Kalogeropoulos A, Levy DAL, Nielsen RK (2017) Reuters digital news report 2017, via https://reuter-sinstitute.politics.ox.ac.uk/sites/default/files/Digital%20News%20Report%202017%20web_0.pdf (doawnload 24 Juli 2017)

Nguyen TT, Hui PM, Harper FM, Terveen L, Konstan JA (2014) Exploring the filter bubble: the effect of using recommender systems on content diversity. In: WWW 2014 proceedings of the 23rd international conference on World wide web, pp 677–686

Oh E, Reeves TC (2014) Generational differences and the integration of technology in learning, instruction, and performance. In: Spector JM, Merrill MD, Elen J, Bishop ML (eds) Handbook of research on educational communications and technology. Springer Science + Business Media, New York, pp 819–828

Ovens C (2017) Filterblasen—Ausgangspunkte einer neuen fremdverschuldeten Unmündigkeit? In: Schmidt JH, Kinder-Kurlanda K, Steg-bauer C, Zurawski N (Hrsg.) Algorithmen, Kommunikation und Gesellschaft, Sonderausgabe von kommunikation@gesellschaft, 18., Beitrag 7

Pagel P (2017) Die Digitalisierung der Welt. Wirtschaftsinformatik und Management 9(1):3

Pariser E (2011) The filter bubble. What the internet is hiding from you. The Penguin Press, New York

Piller F, Zanner S (2001) Mass Customization und Personalisierung im Electronic Business. Das Wirtschaftsstudium (WISU) 30(1):88–96

Rader E, Gray R (2015) Understanding User Beliefs about Algorithmic Curation in the Facebook News Feed. In: Proceedings of the 33rd annual ACM conference on human factors in computing systems, Seoul: ACM, pp 173–182

Reichwald R, Piller FT (2002) Mass Customization-Konzepte im Electronic Business. In: Rolf Weiber (Hrsg.) Handbuch Electronic Business. Informationstechnologien—Electronic Commerce –Geschäftsprozesse, 2. Aufl., Wiesbaden: Gabler, pp 469–494

Resnick P, Garrett RK, Kriplean T, Munson SA, Stroud NJ (2013) Bursting your (filter) bubble: strategies for promoting diverse exposure. In: CSCW 2013 Proceedings of the 2013 conference on computer supported cooperative work companion, pp 95–100

Schackmann J, Schü J (2001) Personalisierte Portale. Wirtschaftsinformatik 43(6):623–625

Schwertler W (2006) Strategisches Affinity-Group-Management—Wettbewerbsvorteile durch ein neues Zielgruppenverständnis. Springer, Wiesbaden

Shahd M, Grimm F, Weber M (2016) Jedes dritte Unternehmen nutzt Big Data, via https://www.bitkom.org/Presse/Presseinformation/Jedes-dritte-Unternehmen-nutzt-Big-Data.html (download 20. Juni 2017)

Sontos HC, Varnum MEW, Grossmann I (2017) Global increases in individualism. Psychol Sci Online First. https://doi.org/10.1177/0956797617700622

Smith NC, Cooper-Martin E (1997) Ethics and target marketing: the role of product harm and consumer vulnerability. J Market 61(3):1–20

Stalder F, Mayer C (2009) Der zweite Index. Suchmaschinen, Personalisierung und Überwachung. In: Becker K, Stalder F (eds) Deep Search. Studienverlag, Politik des Suchens jenseits von Google, Innsbruck, pp 112–131

Vor dem Esche J, Henning-Thurau T (2014) German digitalization consumer report, digitalization think lab. Marketing Center Münster, Roland Berger Strategy Consultants

Weiber R, Krämer T (2002) Paradoxien des Electronic Business und empirische Befunde. In: Weiber R (Hrsg.) Handbuch Electronic Business. Informationstechnologien—Electronic Commerce—Geschäftsprozesse, 2. Aufl., Wiesbaden, Gabler Verlag, pp 181–210

Wirtz BW (2016) Electronic business, 5th edn. Gabler Verlag, Wiesbaden

Katharina Klug is an expert in innovative marketing. As professor of marketing at the Fresenius-University of Applied Science (department of design, AMD) her research focus is on alternative methodologies of marketing communication such as guerilla marketing and messenger marketing. Her further research interests are sustainable consumption and consumer lifestyles. Katharina Klug received a diploma in business administration from the Technical University of Dresden (Germany) and a Ph.D. from the Christian-Albrechts University of Kiel (Germany). Katharina Klug has working experience in strategic marketing and marketing research in various branches of industry.

Charlotte Strang received a Bachelor of Arts in Fashion and Design Management from AMD (Akademie Mode and Design, Munich) in 2017. In her bachelor thesis, she analyzed consumers' perception of filter bubble effects in social media and search engines. Charlotte Strang is currently enrolled in a degree in Computer Science (B.Sc.) in Leipzig, Germany.

Chapter 13
Cyberbullying Endangers Our Society

Uwe Leest

1 Introduction

The Internet made a major change for our society in communication and exchange of information. Many children and young adults spend more and more time online and in social networks. Smartphones give the opportunity to be in the internet and communicate online 24 h a day. Technological progress opens up many new possibilities to communicate and establish contacts. These changes have created many positive aspects but also problems. In the virtual world many personal information are shared and trust is built up to strangers. Both, trust and shared information can be misused which can lead to cyberbullying, cyberstalking, sexual harassment etc. Therefore a responsible handling of media is inevitable for children and young adults to protect them from possible danger and prevent them from becoming wrongdoer themselves.

2 Changes of Communication and Trust Through Digitalization

The invention of the World Wide Web brought a revolution of information exchange to our society in extent comparable with the invention of the letterpress, electricity or automobile. In the beginning of the 90s only a few people suspected how this upcoming virtual world would change our real one.

Digitalization, especially from the beginning of the 21st century opens up new horizons and opportunities but also dangers and risks. New media and technologies have a major influence on our way of life and communication.

U. Leest (✉)
Bündnis gegen Cybermobbing e.V., Leopoldstraße 1, 76133 Karlsruhe, Germany
e-mail: u.leest@buendnis-gegen-cybermobbing.de

T. Osburg and S. Heinecke (eds.), *Media Trust in a Digital World*,
https://doi.org/10.1007/978-3-030-30774-5_13

Children and young adults get in touch with these new technologies early these days which influences their development and our society. Prensky (2001) names young adults as *digital natives*. They are the first generation to grow up with new technologies and media. They are surrounded by computers, internet, smartphones and games their whole lives. These new technologies make an important part of children and young adults. Many of them can't imagine a life without laptop, tablet, smartphone, internet, social network or instant messaging.

The so called *digital immigrants* (Prensky 2001) who didn't grow up with new media are often sceptical of new technologies and have to learn the language of new media whereas young adults rely on them and utilize their opportunities. This has consequences for the working environment, corporate world, forms of communication, way of learning, etc.

Phoning has lost its significance as well as handwritten letters. Personal conversation also fades into the background. Especially young adults prefer to communicate through text messages. This leads increasingly to asynchronous communication where conversational partners don't communicate at the same time or place.

Many young adults have lots of social contacts to communicate with. It's not an exception for them to receive hundreds of messages a day. Communication becomes more superficial, inattentive and less personal through this plurality of messages.

It is inevitable to connect online through social networks to be up to date about news and trends nowadays no matter of political, private or commercial reasons. Relevant information are shared and spread within social networks such as appointments, invitations to events or current news. Many people, pupils and students who aren't registered in social networks feel excluded because of the rising communication via platforms like facebook or instant messengers like WhatsApp.

There is a variety of opportunities to get in touch with people in the whole world through the internet which opens up new chances. One of the new phenomena is called *sharing economy* which means the sharing of services online such as platforms like BlaBlaCar or Airbnb. People trust strangers entering their cars or even staying in their homes. How is this possible? Many institutions become needless through new opportunities of direct contacting. People start trusting more in other people than in institutions. An explicit example is the lack of trust in banks and the rising popularity for crypto currency which make institutions needless for the transaction because of the blockchain technology (Botsman 2015).

How do we decide which people are trustworthy in the internet? Important criterions therefore are evaluations of other users. Especially in online platforms like BlaBlaCar and Airbnb evaluations and reputations of providers, guests and passengers are essential to decide whether someone is trustworthy or not. Ratings are the basis of most consumers to decide whether they enter someone's car or stay at someone's place or not (Leest and Schneider 2017, 75).

Information which we find online about other people is important for this decision too. The majority of young adults' attitude towards people they meet during their activities online is sceptical at first. Nevertheless the extent of trust we face a person is dependent on the amount and type of information we find in social networks and online.

Trust in content of websites depends on their layout and design. The credibility of news and information rises whenever a website is designed accurate in order to a quick and good readability especially on the smartphone.

3 Usage Habits of Young Adults

Many children and young adults can't imagine a life without the internet. Pupils spend their time online several hours a day with a rising tendency. The average use of the internet was 2.4 h in 2013 whereas it has risen up to 3 h in 2017 (cp. Leest and Schneider 2017, 68ff for the following data). Smartphones enable a flexible access to the internet in order to time and location which resolve computers of usage.

Equivalent to the increasing use of the internet different internet activities have an explicit higher frequency of use. The internet is primarily still needed to do research on information about school and hobbies. Other activities lie within music downloads, games, movies (85%), shopping and selling (70%) and looking for advice with problems (66%). Pupils are also amenable to downside aspects of the internet such as porn websites (23%), websites with radical content (16%) and every tenth becomes criminal through sending virus infected e-mails or hacking into stranger websites. Even if those numbers seem to be comparatively low they have to be seen as a warning. In addition the use of instant messaging services, photo portals get more influence whereas the use of chatrooms and social networks decrease.

4 Dangers and Risks

Digitalization and technological progress have not only brought many new opportunities and chances to ease our lives but also created new dangers and risks. Especially children and young adults are vulnerable online which can have major impacts.

There is a lot of content in the internet which is inappropriate for young people. Many parents check the internet use of their children poorly or even not at all. On the one hand missing knowledge can be a reason on the other hand a great number of children and young adults can use the internet via smartphones unattended.

Internet and social networks also open up new ways to villainize, defame, stalk or sexual harass people. A big problem which came up the last years is cyberbullying. According to the Cyberlife study II (Leest and Schneider 2017, 81) 13% of the participated pupils were already involved in this kind of bullying. This equals 1.4 million children and young adults in absolute numbers. Therefore it is obvious that cyberbullying is a wide spread issue rather than an individual case.

Cyberbullying develops the same drive as conventional bullying. People involved are threatened (to death), exposed, offended, sexual harassed or excluded. Smartphones, tablets, computers, etc. therefore function as tools. The internet enables wrongdoers to interact with their victims in a more unrestrained manner. Often wrongdoers can act anonymously without facing consequences.

The level of inhibition is much lower than in our real life and the reactions of victims are unseen. Compassion and empathy are faded out. Tears online are not seen!

The Internet never forgets and it is present to all times. Affected people can't detract derision. No matter where they are the humiliation can be seen online by everyone at all times. Bullying develops group dynamics which get intensified by the internet in a multiple manner. External people can support wrongdoers easily with little clicks. The dissolute behaviour of wrongdoers, the permanent present of the internet and the increasing group dynamics make sure that cyberbullying grows to a threat which excels conventional bullying.

Cybermobbing is not just teasing and jokes beyond classmates it's to be seen as a crime. The impact of cyberbullying can be tremendous: decline in school performance, refusing of school, symptoms of stress, anxiety, depression, unable to fulfill training or a profession to the point of suicide danger.

Another problem spreading in the internet is *hate speech*. In difference to cyberbullying hate speech includes a group which is often a minority rather than a single person. The evident anonymity in the internet leads many people to spread their radical opinions and support like-minded people. In real life many of those wouldn't have the heart to express their opinion in public.

A very high risk for children and young adults lies within the phenomena of *grooming*. It's a special type of sexual harassment, where adults get in touch with minors online. Many social media profiles are a fake image of the counterpart. Some of them are even imaginary. The communicative network of people is unlimited. Everybody is able to get, provide or share information. This makes misuse of information by adults to deceive minors very easy. After building up trust one is asked about information referring interests, place of residence, sexual experiences or even for photos or a meeting. Even though young people are basically sceptical of strangers in the internet a meeting with the internet acquaintance happens in 14% of the cases (Leest and Schneider 2017, 75).

Another danger is the new trend of *sexting* which means the exchange of sexual messages and pictures online. The risk which comes with sending those messages is forgotten quite often. The images which are usually meant for certain people can be shared and spread online easily. The pictured person can be exposed through bullying and sexual harassment. The pictures can also function as a pressurising medium to blackmail a person.

Stalking described as obsessive prosecution which comes with disturbance and harassment is becoming more easily. It's easier to get in touch through a permanent reachability on different online platforms and channels. It's possible to block or delete a certain contact indeed but there are lots of ways to connect e.g. through a different nickname or mobile number.

These aspects are only examples of possible risks and dangers for children and young adults, but there is even more. It takes a while for the providers of social network platforms to take down certain content and until then a lot of damage happened already. The distressing message or image can be saved on private devices by that time.

Therefore it's inevitable to train children for their proper handling of media and point out dangers and consequences. Not only children and young adults have to gain media competence but also parents and teachers. They belong to the so called digital immigrants, which means they are not familiar with new technologies and the opportunities coming with it. They often don't know how to protect children and young adults against bad influence online. Parents are not familiar with the newest trends online which makes it hard for them to know what their children are doing in their free time. Even though parents and teachers are told about dangers like cyberbullying and grooming it is difficult for them to act effectively in urgent cases and solve the problem.

Harm caused by cyberbullying which has already been done is nearly impossible to withdraw. Damaged reputation is hard to rebuild which has negative consequences. As already mentioned the reputation of someone in the internet is getting more important in order to gain trust. This concerns selling or providing a service but also employers which take a look at online activities of their potential applicants.

Beside a good reputation which is hard to rebuild the psychological damage should not be underrated. Deleting messages, contacts or images don't mean bullying stops. Victims are often struggling with troubles and consequences long after. Therefore prevention is necessary to sensitize parents and teachers for cyberbullying.

5 Possible Actions

To react successfully to cyberbullying it is important to understand which aspects of the internet intensify conventional bullying.

On this point the anonymity of users play a special role. It makes wrongdoers lose their inhibitions because they only fear consequences infrequently. It also complicates criminal proceedings. Victims can't defend themselves against persons they don't know. They feel helpless to a strong manner. Anonymity strengthens other aspects of cybercrime too. Therefore it is of interest to teach children and young adults the handling of words and images online already in primary schools to show them they don't get a direct reaction like in a conversation. They have to learn that anonymity opens up new possibilities which also involve responsibilities. Pupils must be pointed out about the harm they can make with bullying in the internet and consequences for wrongdoers and victims have to be shown to them. Cyberbullying is a type of violence which has tremendous consequences. Many wrongdoers do it out of fun without knowledge of the outcome they create.

In General schools should spend more time in media education with online skills as one focus. This should already start in primary school. On the one hand technical questions should be explained like: how children and young adults should present themselves online and how not to? How do you handle the internet referring the variety of content and opportunities? On the other hand social skills have to be supported. There has to be a boundary between freedom of opinion and violation of someone's dignity. A respectful and mindful cooperation both in real life and in virtual life should be promoted.

Many schools do prevention work but not to an adequate extent. This often includes single workshops or advanced training but long term arrangements stay absent. Education policy has to set new frames for education and training. Children and young adults have to be sensitized of dangers and risks as well as chances and opportunities of cyberspace. Media education should start in nursery homes and be implemented in school.

Even though subjects like media competence and education are becoming more and more important and new technologies are used at school it often contains the more technical aspects like how to handle a software program or how to edit a text. The topic how to act online appropriately is neglected as well as dangers and risks.

Experiences show that parents and teachers play a special role when it comes to cyberbullying. But they often feel inadequate prepared and they are missing out on knowledge. It's inevitable to provide an improved teachers training together with good class material and lessons. This not only helps with a more responsible handling of the internet and social networks but can also track down urgent cases and react appropriately to them.

A big responsibility also lies within the parents. Many of them are not checking up on their children's life online. The parents' missing knowledge and skills about new technologies can be a reason for the poor handling of new media. Still it is important for them to be interested in the media consume of their children in order to regulate and control them. Schools can provide training especially for parents to help them gain knowledge and skills about new media.

Like already mentioned not only parents but also young adults feel overwhelmed with cyberbullying incidents and often they don't know how to act. Therefore a certificated online consulting portal or a relief portal such as "Gewalt gegen Frauen" should be introduced by the ministry of family in whole Germany. Consequently children and parents would have a counsellor who could help them to solve problems before they even come up.

At last an introduction of a cyberbullying law would make sense. By the means of technological development and new opportunities which are coming with it legislative processes often drag behind. It's not clear to everyone that cyberbullying is a crime and not only an innocent prank beyond kids. An adequate law would be a sign for wrongdoers and victims of cyberbullying to show that it' not a trivial offence.

6 Future Prospects

Digitalization brings many changes for our society with it. The internet is an irreplaceable part of our working life. Customer acquisition is not longer done with telephones but automated e-mail marketing and a bigger part of personal counselling is replaced by homepages and social media channels.

The pursuit of efficiency economizes on more and more jobs as well as robotics and artificial intelligence. The discontent in society is omnipresent especially in the internet. Not only young adults have to face threats and verbal insults but also people from different parts of the society such as politicians, actors or journalists. Respect is dependent on closeness but that's often what's missing in our modern world of communication which is embossed by a rapid spirit of time and anonymity. Listening and understanding have to be rediscovered in order to build up trust without losing respect for each other.

The internet should become a respectful space enabling new chances for improvement and prevent wrongdoers of misusing it for criminal purposes. The internet helps the world growing together whereby it's possible to create a better place for all people. All of us are invited to see those changes as an opportunity to keep the dignity of people in future times.

References

Botsman R (2015) The changing rules of trust in the digital age. In: Harvard Business Review, 20 October 2015. https://hbr.org/2015/10/the-changing-rules-of-trust-in-the-digital-age. Accessed 20 Nov 2018

Leest U, Schneider C (2017) Cyberlife II Studie, Bündnis gegen Cybermobbing e.V. https://www.buendnis-gegen-cybermobbing.de/fileadmin/pdf/studien/2016_05_02_Cybermobbing_2017End.pdf. Accessed Nov 20 2018

Prensky M (2001) Digital natives, digital immigrants. On the Horizon 9(5):1–6

Uwe Leest is the chairman of the Bündnis gegen Cybermobbing e.V. (alliance against cyberbullying) and the managing director of the COBUS Marktforschung GmbH (COBUS market research GmbH). Since 20 years he has occupied himself with social and political topics in the society. As a member of the Bundesverband Deutscher Markt- und Sozialforscher e.V. (federation of German market and social researchers) as well as in the European Society for Opinion and Marketing Research (Esomar) he has an overview of the changes in societies in Europe. Uwe Leest completed his studies in Telecommunication Engineering in Dortmund and holds a Master degree in Marketing and Sales from the Free University of Berlin (FU Berlin). In addition he has a formation as a coach and consultant.

Part III
Competencies and Markets

Chapter 14
Implementing Artificial Intelligence in Organizations and the Special Role of Trust

Johannes Bruhn and Matthias Anderer

1 AI Present and Future—And Back to Present

Artificial Intelligence (AI) touches our lives every day. Whenever you open your e-Mail account, an AI algorithm has sorted out what it considers to be spam mail to you. By the time you receive your search results in a Google search, the advertising spaces on the results page have been auctioned by algorithms. This is based on your surfing habits stored in commercial data bases, sociodemographic information collected from your social network profiles, and many other resources. The aim here is to match all offers to your potential needs profile as precisely as possible. Even the order of your Facebook timeline and YouTube recommendation list is arranged by an algorithm to keep you on the site as long as possible. Needless to say that Amazon, the World's biggest retail store, bases its services heavily on the use of smart algorithms.

So what is AI? Given that intelligence itself has several definitions and is quite hard to narrow down, *artificial* intelligence is similarly hard to define. Following the notion that everything that humans are capable of doing is more or less intelligent, we will go with the definition that AI is the skill of machines to perform human tasks. This includes for example the extraction of information from text, classifying pictures and physical objects like vegetables by type or quality. Of course, this is a very simplified definition, but we feel it is helpful for getting a grasp on AI without getting lost in unnecessary details.

Another important term is "machine learning". Oftentimes used as a drop-in replacement for the term AI it is actually a sub-set. While AI can be achieved by any programming means, as seen in "Deep Blue", the super computer program that beat

J. Bruhn (✉) · M. Anderer
Hochschule Fresenius, Infanteriestr. 11a, 80797 Munich, Germany
e-mail: johannes.bruhn@hs-fresenius.de

M. Anderer
e-mail: matthias.anderer@googlemail.com

T. Osburg and S. Heinecke (eds.), *Media Trust in a Digital World*,
https://doi.org/10.1007/978-3-030-30774-5_14

Kasparov in chess, machine learning always refers to a setting in which the machine behavior is learned from data. This is important to keep in mind, as the result can only be as good as the data you work with. If in the historic data minorities have been discriminated—the machine will also discriminate minorities. If the machine learned to kill any human in sight from historic data, it will kill any human in sight. This does not mean the machine has an 'evil mind', but that is follows the data it was trained on.

A popular example of bad training data is the Microsoft Tay chatbot. The use of unfiltered Twitter data led to a deeply racist bot. The algorithm was not flawed but Twitter users fed the bot with racist and antisocial input—so this is what the bot learned.

There is a big change happening right now. Public perception of AI is shifting away from "*AI is mainly for big Silicon Valley platform companies*". Artificial intelligence is increasingly considered valuable and potentially applicable in the context of the physical, non-virtual industrial world. A big proponent of this development is the fact that in very narrow "real-world" tasks, machines are starting to perform en par with humans. For instance, image classification and recognition are being utilized across diverse fields ranging from online clothing stores to quality assurance in production. The performance of existing AI models on clear and undistorted images is comparable to that of humans, though human performance still exceeds machine learning when images are blurred or contain a lot of optical noise (Dodge and Karam 2017). Another great example of AI-powered visual recognition is the detection of cancer metastases in medical imagery—a task that computers perform better at than doctors in some fields (Liu et al. 2017).

A task less critical but widely in demand is the automatic transcription of spoken language. With the ever-increasing number of global business meetings, the need to document, understand and sort participants' contributions is also increasing.

AI models that can transcribe spoken language, while detecting and marking the respective speaker, will probably make team assistants' lives much easier. The human level error rate in a simple transcription task—transcribing a phone call between two persons—was surpassed by models developed at Microsoft research—with the limitation that again noise can be a great problem (Xiong et al. 2017).

Looking forward, there is more to come. In 2017, a team of researchers from Oxford and Yale conducted a survey among renown AI researchers (n = 352) asking when AI will exceed human performance (Grace et al. 2017). The results: the median estimate for AI systems to provide phone-banking services at the level of human operators "without annoying customers more than humans" was 8.2 years. According to these experts, AI systems will be able to fold laundry as well as humans in 5.6 years, or to write concise, efficient, human-readable Python code to implement simple algorithms in 8.2 years. These estimates indicate that AI might be just around the corner for some industries and not too far away from re-shaping *all* industries in the life span of many people living today.

This chapter builds upon the assumption that early adopters of AI will have considerable advantages in their markets. When implementation efforts, running costs and error rates are low enough, AI will—at least for single or well-defined tasks—provide great scalability effects and other advantages to those who dare to set out to explore uncharted land. But to lift the potential of AI, early adopters in organizations are confronted with a plethora of new questions and tasks. Only a minority of managers consider themselves computer-savvy above average standards. It is hard for everybody in charge to assess chances and risks that drive or hinder the implementation of AI. It is hard to take good choices where to start, and to foresee changes in skills needed by those involved in AI-supported processes.

Apart from that, a multitude of fuzzy soft factors must be managed, e g. the implications on workers' motivation and their willingness to cooperate with machines that they feel might eventually kill their jobs. Probably one of the biggest challenges (if not the biggest), is to manage workers' trust in AI systems and their computational results. There has been a number of incidents in the history of technology application where either lacking trust or excessive confidence in technology lead to a rejection by technology users. In other cases, problems in human-machine-trust rendered less-than-optimal results or even catastrophic outcomes. Trust in machines thus plays a crucial role for the success of AI implementation.

We believe that the answers to all of the questions and problems raised in the previous paragraph can be molded into four paradigms, which we will elaborate in the next chapter. These four paradigms should be considered as roughly sculpted but evidence-driven claims about what matters most when AI is introduced. While these are work in progress, we so far have not come across any other hands-on, straightforward, concise, non-commercial and easy-to-grasp guideline for managers who want to introduce AI in their area of responsibility.

Before we go into more detail, let us give a word of caution: the common picture of AI, its benefits and pitfalls, is still heavily painted by blockbuster movies and TV series on Netflix and Amazon (Dihal et al. 2018). There is also a myriad of books depicting either some kind of utopia, dystopia, or both, created by future superhuman AI. AI is a catchy and fascinating subject because it seems to offer endless possibilities and potentials, especially when we extrapolate the current rapid progress in this field.

But returning to the now, there is very little knowledge about the real affordances and constraints of today's AI. Making AI work here and now requires a learning process similar to any other new technology. Therefore, organizations will have to give themselves longer trial periods, make room to experiment with AI and capitalize on knowledge gained from real-world learning. There is no point in rushing this. The present public discourse on ethical problems created by AI systems implemented without sufficiently checking side effects should warn us to take enough time upfront to be sure everything works as it should.

2 The Four Paradigms of AI Implementation

2.1 The First Things First *Paradigm*

When implementing AI, it is smart to start with simple end-to-end processes that are well-known and performed the same way all through the organization. Additionally, the processes will need some tweaking to realize the full potential of automation. Finally, AI algorithms will need sufficient amounts of data for training.

So where should one start? The obvious answer is to start with the technical side, such as accessible data or digital interfaces. Yet, an even more important question is: *what are the real business processes in our company*? Ask yourself where you already have processes in place that lend themselves for AI. Making smart decisions about where to put the lever first will render quick experiences and subsequently lead to tangible benefits.

Start with business processes that have simple and clear entry and leave points for data. Do not try to implement a sophisticated chatbot service for your most profitable client group right off the bat. The implementation might force you to process data from multiple databases and to connect an abundant number of incompatible interfaces. We should leave that to the time when we are experienced AI implementers. For the time being, we believe it is wiser to gain experience with simple end-to-end processes that are not overly critical to your core business, but eat up considerable amounts of your employees' working time. These will prove the point that implementing AI can indeed create real and measurable value.

However, identifying the right processes will very likely not be enough. These processes will need adaptation and tweaking to become real AI champions. An often-cited comparison is the introduction of the electric motor: when factories were powered by steam engines, one of the most important design goals was to locate machines with high power consumption near to the steam engine, so that stress in the central rotating shaft could be minimized. When engineers replaced the steam engine with electric engines, they followed that old principle of chaining up their machines along a shaft with transmission belts—the use of electricity thus leading to virtually no efficiency gain. Then they realized a crucial point: the layout of the production plant had to be adapted first. Therefore, the sole central electric engine was replaced by multiple electrical power sources, located in or nearby the contraptions doing the actual work. Supplying power for these new engines via inexpensive and flexibly installable electrical wires made factory layout changes and process redesign much easier, and the shift to electric energy finally boosted productivity. It is important to point out that this boost was not simply caused by a new technology replacing an old one. What made the difference was that the new technology made better and more efficient processes possible (Devine 1983).

The same holds true for AI—if we try to install it into completely unchanged business processes, we cannot hope for high gains. Instead, we will have to find the right processes, i.e. those that are simple, well defined and proven to exist in reality and not only on paper. Having identified these processes, chances are good we will have to alter them to make them fit for AI use.

A great example is the processing of paper forms. While this problem might vanish in the future, it is today of great concern in many industries. Possible examples are banks processing customer forms, written drug prescriptions from doctors, or simple paper-based sign-up forms in a mom and pop shop. To fully leverage AI possibilities and at the same time ensure a human supervision, the process will have to be transformed from a human-based data entry job to a fully digitized data entry that is only presented to a human for final approval.

Take Amazon's warehouse logistics as another example. Amazon redesigned its warehouse after devising a system in which you will not find pickers walking up and down long isles of storage racks trying to find an item on their picklists. In place of the humans, the storage racks move. Whenever an item is needed, a robot picks up the specially designed rack and brings it to a packing station where a human picks the item and packs the parcel. This fundamental alteration of the process saves time and accelerates the delivery process significantly, as there are literally armies of robots that travel each warehouse (Amazon Robotics LLC 2018). The concept of moving the racks and not the people is quite an extreme example for redesigning a process for automation; nevertheless, it shows that ingenuity and persistence is needed to create significant benefits.

When thinking about where to start implementing AI, data plays a crucial role. Most of the promise AI has shown in recent years is based on advances in machine learning, which requires training data in sufficient amounts and of good quality. Before starting your very first AI projects, there are two basic questions to ask. What is the simplest possible algorithm I can choose? And: what amount and type of data do I need to train it? In many cases, we have seen a tendency to choose overly complex algorithms to have a project proposal that sounds highly forward thinking and modern. This approach however is a first indicator that not enough thought and knowledge was involved in the planning process. For many cases—especially when talking about tabular data as found in most databases in most companies—very robust and simple approaches like XGBoost (Chen and Guestrin 2016) are available. What is more, the more complexity we choose for our algorithm, the more data we will generally need to train it. This leads to the second point—if we do not have huge amounts of clean and organized data we should generally aim for simple (i.e. low complexity) algorithmic approaches.

So far, we have a sound understanding of the first processes we want to enhance by the application of AI, and we are sure that these processes are handled the same throughout the enterprise. We are aware we will probably have to tweak them to make the most of digitizing them. We have analyzed the available data and have a good feeling as to how complex the algorithm can be that we train with this data. Are there more criteria to consider when we look for tasks prone to getting automated by AI? The answer is a definite yes: we should especially target processes that are dull and that people hate doing. This is explained in more detail in the next paradigm.

2.2 *The* Kill the Dull Tasks *Paradigm*

When it comes to dull tasks, substituting human labor through AI-powered computer work has the potential for realizing many great benefits. Freeing workers from performing dull tasks that cause stress by demanding too little from their brains will create more time for interesting and satisfying tasks with the potential to create more value.

There is a huge and far back reaching body of scientific evidence—most probably corresponding to your personal experience—saying that performing dull, tedious and boring tasks at work induces stress and affects well-being and health (Thackray 1981; Johansson 1989; Frankenhaeuser and Gardell 2010). Yet, even the dullest jobs pay bills and put people into work.

In this chapter, we will not discuss at length the societal implications that a probable, future large-scale introduction of AI will have on the working world. Just allow us some thoughts on the topic that give an indication of the complexity of the problem. While it is commonplace to assume that the rise of AI will kill jobs in large quantities, some argue that economic data indicate we are not even close to a job-killing effect of automation (Surowieki 2017). Others predict a decrease in current jobs but see strong spillover effects, i.e. a raise in jobs that we do not even know about, making up for at least some of the losses (Autor and Salomons 2017; McKinsey Global Institute 2017).

It seems safe to say that it is not likely that a large number of jobs can or will be *fully* automated in the near future. For example, of the 270 occupations that were counted in the US census from 1950, only one (elevator operator) was swept away by automation by 2010. In many occupations, partial automation actually resulted in more jobs over time (Bessen 2016). Then again, there will be a significant shift in jobs, even if there are new jobs. This will result in a need to upskill large quantities of workers. Ultimately, given this high level of uncertainty and unpredictability, let us refrain from futurological predictions of AI effects on employment rates, and let us go back to the topic of dull tasks.

There is a myriad of dull tasks in the working world that have neither a practical nor a logical reason for humans performing them. Everybody knows these tasks in an organization. Just ask: which tasks kill the motivation of our staff, are boring, tiring, and the usual suspects to procrastination? Think of travel reimbursement, transcription of handwritten papers, exporting or extracting data from a system, reformatting and entering them into another one, formatting text or presentation slides, taking down meeting minutes, assessing standardized data using standardized criteria, archiving, and so on. All these tasks demand too little from our brains and thus feel dull and tedious to us. Nevertheless, the majority of qualified workers has to perform them on a regular basis, and in some cases, they even compose the core of their job.

What if we used this time to do something more fulfilling and challenging? What if we did not get distracted by tedious micro jobs disrupting our workdays? What if we could devote our energy to things we consider more relevant? This is why the 'kill the dull jobs paradigm' has the potential to boost both productivity and employee satisfaction at the same time. Freeing people from unpleasant and wearisome work gives them more space to be creative and more time to do things they are interested in, see more value in, and thus will perform better at.

One thing cannot be overstated: this is not a money saving approach, even if saving money can be a beneficial side effect of killing dull jobs. However, just trying to save money means aiming too low. The money saving approach in AI is equivalent to replacing the central steam engine with a new electrical engine, but apart from that holding on to the same old processes powered by bulky transmission belts. Killing dull tasks is much more about freeing your employees' time, energy and attention for doing things that are more suited for them, make more sense to them and most probably directed their vocational choice in the first place. It is much more a strategy of expansion, quality enhancement, process and product innovation than a strategy of cost cutting by dismissing half of one's staff.

2.3 The Everyone's a Manager *Paradigm*

In the AI economy, workers will also be managers in that they will orchestrate an array of helper AIs. Their managers' jobs will change, too, since planning and communicating with workers will have to be more precise and obliging. All that will call for different skill- and mind-sets and therefore altered educational systems.

With dull tasks widely vanished from the working environment, future workers will encounter a completely new challenge. They will have to manage and orchestrate a variety of sophisticated helper AIs. Early ideas of such tools can already be seen today. With one of the most common problems in business being appointment coordination, startups like X.ai (2018) try to solve this task for you. In more "hands-on" industries like construction, big players like Komatsu are pushing for intelligent agents like automated bulldozers orchestrated by a human planner with a tablet (Nikkei 2017). While this development has the potential to boost productivity and enable single human beings or working groups to achieve superior results, it also bears a significant challenge: for this setup to work well, *everybody has to be a manager.*

What does that mean?

For workers: In our definition, the term *managing* means setting goals, outlining specific deliverables that lead to those goals and assigning workers to achieve those deliverables. At the same time, the manager has to know the capabilities and limitations of his or her workers and trust they will do that job correctly. Whenever managers do not fulfil these requirements, the results of the managed workforce are negative—and the manager is held responsible for the work delivered. When we transfer this to the interaction of *workers acting as managers* of their AI helpers, most or all workers of tomorrow will have to have the ability to set realistic goals, define and prepare tasks for the AI to accomplish, and trust the results and the inner workings of the AI. Like real managers, they will be held responsible for achieving the overall goals. Many jobs will carry more responsibility and will be intellectually more demanding. Workers that up to now receive and execute detailed job descriptions and to-to lists will in the future only receive deliverables from their superiors. They will have to perform well at translating the deliverable into sub-goals, transforming sub-goals into sub-tasks and processes, managing interdependences, assuring a smart order of execution, checking if the processes are carried out as intended, and so on. Therefore, increased levels of uncertainty and freedom, less detailed instructions and more responsibility for process and result quality will be characteristic of a big portion of jobs in the future. Working with AI will demand skills from workers that today are typical only for managers.

For Managers: The clear strength of AI today is acting in cognitive domains that require a considerable degree of expertise in a confined subject matter area. Deep domain expertise is an important skill in managers and will still be an important factor for getting promoted in future scenarios. But since AI systems will contain a lot of (in many cases super-human) domain expertise to enhance human management decisions, the required domain knowledge of managers will—even more than today—have to be broad instead of deep. They will need to understand the results the AI gives them without necessarily having the capability to produce the results themselves. They will have to be experts in testing plausibility and assessing error probabilities. Judging will be at the core of their jobs more than ever. At the same time, the importance of methodological and social managerial skills will increase. Compared to today, many managers will have to be much clearer in planning and communicating deliverables and goals, since, when working results are more data-driven, there will be less space for ambiguous and unclear management jargon. The natural and continuous development and improvement of their team members' skills will be of paramount importance for the success of the company. Especially this point is often stressed in many discussions today, but very seldom is developmental effectiveness measured or valued.

For both: Orchestrating a number of AI helper programs will require skills in planning, project and process management, workplace organization and quality assurance. Furthermore, managers and their team members will have to build trust in their ability to acquire new skills continuously, since the development of their artificial co-workers will proceed at a relatively swift pace.

The topics above all call for a change in the way we are trained for work. More learning opportunities will need to be offered for acquiring skills in planning, delegation, quality assurance, and project management in schools as well as in academic and professional training. Professional domain knowledge will still be important and in demand, but one-track experts will have a harder time to make a career for themselves. At the same time, general skill levels expectations by employers will rise. This will put a strong emphasis on continuous re- and upskilling both in managers and workers. Since training and reskilling takes time, it is important to consider this point very early on. If an organization, division, working group or other entity within an enterprise is ready and willing to deploy AI at scale, it seems wise for them to start training staff in AI in general and more precisely in the skills described above as soon as possible, since these skills will act as a booster to productivity.

To put it a different way: even a multitude of sophisticated AI systems will not render satisfactory results for a company if staff members do not know how to orchestrate them. Begin as early as possible with identifying staff on all hierarchical levels that values the help of AI and embraces the change process leading to AI, and upskill these individuals in the mentioned fields if necessary. Sufficient skills are also a key for the last paradigm, which deals with the crucial topic of trust.

2.4 *The* Trust Building *Paradigm*

Lacking trust in technology—especially when it takes or influences decisions as deeply as AI does—can result in an organizational rejection that nullifies all potential beneficial effects of AI. Therefore, special care must be taken to assure enough trust in these systems.

In a world of blended processes—in which the baseload of work is done by AIs and the overall orchestration is done by humans—one of the biggest or even the biggest question will be 'how can trust be built between humans and machines'? Imagine you have a new colleague, helping you out with a task. The task is absolutely clear to you and you have a clear expectation of the outcome. How will you feel when the result is different from what you expected? You will probably lose trust, and immediately start to question the proficiency of your helper. Trust is built when we can predict another's actions. When Watson for Oncology, a commercial medical AI system and part of the IBM Watson product family, started assisting doctors in cancer diagnosis and treatment, this became quite evident. Whenever Watson recommended a treatment the doctors would have preferred anyway, the machine's contribution was not seen as valuable. But when Watson recommended a treatment deviating from the doctors' view, they would question Watsons's accurateness and competence (Ross and Swetlitz 2017).

Things get even worse when a common bias that we humans often fall victim to sets in: we use a small number of observations as evidence for a more general fact. Scientifically, this is called the representativeness bias. For example, if we flip a coin three times and it always shows head, we are inclined to think that "something is wrong" and the coin might be tampered with (Thaler and Sunstein 2009). What we do not put into the equation is that such small sample sizes have no significant statistical meaning. Due to this human bias, in the beginning of a new relationship there is a high risk of losing trust by a few miscommunications. With AI entering the game, a further case of "error", or more precisely "miscommunication", might surface every time the machine proposes solutions that look strange to a human or somehow do not "feel right"—even if these solutions are in fact statistically optimal or at least better than human 'gut-feeling' solutions.

This effect even applies when results produced by an algorithm are not only *probably* better, but *verifiably* better than human results. To illustrate that with a personal example: When one of the authors used a very straightforward algorithm to forecast the gross revenue of a company based on historic data, in back-testing (forecasting the last historical year and comparing it to the human planning in that year) the algorithm performed way better than the company's human controllers. Yet, some stakeholders in charge of the top line were reluctant to work with the machine results because they would not trust the algorithm. In their opinion, business was not predictable because there were so many unknown unknowns. What these humans did was rightfully taking into account that "black swans" are not predictable—so they took the machine result with a grain of salt. What they failed at, however, was the assumed probability for such a black swan. In their mind, every business year held several of such events—while we could show that historic data indicated a very stable and predictable business that could be forecasted with simple statistical tools. Another aspect of this example that we surely do not want to judge: when a machine is better in doing a job you were supposed to do well the last years, you will most likely push back and try to justify your historic performance. This personal experience is supported by research coining this phenomenon "algorithm aversion" (Dietvorst et al. 2014).

To us, trust is the most important human factor to be able to make use of and learn from AI. But overly trusting in AI can not only keep us from benefitting from AI, but also throw us in deep trouble. The reason is that the same bias that we develop when the machine fails three times (making us think it is generally flawed) applies to three immediate successes of the machine. When being convinced by the results of a small number of encounters we tend to build *unjustified trust*. This can lead to humans using AI for purposes it was not designed for.

When in March 2018, a Tesla Model X crashed into a concrete highway lane divider, burst into flames, and killed the driver, it was set to autopilot mode. This self-driving feature is built upon a sophisticated AI software that simultaneously processes camera pictures as well as ultrasonic and radar signals (Tesla Inc. 2018). Prior to the accident, the driver did not have his hands on the steering wheel (which he was supposed to) for 6 s and was consequently warned by a multitude of optical and acoustic alerts (Stewart 2018). It seems that he was overly trusting in his car's technology—maybe because the machine performed flawlessly in his perception prior to the fatal accident.

Using AI in unintended fields might lead to scenarios in which the AI intended for the processing of uncritical handwritten forms is also used for the processing of multi-million Dollar orders, a use case that we clearly do not want or recommend.

Adequate trust in AI therefore means: we know exactly what the system was designed for, we use it according to its intended purpose, we have a good feeling of how often a system is right, and also, for which examples it is right (Lipton 2016). This raises a crucial question: how we can accomplish that in a given organization, all relevant people trust the AI in the right amount and consistent across divisions? This is what the *trust building* paradigm is all about. Yet, there is no single or easy answer how to tackle this challenge. In fact, from our view, there is a whole array of measures, some relating to humans and others to machines that have to be selected and arranged wisely in order to build sufficient and consistent trust:

Training will serve very well when (a) the workforce needs to acquire a robust concept of what AI can do and what it cannot do and (b) when specific employees have to execute new tasks associated with AI. It is important to understand that for the latter scenario, training to use the AI system alone will not be sufficient if not increasing the potential risk of overestimation. To get a balanced view of what AI can do and what the fundamental limitations are, every employee has to acquire a basic understanding of key concepts in AI and machine learning.

Buying external expertise and consultancy will be the right solution when it comes to (a) integrating the technology, (b) transforming the organization, (c) helping with quality assurance [for example, Accenture lately launched a service to make customer AIs "bias-free" (Accenture UK 2018)], (d) troubleshooting, when internal experts have trouble solving problems. Given that expertise in designing and implementing AI solutions is a very scarce resource, it is of great importance to build a network of external partners and suppliers in order to develop successful projects. A trend that the authors observe too often is that companies seek to do everything with internal experts (after all AI is top priority) and realize too late that attracting the right talent to build up adequate internal capabilities takes too long or is not possible at all.

Transparency or more precisely a lack thereof is a major root cause for lacking trust, as today's AI is in most cases unable to explain its "reasoning". The black-box character of the actual algorithmic process keeps coworkers from evaluating the "reasons" by which the AI system came to its "decisions". One research approach, as seen in the DARPA funded Explainable Artificial Intelligence (XAI) program, is to address this issue by designing AI that can "explain" its decisions to humans, be it developers or users. However, this approach will still have to live up to human expectation, and the transparency issue (despite the EU's General Data Protection Regulation, GDPR, from May 2018) will continue to be problematic for the near future. Here, trust-building means accepting the opaqueness of the algorithmic calculation and painstakingly testing and checking the machine's outputs even more so that its inherent lack of transparency can be cushioned to some extent.

Auditing and certification. On 18 April 2018, the American FDA (Federal Food and Drug Administration) approved a device for detecting diabetes-related eye problems (diabetic retinopathy) based on AI-driven software. The device received official authorization to provide diagnostics without the need for an additional clinician to confirm the result. Having AI software audited and certified will help greatly in building trust into these systems. While industries outside the medical field are still figuring out how to certify machinery and algorithms heavily based on AI, this is a promising example of how certification of technical systems might look like in the future—leaving the path of formal mathematical proof towards a more statistical approach.

Industry Benchmarking is a standard procedure in many procurement decisions. Knowing that a system performs well in other organizations and benefitting from real experience of other customers can help in building trust in AI. It may be worthwhile to start with commercially available systems that have proven their reliability and trustworthiness many times before designing your own custom AI system.

Interface Design plays a major role for trust building. Research in human-machine interaction has showed profound effects of interface design, clarity, unmistakability and even natural language on trust (Madhavan and Wiegmann 2004). For example, it has been shown that the voice and accent of a chatbot influences trust put into the system (Torre et al. 2018). Good design can therefore help to make AI systems trustworthy in the eyes of their users.

Having trusted employees lead AI implementation projects. While this idea may seem a little bit obvious and simplistic, it is always a smart move to lend out trust from people that are considered trustworthy by many for building trust in things we want to be trusted in. So when thinking about who lead an AI implementation project, do not only think about the tech wizards. Pick senior people with a good and well-respected common sense and a good inner compass for results that can be trusted. There is an additional benefit for this strategy: this kind of people is likely to flag early when things take a wrong turn, thus adding further to a trustworthy implementation process and trusted AI results.

Bug bounty programs in development and test phases. While building trust in AI through education and fostering community exchange are necessary steps, we propose to also build trust through trying to break the system. Everyone should be invited to challenge and break the desired AI solutions in a safe testing and experimenting phase. This approach will bring two advantages. If there are flaws in the system, they might be uncovered by the wisdom of the crowd—employees with a strong domain expertise might be much smarter in coming up with hard test cases then the AI-savvy development team. On the other hand, if the system withstands the naysayers and sceptics trying hard to show that they are right by breaking it, they will start to accept it.

Know-my-limits workshops: We propose to establish know-my-limits formats that walk all potential users through boundary cases of an AI solution. By experiencing the errors a system makes in certain conditions, humans will start to establish a feeling for the system and will be cautioned against overestimation and building unjustified general trust.

As we have seen, trust in AI is a major problem, one that even has the potential to divide societies by creating AI-savvy elites and social classes not believing and therefore not benefitting from AI (Polonski 2018). Even the UN recently turned its attention to the issue: anyone planning a project concerned with building trust in AI can apply to https://www.trustfactory.ai in order to ask for UN funding of that project or idea. The trust-building paradigm claims that it is of paramount importance to put the dimension of trust into the equation when establishing AI systems. Without dedicated work on trust-building, AI implementation projects might be prone to fail. From all we know, trust seems to be the most important human factor to consider and to actively address when implementing AI.

3 Conclusion

In this chapter, we tried to outline a "survival guide" for those managers that are willing or urged to start using AI solutions in their areas of responsibility. The experience-based hypothesis behind our approach is that many managers feel lost, at least to a certain extent, when confronted with this need or wish.

We structured our recommendations along four paradigms, each one describing research findings and practical evidence, deriving concrete action points from these. While we do not claim this to be a comprehensive list, we feel it might be a good starting point for everyone struggling with the obvious complexity of the task of introducing AI.

In describing our paradigms, we addressed *organizational factors* such as finding the right tasks and processes for automation, or process redesign for maximum benefit of AI usage. Furthermore, we pointed to the importance of *human factors* that will significantly influence AI implementation success: Are tasks that are subject to automation sufficiently unpopular (the automation of unpopular dull tasks will create better acceptance of AI)? When the AI is in place—will managers and staff live up to the heightened skill expectations created by their virtual colleagues (this calls for constant upskilling on both levels)? And even if results rendered by AI systems are bullet-proof and verifiable (a rare case)—will workers trust them (do not take that for granted)? What does it take to make an AI system trustworthy, when its internal workings are mostly opaque (a number of measures, finding the right combination of them being the key)?

Our emphasis of human factors is perfectly in line with a common rule of thumb that for every Euro spent on IT infrastructure, around seven Euros should be spent on change and transformation. Providing technology is only one side of the coin. The other side is addressing AI coworkers' and managers' needs so that they and the new technical systems complement each other seamlessly.

While AI implementation seems to be a rough ride especially concerning the necessary change in the humans involved, if is done right, it carries the promise of multiple benefits:

- Employees are both more efficient and more content with their jobs, because they are freed from repetitive and dull jobs, and have better, more satisfying ways to make use of their skills
- Managers can focus more on strategy and judging work since AI can take over much of their administrative work
- The success of AI in initial areas will trigger the use of AI in others. That way, scale effects will come into effect. With AI implementation expertise rising, speed and ease of AI implementation will increase, while implementation cost will gradually decrease
- Perspectively, innovation cycles will accelerate and the risk in prototyping new products and services will decrease
- When successfully using AI, the external picture of the organization can improve and gain in attractiveness

- All of the above will give the organization multiple competitive advantages and market benefits
- After an initial trial and investment period a huge potential ROI will be seen through lowered transaction and production costs.

We hope we have demonstrated that the journey towards an AI-driven future is a question of finding the right balance. We need to give AI a chance while at the same time not overestimating its capabilities. We have to invest into promising projects while dampening ROI expectations derived from established software projects. We have to push towards automated processes while at the same time addressing the fears and potentially lacking trust of our employees.

This balancing act will be an exciting transformation for everyone, the institutions we all work in and the society we are part of. Maybe this chapter provided you with a few helpful ideas for this journey. We would be delighted to exchange thoughts with everyone who is interested in this fascinating topic.

References

Accenture UK (2018) Creating smarter artificial intelligence by eliminating bias. Retrieved from https://www.accenture.com/gb-en/blogs/blogs-creating-smarter-artificial-intelligence

Amazon Robotics LLC (2018) Amazon robotics—vision. Retrieved from https://www.amazonrobotics.com/#/vision

Autor D, Salomons A (2017) Does productivity growth threaten employment? Retrieved from https://www.ecbforum.eu/uploads/originals/2017/speakers/papers/D_Autor_A_Salomons_Does_productivity_growth_threaten_employment_Final_Draft_20170619.pdf

Bessen JE (2016) How computer automation affects occupations: technology, jobs, and skills (Law & economics working paper no. 15-49). Boston University School of Law

Chen T, Guestrin C (2016) XGBoost: a scalable tree boosting system. Retrieved from https://arxiv.org/abs/1603.02754

Devine WD Jr (1983) From shafts to wires: historical perspective on electrification. J Econ Hist 43(2):347–372

Dietvorst BJ, Simmons JP, Massey C (2014) Algorithm aversion: people erroneously avoid algorithms after seeing them err. J Exp Psychol Gen 144(1):114–126

Dihal K, Dillon S, Singler B (2018) From homer to HAL—3,000 years of AI narratives. University of Cambridge Research Horizons Magazine, vol 35, pp 28–29. Retrieved from https://www.cam.ac.uk/system/files/issue_35_research_horizons_new.pdf

Dodge S, Karam L (2017) A study and comparison of human and deep learning recognition performance under visual distortions. Retrieved from https://arxiv.org/abs/1705.02498

Frankenhaeuser M, Gardell B (2010) Underload and overload in working life: outline of a multidisciplinary approach. J Hum Stress 2(3):35–46

Grace K, Salvatier J, Dafoe A, Zhang B, Evans O (2017) When will AI exceed human performance? Evidence from AI experts. Retrieved from https://arxiv.org/abs/1705.08807

Johansson G (1989) Job demands and stress reactions in repetitive and uneventful monotony at work. Int J Health Serv 19(2):365–377

Lipton Z (2016) The mythos of model interpretability. Retrieved from https://arxiv.org/abs/1606.03490

Liu Y, Gadepalli K, Norouzi M, Dahl GE, Kohlberger T, Boyko A, Venugopalan S, Timofeev A, Nelson PQ, Corrado GS, Hipp JD, Peng L, Stumpe MC (2017) Detecting cancer metastases on gigapixel pathology images. Retrieved from https://arxiv.org/abs/1703.02442

Madhavan P, Wiegmann DA (2004) A new look at the dynamics of human-automation trust: is trust in humans comparable to trust in machines? In: Proceedings of the human factors and ergonomics society 48th annual meeting, Santa Monica

McKinsey Global Institute (2017) A future that works: automation, employment and productivity. Retrieved from https://www.mckinsey.com/~/media/mckinsey/featured%20insights/Digital%20Disruption/Harnessing%20automation%20for%20a%20future%20that%20works/MGI-A-future-that-works-Executive-summary.ashx

Nikkei (2017) Nvidia to help Komatsu automate construction machinery. Retrieved from https://asia.nikkei.com/Business/Deals/Nvidia-to-help-Komatsu-automate-construction-machinery

Polonski V (2018) Humans don't trust ai predictions—here's how to fix it. Retrieved from https://www.oecd-forum.org/users/80891-dr-vyacheslav-polonski/posts/29988-humans-don-t-trust-artificial-intelligence-predictions-here-s-how-to-fix-it

Ross C, Swetlitz I (2017) IBM pitched its Watson supercomputer as a revolution in cancer care. It's nowhere close. Retrieved from https://www.statnews.com/2017/09/05/watson-ibm-cancer/

Stewart J (2018) Tesla's autopilot was involved in another deadly car crash. Retrieved from https://www.wired.com/story/tesla-autopilot-self-driving-crash-california/

Surowieki J (2017) Robocalypse not. Retrieved from https://www.wired.com/2017/08/robots-will-not-take-your-job/

Tesla Inc (2018) Full self-driving hardware on all cars. Retrieved from https://www.tesla.com/autopilot

Thackray RI (1981) The stress of boredom and monotony: a consideration of the evidence. Psychosom Med 43(2). Retrieved from https://pdfs.semanticscholar.org/a856/7c2944287154b2d92fe1938fbcb2e3a21be0.pdf

Thaler R, Sunstein C (2009) Nudge: improving decisions about health, wealth and happiness. Penguin, London

Torre I, Goslin J, White L, Zanatto D (2018) Trust in artificial voices: a "congruency effect" of first impressions and behavioural experience. In: Proceedings of APAScience '18: technology, mind, and society (TechMindSociety '18), New York

X.ai (2018) AI scheduled meetings for smarter work days. Retrieved from https://x.ai/

Xiong W, Wu L, Alleva F, Droppo J, Huang X, Stolcke A (2017) The Microsoft 2017 conversational speech recognition system. Retrieved from https://arxiv.org/abs/1708.06073

Johannes Bruhn is a professor of Organizational Psychology and Business Ethics at Fresenius University of Applied Studies, Munich. He started his professional career as a musician and arranger in a highly digitized recording studio, developing an ever-growing interest for the effects of technology on human life. After earning his doctorate degree in Learning Sciences and Educational Psychology examining cooperative learning in computer networks, he worked in the consulting business and the financial industry for 18 years, the last 8 years in managerial roles in a Dax 30 corporation. In his current scientific work, Johannes specializes in the organizational, societal and ethical implications of the introduction of artificial intelligence.

Matthias Anderer is a Munich-based technology consultant with a focus on digitalization and artificial intelligence. He combines experience in aerospace engineering, strategy consulting (Bain & Company) as well as startup mentoring and coaching. His clients are mostly DAX and MDAX corporations, Munich Re being one of them. Matthias seeks to bridge the communicational gap between business and technology mind-sets. While understanding both worlds he is sure real progress can only be made when business deciders have a solid understanding of technology trends and technology experts leave their filter bubble.

Chapter 15
The Blockchain Technology in the Media Sector

Natalie Buciek and Philipp Sandner

1 Introduction

> Every informed person needs to know about Bitcoin because it might be one of the world's most important developments. (Louw 2013)

Since the introduction of the Bitcoin protocol in 2008 by an anonymous person or group under the pseudonym Satoshi Nakamoto, the underlying blockchain technology has turned out to be a potentially disruptive or promising breakthrough technology. Many companies, institutions, entrepreneurs, banks and even governments try to engage with and invest heavily into the technology even though it still seems to be in an early stage of adoption. The technology shows the potential not only to disrupt existing but also to enable new business models particularly in instances where record-keeping and auditable data is of vital importance, such as in the Media Industry. The question arises, what makes this technology so appealing?

In its core, the technology allows for the substitution of one of the most important actors in our society, the middleman. This is because it is based on cryptographic proof instead of trust (Nakamoto 2008, 1). With the introduction of a peer-to-peer distributed ledger technology (DLT) many industries integrated with the internet can adopt to a trustless, secure and immutable asset management, which does not only allow for transactions of cryptocurrencies, but more importantly for transactions of any units of value. Since the Media industry relies heavily on third parties, this potential of DLTs and DLT-enabled smart contracts could be extremely disruptive as it can offer for instance solutions for complex financial services such as crowdfunding

N. Buciek (✉)
Daimler AG, Stuttgart, Germany
e-mail: natalie.buciek@icloud.com

P. Sandner
Frankfurt School of Finance and Management gGmbH, Adickesallee 32-34, 60322 Frankfurt am Main, Germany
e-mail: email@philipp-sander.de

T. Osburg and S. Heinecke (eds.), *Media Trust in a Digital World*,
https://doi.org/10.1007/978-3-030-30774-5_15

or micropayments, or more general self-executing smart contracts not requiring any middlemen for its execution. Next to the absence of central control over the system, the blockchain technology possesses further fundamental properties. Those are the transparency of all transactions, the immutability and indelibility of entries to the ledger, the anonymity of participants and the relatively small transaction costs. These properties allow for a transparent, integrated and secure solution for digital and intellectual property rights management in a sector, which is becoming more and more complex in the light of digitization. Despite of all the advantages the technology offers, it is still in an early phase of development introducing challenges, which must be addressed by experimenting with the technology, in order to scoop maximum value from it.

To fully understand the potential of DLTs in the Media sector, in a first step the technology will be examined with regard to Bitcoin. Following this, Smart Contracts as an application enabled by the technology will be introduced. Finally, the benefits of the technology will be elaborated in context to the media sector as well as the challenges it faces.

2 The Blockchain Technology

The blockchain technology is the innovation underpinning all current smart contract developments and cryptocurrency approaches. The aim of this chapter is to give an overview over the functioning of the complex technology by referencing it to its foremost application known as Bitcoin. Blockchain technology in its core provides a mechanism to enable transactions through computer networks not reliant on intermediaries to verify or to monitor the integrity of the transactions effected (Morabito 2017, 23). Before the invention of blockchain technology, it was not possible to coordinate such transactions over the internet without a central instance ensuring the integrity of the data. Through the concept of a distributed consensus ledger, where the ledger is stored and maintained on a distributed network of computers, transactions are permanently recorded in transaction blocks. All confirmed and validated blocks are linked and added from the original, known as the genesis block, to the most current block, hence the name blockchain.

Blockchain is only one type of Distributed Ledger Technologies and will be used here to describe the functioning of Bitcoin, but there are other DLT types used for smart contracts and hence are implementable within the Media Sector. In the following, an explanation of the blockchain technology will be given through a reference to Bitcoin functionality since it is intrinsically linked to it. However, Bitcoin is also only one of the numerous possible applications of the blockchain and insofar DLT technology.

2.1 *Functionality of Blockchain Technology Explained Through Bitcoin*

The cryptocurrency bitcoin was introduced in 2008 by an anonymous group or person under the pseudonym Satoshi Nakamoto in "Bitcoin: A Peer-to-Peer Electronic Cash System" as a solution to the problem of frictions and high transaction costs in E-Commerce emerging from the trust-based model (Nakamoto 2008). Nakamoto proposed a peer-to-peer payment system, which relies on a chain of hash-based proof of work, eliminating the necessity of a trusted third party such as a financial institution to conduct transactions. As the digital currency bitcoin relies on a decentralized blockchain, it is therefore unlike other fiat currencies not dependent on any bank or government (Wright and De Filippi 2015, 9).

The word Bitcoin is an ambivalent term, as it not only refers to the currency, but also to the network, the reference implementation and the protocol. Hence, in this paper Bitcoin with capital letter "B" references the protocol, bitcoin with lowercase "b" a unit of the digital currency, Bitcoin Core denotes the reference implementation and the network will be denoted as (Peer-to-Peer) network.

On a very high level, Bitcoin can be described as a digital currency protocol protected by cryptographic processes and maintained by a Peer-to-Peer network, where ownership of bitcoins is passed via transactions, which are being validated through a process called mining and finally the order of those transactions is protected in the blockchain. The security of transactions as well as the decentralized maintenance of the blockchain are enabled through cryptographic processes, which will be examined first.

2.1.1 Cryptographic Processes

Bitcoin in its core is a cryptocurrency. The word itself stresses the importance of its underlying cryptographic processes, which will shortly be discussed in this chapter. Originally, Bitcoin makes use of three different cryptographic concepts, which are not new in fact, but their combination is unique up to the invention of Bitcoin: public key cryptography, cryptographic hash functions and symmetric key cryptography (Franco 2015, 52).

Whereas the latter method of symmetric encryption works with secret keys, therefore also known as secret key cryptography, the former method of public key cryptography works partly with public and partly with private keys. In this context, it is also referred to as asymmetric cryptography (Schmeh 2013, 41). Symmetric key cryptography in Bitcoin is used to secure private keys, which are used to sign transactions in the Bitcoin Core[1] Wallet. Symmetric key encryption can be described analogue to a safe with one key. This single key is used both to lock (encrypt) and to unlock (decrypt) the safe (Franco 2015, 53). More important for this work is the acknowledgement of public key encryption. According to the safe analogy for symmetric encryption, in public key encryption a pair of keys is needed, firstly, the public key, to lock the safe, and secondly, the private key, to unlock it (Franco 2015, 53).

Whenever two parties want to communicate over an insecure channel such as the internet through symmetric encryption, they need to ensure beforehand to interchange the secret keys to decrypt the message, leaving no place for anonymity. Otherwise, their message would be vulnerable to attacks. Differently than with symmetric cryptography, in public key encryption a pair of keys is created consisting on the one hand of the public key, which is used to receive a message or in the case of Bitcoin monetary units and can be distributed widely and on the other hand the private key which is used to sign transactions and must be kept private. It is possible to calculate the public out of the private key, but not the other way around. The key pair is thus connected through a one-way function. In Bitcoin the public key or the Bitcoin address derived from it represents a pseudo-anonymous network participant. The pseudo-anonymity in the Bitcoin blockchain is granted through the feature, that public keys are not connected with a real-world identity (Pilkington 2016, 226). The private key then enables this participant to prove his entitlement to this pseudonym. Each person can take on several pseudonyms by creating an arbitrary number of key pairs (Berentsen and Schär 2017, 119).

Many fundamental functionalities within Bitcoin are based on hash functions. Such functions generate a digital fingerprint for messages of arbitrary length, taking as input a string of arbitrary length and returning a string with predetermined length, named the hash value (Badev and Chen 2014, 9). The input data hereby is often referred to as message and the output as digest. Hash functions are deterministic functions in so far that the same input will always generate the same output, whereas a slightest change to the input changes the output completely. A simple exemplary application of hash functions is the checksum within International Bank Account Numbers, short IBAN. Mistyping of this number leads to a dissimilarity of the checksum with the entered account number and thus to an invalid transaction order, which can immediately be indicated to the person initiating the transaction (Berentsen and Schär 2017, 141).

Bitcoin uses cryptographic hash functions in its protocol which require three more conditions to hold over regular hash functions: Firstly, one-wayness, meaning that for a given hash value its associated input data must be computationally infeasible to revert. Secondly, through weak collision resistance it is secured that an input has a unique hash value which does not apply to another input. And thirdly, strong collision resistance implies that it is computationally impossible to find two input data points resulting in the same hash value (Franco 2015, 96).

[1]Bitcoin Core references the open source implementation, a single computer program including two services: The Bitcoin Core Wallet and the Bitcoin Core Server, which implements a network node (Franco 2015, 19).

2.1.2 Peer-to-Peer Network

The Bitcoin protocol is structured as a peer-to-peer (P2P) network, meaning that it consists of a system of interconnected computers, each individually referred to as node. Information within the network is exchanged through computer nodes in such a way, that every node receives and stores the data submitted to the network. Each node has its own copy of the blockchain, which is downloaded when the computer firstly connects to the network and updated and synchronized with the other nodes through the P2P protocol (Kakavand et al. 2017, 9). There exists no hierarchy in the network as all nodes are equal (Antonopoulos 2014, 139). Given this decentralized nature of the network, the absence of a central server impedes possible client/server-related attacks (Morabito 2017, 64). Whereas in a centralized network, the failure of a central participant can lead to fatal consequences, in a P2P architecture each participant is replaceable (Berentsen and Schär 2017, 96). Figure 1 illustrates the different network types.

The design of a P2P network allows for adaptation, self-organization, high performance, availability through massive replication and robustness against defaults, as there is no single point of failure (Daswani et al. 2003, 1). However, it also leads to higher complexity, as P2P systems present certain challenges, such as the possibility of intentional manipulation through malicious intent,[2] the possibility of incorrect information and the need to assure for transactions to be performed only once and completely, analogue a database transaction (Schütte et al. 2017, 11).

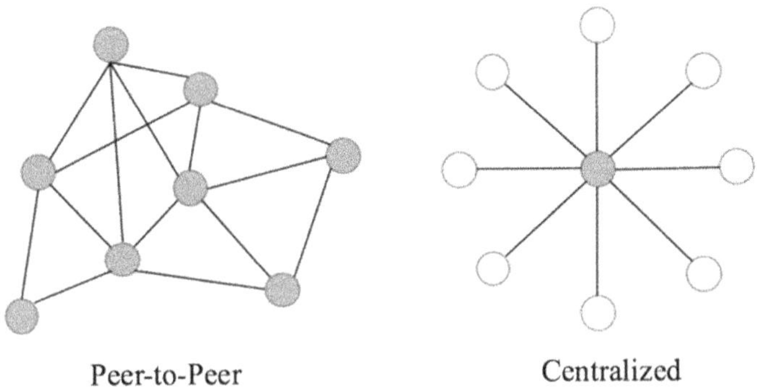

Fig. 1 Different network types. Adapted from Berentsen and Schär (2017, 96)

[2]A common problem in P2P networks is the Byzantine Generals Problem (Lamport et al. 1982), which assumes that in distributed systems some participants misbehave, leading to a malfunction of the system.

2.2 Blockchain

The blockchain constitutes the core of the Bitcoin network. Simply speaking it is the record of all confirmed transactions ever completed in the network. Within this decentralized database all transactions realized within the Bitcoin system are depicted in a chronological order from the genesis block[3] up to the most recent and each block referring to its predecessor in the chain. The ledger is available to anyone in the network and transparent in so far, that the path of all transactions is traceable (Halaburda and Sarvary 2016, 104). The final step in a transaction process is the assembly of newly created blocks into the blockchain and the selection of the chain, where most Proof-of-Work has been done (Antonopoulos 2014, 202).

Once a block is finally validated it gets linked to its predecessor block in a linear and chronological order, such that a chain of blocks is formed, hence the name blockchain. The ledger and each P2P network participants copy of it gets updated and thus each transaction recorded in the transparent public ledger is immutable (Kiviat 2015, 579).

2.3 Alternative Blockchain Design

Whereas the term *blockchain* originally refers to the above described Bitcoin protocol, the present day understanding of the term goes beyond it, to a "myriad of nascent distributed ledger technologies", which are associated with or evolved from the Bitcoin concept (Lai and Chuen 2017, 146). Being open source, Bitcoin has been copied and modified over a thousand times, leading to so-called altcoins, alternative cryptocurrencies. Most altcoins only introduced little changes to the protocol, for example the average time between blocks. More complex technical changes are related for instance to the hashing algorithm or the consensus mechanism. On another level, changes have been made to the idea of blockchain itself, using it not only for cryptocurrencies, but for applications beyond. Next to architectural adjustments to the introduced Bitcoin blockchain in its degree of access rights and underlying distributed consensus protocol, a differentiation of specific and generic blockchain designs is important to understand the concept of smart contracts.

Whereas some protocols, such as Bitcoin, are designed highly specialized with one purpose, to perform a specific task, i.e. tracking assets and transferring value, other protocols pursue a more general purpose. Such general-purpose platforms enable users to write own programs which will be stored on the blockchain and executed automatically in a distributed manner (Mattila 2016, 9).

An example of such a platform is Ethereum, "a blockchain with a built-in Turing-complete programming language, allowing anyone to write smart contracts and

---

[3]The genesis block is the first block ever created. It is statically encoded within the Bitcoin Core and acts as a secure "root" where a trusted blockchain can be built on (Antonopoulos 2014, 166).

decentralized applications where they can create their own arbitrary rules of ownership, transaction formats and state transition functions" (Buterin 2014, 13). Even though Ethereum has its own cryptocurrency, called ether, it moves far beyond just being a cryptocurrency. It can be understood as a virtual machine enabling all kinds of applications by providing an infrastructure able to run all blockchains and protocols (Swan 2015, 21). This project, as well as other further development projects of the Bitcoin protocol therefore enables what has come to be known as Blockchain 2.0 and hence, the implementation of smart contracts.

3 Smart Contracts

Blockchain 1.0 is a generic term for the decentralization of money and payments enabled by Bitcoin as described above, and other cryptocurrencies. Conversely Blockchain 2.0 stands for the "decentralization of markets more generally" and insofar goes beyond the transfer of currency to the transfer of any kind of assets using the blockchain (Swan 2015, 9). An illustrative example of this new sphere is for Blockchain 1.0 to be understood as the protocol stack of the Web providing the infrastructure for applications, such as Amazon or Netflix to be built on top of it (Swan 2015, 9f.). Therefore, the described blockchain functionality can be used in a modified way as an infrastructure to build, capture and execute smart contracts on top of it. How such smart contracts function should be explained in this chapter.

Smart contracts are a key emerging use case of blockchain or more generally distributed ledger technology and are considered as "one of the first truly disruptive advancements to the practice of law since the invention of the printing press" (Wright and De Filippi 2015, 10). As of today, and similarly to the problem Nakamoto identified for online transactions, entering an agreement, especially with an unknown person, requires a third party to enforce what has been agreed on. Therefore, distributed consensus ledger networks provide an ideal basis for such agreements since the network acts as an honest intermediary through game theoretic incentives. A Bitcoin transaction already can be seen as a very simple contract for the transaction of cryptocurrency between two or more parties. Smart contracts additionally possess the ability to attach conditions and features to a given transaction and can have internal state and feature loops (Peters and Panayi 2016). The verification of this transaction works by the consensus mechanism of DLTs in the same way bitcoin transactions get verified by every node in the network. This enables the automatic performance and conclusion of such contracts, which are also executed by each node in the network. The DLT hereby constitutes an explicit and decentralized register of all kinds of data. Also, other related concepts are conceivable within the development of smart contracts. Such concepts are not limited to the sole transfer of cryptocurrencies, but instead nearly everything that changes state over time. Insofar, for instance micropayments or ownership of real-world assets or smart property, property with access to the distributed ledger, can be controlled via smart contracts.

Micropayments can be understood as transactions of very small amounts, which are not viable within existing payment methods since the transaction fees would already account for a relatively large amount of the transaction (Franco 2015, 186f.). Hence, Bitcoin and other cryptocurrencies with low transaction fees can be used to embed smart contracts for micropayments.

4 The Distributed Ledger Technology in the Media Sector

In exchange for money or data, media such as news, information, music, movies or marketing material are provided to the customer. In light of digitization however, the market power has shifted from the content creators, artists or rights owners to the many intermediaries and service layers in the media value chain. Additionally, digitization has led to the copying and distribution of content leading to a lack of control and trust in the media content management.

This lack could be addressed through smart-contract-interfaces in the process of content production, aggregation, distribution and consumption, such that content creators and everyone involved in the creative process gets paid effectively by bypassing the intermediaries and linking the content directly to the content creator reducing the possibility of copyright infringement. As the British singer and songwriter Imogen Heap has stated:

> We are at an amazing point in history for artists. A revolution is going to happen, and next year it's going to take over. It's the ability of artists to have the control and the say of what they do with their music at large. The answer to this is the Blockchain. (Perez 2015)

Even though this revolution is only just beginning to happen, it has already brought up initiatives working with and investing in the technology in the media sector such as ujomusic[4] or the media start-up BOT Labs[5] and it seems like a matter of time that the technology will unfold its full potential. DLTs present an opportunity to fundamentally change how artists, writers, content creators and their consumers can exchange content and establish trust between them without trusted intermediaries.

For the media sector, the DLT seems to offer solutions primarily within the realms of payment and business models, such as micropayment-based pricing models, copyright tracking, or the targeting of budgets through direct linkage to the respective content. Far more applications are thinkable, however considering the early stage of advancement of the technology, payment-based solutions are in focus here since they already have been proved to work. There are several use cases to demonstrate the benefit of DLT for the media sector, out of which the following four use cases a Deloitte report reveals, will be described here (Deloitte 2017):

---

[4]https://ujomusic.com/.

[5]https://www.burda.com/de/news/?tag=bot-labs.

1. **New pricing models for paid content**
   The shift to more digital business models has led to a shift in demand for consumers. Instead of committing to one newspaper, TV or Radio channel, consumers are more and more demanding flexibility through pay-per-use-models as evidenced by the success of streaming services. Whereas transaction costs have made it more difficult to profitably and competitively market small bundles or low-priced content items, with DLT enabled micro-payments this flexibility could be provided by selling for cent-prices without excessive transaction costs.
2. **Content bypassing aggregators**
   While ad-based distribution models will continue to be crucial in the next decade, the intermediaries between the potential advertiser and the content creator could become less important or even obsolete through a DLT solution, since it allows for an exact tracking of content usage and thus enables the direct allocation of advertising budgets. Content creators are enabled to tie up digital copies of the content in a distributed ledger and sell them directly to their customers through DLT-enabled micro-payments.
3. **Distribution of royalty payments**
   Another payment model refers to royalty payments in the music industry. Whenever music is streamed online, played on radio, TV or on any other occasion, the artist should receive such a payment in a contractually defined split. This however builds on multiple contracts between the parties involved and thus leads to contractual complexities. On a shared distributed ledger however, a music directory could be included with the original digital music file associated to the relevant content creators leading to a more transparent and efficient distribution of royalties.
4. **Secure and transparent customer-to-customer sales**
   DLT enables content rights owners to leverage consumer-to-consumer sales and thus build up additional sources of revenue. The ongoing problems with illegal file sharing for the media industry could potentially be solved by DLT solutions by giving content owners full control and visibility of the consumption and peer-to-peer distribution of their content. As an example, a subscriber could access their distributed ledger content and share it with a friend, but then being charged directly for the content shared. This would not only permit for easy and legal sharing of paid content, but also for additional revenue streams for copyright holders (Deloitte 2017).

Next to the use cases displayed above, there are already some real-world applications of the DLT in the media sector in place. One example is Spotify having acquired the blockchain startup Mediachain, which has specialized on the development of a distributed database, where original creators and authors are linked to the content they create (Rath 2017). Other examples of platforms using the DLT for digital-rights-management or royalty payments are Ujo, Musicoin, DotMusic or Reveleator, just to name few. However, since the technology is still in an early phase of development, it will take time for more use cases to be elaborated and experienced with it in order to unfold its full potential.

5 Conclusion

The examination of the blockchain as a distributed ledger technology has shown, how it enables the redistribution of power from central actors to a network of equal peers, the transparency of transactions, immutability and indelibility of entries to the ledger, the anonymity of participants and relatively small transaction costs. Insofar, the technology can be seen as a promising breakthrough technology especially in areas, where trustful records of transactions and auditable data are needed, such as the media sector.

The use cases presented demonstrate only few of the numerous possible applications of DLT in the media sector. However, the cases have shown, that the immutability and trustless nature of the DLT grants transparency and efficiency through automation of execution and direct payments to content creators. This leads to a simplified digital media management by bypassing aggregators and intermediaries and securing micro-payments of advertising or pay-per-use models as well as the prevention of piracy. However, next to the many potential benefits a DLT solution might offer for the media sector, there are still some challenges which must be faced to enable a widespread adoption. On the one hand the technology is not yet robust enough and still needs to overcome several technical, legal and regulatory, public perception, implementation as well as market and business-model related challenges to realize its full potential. It might take some more years for the technology to bring returns to the ones investing in it. But on the other hand, all the advantages of an innovation are often not apparent at the beginning of its development. Businesses in the media sector will have to analyze and validate the technology to determine whether it might add value. Similar to other innovative technologies, the DLT and DLT-enabled smart contracts will inevitably go through a long process of development, within which experiments, use cases as well as research within all relevant interdisciplinary fields covered by the technology will sequentially unfold its actual potential.

References

Antonopoulos A (2014) Mastering bitcoin: unlocking digital crypto-currencies. O'Reilly, Sebastopol, CA

Badev AI, Chen M (2014) Bitcoin: technical background and data analysis. FEDS working paper no. 2014-104. https://www.federalreserve.gov/econresdata/feds/2014/files/2014104pap.pdf. Accessed 05 May 2018

Berentsen A, Schär F (2017) Bitcoin, blockchain und kryptoassets. BoD—Books on Demand, Norderstedt

Buterin V (2014) Ethereum white paper, published on a next generation smart contract & decentralized application platform. http://www.the-blockchain.com/docs/Ethereum_white_paper-a_next_generation_smart_contract_and_decentralized_application_platform-vitalik-buterin.pdf. Accessed 12 May 2018

Daswani N, Garcia-Molina H, Yang B (2003) Open problems in data-sharing peer-to-peer systems. Database theory—ICDT, pp 1–15

Deloitte M (2017) Blockchain@Media: a new game changer for the media industry? Blockchain Institute

Franco P (2015) Understanding bitcoin: cryptography, engineering and economics. Wiley, Chichester

Halaburda H, Sarvary M (2016) Beyond bitcoin: the economics of digital currencies. Palgrave Macmillan, Hampshire

Kakavand H, Kost De Sevres N, Chilton B (2017) The blockchain revolution: an analysis of regulation and technology related to distributed ledger technologies. https://ssrn.com/abstract=2849251. Accessed 05 May 2018

Kiviat T (2015) Beyond bitcoin: issues in regulating blockchain transactions. Duke Law J 65(3):569–608

Lai R, Chuen DL (2017) Blockchain—from public to private. In: Chuen D, Deng R (eds) Handbook of blockchain, digital finance and inclusion, vol 2. Academic Press, Cambridge

Lamport L, Shostak R, Pease M (1982) The byzantine generals problem. ACM Trans Program Lang Syst 4(3):382–401

Louw L (2013) BusinessDay. https://www.businesslive.co.za/bd/opinion/columnists/2013-10-23-the-bitcoin-revolution-could-change-government/. Accessed 12 May 2018

Mattila J (2016) The blockchain phenomenon: the disruptive potential of distributed consensus architectures (B. University of California, eds). BRIE working paper 2016-1. http://www.brie.berkeley.edu/wp-content/uploads/2015/02/Juri-Mattila-.pdf. Accessed 12 May 2018

Morabito V (2017) Business innovation through blockchain: the B3 perspective. Springer, Cham

Nakamoto S (2008). Bitcoin: a peer-to-peer electronic cash system. https://bitcoin.org/bitcoin.pdf. Accessed 05 May 2018

Perez YB (2015) Grammy winner Imogen Heap: blockchain tech can empower artists. https://www.coindesk.com/grammy-award-nominee-touts-benefits-of-blockchain-tech/. Accessed 23 May 2018

Peters G, Panayi E (2016) Understanding modern banking ledgers through blockchain technologies: future of transaction processing and smart contracts on the internet of money. In: Tasca P, Aste T, Pelizzon L, Perony N (eds) Banking beyond banks and money. Springer, Cham, pp 239–278

Pilkington M (2016) Blockchain technology: principles and applications. In: Olleros F, Zhegu M (eds) Research handbook on digital transformations. Edward Elgar Publishing, Cheltenham

Rath J (2017) Spotify acquired blockchain startup mediachain. https://www.businessinsider.de/spotify-acquired-blockchain-startup-mediachain-2017-4?r=US&IR=T. Accessed 12 May 2018

Schmeh K (2013) Kryptografie: Verfahren, Protokolle, Infrastrukturen (5th revised and updated edition). dpunkt.verlag, Heidelberg

Schütte J, Fridgen G, Prinz W et al (2017) Blockchain: Technologien, Forschungsfragen und Anwendungen. https://www.aisec.fraunhofer.de/content/dam/aisec/Dokumente/Publikationen/Studien_TechReports/deutsch/FhG-Positionspapier-Blockchain.pdf. Accessed 05 May 2018

Swan M (2015) Blockchain: blueprint for a new economy. O'Reilly Media, Sebastopol

Wright A, De Filippi P (2015). Decentralized blockchain technology and the rise of lex cryptographia. https://ssrn.com/abstract=2580664. Accessed 05 May 2018

Natalie Buciek works in the field of international controlling for a German automotive corporation. She studied politics, sociology and European economics at the Julius-Maximilians-University of Würzburg, the University of Granada, the University for Development of Santiago de Chile and the Otto-Friedrich-University of Bamberg. Her areas of expertise include Financial Sciences, the Distributed Ledger Technology and Smart Contracts.

Philipp Sandner is professor and head of the Frankfurt School Blockchain Center at the Frankfurt School of Finance and Management. His expertise in particular includes blockchain technology, crypto assets, initial coin offerings (ICOs), digital transformation and entrepreneurship. He advises companies concerning their blockchain activities, e.g. the first European crypto fund or startups in Consensys' Token Foundry program. Philipp is a member of the FinTechRat of the Federal Ministry of Finance and also engaged in the Blockchain Observatory established by the European Union and, additionally, founding member of the German Blockchain Association e.V. and the Multichain Asset Managers Association. Before joining Frankfurt School, he co-founded a consulting company specialized in the area of innovation strategy IP and technology transfer. He has been research fellow at the Technical University Munich, the Ludwig-Maximilians-University Munich and the Berkeley Center for Law and Technology. Previous to that, he studied business administration focusing on computer science at the University Mannheim.

Chapter 16
Trust Me if You Can: From Media Competence to Digital Competence

Stephanie Heinecke, Maria Berg and Ludwig Hinkofer

1 Introduction

Reports about the number of computers in schools, the need for children to learn code, or data privacy issues shape the discussion on education in a digital world. In Germany, almost every debate goes along with the words "too little" and "too slow". Is this a battle in order to gain public attention? Or do we actually have a serious problem?

Traditionally, *media competence* was the buzzword for such discussions. Today, *digital competence* is used much more. This article asks to broaden the view and open the debate for a long-term understanding of digitization and its impacts on society and education. Based on reflections on the academic conceptions of media competence, the text discusses the relevance and impact of digital skills. Education in this sense is not limited to children and teenagers, but is essential for persons of all ages. Understanding digital competence as a circle of lifelong learning, it includes individual digital skills, digital social competence, socio-political participation, and employability. People need to trust in their own skills to deal with the changes that our societies are facing. Self-efficacy will be a key resource in the digital world, digital competence can be used as a toolbox to get there.

S. Heinecke (✉) · M. Berg · L. Hinkofer
Hochschule Fresenius, Infanteriestraße 11a, 80797 Munich, Germany
e-mail: stephanie.heinecke@hs-fresenius.de

M. Berg
e-mail: maria.berg@hs-fresenius.de

L. Hinkofer
e-mail: hinkofer@hs-fresenius.de

T. Osburg and S. Heinecke (eds.), *Media Trust in a Digital World*,
https://doi.org/10.1007/978-3-030-30774-5_16

2 Relevance: From Media Usage to a Digital Life

Our children intuitively know how to use a tablet before they can talk. We share our daily life in social networks—why not, we think, we don't have anything to hide. We track our sports activities, we talk to Alexa and Siri and advertisement tells us that this is appropriate in the age of digitalization. We are users, consumers, and customers in a digital media world. However, the future job market will need creators and innovators for the tasks machines cannot accomplish. But: Will we all need to learn how to code, as chancellor Angela Merkel pointed out during the opening ceremony at CeBIT 2017 (Merkel 2017)? Or will we need to integrate digital tools and thinking in a much broader sense into our daily life?

Over the last few decades, convenience and usability paved the path for both digital media content and devices. People know about risks and dangers, the lacks in the protection of personal data, misinformation or security issues. Still, only very few of us take appropriate measures. Sara Hofman (Deutsches Institut für Sicherheit und Vertrauen im Internet 2017) explains that consumers often value personal benefit higher than trust. Regarding trust in digital communication, she points out two aspects to be aware of: trust in technology (e.g. online technology, platforms such as Facebook etc.) and trust in the communicator (people and organizations).

Both aspects play an essential role in today's media system. On the content side, we know about the media logic, meaning the way the media select, present and interpret news (Meyen et al. 2014). We know about journalistic values and we ideally have an intuition whether a media brand is following these guidelines—so we trust in them (or not). However, this attitude is not innate but needs to be acquired, even more so in times with rapidly changing structures among the communicators. On the technological side, convergence is key. Media content is available on numerous digital platforms and devices. Still, usage is not a sole topic of classical media usage anymore. Social interaction, daily life and business are integral parts of the digital offerings. Keeping up with this development is an essential skill for any kind of participation in the 21st century.

For the educational system, there are some challenges regarding following the speed of digital innovation. Still, media competence and digital skills are not exclusive topics for educational institutions. Private companies and initiatives see the urgent need to quicken the process of digitalized education, even more so in times of skills shortage, digital business models and social movements on digital platforms. To name only a few: in Germany, companies such as Lego, Apple or Google enter classrooms, providing state of the art technology for lessons and, moreover, establish trust in their brands (Töpper 2017). Timotheus Höttges, CEO of *Deutsche Telekom*, criticizes the educational system for the lack of digital tools (starting with very basic things such as broadband speed), subjects (coding—heavily discussed, still: yes!) and accordingly trained teachers. Finally, it's the mindset that matters: in a digital world, creativity, courage and the ability to try things out are more important than ever (Höttges 2018).

So: what does it take? This text bridges the gap between the classic research models of media competence to concepts in terms of digital competence. It discusses both theoretical approaches and the practical needs of today's industry. Key driver of the argumentation is the factor "trust": Digital competence with all its implication can increase trust (if appropriate) and be a guideline to navigate through the digital world. Finally, this idea is not only a claim for education, but rather an appeal for lifelong learning.

3 Media Competence: Terms and Reflections

Several academic subjects discuss issues of media competence, above all educational sciences and communication studies. To find a common understanding of terms and definitions, there are three key questions:

First: which media are we talking about? Even in times of digitization and mediatization, we see very different approaches within communication studies to what exactly the term "medium" may mean. In the past, most authors used the understanding of mass communication as some kind of front line and limitation for their subject (Birkner 2017). However: the world has changed. We see more and more convergence of public and private communication in all kinds of interactions. So there is a strong need to broaden the academic perspective, especially when it comes to media competence as a competent usage of all the things that we colloquially understand as some kind of "media". In this sense, Krotz (2015) defines three kinds of media in today's media system:

- Mass media with standardized content for a mass audience (e.g. television, newspapers);
- Media for interpersonal communication (e.g. phone, chat);
- Interactive media for communication with hard-/software systems (e.g. robots, gaming).

As this text will show, a contemporary understanding of media competence must comprise all three dimensions. Besides, there is need for discussion regarding the term media competence on its own in today's world.

The second question is: what exactly is competence? From a psychological point of view, the term is important regarding applied performance (Hartig and Klieme 2006). In educational science, competences characterize objectives in the educational system (ibid., 128). Roth (1971) used the term in this context: maturity is a competence for responsible action (Roth 1971, 180). In his interpretation, there are three aspects: self-competence, professional competence and social competence. Baacke (whose concept will be discussed shortly) based his ideas of media competence on Habermas' theory of communicative competence, which describes the aim of media competence as giving people conflict-solving skills in a democratic society. For Baacke, competence is both an ability to strive for and at the same time a presuming skill (Baacke 1973).

The third question asks for the purpose of media competence: why do we need a competent use of media? As a key qualification in a democratic society, media competence is often discussed as a political goal. Generating publicity and providing a platform for information and discussion is the primary function of mass media in a political context (Strohmeier 2004). Therefore, media competence is part of democratic competences (Gapski et al. 2017) and an essential social task that must reach all parts of the population (Aufenanger 2003).

For sure, there is no general answer to the three key issues addressed here. But the relevancy in times of digitization is out of question. Which media channels do we use for which purpose? What kind of competences are necessary to fulfil the strong socio-political demand enclosed in traditional models of media competence?

There is no doubt about the importance of an education in terms of media competence. Still, there are only very little findings about the individual characteristics of media related competences. The current approaches to measure media competence mostly focus on single aspects (Trepte and Reinecke 2013) since the theoretical foundation is complex and hard to capture. For an overview, see Hermida et al. (2017) who discuss current and future approaches to measure media competence.

The actual media usage in terms of mass communication has been rising significantly over the last 50 years. Figure 1 shows data from the *ARD/ZDF-Langzeitstudie Massenkommunikation* with daily media usage rising from 3:14 h in the year 1964 to 9:26 h in the year 2015.

The increasing usage over time corresponds to an increasing number of media available. At the same time, mobile Internet usage has increased clearly. In 2015,

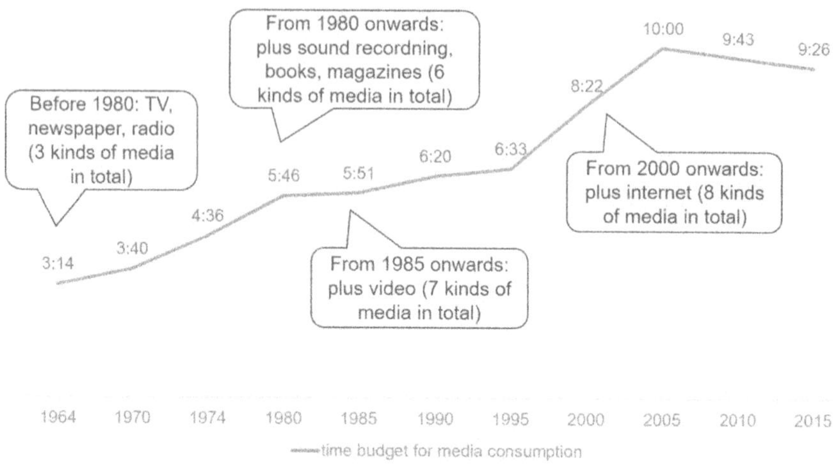

In hours:minutes, participants 14 years and older
Basis: FRG total (until 1990 only West German states), Mon-Sun (until 1990 Mon-Sat), 5:00 a.m.-12:00 p.m.; 1964: people 15 years and older, 5:00 a.m. – 1:00 a:m.; until 2005 German people, from 2010 onwards German speaking people.

Fig. 1 Time budget for media consumption from 1964 to 2015. *Source* Own illustration based on Breunig and van Eimeren (2015, 506)

18% of respondents in the *ARD/ZDF Onlinestudie* used mobile Internet offers daily. In 2017, this number increased to 30% of respondents (Koch and Frees 2015, 437). When looking at the young target group of people from 14 to 29 years, values are more than twice as high (2015: 47%, 2017: 63%). According to Koch and Frees, mobile devices lead to more frequent and longer Internet usage. Still, does more frequent media usage qualify people as media experts? Certainly not. To some extent, media usage needs a certain competence. From actual media usage, new skills arise. Therefore, usage and competence condition each other. Several models for media competence reflect this process-driven approach. For example, Tulodziecki (2011), Moser (2010) or Riesmeyer et al. (2016) give an overview on the different theoretical approaches to media competence. Hereinafter, this text will show some exemplary approaches and on this basis develop an argumentation towards digital competence.

4 Conceptions: Approaches to Media Competence

In German speaking countries, Dieter Baacke's habilitation thesis (1973) is the pioneering work in terms of media competence (Groeben 2003; Tulodziecki 2011; Moser 2010). According to Groeben, it was the starting point for different models from social, educational, and individual perspectives. They all have two things in common: fist, they try to split the concept into sublevels. Second, they put an emphasis on the need for these sublevels, defined as individual abilities and skills that are necessary to survive in media society (Groeben 2003).

Baacke (1997) defines four aspects, which empower the media user to handle new ways of information processing in a confident way (Baacke 1997). This approach has become known as the *Bielefelder Medienkompetenzmodell*. According to Baacke, media competence has a mediatory dimension, *media critique*. This aspect asks the media user to analyse social processes, to reflect and apply them to his or her own acting in a socially responsible way. Baacke's second dimension refers to *media science*. On the one hand, it consists of knowledge about media and media systems. On the other hand, the term includes the ability to actually handle media devices (Baacke 1997). Both *media critique* and *media science* are the foundation for the goal-oriented dimensions *media use* and *media design*. *Media use* includes both a receptive and an interactive aspect. *Media design* includes innovation and creativity. This dimension aims at the ability to construct, change, and develop media offers (Baacke 1997).

Psychologist Groeben (2003) took a broader approach to model media competence. His process-oriented model highlights individual growth and intellectual and personal development. Groeben understands human beings as socially capable subjects (Groeben 2003, 42). It is not only about using media, but also about taking advantage of it. According to this model, *media knowledge* and *consciousness of mediality* (in German: *Medialitätsbewusstsein*) are prerequisites for all other dimensions. The first of these aspects is similar to Baackes *media science*. On the one hand, it is about the general conditions and categories of media, their intention and effects.

On the other hand, this dimension includes the knowledge about differences between the reality in everyday life and the reality constructed by the media. The more differentiated this basis is, the more specific the next step of media competence is in Groeben's model: *media specific patterns of reception*. This term covers a wide area from technical skills to complex cognitive processing patters. In this context, emotional motives as drivers for media usage play an important role. Groeben explains that many people use media content made for entertainment falsely as a source for information and vice versa. The next dimension is about *media-related enjoyment* and a new addition to the concept of media competence compared to other models. Groeben argues that there is actually a certain competence needed in order to enjoy media entertainment without getting lost in the multiple offerings or becoming addicted to them. The dimension of *media critique* is already explained well by different authors (e.g. Baacke 1997; Aufenanger 2003; Moser 2010). According to Groeben, it refers to both content-related and formal aspects of media products. *Selection and combination of media usage* is essential for the ability to act in a social context, even more so in a world with a surplus of media offerings, since selection includes the aspect of orientation. The dimension *productive patterns of participation* is also part of other authors' work (for example partially in Baacke's *media design*). It comprises more than just media usage and puts an increasing emphasis on media production: the development of today's media landscape offers many ways of active participation, which can be an essential part of self-expression. Therefore, it's not just about the usage of interactive media, but also about one's own content creation. This aspect has gained importance enormously. Finally, the last dimension *follow-up communication* especially refers to the processual approach of Groeben's model. Other aspects, such as *media-related enjoyment* and *media critique*, are closely linked to it. If media usage is followed by a discussion, users are able to expand their corresponding competences. Follow-up communication about media use is relevant for the development of media competence in general, right up to the overall goal of a socially capable subject (Groeben 2003, 39).

Riesmeyer et al. (2016) continue this idea of a processual model and apply it especially to online media. Regarding media competence, the authors see the transition from knowledge to action as a central point in the overarching construct of media competence. Similar to Roth's (1971) definition, they differentiate in *expertise*, *self-competence*, and *social competence*. Their idea of *expertise* is broader than Baacke's *media science* and Groebens *media knowledge*. It includes not only traditional knowledge about media structures and techniques, but also has a social component. Social discourse on media competence (compare Groeben's *follow-up communication*) is modelled as a sub-dimension to *expertise*: only discourse can lead to autonomous decision-making (Riesmeyer et al. 2016).

This knowledge becomes action: evaluative, emotional, motivational, and creative skills make up the dimension *self-compentence*. Theoretical approaches to media competence have focused on *evaluative skills* for a long time. Baacke (1997) and Groeben (2003) see these aspects in the context of critical thinking. According to Riesmeyer et al., *emotional skills* include the processing and handling of emotions that arise during online media usage. Groeben summarized them in *media-specific patterns of reception* and *media-related enjoyment*. His idea of *selection* is included in Riesmeyer et al.'s *motivational skills*. This term refers to whether media users can fulfil their needs by media usage. *Creative skills* are becoming more important. As discussed before, also other approaches to media competence point out the importance of this aspect (e.g. Baacke 1997; Aufenanger 2003; Groeben 2003; Schorb and Wagner 2013). In the online world, these aspects are part of the digital identity. Therefore, they are part of the dimension *self-competence* (different from Baacke, *media critique* and *media science* are an essential requirement for *media design* in his model).

According to Riesmeyer et al., online and especially social media require a certain amount of *social competence*, the third dimension featured in their model. Media competence in the digital world is not just about individual media usage, but also has a high impact on social behaviour and relationships among the community. *Social competence* includes *participatory skills* (how to interact with others/treat others), *integrative skills* (referring to follow-up communication), and *moral skills* (aligning one's behaviour to social standards) (Riesmeyer et al. 2016).

In an international context, researchers often use the term *media literacy*, but cite German articles mostly using the term *media competence*. Still, presuming not least due to the language barrier, they refer to the German publications not too prominently, even though there are many parallels. UK researcher Sonia Livingstone for example defines media literacy as "the ability to access, analyse, evaluate and create messages across a variety of contexts" (Livingstone 2004, 3). This is very similar to the approach of the European Commission, which is a common understanding for initiatives within the European Union: media literacy is described as "a matter of inclusion and citizenship in today's information society. It is a fundamental skill not only for young people but also for adults and elderly people, parents, teachers, and media professionals. Media literacy is today regarded as one of the key pre-requisites for an active and full citizenship in order to prevent and diminish risks of exclusion from community life" (Ding 2011, 5). These aims are part of the *EUROPE 2020 Strategy* and the *Digital Agenda* for Europe: "the digital era should be about empowerment and emancipation of citizens. Lack of background knowledge, literacy or skills should not be a barrier to accessing the new opportunities offered by the media and the information society" (Ding 2011, 5).

The academic discourse in the US has—among others—been shaped by the work of Renee Hobbs. She is co-editor of the Journal of *Media Literacy Education*, published by the *National Association for Media Literacy Education* (NAMLE). NAMLE defines media literacy similar to the definition of the European Commission, but puts an additional emphasis on action: "Media Literacy: the ability to access, analyse, evaluate, create, and act using all forms of communication is interdisciplinary by nature. Media literacy represents a necessary, inevitable, and realistic response to the complex, ever-changing electronic environment and communication cornucopia that surround us." (Namle 2018, n.p.).

German and international concepts have several overlaps: Baacke's (1997) or Groeben's (2003) *media critique* and, resulting from these aspects, (receptive) *media usage* are analogue to Livingstone's dimension *analysis* and *evaluation*. All approaches discussed include a dimension of *media design* (e.g. Baacke 1997), *creative skills* (Riesmeyer et al. 2016), or *content creation* (Livingstone 2004). International research points out two aspects: the context of media content production (in German literature: see Riesmeyer et al.) and media usage for socio-political goals (Hobbs 1998). Due to the digitization of the media industry, English-speaking texts increasingly use the term *digital literacy* to discuss topics previously called *media literacy*. There are different interpretations of the concept and the terms used, Bawden (2008) and Koltay (2011) provide an overview, including the historical development and differences to other approaches.

5 Shifts: From Media Competence to Digital Competence

Most of the approaches discussed above come from an educational context and refer to children and teenagers. It is obvious that digitization has an enormous impact on the skills needed today and in our future society. Still, not only the youth, but all people of all ages will need more and more (digital) media related skills to master their life. It is essential to keep up with the technological progress—not everybody in every aspect, but we will need a broad understanding of all kind of media in general, digital applications and their effects. They will become (and already are!) an essential part in multiple dimensions: in private life, in professional contexts, or in terms of social and political participation.

For sure, there still will be jobs that are less affected by digitization. Of course, everyone can decide, to what extend he or she wants to use digital devices and applications in their private lives. Still: the general development is unstoppable and it concerns even fields that haven't unfolded their digital potential yet. Just some keywords: smart home, digital administrative offices, mobility. When our fridge automatically orders new milk from an online store, this does not seem to be an issue of media literacy at first sight. In fact it is: how is my personal information used and stored, how does the fridge or the store track my usage habits for my next orders and why does my smartphone actually display ads for pizza delivery services every Sunday evening? It hardly will be possible to ignore all these developments for one's own life—not at least because they will make our lives easier.

This text promotes an approach to broaden the view on the abilities and skills needed to deal with the digital world. Despite all technological developments, contemporary media literacy or digital literacy must comprise more aspects than just the technical knowledge on how to deal with the latest devices. Learning processes and their consequences play an important part in this discussion. In Germany, child psychiatrist Manfred Spitzer is one of the strongest critics. He argues (Spitzer 2012) that from a neuroscientific point of view, the early contact with digital media can affect the brain development in a negative way. The title of his book *Digital Dementia* is therefore meant in the literal sense and not just a clever marketing buzzword and alliteration. The discussion about Spitzer's work and the reliability of his argumentation is highly controversial (exemplary: Keine Bildung ohne Medien 2012), both in the academic and public context. Still, the issue itself is obvious: most adults know the impact of smart digital devices on their media usage behaviour from their very own experience. It is hard to stop once acquired usage habits and withdraw from the ever-ongoing flood of information. Children's brains are still in development, they need to learn how to process and filter stimuli before they can take any deliberate decision regarding usage. From this point of view, the urgency of the appeal in general is obvious.

Of course, possibly one-sided argumentation and arbitrary selection of studies need to be discussed and analysed within the academic world. However, it is important that this discussion is open to a broad audience, since digitization will progress with all its consequences. Even though there are counter-movements such as *digital detox*, the general trend is obvious and unstoppable, and it will shape our future significantly. The skills needed to navigate through this digital world do not only include the use of digital tools and devices, but also and more than ever the ability to reflect one's own behaviour in this changing environment (which might sound pretty traditional, but is essential). Therefore, *digital competence*, as we will call it in this text, must be understood as a combination of both analogue and digital competences. The user needs to build trust in their very own media and digital usage behaviour and, by doing so, will increase their knowledge and ability to act.

In an international context, *DQ Institute* provides an exemplary conceptualization of digital competence. They are a "public-private-civic-academic coalition" (DQ Institute 2018), working in association with the *World Economic Forum* and supported by collaborating companies and initiatives (among them: *Google*, *Unicef*, *Twitter SINGTEL*). The term DQ follows the terminology of IQ and EQ as a core competency. DQ is "the sum of social, emotional, and cognitive abilities that enable individuals to face the challenges and adapt to the demands of digital life" (DQ Institute 2018). For DQ Institute, digital intelligence comprises three key areas: digital citizenship, digital creativity, and digital entrepreneurship. The current campaign *#DQEveryChild* aims at children aged between eight and twelve to develop digital citizenship. With a global pilot launch in March 2017, the strategy aims to roll out DQ education to more than 100 nations by 2020. DQ Institute splits DQ into eight dimensions (DQ Institute 2018):

- Digital Rights: freedom of speech, intellectual property rights, privacy
- Digital Literacy: computational thinking, content creation, critical thinking
- Digital Communication: online collaboration, online communication, digital footprints
- Digital Emotional Intelligence: social and emotional awareness, emotional awareness and regulation, empathy
- Digital Security: password protection, Internet security, mobile security
- Digital Safety: behavioural risks, content risks, contact risks
- Digital Use: screen time, digital health, community participation
- Digital Identity: digital citizen, digital co-creator, digital entrepreneur.

This is an exemplary approach to the areas that should be focused on in the discussion—may it be in the traditional education system or in additional efforts. Compared to the classic models for media literacy, there are some parallels, for example when it comes to social participation, general conditions of media, and the ability to produce one's own content (Baacke 1997; Groeben 2003). At the same time, the points raised can be split into expertise, self-competence, and social competence as Riesmeyer et al. (2016) suggest. So: what's new? There is a noteworthy conceptual separation between *digital literacy* and other aspects. DQ has a strong focus on technological aspects. Knowledge in terms of *digital security* and *digital safety* exceeds the risks of traditional media usage. This may not be underrated. People can only align their media/digital usage behaviour to such dangers when they are aware of the possible threats and consequences. This is essential for trust in technologies that will profoundly influence the life of our and future generations.

6 Trust Me if You Can: About Competence, Trust and Lifelong Learning

There is a clear need for education and action. As an Ipsos (2017) survey shows, people have mixed feelings about digitization. In Germany, every second person is afraid of cyber-crime. This fear is shared both by people who consider themselves to have a high competence in online applications and the average respondent (48% agreement in both groups, see Fig. 2). This is remarkable, since the "expert" group is much more positive regarding all other impacts of digitization obtained for the study.

In a joint project, the German *Institut für Sicherheit und Vertrauen im Internet* (DIVSI) and *iRights.Lab* also asked about trust in a digital world with a special focus on communication issues. The study's authors Lahmann and Kreutzer (2017a) trace back trust in its original sense to an interpersonal relationship. They combine this view with Luhmann's idea of trust in the system, since the complex world is not

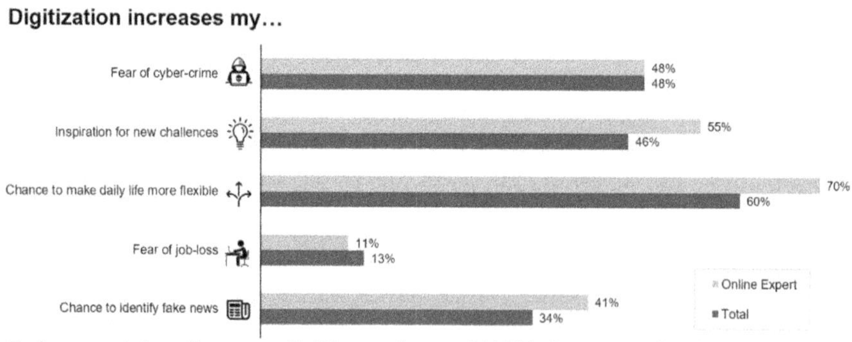

Basis: representative online survey of 1.000 respondents aged 16-70 in Germany, conducted April 21-25 2017, top-2 values of a five-point-scale

Fig. 2 Attitudes towards digitization. *Source* Translation and adaption of Ipsos (2017)

only based on interpersonal relationships. Trust in functions, roles, and systems is necessary to be capable of acting in the society (Lahmann and Kreutzer 2017a). In a digital society, trust in the security of communication processes is essential: senders of any information expect that the content cannot fall into the wrong hands. The identities of people involved in the communication process must be real and clear. It must be ensured that information cannot be distorted and that it should reach the right recipient within a short period. The expectations among the recipients regarding information are very similar (ibid.).

Similar to Ipsos, DIVSI's surveys show ongoing reservations regarding digital communication issues. The complexity of processes is hardly transparent. For example, there are several additional parties involved in telecommunication processes than just sender and receiver: email provider, service provider, and manufacturers of communication devices, to name only a few. Criminal activities such as phishing undermine trust. Media coverage of hacker attacks, data lacks, and other incidents seem to confirm reservations. The authors suggest some ideas for improvement, for example technological security, transparency, usability, and alternative offerings without price discrimination (Lahmann and Kreutzer 2017b).

To sum up: there is a clear demand for rework and optimization on the providers' side. Still, the user is in a responsible position, too. Trust is always based on an individual valuation. *Digital competence* is a prerequisite and, as we understand it in this text, consists of different aspects, namely:

- Individual digital skills;
- Digital social competence;
- Socio-political participation;
- Employability.

There are two directions to take into consideration regarding the development of individual digital skills: application-specific skills and the conscious self-management. Regarding applications, there will be the need for some standard skills regarding general knowledge. Other skills will be relevant only for special groups of people. There is a highly controversial debate regarding the question, which skills will be essential and which will not. At the very beginning of this text, we mentioned the public and political appeal for coding. For many people, coding is just a buzzword for any digital skill. It should be so much more: it is necessary to combine technological knowledge and skills such as creativity and innovative thinking for educational and professional purposes. This way, coding (to remain with the example) can be a tool to enable new forms of creativity. This will be even more relevant since AI is strongly on the rise and will play an essential part in tomorrow's both private and business ecosystems. Beside application-specific skills, the individual handling of the digital world's challenges is enormously important. It includes both one's own (passive) usage behaviour and the reflexion on digital content, its effects, and the motivations and processes behind content creation.

All aspects have an ever-increasing effect on people. It's necessary to find a conscious and open-minded access to media, digital communication tools, and applications to avoid a looming "digital divide". Digital competence will be an essential skill to deal with everyday life and—in a next step—to participate in social life and the processes in a democratic society. Digital authorities, digital referendums, and digital elections are already reality in several countries. Therefore, the corresponding skills and mindsets must be part of the curriculum at schools and in academic and further education. The shifting demands of the job (*employability*) market push the need for action in a strong way. The crucial point is: this is an ongoing process with no final goal, but must always be adapted to the changing world in the spirit of *lifelong learning*. The requirements on all levels explained are shifting and demand an ongoing development. Figure 3 summarizes the key elements in a *circle of lifelong learning* in a digital world.

Without ignoring the other aspects, employability is a key issue for social cohesion. Almost 10% of Germans are afraid of a job-loss due to digitization, as the survey by Ipsos in Fig. 2 points out (Ipsos 2017). The survey *Zukunftsmonitor* by the German Bundesinstitut für Bildung und Forschung (2017) asked about impacts of digitization in the job market in general by 2030 (this year is reference for the following data explained). 81% of respondents fear that people will be left behind in career terms by future technological development. 84% assume that the pay gap will widen due to digitization. The survey shows people's broad awareness of the consequences on the individual level: 90% of respondents consider lifelong learning as an indispensable requirement for professional success in the year 2030. Still, the personal readiness is not the only crucial factor. 85% of respondents see urgent

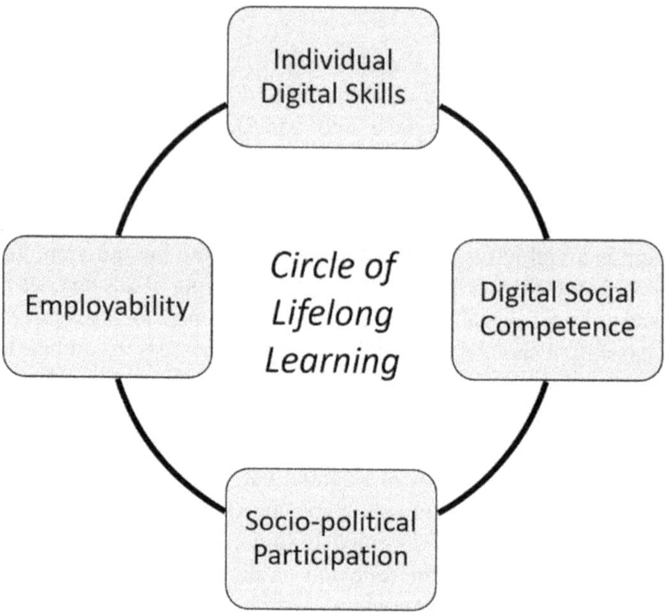

Fig. 3 Circle of lifelong learning in a digital world. *Source* Own illustration

need for action when it comes to the contents of education and professional training (Bundesministerium für Bildung und Forschung 2017).

Many voices criticize the traditional German education system for deficits and slow counteractions (e.g. Höttges 2018). There are several initiatives and further training options by public and private facilities, for an overview see for example Deutscher Bildungsserver (2018) or Bundesministerium für Familie, Senioren, Frauen und Jugend (2017). However, large enterprises have entered the market for education, too. Their offerings address all age groups and boost both STEM skills (in German: MINT) and digital competence in general. To name only a few: Deutsche Telekom Stiftung (2018) promotes several educational activities in the digital world with specific projects. *Lego*, key player in the toy industry, has had an own product line Lego Education (2018) for pedagogic material for more than 30 years. Today, there are products to develop coding skills even for elementary schools. Teacher trainings are part of the programme, too. *Google*'s *Zukunftswerkstatt* offers free online and offline courses for several topics regarding digital tools and innovation. They approach a broad target group from trainees and students, private citizens, and the self-employed up to mid-size companies.

To sum it up: the claim for lifelong learning is nothing new and challenges the political agenda both on national and EU-wide context (for discussion, see Münk 2017; Münk and Walter 2017). Educational systems and society already deal with multiple issues and still will have to deal with them over the next years. To promote *digital competence*, joint efforts in accordance with the dimensions mentioned above are indispensable.

7 What's Next: From Digital Competence to a Meaningful Life in a Digital World

It is certain that there is a strong need not only for further research and concepts, but also for a consequent implementation. Just one of the tricky questions is: Who are the best teachers for digital competence? Research assumes that *digital natives* (children and teenagers who grew up with the Internet and digital devices) have a fundamental different relationship to digital media and communication than *digital immigrants* (Prensky 2001a, b). They got their socialization in a digital world and are often more familiar with applications and devices than the generation of their teachers. Prensky points out: "our Digital Immigrant instructors, who speak an outdated language (that of the pre-digital age), are struggling to teach a population that speaks an entirely new language" (Prensky 2001a, 3). Still, it can be assumed that the teacher generation has more expertise when it comes to critical thinking, individual responsibility and deliberate acting—skills that are essential in today's world, as this text has shown.

Starting from the traditional understanding of media literacy, this text discussed contemporary ideas in terms of *digital competence*. The picture of a *circle of lifelong learning* represents four key aspects to be aware of: individual digital skills, digital social competence, socio-political participation, and employability. Trust in a digital world will only be possible when people can both trust in their practical skills and in their ability to reflect on their actions and on changes in the world around. Therefore, we stipulate to bring knowledge from the analogue and the digital world together in order to build up the competences necessary in a world of digital change.

What's next? Marc Prensky discussed his own concept assuming that "the distinction between digital natives and digital immigrants will become less relevant" (Prensky 2009, 3) over time. He introduced a new term, *digital wisdom*. For Prensky, there are two aspects to take into consideration: "Wisdom arising *from* the use of digital technology to access cognitive power beyond our innate capacity and (…) wisdom *in* the prudent use of technology to enhance our capabilities" (Prensky 2009, 3 emphasis in original).

For the first aspect, digital technology will be a key driver for deliberate decisions. There has never been as much information available as it is today and it is only one click away. Data analytics have the power to capture and calculate much more material than traditional scientific experiments; AI produces results without "knowing" anything about the issue itself. According to Prensky, this will enhance human thinking and might lead to new ways of reception of information in the years to come. But he also points out the need for the "what if" question, a very human kind of wisdom with a huge ethical dimension. Theoretically, anything producing any kind of data could be analysed. Systems will get better the more data they get. Prensky is very aware that this will (and already does!) lead to moral questions.

How does Prensky's idea of digital wisdom now correspond to the concept of digital competence explained in this text? Digital competence asks for the needs (*what and why?*), digital wisdom for the consequences in a digitally enhanced world (*to what end?*). The public discussion on both issues is in full swing and this chapter could end now with a list of elaborated recommendations on how to get things done. It doesn't.

Instead, let us take a step back and have a final look at the human factor. An education in terms of digital competence, lifelong learning, and digital wisdom will only reach people when they are open for these developments. Digitization is changing our daily and social life, our health, and our work to a huge extent. In a globally connected world, the consequences are often beyond our own power. Social change is actually happening. Who will be suspended, who will win from digitization? We are moving at full throttle. This can be scary, and people's reservations about the unknown should never be underrated. Fear is a strong driver. There are many options and little control at the very same time.

This can bring people back to the very fundamental question of a meaningful life—and this might be good news. So this chapter will end with a call for a human-centric view: every development starts at each person's very own interpretation of meaning, may it be conscious or not. If people do not understand the things that are going on, they can hardly find their individual way of dealing with them.

Self-efficacy and self-determination have always been key elements of people's emotional stability, so it is essential to spread these abilities into the digital world. We will struggle, if we see change as a threat. Digital competence is a toolbox to enable people to adapt flexibly to the developments that are taking place and those that are still to come. It will be a key resource to navigate, select, master, and reflect the challenges in a digital world and essential for building trust in our future.

References

Aufenanger S (2003) Medienkompetenz und Medienbildung. In: ajs-informationen, issue 1, pp 1–9. http://ajs-bw.de/media/files/ajs-info/ausgaben_altbis05/aufenanger.pdf. Accessed 05 Mar 2018

Baacke D (1973) Kommunikation und Kompetenz. Grundlagen einer Didaktik der Kommunikation und ihrer Medien. Juventa Verlag, München

Baacke D (1997) Medienpädagogik. Niemeyer, Tübingen

Bawden D (2008) Origins and concepts of digital literacy. In: Lankshear C, Knobel M (eds) Digital literacies. Concepts, policies and practices. Peter Lang, New York, pp 17–32

Birkner T (2017) Medialisierung und Mediatisierung. Nomos, Baden-Baden

Breunig C, van Eimeren B (2015): 50 Jahre „Massenkommunikation": Trends in der Nutzung und Bewertung der Medien. Ergebnisse der ARD/ZDF Langzeitstudie 1964–2015. In: Media Perspektiven, issue 11, pp 505–525

Bundesministerium für Bildung und Forschung (2017) ZukunftsMonitor IV: Wissen schaffen – Denken und Arbeiten in der Welt von morgen. https://www.zukunft-verstehen.de/application/files/1814/9070/7629/ZF_IV_ZukunftsMonitor_Ergebnisse_Barrierefrei.pdf. Accessed 05 Mar 2019

Bundesministerium für Familie, Senioren, Frauen und Jugend (2017) Medienkompetenz stärken. https://www.bmfsfj.de/bmfsfj/themen/kinder-und-jugend/medienkompetenz/medienkompetenz-staerken/75350. Accessed 20 Apr 2019

Deutsche Telekom Stiftung (2018) Bildung besser machen – Unsere Handlungsfelder und Projekte. https://www.telekom-stiftung.de/projekte. Accessed 20 Apr 2018

Deutscher Bildungsserver (2018) Medienkompetenz. https://www.bildungsserver.de/Medienkompetenz-2924-de.html. Accessed 20 Apr 2018

Deutsches Institut für Sicherheit und Vertrauen im Internet (DIVSI) (2017) Vertrauen in Kommunikation im digitalen Zeitalter. https://irights-lab.de/wp-content/uploads/2017/11/Studie-Vertrauen-in-digitale-Kommunikation.pdf. Accessed 18 Jan 2019

Ding S (2011) The European Commission's approach to media literacy. In: Livingstone S (ed) Media literacy. Ambitions, policies and measures. http://www.cost-transforming-audiences.eu/system/files/cost_media_literacy_report.pdf. Accessed 12 Apr 2018

DQ Institute (2018) 2018 DQ impact report. https://www.dqinstitute.org/2018dq_impact_report/. Accessed 07 Mar 2018

Gapski H, Oberle M, Staufer W (2017) Einleitung. In: Gapski H, Oberle M, Staufer W (eds) Medienkompetenz. Herausforderungen, politische Bildung und Medienbildung. Bundeszentrale für politische Bildung, Bonn, pp 17–30

Groeben N (2003) Medienkompetenz. In: Mangold R, Vorderer P, Bente G (eds) Lehrbuch der Medienpsychologie. Hogrefe, Stuttgart, Annenberg and Cologne

Hartig J, Klieme E (2006) Kompetenz und Kompetenzdiagnostik. In: Schweizer K (eds) Leistung und Leistungsdiagnostik. Springer, Berlin

Hermida M, Hielscher M, Petko D (2017) Medienkompetenz messen: Die Entwicklung des Medienprofis-Tests in der Schweiz. MedienPädagogik: Zeitschrift für Theorie und Praxis der Medienbildung 17:38–60

Hobbs R (1998) The seven great debates in the media literacy movement. J Commun 48(2):9–29
Höttges T (2018) Wer wagt, hat schon gewonnen! Ein Plädoyer für digitale Bildung. https://www.linkedin.com/pulse/wer-wagt-hat-schon-gewonnen-ein-pl%C3%A4doyer-f%C3%BCr-digitale-tim-h%C3%B6ttges/?trk=eml-email_feed_ecosystem_digest_01-recommended_articles-4-Unknown&midToken=AQETLKR5432Tvw&fromEmail=fromEmail&ut=2ITw4tvw-zE841. Accessed 19 Jan 2018
Ipsos (2017) Jeder Zweite hat Angst, Opfer von Cyberkriminalität zu werden. Pressemitteilung vom 10. Mai 2017. https://www.ipsos.com/sites/default/files/2017-05/Ipsos-PI_Digitalisierung_Mai2017_Cyber-Kriminalitat.pdf. Accessed 05 Mar 2018
Keine Bildung ohne Medien (2012) Medienpädagogisch fundierte Debatten statt Populismus. Pressemitteilung vom 05 September 2012. https://www.dgpuk.de/sites/default/files/PRESSE_KBoM_Digitale-Demenz.pdf. Accessed 05 Feb 2018
Koch W, Frees B (2015) ARD/ZDF-Onlinestudie 2017: Neun von zehn Deutschen online. Ergebnisse aus der Studienreihe „Medien und ihr Publikum" (MiP). In: Media Perspektiven, issue 9, pp 434–446
Koltay T (2011) The media and the literacies: media literacy, information literacy, digital literacy. In: Media Cult Soc 33:211–221
Krotz F (2015) Mediatisierung. In: Hepp A, Krotz F, Lingenberg S, Wimmer J (eds) Handbuch cultural studies und Medienanalyse. Springer VS, Wiesbaden, pp 439–451
Lahmann H, Kreutzer T (2017a) Vertrauen in digitale Kommunikation. Eine Bestandsaufnahme. Diskussionspapier im Projekt „Braucht Deutschland einen Digitalen Kodex?". https://irights-lab.de/wp-content/uploads/2017/11/Themenpapier-1-Vertrauen-in-Kommunikation-%E2%80%93-Bestandsaufnahme.pdf. Accessed 05 Mar 2018
Lahmann H, Kreutzer T (2017b) Wege zur Herstellung von Vertrauen in digitale Kommunikation. Diskussionspapier im Projekt „Braucht Deutschland einen Digitalen Kodex?". https://irights-lab.de/wp-content/uploads/2017/11/Themenpapier-2-Vertrauen-in-Kommunikation-%E2%80%93-Herstellung-von-Vertrauen.pdf. Accessed 05 Mar 2018
Lego Education (2018) Spielerisches Lernen mit LEGO Education. https://education.lego.com/de-de. Accessed 20 Apr 2019
Livingstone S (2004) What is media literacy? Intermedia 32(3):18–20
Merkel A (2017) Rede von Bundeskanzlerin Merkel zur Eröffnung der CeBIT am 19. März 2017. https://www.bundeskanzlerin.de/Content/DE/Rede/2017/03/2017-03-19-rede-merkel-cebit.html. Accessed 05 Mar 2018
Meyen M, Thieroff M, Strenger S (2014) Mass media logic and the mediatization of politics. Journalism Stud 15(3):271–288
Moser H (2010) Einführung in die Medienpädagogik. Aufwachsen im Medienzeitalter. VS Verlag für Sozialwissenschaften, Wiesbaden
Münk D (2017) The dark sides of lifelong learning: Unzeitgemäße Überlegungen zu einem zeitgemäßen problem. In: Münk D, Walter M (eds) Lebenslanges Lernen im soziostrukturellen Wandel. Ambivalenzen der Gestaltung von Berufsbiografien der Moderne. Springer, Wiesbaden, pp 13–38
Münk D, Walter M (eds) (2017) Lebenslanges Lernen im soziostrukturellen Wandel. Ambivalenzen der Gestaltung von Berufsbiografien der Moderne. Springer, Wiesbaden
NAMLE (2018) Media literacy defined. https://namle.net/publications/media-literacy-definitions/. Accessed 12 Apr 2018
Prensky M (2001a) Digital natives, digital immigrants part 1. On the Horizon 9(5):1–6
Prensky M (2001b) Digital natives, digital immigrants part 2: do they really think differently? On the Horizon 9(6):1–6
Prensky M (2009) H. Sapiens digital: from digital immigrants and digital natives to digital wisdom. Innovate J Online Educ 5(3). https://nsuworks.nova.edu/cgi/viewcontent.cgi?article=1020&context=innovate. Accessed 25 Sep 2018

Riesmeyer C, Pfaff-Rüdiger S, Kümpel A (2016) Wenn Wissen zu Handeln wird: Medienkompetenz aus motivationaler Perspektive. In: M&K Medien & Kommunikationswissenschaft, issue 64, pp 36–55

Roth H (1971) Pädagogische Anthropologie. Schroedel, Hannover

Schorb B, Wagner U (2013) Medienkompetenz – Befähigung zur souveränen Lebensführung in einer mediatisierten Gesellechaft. In: Bundesministerium für Familie, Senioren, Frauen und Jugend (ed) Medienkompetenzförderung für Kinder und Jugendliche. Eine Bestandsaufnahme, pp 18–23

Spitzer M (2012) Digitale Demenz. Wie wir uns und unsere Kinder um den Verstand bringen. Droemer, München

Strohmeier G (2004) Politik und Massenmedien. Eine Einführung. Nomos, Baden-Baden

Töpper V (2017) Die wollen doch nur helfen – oder? Google, Legp, Apple im Klassenraum. In: Spiegel Online, 28.10.2017. http://www.spiegel.de/forum/lebenundlernen/google-lego-apple-im-klassenraum-die-wollen-doch-nur-helfen-oder-thread-670678-1.html. Accessed 19 Jan 2018

Trepte S, Reinecke L (2013) Medienpsychologie. W. Kohlhammer GmbH, Stuttgart

Tulodziecki G (2011) Zur Entstehung und Entwicklung zentraler Begriffe bei der pädagogischen Auseinandersetzung mit Medien. In: MedienPädagogik – Zeitschrift für Theorie und Praxis der Medienbildung, issue 20, pp 11–39

Stephanie Heinecke is professor for communication studies at Hochschule Fresenius in Munich. Previously, she worked for 10 years as Head of Research and Knowledge Management at Solon Management Consulting, a strategy consultancy specialised in TIME markets. Stephanie studied communication science at Ludwig Maximilian University of Munich and did her Dr. Phil. in parallel to her work at Solon. Focus of her thesis were issues of mediatization in professional sports. In 2017, she joined Hochschule Fresenius. Her current work and research includes both current issues of media economy and the impact of digital transformation on people, companies, and society.

Maria Berg is research assistant at Fresenius University in Munich. She holds a Master's degree in Communication Studies and a Bachelor's degree in Slavic Studies. Maria previously worked at the PRIX JEUNESSE Foundation and the International Central Institute for Youth and Educational Television (IZI), which is a department of the Bavarian Broadcasting Corporation. There she was responsible for and actively participated in various research projects involving children and television.

Ludwig Hinkofer is vice-dean and academic head of the Faculty of Economics and Media at the Fresenius University of Applied Sciences in Munich, as well as professor and dean for the study programme Media and Communication Management. He studied business administration in Munich, New York and Chambéry and holds a bachelor's degree from the University of Applied Sciences in Munich and a master's degree from the University of Savoie in Chambéry in France. After his studies, he worked as a research assistant at the Institute for Educational Psychology and Empirical Education at the Ludwig-Maximilians-University Munich for more than five years and achieved his Dr. Phil. on Education, Business Administration and Psychology. He has a profound professional background and worked as a consultant and manager in the field of human resources development and e-learning as well as corporate communications for more than 10 years. Ludwig Hinkofer also worked in leading positions at Internet and multimedia agencies. He managed many e-learning projects in Germany and Europe and gained the European E-Learning Award with his team.

Chapter 17
Creating Societal Trust Through Communication to Legitimize Social Entrepreneurship in Russia

Yulia Aray and Anastasia Petrova-Savchenko

1 Introduction

Russian social entrepreneurship has developed relatively recently. Consequently, an institutional role of social entrepreneurship is only just beginning to take shape in Russia. Social entrepreneurship follows a dual logic, combining the logic of the non-profit sector with that of the business sector by pursuing a social mission with the help of business instruments, and as such is considered a hybrid organization (Battilana and Lee 2014; Maier et al. 2016; Mongelli et al. 2013; Santos et al. 2015). Enterprises consisting of potentially conflicting institutional logics (Grenier 2006; Tracey et al. 2011) need to be legitimized in society from the perspective of different stakeholders.

Social entrepreneurs who set themselves both social and economic goals are the actors who may try to create and develop new business models in the areas of state and market failures. At the moment, social entrepreneurs in Russia are usually attracted into these areas by moral motives. Here we pose a question which is crucial to our argument: How many more people with various resources might also be attracted if society tolerated an economic motivation? How big would the flow of profit-oriented people searching for new business opportunities be if society believed that it is good—or at least acceptable—to make money through solving social problems?

People mostly judge social entrepreneurs by their intentions (seeing any egoistic intentions as evil), instead of judging by the social effects brought by their entrepreneurial activities. Here we raise two more fundamental questions: first, why can people not have confidence that searching for business opportunities in solving

Y. Aray (✉) · A. Petrova-Savchenko
Saint Petersburg State University, 3, Volkhovskiy per., 199004 Saint Petersburg, Russian Federation
e-mail: Aray_yulia@gsom.spbu.ru

A. Petrova-Savchenko
e-mail: savchenko@gsom.spbu.ru

T. Osburg and S. Heinecke (eds.), *Media Trust in a Digital World*,
https://doi.org/10.1007/978-3-030-30774-5_17

social problems is beneficial to all parties? Second, why do people fail to believe that the economic interests of social entrepreneurs can add as much to solving social problems as their moral motivation? The egoistic basis of nations' wealth stated by Adam Smith is considered to be natural for market economies. We should probably, therefore, not seek to deny it in social entrepreneurship, which can rarely avoid market competition. We should probably also trust to the common human nature of social entrepreneurs, who bring wealth to their nations by loving both other people and themselves. Denying one half of this nature by letting only pure, selfless angels into the social entrepreneurship field means leaving that field weak and ever-hungry for resources and ideas.

This chapter covers the topic of legitimizing social entrepreneurship in Russia through the creation of trust among different stakeholders. The authors analyse and illustrate with cases how trust in social entrepreneurship is created and sustained through various communication strategies.

2 Social Entrepreneurship: Hybrid Nature, Sources of Legitimization and the Role of Trust

Social entrepreneurship, as "entrepreneurship with an embedded social purpose" (Austin et al. 2006, p. 1), has grown rapidly over the last few years. Not only is there an increasing number of successful examples in the social entrepreneurship sphere all over the world; there is growing interest in the phenomenon from private and public actors at different levels: global (e.g. the Skoll Foundation or the Ashoka Foundation); country-based (e.g. the Foundation of Social Regional Programs "Our Future" in Russia or "Tata Trusts" Foundation in India); and state initiatives (e.g. "Big Society" in the UK, "Social Enterprise Promotion Act" in South Korea).

Social entrepreneurship displays some unique characteristics in contrast to conventional entrepreneurship. For example, "the provision of the product or service is not an end in itself, but an integral part of an intervention to achieve social objectives, thereby contributing to social change" (Mair et al. 2012, p. 353). Some scholars argue that social enterprises create a blended value of economic, social and environmental returns (Emerson 2003). Taking into account the blended nature of social enterprises, they are considered to be hybrid organizations (Battilana and Lee 2014). Battilana and Lee (2014, p. 397) define hybrid organizations "as the activities, structures, processes and meanings by which organizations make sense of and combine multiple organizational forms". The creation of blended value very often becomes a source of tensions between these components of blended value would appear to be especially acute in hybrid organizations and could lead, for example, to so-called "mission drift", which occurs when an organization diverges from its main purpose (Cornforth 2014; Young and Kim 2015).

Pressures may come from the external environment and different stakeholders (Ebrahim et al. 2014). The dual mission and the two main logics (commercial and social) may be seen to be in contradiction and may create tensions (Alegre 2015; Costanzo et al. 2014; Jäger and Beyes 2009). Tensions may also arise between constituents: customers (commercial) and beneficiaries (social) (Battilana et al. 2015). Tensions are, of course, not exclusive to social enterprises (Lallemand-Stempak 2015); however, considerable attention has been paid to the importance of the different types of tensions that exist within hybrid organizations such as social enterprises.

Moreover, enterprises consisting of potentially conflicting institutional logics (Grenier 2006; Tracey et al. 2011), need to be legitimated in society from the perspective of different stakeholders. Legitimacy can be considered to be "generalized perception or assumption that the actions of an entity are socially desirable, proper or appropriate within some socially constructed system of norms, value, beliefs and definitions" (Suchman 1995, p. 574). Suchman (1995) offers three types of legitimization (pragmatic, moral and cognitive legitimacy), ought to be taken into consideration in social entrepreneurship. *Pragmatic* legitimacy is based on a kind of exchange calculation of the expected value of the focal organization's activity to immediate stakeholder groups: "If we get anything out of this, then we consider it legitimate" (Dart 2004, p. 416).

Moral legitimacy refers to legitimacy that is normative and based on an evaluation of whether an activity of a focal organization is the proper one (relative to external norms) rather than whether it specifically benefits those who are making the evaluation: "the right thing to do" (Suchman 1995, p. 579). *Cognitive* legitimacy refers to legitimacy at the level of taken-for-granted (Hannan and Freeman 1986) rather than the level of evaluation. The institutional role of social entrepreneurship is just being moulded in Russia, so legitimization there of the phenomenon constitutes a high priority for all participants, and primarily for the social entrepreneurs themselves. Social entrepreneurship in Russia achieves pragmatic legitimacy: public authorities and corporations (Blagov and Aray 2016) recognize it as a necessary mechanism for creating social goods, but it does not achieve moral and cognitive legitimacy. And one of the main reasons for that, as social entrepreneurs point out, is a low level of societal trust in private initiatives being capable of resolving social problems (Aray and Petrova-Savchenko 2018).

Any social phenomenon can be legitimized through trust building. Lucas and Lovaglia (2015) propose that "fundamental theoretical level legitimation and institutionalization build trust. Individuals come to accept as legitimate those aspects of the social world that they trust will operate to produce outcomes favorable to the group or organization" (p. 230). Moreover, trust can be considered as an informal institution, in other words, as "socially shared rules, usually unwritten, that are created, communicated, and enforced outside of officially sanctioned channels" (Helmke and Levitsky 2004, p. 727) and trust acts as a sanctioning mechanism. Thus, as Welter and Smallbone (2011) point out, trust "can perform an important role in either complementing or substituting for the formal institutional framework" (p. 118). They emphasize that "research undertaken in a context of low institutional trust, such as in the former post-Soviet countries, often emphasizes the role of trust in substituting for an incomplete institutional framework".

For the last decade the concept of "trust" has been much discussed in different research spheres such as psychology, sociology and cultural studies, as well as in economics and management. Trust is recognized as an important element in entrepreneurship especially for new ventures (Liao and Welsch 2005; Zahra et al. 2006) and for innovative enterprises (Aldrich 2000). Being a multidisciplinary concept, it does not have a unified definition. We use the common understanding of the word, namely. that trust is based on a perception of the probability that other agents will behave in an expected, predictable way and fulfil their obligations without the need for special sanctions (Coleman 1988; Gambetta 1988).

3 Social Entrepreneurship in Russia: Challenges to Legitimacy

Russia is considered to be a society in which there is a low level of trust (Polishchuk 2009; Pehilvanova 2009). The decline in political and civic trust from earlier levels was greatly increased by regime change in the country: in post-communist society the role of the state in the creation of public good was diminished dramatically and "the radical and largely chaotic changes the post-Soviet period have made preoccupation with one's own economic welfare the top priority" (Polishchuk 2009, p. 82). "Civic initiatives were not cultivated during the Soviet era" (Polishchuk 2009, p. 82), and do not play a significant role in society nowadays due to lack of social capital, which can be defined as "a culture of trust and tolerance, in which extensive networks of voluntary associations emerge" (Inglehart 1997, p. 188) and as the "actual and potential assets embedded in relationships among individuals, communities, networks, and societies" (Mair and Marti 2006, p. 41). Thus, civic initiatives in the social sphere are not widely accepted in Russian society.

Social entrepreneurship is a rather new phenomenon in Russia and its status has been "semi-official" till recently, i.e. it did not have a specific legal status, and it did not exist "de jure" (Blagov and Aray 2016) till 2019. The current perceived legitimacy and level of trust regarding social entrepreneurship in Russia was examined in a 5-year survey conducted by the authors. The survey was carried out in the 2014–2018 period by the PwC Center for Corporate Social Responsibility, Graduate School of Management, St Petersburg State University and included 157 social entrepreneurs from different parts of Russia (active respondents who constitute a 54% response rate out of 290 social entrepreneurs).

The authors used questionnaires and semi-structured interviews covering various aspects of social entrepreneurs' activities, including: reasons for undertaking social entrepreneurship activities, their self-identification, development, social arenas chosen, managerial aspects (financial, HR, etc.), as well as problems and obstacles they face in everyday transactions and the institutional environment. The research results revealed that lack of trust in private social initiatives is one of the key obstacles to

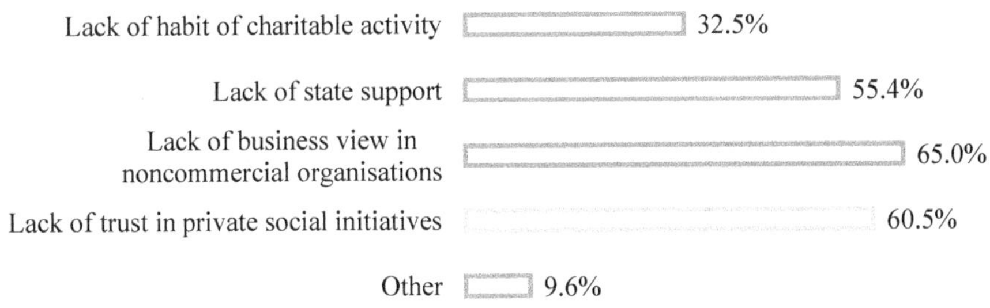

Chart 1 Factors that hamper the development of social entrepreneurship in Russia

the development and prospering of social entrepreneurship. Sixty per cent of respondents reported that their good intentions might not develop into initiatives due to society not believing in empathy prevailing over egoistic motives (see Chart 1). Social entrepreneurs see trust as an even more important factor than state support or the habit of charitable activity on the part of citizens and organizations.

It is not unreasonable to assume that in the Russian social environment the presumption of egoistic intention is dominant. Social initiatives are viewed with a great of and have to display a great deal of evidence of both good intentions and concrete results from their activities in order to gain trust. If this does not happen, social entrepreneurs face difficulties in gaining access to important resources, including financial ones, which are crucial for starting and developing a new initiative. Social entrepreneurs often get trapped in a vicious circle: they present a set of social and economic motives to stakeholders in order to get resources, but they cannot receive those resources until they demonstrate some substantial results from their activities, results that are valuable enough to solve specific social problems. In turn, substantial results cannot be achieved until an organization gains access to resources.

Our research leads us to make the observation that implies that Russian society does not generally support the idea that social initiatives should bring benefit to their creators as well as to participants. Even if a social enterprise does not ask communities for any resources, it will often face questioning of its right to make money. The view seems to be that if you call yourself "social", you should be 100% "social" (giving everything away for the good of others); if not, you are assumed to be merely exploiting a "social" tag to find business opportunities. It is sometimes hard to justify even administrative costs. Acting and potential social entrepreneurs coming to study at Graduate School of Management, St Petersburg State University were obliged to prepare a business plan as their final study project. While preparing, some of them would forget to include their salaries in the costs. They would interpret salaries as an immoral benefit taken from "the needy" instead of seeing them as simple resources necessary for their own survival and continued professional activity. Showing profits for a social enterprise may be somewhat dangerous as it may risk losing public trust.

We suggest that an attitude described above hinders the development of social entrepreneurship. Social entrepreneurship mainly arises in the areas of state and market failures. There are areas where state government would not spend money due to the presence of more urgent social matters and obvious limits of the state budget. These areas would similarly not appeal to business due to a lack of any profit potential. In Russia, the areas which involve some social problems and suffer from a lack of state or business attention include garbage processing, clothes and footwear recycling, recruitment of disabled people or youngsters coming from orphanages, care for elderly people, and rehabilitation services. These areas are usually served by non-commercial organizations, but they suffer from two general problems. First, most non-commercial organizations are highly vulnerable as they depend on donated resources. The influx of these resources depends on the visibility and prominence in the public's mind of the social problem concerned and the economic status of the givers. As soon as people and organizations involved in a charity face their own economic problems, many of them stop donating. If an economic crisis happens (which it does far from rarely in Russia), the flow of donations may become so feeble that a non-commercial organization would be forced to stop its activities. Second, the combined efforts of non-commercial organizations are sometimes not enough to make a serious impact on a given social problem.

The social entrepreneurs' desire to be sustainable through profits (see Chart 2) lends support to the idea that society should develop trust in social initiatives that are enhanced by an economic orientation. Legitimization of such an approach in Russian society would direct more resources towards the solution of current social problems. At the same time, an increased level of trust in social entrepreneurs would stimulate the emergence of various partnerships—with businesses, NGOs and the state.

The authors have also found that lack of trust in social entrepreneurship is partly caused by its absence from or non-representation in Russian law. [1] Social entrepreneurs are deeply worried about the fact that they simply do not formally exist and see the development of laws stating, regulating and defining their status as an urgent need (see Chart 3).

When they start their activities, social entrepreneurs must choose between taking the legal form of a commercial or a non-commercial organization. If they select the first option, stakeholders often see their social goal as an obstacle to potential

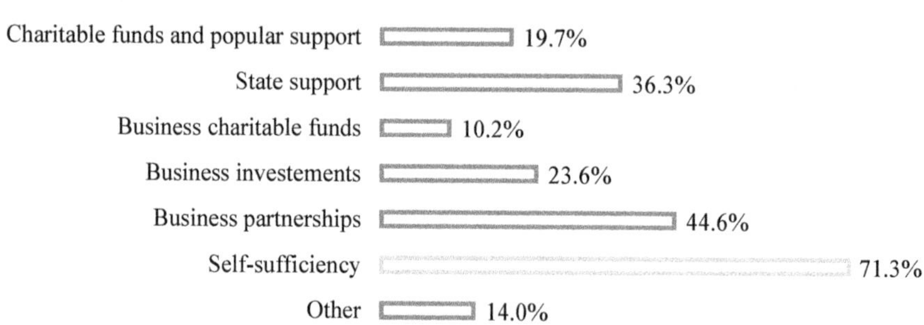

Chart 2 Factors of Russian social entrepreneurs' survival stated by social entrepreneurs

[1] Social Entrepreneurship has been legally defined through the amendments to the law about development to small and medium enterprises (No. 243 - 3) only on 26.07.2019.

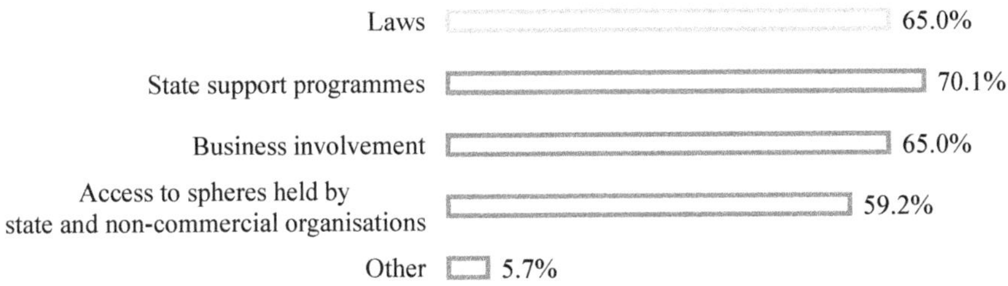

Chart 3 Current needs of Russian social entrepreneurs

relationships (because pursuing social benefit may be harmful for profit generation). If they choose the second option, stakeholders might often deny their right to even think about profitability, as has been outlined earlier. Social entrepreneurs thus find themselves trapped in a dilemma with no good outcome possible: whichever legal form of organization they choose would earn stakeholders' distrust—either from a business perspective or a social one. Any attempt to informally position oneself as a social entrepreneur while formally choosing a commercial or non-commercial legal form usually fails due to low awareness of social entrepreneurship term in Russian society. This is confirmed by the results of an 8-year study conducted by Zircon (see Chart 4).

Only about 6–7% of respondents could define social entrepreneurship, and about 70% of them had never heard of it. When asked about the possibility of specific organizations combining social and economic goals appearing, 17% of respondents replied that it is generally impossible; 26% thought that it is very unlikely; 18% suppose it may happen in the long term; 14% assume it is possible in the short term; and only 16% believe that social entrepreneurs exist. It is therefore hardly surprising that people do not trust existing social entrepreneurs.

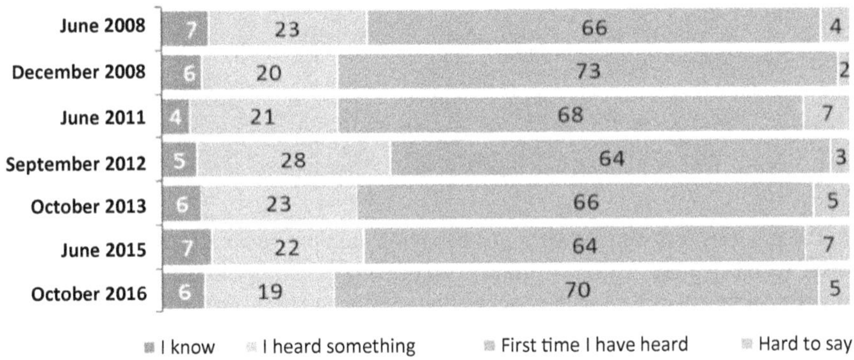

Chart 4 Awareness in Russian society of social entrepreneurship as a term

4 Trust Through Communication

There are certain representative social entrepreneurs who have succeeded in winning stakeholders' trust. Among these should be mentioned the "Spasibo!" ("Thank you!" «Спасибо!») charity shop that began operating in St. Petersburg (Russia's second-largest city) in 2010. Its business model involved the city's inhabitants bringing clothes and footwear that they did not need any more to the charity shop, which would subsequently either give those things to those in need or sell them. The profits gained from selling second-hand clothes and footwear would go to help other charities' funds. As the "Spasibo!" founder Julia Titova noted, it would be impossible to persuade people to donate their clothes and footwear for free (especially if they were to be sold) if the charity shop failed to clearly show where any profits produced thereby went. Thus, "Spasibo!" has issued detailed reports with information about which non-commercial organizations they support and how much money was given to charitable causes. Their efforts to build a sustainable business model based on people's trust has led to the creation of a chain of several charity shops in St Petersburg. Additionally, their model has been taken up by people in other cities and towns as an example for their own charity shops.

The modern economic system has become complex, and actors need more trust-based relationships. As Power (2007) suggested, such relationships have created an ecosystem "of actors and systems that can act for the principals in economic settings and, thus, reduce their risk. These include internal control systems, public disclosures and regulation, and a third party audit 'industry'" (Nicholls 2009, p. 758). As can be seen from the case discussed above, one social entrepreneur applied the disclosure of the company's activities to build up trust among stakeholders. It is important to emphasize that the information presented should aim to give "equal strategic attention to capturing and disclosing social and financial value creation in combination" (Nicholls 2009, p. 759).

There is also the interesting case of the Raoul Charity Foundation (Фонд «Рауль»), which is working on a solution to an important problem for Russian society, namely, the isolation from social and economic life suffered by graduates of correctional boarding schools. The Raoul organization helps them get employed by corporations who are developing programmes of corporate social responsibility and require a low-skilled workforce. Raoul encountered a certain level of distrust from two key stakeholders—non-profit organizations interacting with correctional boarding schools graduates and graduates themselves. The non-profit organizations did not show the appropriate initiative and interest in achieving results. As for the graduates themselves, they tend to not trust anyone at all; at the same time, they constantly get into situations in which they are in need of a person who is ready to support them, help them make a choice and give them advice when most needed.

Raoul decided that it should appoint a mentor to every young person involved in its programme. Specialists state that a long-term, unbroken contact helps correctional boarding schools' graduates, who are mainly orphans, to compensate for the aspects of their life related to lacking a family. They acquire a person interested in their everyday achievements, even minor ones. Mentors as mediators have helped to overcome the high level of distrust previously existing between Raoul, non-commercial organizations and correctional boarding schools' graduates. By 2018 the number of mentors in the program had reached 1021 people. Here we can see an indication of the crucial importance of personal relationships and everyday personal contacts in social entrepreneurs' activities. As a result, Raoul has succeeded in creating a network of stakeholders consisting of non-profit organizations, corporations, correctional boarding schools, mentors and graduates, all of whom support this social entrepreneur in its activities and initiatives.

Many authors stress the role of social networks trust in creating and developing new organizations (Liao and Welsch 2005; Zahra et al. 2006). Anderson and Jack (2002) suggest that networks contain trust, which works as "glue and lubricant" holding networks together. Moreover, networks assist a new venture in creating legitimacy (Welter and Smallbone 2009). Building up trust within their network is of high priority for social entrepreneurs as it can guarantee and assist them in developing legitimacy in a particular market (Welter and Smallbone 2009). As can be seen from "Raoul" case discussed above, a social entrepreneur put the effort into communicating with the most closely involved stakeholders whose support was urgently required and creating trustworthy relations that helped it develop its operations. The establishment of mutually trusted relationships seems to be much more important in social entrepreneurship that in business entrepreneurship.

A third example is a "Tibozh" («Тибож») factory that produces footwear and accessories while employing only people with disabilities. They developed the idea that gaining trust would only be possible if as many people as possible got to know about the factory and its social mission. Due to people awareness the factory was able to rely on its word-of-mouth reputation which would, later on, bring B2C and B2B customers as well as business partners. Gradually, as the factory grew, they started to develop a media presence in social networks and also enrolled in a Boomstarter fundraising project which helped to increase customer awareness and gather orders.

Very often, in the initial stages of venture creation entrepreneurs rely heavily on personal networks, trying to build up trust among "friends of friends". However, as Welter and Kautonen (2005) emphasize, whereas "social relations based on personal trust are functional as a basis for business in the initial phase, an over-extensive reliance on social networks can become a liability when the business develops" (p. 369). As can be seen from the case discussed above, that social entrepreneur gradually extended the communication tools for building trust not only within the network of known stakeholders, but far beyond that, through social media and crowdfunding platforms. Such a strategy allowed the company to attract additional resources, create new opportunities and enhance legitimacy among a wider range of stakeholders.

5 Summary

This chapter contributes to understanding the role of trust in social entrepreneurship legitimization. Social entrepreneurship, having a dual nature and being a rather new phenomenon in Russia, needs to gain societal legitimacy to sustain its existence in the long term. The role of trust as an important mechanism for enhancing social entrepreneurship legitimization is discussed in this chapter. Different strategies for creating and developing trust are sketched out:

- social entrepreneurs use disclosure of information about companies' operations to build up trust among stakeholders;
- social entrepreneurs put effort into creating trust in their networks through transparent communications with different stakeholders;
- social entrepreneurs gradually extend the communication tools for building trust beyond the narrow network of immediate stakeholders.

References

Aldrich H (2000) Entrepreneurial strategies in new organizational populations. In: Swedberg R (ed) Entrepreneurship: the social science view. Oxford University Press, Oxford, pp 211–228

Alegre I (2015) Social and economic tension in social enterprises: does it exist? Soc Bus 5(1):17–32. https://doi.org/10.1362/204440815X14267607784767

Anderson AR, Jack SL (2002) The articulation of social capital in entrepreneurial networks: a glue ora lubricant? Entrepreneurship Reg Dev 14:193–210

Aray Y, Petrova-Savchenko A (2018) Social entrepreneurship in Russia: current trends and opportunities for development. In: Proceedings of GSOM emerging markets conference. St. Petersburg University Graduate School of Management, pp 60–61

Austin J, Stevenson H, Wei-Skillern J (2006) Social and commercial entrepreneurship: same, different or both? Entrepreneurship Theor Pract 30(1):1–22

Battilana J, Lee M (2014) Advancing research on hybrids organizing—insights from the study of social enterprises. Acad Manage Ann 8(1):397–441

Battilana J, Sengul M, Pache A-C, Model J (2015) Harnessing productive tensions in hybrid organizations: the case of work integration social enterprises. Acad Manage J 58(6):1658–1685

Blagov Y, Aray Y (2016) Developing social entrepreneurship models in Russian legal and socio-economic context. In: Proceedings of GSOM emerging markets conference. St. Petersburg University Graduate School of Management, pp 49–51

Coleman JS (1988) Social capital in the creation of human capital. Am J Sociol 94:95–120

Cornforth C (2014) Understanding and combating mission drift in social enterprises. Soc Enterp J 10(1):3–20

Costanzo LA, Vurro C, Foster D, Servato F, Perrini F (2014) Dual-mission management in social entrepreneurship: qualitative evidence from social firms in the United Kingdom. J Small Bus Manage 52(4):655–677

Dart R (2004) The legitimacy of social enterprise nonprofit. Manage Leadersh 14(4):411–424

Ebrahim A, Battilana J, Mair J (2014) The governance of social enterprises: mission drift and accountability challenges in hybrid organizations. Res Organ Behav 34:81–100

Emerson J (2003) Where money meets mission: breaking down the firewalls between foundation investments and programming. Stanford Soc Innov Rev. Available at: www.blendedvalue.org/wp-content/uploads/2004/02/pdf-money-meets-mission.pdf

Gambetta DG (ed) (1988) Trust: making and breaking cooperative relations. Basil Blackwell, New York

Grenier P (2006) Social entrepreneurship: agency in a globalizing world. In: Nicholls A (ed) Social entrepreneurship. New models of sustainable social change. Oxford University Press, Oxford

Hannan MT, Freeman J (1986) Where do organizations come from? Sociol Forum 1(1):50–72
Helmke G, Levitsky S (2004) Informal institutions and comparative politics: a research agenda. Perspect Politics 2(04):725–740
Inglehart R (1997) Modernization and post-modernization: cultural, economic, and political change in 43 societies. Princeton University Press, Princeton, NJ
Jäger UP, Beyes T (2009) Strategizing in NPOs: a case study on the practice of organizational change between social mission and economic rationale. Voluntas 21:82–100
Lallemand-Stempak N (2015) Rôle de la planification stratégique dans l'évolution des entreprises sociales. Revue française de gestion 247:101–117
Liao J, Welsch H (2005) Roles of social capital in venture creation: key dimensions and research implications. J Small Bus Manage 43(4):345–362
Lucas JW, Lovaglia MJ (2015) Legitimation and institutionalization as trust-building: reducing resistance to power and influence in organizations. Adv Group Processes 23:229–252
Maier F, Meyer M, Steinbereithner M (2016) Nonprofit organizations becoming business-like: a systematic review. Nonprofit Voluntary Sect Q 45(1):64–86
Mair J, Marti I (2006) Social entrepreneurship research: a source of explanation, prediction, and delight. J World Bus 41(1):6–44
Mair J, Battilana J, Cardenas J (2012) Organizing for society: a typology of social entrepreneuring models. J Bus Ethics 111(3):353–373
Mongelli L, Rullani F, Versari P (2013) Hybridization of diverging institutional logics through the 'common tone': the case of social entrepreneurship. In: EMES-SOCENT conference selected papers, no. LG13-46, Liège, 4th EMES international research conference on social enterprise, 18p
Nicholls A (2009) 'We do good things, don't we?': 'Blended Value Accounting' in social entrepreneurship. Acc Organ Soc 34:755–769
Pehilvanova P (2009) The decline of trust in post-communist societies: the case of Bulgaria and Russia. Contemp Issues 2(1):32–47
Polishchuk L (2009) Corporate social responsibility or government regulation? An analysis of institutional choice. Probl Econ Trans 52(8):73–94
Power M (2007) Organized uncertainty: designing a world of risk management. Oxford University Press, Oxford
Santos F, Pache A-C, Birkholz C (2015) Making hybrids work: aligning business models and organizational design for social enterprises. Calif Manage Rev 57(3):36–58
Suchman MC (1995) Managing legitimacy: strategic and institutional approaches. Acad Manage Rev 20:571–610
Tracey P, Nelson P, Jarvis O (2011) Bridging institutional entrepreneurship and the creation of new organization forms: a multilevel model. Organ Sci 22(1):60–80
Welter F, Kautonen T (2005) Trust, social networks and enterprise development: exploring evidence from east and west Germany. Int Entrepreneurship Manage J 1:367–379
Welter F, Smallbone D (2009) The emergence of entrepreneurial potential in transition environments: a challenge for entrepreneurship theory or a developmental perspective? In Smallbone D, Landström H, Jones-Evans D (eds) Entrepreneurship and growth in local, regional and national economies. Edward Elgar Cheltenham, UK
Welter F, Smallbone D (2011) Institutional perspectives on entrepreneurial behavior in challenging environments. J Small Bus Manage 49(1):107–125
Young DR, Kim C (2015) Can social enterprises remain sustainable and mission-focused? Applying resiliency theory. Soc Enterp J 11(3):233–259
Zahra S, Yavuz RI, Ucbasaran D (2006) How much do you trust me? The dark side of relational trust in new business creation in established companies. Entrepreneurship Theor Pract 30(4):541–559

Yulia Aray is Senior Lecturer of Strategic and International Management Department of Graduate School of Management, Saint-Petersburg State University. Her main research interests are connected with social entrepreneurship, sustainability and corporate social responsibility. Dr. Yulia Aray is an expert in the field of business models of firms working in social entrepreneurship with more than 25 publications in Russian and English.

Anastasia Petrova-Savchenko is Senior Lecturer of Strategic and International Management Department of Graduate School of Management, Saint-Petersburg State University. Her main research interests are connected with corporate social performance management, business ethics and social entrepreneurship. Dr. Anastasia Petrova-Savchenko is conducting related learning courses in Graduate School of Management and is an author of more than 25 publications in Russian and English.

Chapter 18
Digital Marketing and Communication for Social Enterprises

Chinmoy Bandyopadhyay and Subhasis Ray

1 Introduction

After information technology revolution, digital presence and connectivity has become indispensable for any business (Malecki and Moriset 2007). The power has shifted from the producers to the consumers as the consumers are more informed and connected than before (Wuyts et al. 2011). Thus, currently, the fate of any business and their offerings depends to a great extent on the reviews and feedback of the consumers (Lee et al. 2008; Sen and Lerman 2007; Zhu and Zhang 2010). Also, the decisions related to the purchase of products/services is now being taken more and more by the young people. Young consumers are tech savvy and inclined to purchase online (Engel et al. 2011). From the side of the organization, digital connectivity makes it easy to reach more and more people at a low cost (Levy and Birkner 2011). For instance, organizations can leverage the social media or any other online medium to spread good words about them through pleased consumers (Dellarocas 2003; Duan and Whinston 2008a; Lipsman et al. 2012). This allows organizations to have dialogues with the consumers, understand their needs in a much better way and hence serve them better (Alalwan et al. 2017; Simmons 2008). Therefore, the use of digital medium can dismantle the geographical boundaries by connecting global consumers with the offerings of a business (Hanna et al. 2011; Singh et al. 2012). Small businesses stand to benefit from cost-effective tools like e-marketing, particularly because they don't have resources to carry out traditional marketing activities (Eid and El-Gohary 2013).

Social enterprises (SEs), as defined by prior works, further their social cause through revenues generated from business operations (Bacq and Janssen 2011;

C. Bandyopadhyay (✉) · S. Ray
Xavier Institute of Management, Xavier University, Bhubaneswar, Odisha 751013, India
e-mail: chinmoy.mcet@gmail.com

S. Ray
e-mail: sray@ximb.ac.in

T. Osburg and S. Heinecke (eds.), *Media Trust in a Digital World*,
https://doi.org/10.1007/978-3-030-30774-5_18

Collavo 2018; Mair and Marti 2006; Weerawardena and Mort 2006). Seen this way, SEs are organizations that are expected to give equal weight to social and economic goals by incorporating them at the strategic level (Battilana and Lee 2014). SEs, like other organizations that are involved in selling products and services, need marketing. Although marketing is important for the long-term existence of SEs, they face challenges regarding the lack of resources and thus lack a robust distribution setup. Hence, digital marketing tools can be advantageous for SEs because like small businesses, they lack resources to invest in full-fledged marketing operations (Bull and Crompton 2006; Peattie and Morley 2008). In addition, SEs encounters the problem of lower awareness and trust among different stakeholders (Cornelius et al. 2008; Spear et al. 2009). Moreover, SEs often offer regional and local products, which are very expensive to make available to the consumers through physical distribution setup. Therefore, SEs need cost-effective way to promote their offerings and make people aware about their cause and also to gain the trust and support of their stakeholders (Bandyopadhyay and Ray 2019a). For example, a video by a SE, showing their offerings or their operation may go viral and that will spread the name of that SE in a cost-effective way.

While it is well documented that the digital marketing tools are useful for SEs (Mallin and Finkle 2007; Wong and Tse 2016), there is little guidance from academia on how SEs utilize these tools to market their products/services to digitally connected consumers. Numerous researchers also have highlighted the need of exploring the way SEs use digital marketing tools (Bandyopadhyay and Ray 2019b; Kannampuzha and Suoranta 2016). With this limited past discussion, the present study seeks to capture the experience and learning of social entrepreneurs of using digital marketing tools. Using the views of the social entrepreneurs, we show that usage of digital marketing tools helps SEs overcome the issue of lower resources, awareness, and trust by connecting them to key stakeholders.

2 Literature Review

Digital Marketing

In a time when customers are increasingly purchasing their products online (Leeflang et al. 2014), organizations with better knowledge and setup of digital platforms will have edge over others (Albuquerque et al. 2012). Marketing has entered the era of digital transactions, thus digital marketing has become a useful approach for almost all kinds of organizations (Simmons 2008; Tiago and Veríssimo 2014; Wind and Mahajan 2002). With present upsurge of smartphones, more and more companies have started considering online platforms to advertise their offerings (Bleier and Eisenbeiss 2015; Okazaki et al. 2007). Nowadays, digital platforms have made it possible for customers to gather information on the options available in the market before purchasing anything (Ratchford et al. 2007; Ward and Lee 2000). Hence, the power of the consumers have increased as they are now more connected and informed (Pitt et al. 2002).

In present day, it is not only about the relationship between the organization and the customers. The customers are also connected with each other through different online platforms. Hence, the snowball effect of people talking to each other about the products and services is really crucial (Barnes et al. 2012; Trusov et al. 2009). People tend to trust their peers more than the companies that offering products/services. Hence, more than ever, customers take purchase decisions based on the feedback of other consumers (Forman et al. 2008; Godes and Silva 2012; Häubl and Trifts 2000; Mangold and Faulds 2009). These feedback from the consumers in the online platforms are much more important for service providing firms. As services are generally intangible and therefore the assessment of the existing users is important (Duan et al. 2008b; Kim et al. 2016; Litvin et al. 2008; Liu 2006; Sotiriadis and Van Zyl 2013; Zhu and Zhang 2010). Hence, online reviews can influence how customers see a firm and its offerings and eventually build trust and credibility (Awad and Ragowsky 2008; Sparks and Browning 2011). Taking it one step further, few consumers also share their experiences of using products/services through self-made videos, which get shared across a large audience (Berthon et al. 2008). Therefore, the presence of an organization in social media platforms such as Facebook and Twitter is important (Bulearca and Bulearca 2010; Dwivedi et al. 2015; Harris and Rae 2009).

Presently, more and more young people are taking the purchase decision. The younger generation is inclined to make online purchases. This, in turn, has increased the importance of adopting an online mode of marketing products and services (Durkin et al. 2013). Millennials often get tempted to purchase online through digital media due to several reasons such as convenience, frequent discounts, range of products, user reviews, and so forth (Smith 2011; Taken Smith 2012).

Using the digital medium, organizations can have relationships with the target customers (Bughin 2014). The essence of this interactivity is that it can open the way for customization of the offerings (Ansari and Mela 2003). Therefore, these digitally enabled relationship between the organizations and their customers also set the foundation for co-creation of value (Kierzkowski et al. 1996; See-To and Ho 2014). This approach can be advantageous as more and more customers have started involving themselves in the product designing process (Franke and Schreier 2010). The digital relationship with the customers even presents an opportunity for small organization to seek financial aid from the customers (Ordanini et al. 2011; Whitla 2009).

Most firms, whether small or big, get benefitted by communities of consumers who are fan of their brand (McAlexander et al. 2002; Muniz and O'guinn 2001; Schau et al. 2009). Digital platforms make it easier for the firms to form, maintain, and track these online communities (Chi 2011; Szmigin et al. 2005). For instance, awareness and popularity of a brand can be increased through Facebook fan pages (De Vries et al. 2012; Gummerus et al. 2012). The presence of theses online communities results in consumer engagement and subsequently the firms may gain trust from the consumers (Brodie et al. 2013; Habibi et al. 2014).

Taken together, with the upsurge of digital media usage, firms are increasingly relying on digital marketing tools to sell their offerings. These tools not only just take them closer to the customers but also help them gaining entry to the conversations between the customers in a cost-effective way. Doing so allows the firms to address specific needs of the customers and to become more effective, transparent, and trustworthy. As noted in the following section, digital marketing helps SEs to understand and address the needs of the consumers in a cost-effective way.

Need for Digital Marketing in Social Enterprises

As noted earlier, the inflow of financial resources is important for SEs to accomplish their social objectives in a larger way and for a longer period. To get financial resources, SEs need support from different stakeholders such as the investors and customers. Whether an investor will invest in a SE or a customer will purchase the offerings of the SE often comes down to the marketing strategies (Jenner 2016; Madill et al. 2010). However, due to some organizational issues in SEs, it seems appropriate to use digital marketing tools in SE context. As described below, the budget allocated for marketing activities in SEs remains remarkably low. Also, the success of SEs depends on the level of awareness among the stakeholders. In addition, it could be valuable for SEs to be transparent to gain the trust and support from the stakeholders (Bandyopadhyay and Ray 2019b).

SEs are often confronted with the issue of lack of budget for marketing activities. Consequently, they lack the arrangement and skilled manpower to plan and implement a traditional full-length marketing activities (Doherty et al. 2009; Mitchell et al. 2016; Peattie and Morley 2008). For the same reason, SEs lack a physical distribution set up like the big players in the market. As a remedy, they may use the potential of online platforms. Another problem is that SEs often sell indigenous products or crafts made by the artisans to urban customers with a taste for these kinds of products. For them it is important to put their products in an online platform because these customers are located in different places and they often search for such products online. Moreover, the online presence also helps SEs in demonstrating the social impact by showcasing success stories through photos, videos, blogs, Facebook posts, and the like. For example, *Rangsutra* is a SE based in India. Not only they sell the garments made by local artisans online, they also post the stories of successful artisans.

In order to be effective and successful, SEs need people to know about their organization (Bhattacharya 2013; Singh et al. 2015). One part of this process is related to spreading awareness about the social impact. The other part is associated to the communications regarding the quality and attributes of the offerings.

Finally, given the need for support from different stakeholders, SEs often try to become more credible as an organization. To gain trust, it is important to maintain transparency (Bandyopadhyay and Ray 2019b). The first and an important step towards enacting transparency is to make information available to wider audience. Doing so could help SEs in becoming more credible and trustworthy. Uploading information in an online platform appears to be a faster and cost-effective way.

3 Methodology

For this study, we interviewed eight social entrepreneurs who operates in different parts of India. All the social entrepreneurs we interviewed, had adopted digital marketing tools as part of their marketing approach. The line of questioning was based around the kind of digital marketing approach or tools they generally use and their experience of using them. Findings of the study are inferred from the eight interviews with the social entrepreneurs. The average time of those interviews were around one hour. All the interviews are transcribed and then analyzed to generate useful findings. The following table presents information about all the eight SEs selected for the present study.

Social enterprises	Products/services	Geographical location
SE1	Handloom products	Bhubaneswar, India
SE2	Organic food products	Bhubaneswar, India
SE3	Organic food products	Kolkata, India
SE4	Handloom products	Bangalore, India
SE5	Organic farming services	Bangalore, India
SE6	Plastic free containers	Bangalore, India
SE7	Volunteering services	Jaipur, India
SE8	Himalayan organic food products	Khairoli, India

4 Findings

Our interaction with the social entrepreneurs provided insight into the way they use digital marketing tools and the variety of potential benefits that these tools have.

Attracting Volunteers

SEs often are short of talented people, therefore use of digital tools may go a long way in attracting new talents by showcasing their social impact. Similar to the process of choosing a product or service, young generation of people go online to find information before deciding to work for any organization. Hence, keeping the online audience informed about the unique attributes and operations of a SE seems to be a good way of acquiring prospective employees or volunteers too. As noted by one of the social entrepreneurs, "So, aggregating them on a web platform, for example, a mobile app where they (volunteers) can scroll and they can see what all activities are happening in the city in upcoming days, who is conducting what activity and what is required of them. The availability of this kinds of information helps people to join and serve" (SE7).

Informative Apps to Appeal to the Investors

The presence of a well-designed and information rich website or app is critical for the visibility of a firm among key stakeholders and building relationship with them (Pratt et al. 2008; Uzunoğlu and Kip 2014). For instance, investors may make sense of a SE through an appealing and informative website or app. As the entrepreneur of SE4 observed:

> What holds all the business operations together, which we called *connect* which is using digital technology and having a technology base that holds this whole thing together. Whether it is the supply chain itself, transparency, visibility of supply chains, payments- how the payments bflow up and down in the system. So that's all being done digitally and it is been done through a set of apps that people can have access to… So, this is how we communicate to our funders saying that look it is not just going and doing one thing but we are taking care of all at the same time.

Supply Chain Management

When dealing with the expenses involved with supply chain, SEs often try to take the shortest path. Online platform helps them in this regard by allowing them to showcase their products through their website and social media. They then can track and manage the incoming orders by themselves through these online mediums. This enables them to keep control of the supply chain to a great extent, as is evident in one social entrepreneurs' comment on using online platforms: "we try to keep our supply chain as short as possible. And also as we are targeting urban consumers, we use online platforms rather than traditional channels" (SE2).

Gaining Trust and Credibility by Maintaining Transparency

The view of few participants of this study illustrates that proper flow of information between the organization and the stakeholders is key. Our findings suggest that the stakeholders must have access to relevant information about the operations of the SEs. As the entrepreneur of SE3 said when discussing about gaining the trust of the producers: "We have developed an ICT platform. So, the farmers and others will get information such as pricing, how much did we sell, and so forth. So, everything should be transparent, nothing we should hide from them. And, then gradually you can gain trust". Similarly, another participant reported that it is important to provide regular updates to the customers to keep them engaged and it also helps to add credibility to their organization: "…there is a farmer app and there is customer app. Everything that is happening, the farmer is actually capturing it in his farmer app. So we would know exactly what seed was planted in which bed…keeping the customers updated through the app helps in building trust" (SE5).

Building Awareness About the Social and Economic Benefits

When probed about how they spread awareness about their mission and offerings, participants echoed the issue of lower budget. To counter this issue, they seem to use a range of innovative ways mainly by utilizing social media. For instance, one social entrepreneur said the following about using YouTube videos to generate awareness:

> …so basically those are good small crisp videos which are talking about how each one of us can make a difference in terms of our everyday life by decreasing use of plastics in a very simple way. It is not very difficult at all. Most of the videos have little children who spoken with focus and because they are the best advocate. Parents usually like to listen to their kids saying good things so they eventually follow them. So that is one of the means that we're using, and it seems to have worked quite well for us (SE6).

Further, one of the participants discussed how their presence in different online news portals helps them in spreading good words about their work:

> I think the single most important thing is to continuously build awareness. So, we've been on the radio channels quite regularly and NDTV (national level news channel) has written about us and Better India (online media platform) is having us on their platform, we sell through Better India. Yourstory (online media platform) has written about us. And we continuously are quite active on the social media and we are very sure that you are not always trying to sell off your products there but it's more about building awareness (SE6).

As traditional advertising mediums invlove high investment, social entrepreneurs continuously look for new ways to make people aware of their organizations. One social entrepreneur described it vividly, "Frankly speaking, we do not have the money to carry out full-fledged awareness programs. Creating consumer awareness is very expensive. Earlier, people used to give television advertisements, but it is very expensive. We rely on social media and peer to peer communications" (SE4).

Some SEs also seems to leverage their website to educate the customers by providing information about their products. As mentioned by one participant, "Most of our customers are health conscious young people working in multinational corporations. We generate awareness about the benefits about our products by sharing health tips through our website" (SE8).

Celebrity Endorsement

Some SEs also benefit from the promotional activities involving a popular personalities having huge numbers of followers in social media. One of the social entrepreneurs provided the following account:

Apart from the word-of-mouth, we also use influence marketing. We use people who have a lot of followers and send them one sample product as part of our promotional activity. Suppose, someone has 20,000 followers in Instagram and she posts pictures of her wearing Sari (ethnic wear for women) and jewelries made by us. In that way, more and more people will come to know about our products and will visit our social media pages. That is an effective way of marketing (SE1).

Identifying and Targeting Online Customers

Our findings suggest that SEs often depend on the digital media to identify and target their potential customers. As the participant from SE1 described, "we identify our customers mostly through our social media platforms. We all follow our page on Facebook, Twitter, and Instagram. Mostly we get our customers from these platforms. Also, we get some customers through WhatsApp chats".

The findings also provide evidence that the SEs tend to focus more on the online buyers than their offline counterparts. This implies that the targeting process in SEs driven, to a great extent, by the availability of the customers in the online space. To this point one participant expressed, "We target young customers who purchase products online. On the other hand, old people, although they are more health conscious, do not like to transact online. So, for now, we are not focusing on them" (SE8).

5 Conclusion

While the need of digital tools in SE marketing has been touched upon in earlier studies, we lack understanding on the process or approach adopted by the SEs. In response, we sought to understand and explore the nature of the digital marketing activities in SEs. This paper shows that digital marketing holds special significance for SEs. Used wisely, digital marketing can help SEs to increase their outreach and target customers and build a relationship with them. Our interaction with the social entrepreneurs indicated that digital marketing tools are specifically tailored to meet the resource related issue in SEs. We found that instead of traditional mediums methods, SEs tend to use social media to generate customer awareness at a lower cost. The findings also suggest that social entrepreneurs seem to prefer online channels, as they help them break away from the cost associated with the supply chain intermediaries. Together, these insights suggest that digital media helps in maintaining a transparent system, which is a necessary precondition for building trust. Hence, we argued that by having digital relationship, SEs can gain more trust and credibility from their stakeholders.

These insights are important as they can provide some initial directions towards using digital media to generate awareness and building trust and credibility for SEs. Our study builds on the prior work that mostly focused on the consumers. While these studies have documented different facets of digital marketing approach adopted by firms, the findings of the present study significantly expands current understanding by focusing on the perspectives of the social entrepreneurs.

It could be valuable to carry out a similar study involving a greater number of social enterprises for more comprehensive and insightful results. Moreover, as the present study has only focused on the views of the social entrepreneurs, future research may benefit from perspectives of other stakeholders such as the suppliers, investors, and customers.

References

Alalwan AA, Rana NP, Dwivedi YK, Algharabat R (2017) Social media in marketing: a review and analysis of the existing literature. Telematics Inform 34(7):1177–1190

Albuquerque P, Pavlidis P, Chatow U, Chen KY, Jamal Z (2012) Evaluating promotional activities in an online two-sided market of user-generated content. Mark Sci 31(3):406–432

Ansari A, Mela CF (2003) E-customization. J Mark Res 40(2):131–145

Awad NF, Ragowsky A (2008) Establishing trust in electronic commerce through online word of mouth: an examination across genders. J Manage Inf Syst 24(4):101–121
Bacq S, Janssen F (2011) The multiple faces of social entrepreneurship: a review of definitional issues based on geographical and thematic criteria. Entrepreneurship Reg Dev 23(5–6):373–403
Bandyopadhyay C, Ray S (2019a) Responsible marketing: can social enterprises show the way? J Nonprofit Public Sect Mark 31(2):164–183
Bandyopadhyay C, Ray S (2019b) Social enterprise marketing: review of literature and future research agenda. Mark Intell Planning. https://doi.org/10.1108/MIP-02-2019-0079
Barnes D, Clear F, Dyerson R, Harindranath G, Harris L, Rae A (2012) Web 2.0 and micro-businesses: an exploratory investigation. J Small Bus Enterp Dev 19(4):687–711
Battilana J, Lee M (2014) Advancing research on hybrid organizing—insights from the study of social enterprises. Acad Manage Ann 8(1):397–441
Berthon P, Pitt L, Campbell C (2008) Ad lib: when customers create the ad. Calif Manage Rev 50(4):6–30
Bhattacharya CB (2013) The importance of marketing for social innovation. In: Social innovation. Springer, Berlin, pp 147–154
Bleier A, Eisenbeiss M (2015) Personalized online advertising effectiveness: the interplay of what, when, and where. Mark Sci 34(5):669–688
Brodie RJ, Ilic A, Juric B, Hollebeek L (2013) Consumer engagement in a virtual brand community: an exploratory analysis. J Bus Res 66(1):105–114
Bughin J (2014) Brand success in an era of digital Darwinism. J Brand Strategy 2(4):355–365
Bulearca M, Bulearca S (2010) Twitter: a viable marketing tool for SMEs? Global Bus Manage Res 2(4):296–309
Bull M, Crompton H (2006) Business practices in social enterprises. Soc Enterp J 2(1):42–60
Chi HH (2011) Interactive digital advertising vs. virtual brand community: exploratory study of user motivation and social media marketing responses in Taiwan. J Interact Advertising 12(1):44–61
Collavo T (2018) Unpacking social entrepreneurship: exploring the definition chaos and its consequences in England. J Entrepreneurship Manage Innov 14(2):49–82
Cornelius N, Todres M, Janjuha-Jivraj S, Woods A, Wallace J (2008) Corporate social responsibility and the social enterprise. J Bus Ethics 81(2):355–370
Dellarocas C (2003) The digitization of word of mouth: promise and challenges of online feedback mechanisms. Manage Sci 49(10):1407–1424
De Vries L, Gensler S, Leeflang PS (2012) Popularity of brand posts on brand fan pages: an investigation of the effects of social media marketing. J Interact Mark 26(2):83–91
Doherty B, Foster G, Meehan J, Mason C (2009) Management for social enterprise. Sage Publications, Thousand Oaks
Duan W, Gu B, Whinston AB (2008a) The dynamics of online word-of-mouth and product sales—an empirical investigation of the movie industry. J Retail 84(2):233–242
Duan W, Gu B, Whinston AB (2008b) Do online reviews matter?—an empirical investigation of panel data. Decis Support Syst 45(4):1007–1016
Durkin M, McGowan P, McKeown N (2013) Exploring social media adoption in small to medium-sized enterprises in Ireland. J Small Bus Enterp Dev 20(4):716–734
Dwivedi YK, Kapoor KK, Chen H (2015) Social media marketing and advertising. Mark Rev 15(3):289–309
Eid R, El-Gohary H (2013) The impact of E-marketing use on small business enterprises' marketing success. Serv Ind J 33(1):31–50
Engel CJ, Bell RL, Meier RJ, Martin MJ, Rumpel JH (2011) Young consumers in the new marketing ecosystem: an analysis of their usage of interactive technologies. Acad Mark Stud J 15(2):23
Forman C, Ghose A, Wiesenfeld B (2008) Examining the relationship between reviews and sales: the role of reviewer identity disclosure in electronic markets. Inf Syst Res 19(3):291–313
Franke N, Schreier M (2010) Why customers value self-designed products: the importance of process effort and enjoyment. J Prod Innov Manage 27(7):1020–1031

Godes D, Silva JC (2012) Sequential and temporal dynamics of online opinion. Mark Sci 31(3):448–473

Gummerus J, Liljander V, Weman E, Pihlström M (2012) Customer engagement in a Facebook brand community. Manage Res Rev 35(9):857–877

Habibi MR, Laroche M, Richard MO (2014) The roles of brand community and community engagement in building brand trust on social media. Comput Hum Behav 37:152–161

Hanna R, Rohm A, Crittenden VL (2011) We're all connected: the power of the social media ecosystem. Bus Horiz 54(3):265–273

Harris L, Rae A (2009) Social networks: the future of marketing for small business. J Bus Strategy 30(5):24–31

Häubl G, Trifts V (2000) Consumer decision making in online shopping environments: the effects of interactive decision aids. Mark Sci 19(1):4–21

Jenner P (2016) Social enterprise sustainability revisited: an international perspective. Soc Enterp J 12(1):42–60

Kannampuzha MJ, Suoranta M (2016) Bricolage in the marketing efforts of a social enterprise. J Res Mark Entrepreneurship 18(2):176–196

Kierzkowski A, Mcquade S, Waitman R, Zeisser M (1996) Current research: marketing to the digital consumer. Mckinsey Q 22(2):180–183

Kim WG, Li JJ, Brymer RA (2016) The impact of social media reviews on restaurant performance: the moderating role of excellence certificate. Int J Hospitality Manage 55:41–51

Lee J, Park DH, Han I (2008) The effect of negative online consumer reviews on product attitude: an information processing view. Electron Commer Res Appl 7(3):341–352

Leeflang PS, Verhoef PC, Dahlström P, Freundt T (2014) Challenges and solutions for marketing in a digital era. Eur Manage J 32(1):1–12

Levy P, Birkner C (2011) Digital marketing 2011: what you need to know. Mark News 45(3):10–14

Lipsman A, Mudd G, Rich M, Bruich S (2012) The power of "like": how brands reach (and influence) fans through social-media marketing. J Advertising Res 52(1):40–52

Litvin SW, Goldsmith RE, Pan B (2008) Electronic word-of-mouth in hospitality and tourism management. Tour Manage 29(3):458–468

Liu Y (2006) Word of mouth for movies: its dynamics and impact on box office revenue. J Mark 70(3):74–89

Madill J, Brouard F, Hebb T (2010) Canadian social enterprises: an empirical exploration of social transformation, financial self-sufficiency, and innovation. J Nonprofit Public Sect Mark 22(2):135–151

Mair J, Marti I (2006) Social entrepreneurship research: a source of explanation, prediction, and delight. J World Bus 41(1):36–44

Malecki EJ, Moriset B (2007) The digital economy: business organization, production processes and regional developments. Routledge, London

Mallin ML, Finkle TA (2007) Social entrepreneurship and direct marketing. Direct Mark Int J 1(2):68–77

Mangold WG, Faulds DJ (2009) Social media: the new hybrid element of the promotion mix. Bus Horiz 52(4):357–365

McAlexander JH, Schouten JW, Koenig HF (2002) Building brand community. J Mark 66(1):38–54

Mitchell A, Madill J, Chreim S (2016) Social enterprise dualities: implications for social marketing. J Soc Mark 6(2):169–192

Muniz AM, O'guinn TC (2001) Brand community. J Consum Res 27(4):412–432

Okazaki S, Katsukura A, Nishiyama M (2007) How mobile advertising works: the role of trust in improving attitudes and recall. J Advertising Res 47:165–178

Ordanini A, Miceli L, Pizzetti M, Parasuraman A (2011) Crowd-funding: transforming customers into investors through innovative service platforms. J Serv Manage 22(4):443–470

Peattie K, Morley A (2008) Eight paradoxes of the social enterprise research agenda. Soc Enterp J 4(2):91–107

Pitt LF, Berthon PR, Watson RT, Zinkhan GM (2002) The internet and the birth of real consumer power. Bus Horiz 45(4):7
Pratt JA, Yakabov R, Glinski R, Hauser K (2008) Non-profit organisation websites and fundraising. Int J Manage Enterp Dev 6(1):55–79
Ratchford BT, Talukdar D, Lee MS (2007) The impact of the internet on consumers' use of information sources for automobiles: a re-inquiry. J Consum Res 34(1):111–119
Schau HJ, Muñiz AM Jr, Arnould EJ (2009) How brand community practices create value. J Mark 73(5):30–51
See-To EW, Ho KK (2014) Value co-creation and purchase intention in social network sites: the role of electronic word-of-mouth and trust—a theoretical analysis. Comput Hum Behav 31:182–189
Sen S, Lerman D (2007) Why are you telling me this? An examination into negative consumer reviews on the web. J Interact Mark 21(4):76–94
Simmons G (2008) Marketing to postmodern consumers: introducing the internet chameleon. Eur J Mark 42(3/4):299–310
Singh N, Lehnert K, Bostick K (2012) Global social media usage: insights into reaching consumers worldwide. Thunderbird Int Bus Rev 54(5):683–700
Singh A, Saini GK, Majumdar S (2015) Application of social marketing in social entrepreneurship evidence from India. Soc Mark Q 21(3):152–172
Smith KT (2011) Digital marketing strategies that Millennials find appealing, motivating, or just annoying. J Strateg Mark 19(6):489–499
Sotiriadis MD, Van Zyl C (2013) Electronic word-of-mouth and online reviews in tourism services: the use of twitter by tourists. Electron Commer Res 13(1):103–124
Sparks BA, Browning V (2011) The impact of online reviews on hotel booking intentions and perception of trust. Tour Manage 32(6):1310–1323
Spear R, Cornforth C, Aiken M (2009) The governance challenges of social enterprises: evidence from a UK empirical study. Ann Public Coop Econ 80(2):247–273
Szmigin I, Canning L, Reppel AE (2005) Online community: enhancing the relationship marketing concept through customer bonding. Int J Serv Ind Manage 16(5):480–496
Taken Smith K (2012) Longitudinal study of digital marketing strategies targeting Millennials. J Consum Mark 29(2):86–92
Tiago MTPMB, Veríssimo JMC (2014) Digital marketing and social media: why bother? Bus Horiz 57(6):703–708
Trusov M, Bucklin RE, Pauwels K (2009) Effects of word-of-mouth versus traditional marketing: findings from an internet social networking site. J Mark 73(5):90–102
Uzunoğlu E, Kip SM (2014) Brand communication through digital influencers: leveraging blogger engagement. Int J Inf Manage 34(5):592–602
Ward MR, Lee MJ (2000) Internet shopping, consumer search and product branding. J Prod Brand Manage 9(1):6–20
Weerawardena J, Mort GS (2006) Investigating social entrepreneurship: a multidimensional model. J World Bus 41(1):21–35
Whitla P (2009) Crowdsourcing and its application in marketing activities. Contemp Manage Res 5(1)
Wind J, Mahajan V (2002) Digital marketing. Symphonya Emerg Issues Manage 1:43–54
Wong AHK, Tse FWL (2016) Social media, networking, and marketing performance: a study of social enterprises in Hong Kong (HKIBS working paper series 076-1516). Retrieved from Lingnan University website: http://commons.ln.edu.hk/hkibswp/77
Wuyts SH, Dekimpe MG, Gijsbrechts E, Pieters FR (eds) (2011) The connected customer: the changing nature of consumer and business markets. Routledge, London
Zhu F, Zhang X (2010) Impact of online consumer reviews on sales: the moderating role of product and consumer characteristics. J Mark 74(2):133–148

Chinmoy Bandyopadhyay is a doctoral candidate at the Xavier Institute of Management, Xavier University, Bhubaneswar, India. He is currently working in the area of marketing. His doctoral research project focuses on how social enterprises position themselves to multiple stakeholders. Chinmoy holds an MBA degree in Rural Management and a B.Tech degree in Electronics and Communication Engineering. Before joining the doctoral programme, Chinmoy worked as a manager for non-profit organizations in different parts of India. His research has appeared in academic journals such as *Journal of Nonprofit and Public Sector Marketing* and *Marketing Intelligence and Planning*.

Subhasis Ray is a professor of Marketing at the Xavier Institute of Management, Xavier University, Bhubaneswar, India. He has more than 20 years of work experience in corporate and academia. His research interests are in sustainability, marketing, social innovation and entrepreneurship, CSR, emerging markets, and Indian philosophy and religion. He has published several articles in academic journals such as *Journal of Business Research, Marketing Intelligence and Planning, Journal of Nonprofit and Public Sector Marketing, International Journal of Health Care Quality Assurance*, etc. He is also the founder of *Centre for Resettlement, Rehabilitation and Corporate Social Responsibility, India.*

CPSIA information can be obtained
at www.ICGtesting.com
Printed in the USA
LVHW041943281119
638724LV00014B/688/P

9 783030 307738